Quaker Enterprise in Biscuits
Huntley and Palmers of Reading 1822–1972

'There is abundant room for newcomers in the upper ranks of the middle class. It is to the activity and resource of the leading minds in this class that most of those inventions and improvements are due, which enable the working man of today to have comforts and luxuries that were rare or unknown among the richest of a few generations ago. . . . Their profits are sometimes large: but taking one with another they have probably earned for the world a hundred times or more as much as they have earned for themselves.'

A. MARSHALL: *Principles of Economics*
(8th edition 1920) p. 719

Books by the same author

DEMOCRATIC DESPOT:
A LIFE OF NAPOLEON III

DOMESTIC ELECTRICAL APPLIANCES

Quaker Enterprise in Biscuits

Huntley and Palmers of Reading 1822–1972

T. A. B. CORLEY
Senior Lecturer in Economics
University of Reading

HUTCHINSON OF LONDON

HUTCHINSON & CO (*Publishers*) LTD
3 Fitzroy Square, London W1

London Melbourne Sydney Auckland
Wellington Johannesburg Cape Town
and agencies throughout the world

First published 1972

© T. A. B. Corley 1972

Designed and produced by Hutchinson Benham Limited

*This book has been set in Garamond type, printed in Great Britain
on antique wove paper by Anchor Press, and
bound by Wm. Brendon, both of Tiptree, Essex*

ISBN 0 09 111320 2

Contents

PART I *The Origins*

INTRODUCTION: The Quaker Cousinhood ... 3
1 The Huntley Family 1638–1838 ... 11
2 The Palmer Background 1727–1841 ... 23

PART II *The Partnership Era 1841–98*

3 Commencement of the Partnership 1841–6 ... 35
4 Origins of Biscuit Manufacture ... 45
5 The Last Years of Thomas Huntley 1846–57 ... 56
6 The Second Partnership 1857–74 ... 69
7 Exports and International Exhibitions ... 82
8 Life in the Factory 1846–98 ... 96
9 The First Generation: George, Samuel and William Isaac Palmer ... 111
10 The Second Generation 1874–98
    (i) The Seventies and Eighties ... 125
11 The Second Generation 1874–98
    (ii) The Nineties ... 140

PART III *The Twentieth Century*

12 Turn of the Century 1898–1906 ... 155
13 Pre-War 1906–14 ... 166
14 The Great War and its Aftermath: Business Mainly as Usual 1914–16 ... 180
15 The Great War and its Aftermath: Food Control 1916–19 ... 190
16 The Associated Biscuit Manufacturers Ltd. 1919–29 ... 203

17	Depression Years 1929–39	219
18	The Second World War 1939–45	232
19	Restriction 1945–52	244
20	Reappraisal 1953–60	255
21	Reconstruction: (i) A Programme of Change 1960–5	268
22	Reconstruction: (ii) Stage Two and After 1965–72	278
	Notes to Chapters	291
	Appendix I: Wage Rates 1844–1914	303
	Appendix II: Employees' Counties of Birth 1851 and 1861	305
	Appendix III: Turnover and Profits	306
	Appendix IV: Net Output	309
	Index	311

Illustrations

Between pages 144 and 145

The biscuit shop, 72 London Street, Reading
Thomas Huntley, 1853
George Palmer, *c.* 1860
Mary Palmer
Samuel Palmer, aged thirty-five, 1855
The factory, 1851
Entrance to the factory, 1867
George Palmer among his men, 1872
A party at the Acacias, 1870
A party at Marlston House, 1906
George Palmer in later life
The gentlemen in the board room, 1933
The ladies in the sugar-wafer department, 1906
Huntley and Palmers' First XI, 1886
Huntley and Palmers' new offices, built in 1936
Men cutting out biscuits, 1900
One of the thermostatically controlled ovens, 1970
Decorated biscuit tins, 1898
The Board, 1968

Endpapers: Copies of old prints of Huntley & Palmers
Reading factory both thought to be mid-nineteenth century

In mem.
M.E.C.

Preface

Although this book happens to come out in the year of Huntley and Palmers' 150th anniversary, it is not a commemorative history. Instead, it is an independent study of a firm's progress through different phases: from family shop to partnership, to a private limited company, to amalgamation with Peek Frean & Co. Ltd. in a loose federation; and finally, since they were joined by a third firm—W. & R. Jacob & Co. (Liverpool) Ltd.—in 1960, to becoming merged in a homogeneous entity which seeks to combine the beneficial aspects of family control with equal opportunities for everyone.

The surviving documents, to which the author has been given unrestricted access, are remarkably full, no doubt owing to the continuity of one family's management on the same site over the past 125 years. If the lack of correspondence for much of the period means that we do not always know why events happened as they did, the unbroken series of ledgers and account books tell us in great detail exactly how the firm was run.

Huntley and Palmers—and, hopefully, the present history—can claim to be unusual in certain ways. First, as Chapter 4 shows, George Palmer, through his invention of the first continuously running machinery for making fancy biscuits, effectively established a completely new consumer industry, and went on to make the British biscuit known in every country of the world. Second, the firm's Quaker origins help to illuminate facets of British enterprise in the early nineteenth century and of relations between employer and employee later that century that are only partly understood. Thirdly, the events of the 1960s, when Huntley and Palmers, Peek Frean and Jacob's became fully integrated into Associated Biscuits Ltd., form what must be a unique case-study of the successful response of the three controlling families to the needs of consumers and to rivals' pressures in that decade.

The obligations which an author incurs in compiling a book of this kind are many. First of all I must thank John Dunning, Professor of

Economics at Reading University, for suggesting this study to Huntley and Palmers, and Alan Palmer and Lord Palmer (now chairmen of the Associated Biscuit Manufacturers Ltd., and Huntley and Palmers Ltd. respectively) for accepting the suggestion and for making the author's task as straightforward as possible. They have thoroughly vetted successive drafts, but only to ensure that the facts were right; comments backed up by the evidence have been accepted without reservation.

On the family side Dr. Gerald Palmer, senior descendant of George Palmer who has followed the hereditary tradition of public service as M.P. and as President of Reading University's Council, has lent me such family papers as have survived and has been generous both with discussion time and with hospitality. Other members of the family have helped in a number of ways: the Hon. Arnold Palmer, Lady (Eric) Palmer, Miss Felicity Palmer, Geoffrey Palmer, the Hon. Gordon Palmer, the late Reginald Palmer, Richard Palmer, Miss Vera Palmer, William Palmer, Neil Gardiner, David Gardiner, Lady (Arthur) Bryant, Mrs. Dorothy French and Mrs. Olive White. Hector Hanford, Bennet Palmer and C. D. van Namen all contributed helpful boardroom knowledge for Huntley and Palmers, as did Christopher Barber for Associated Biscuits, Richard Carr and E. C. W. Johnson for Peek Frean and L. Victor Smith for Huntley Boorne and Stevens.

Thomas Huntley's descendants Miss Gladys and Miss Marjorie Huntley Wright trustingly sent me some invaluable papers and photographs through the post when we were complete strangers, and have continued to give help and encouragement now that we are good friends. The vital Quaker element in the story could not have been unravelled so thoroughly without the expertise of Edward H. Milligan, Librarian of the Society of Friends in London, and of Leslie Baily and S. C. Morland. C. T. Digby-Jones, Secretary of the National Association of Biscuit Manufacturers, obtained his committee's permission for me to consult the Association's early minutes, which he then made available, and the late Sidney Bailey lucidly explained events in the initial years of the Cake and Biscuit Alliance.

I am also grateful to the late George Palmer, M.P., for leaving to posterity a small but essential packet of letters, without which a good deal of the firm's early history would have remained obscure. The Marquess of Salisbury, K.G., kindly gave me permission to use the papers of his grandfather, sometime Prime Minister, which are now at Christ Church, Oxford, and the Librarian there, Dr. J. F. A. Mason, drew my attention to some interesting documents. The Master of the Royal Household, the Librarian of Windsor Castle and the Deputy Keeper of the Public Records have also been of service. Miss D. J.

Phillips of Reading Public Library's Reference Department and Miss A. Green of the Berkshire Record Office, together with their staffs, and Roger Kneebone, Reading Borough Archivist, have gone to much trouble to answer queries, as have the County Archivists of Dorset, Glamorgan, Gloucestershire, Oxfordshire, Somerset, Staffordshire and Wiltshire, the City Archivist at Bristol and the Dorset County and Gloucester City librarians. F. C. Davis has, with the consent of the company's Board, generously allowed me to make use of his unpublished *History of Peek Frean 1857–1957*.

Among the many individuals who have shared their knowledge with me have been W. Lindahl Brown, Mrs. Armine Edmonds, Mrs. Ina Lamb, Leslie North, Mrs. Clarinda Peto, Miss Muriel Bowman-Smith and E. L. Spicer; and from the academic world Professors T. C. Barker and E. L. Jones, Dr. E. J. T. Collins, Dr. Michael Twyman, A. E. Musson and J. F. Wright. Alec Davis (author of *Package and Print*) and M. J. Franklin have guided me skilfully through the largely unresearched topic of decorated biscuit tins. My children Hilary, Jeremy, Felix and Peter have shown much fortitude of mind over their surviving parent's preoccupation with this work. They have munched their way through most varieties of the company's products and have commented at length both about these and about what little they have understood of its affairs. But for them, the book might have been completed much sooner but would have been a poorer thing. For the labours of typing various drafts, I was fortunate in being able to call on the skills of Christine Brown (herself descended from a line of top managers in the company, from Richard Brown onwards) and of Margaret Lewis.

Convention forbids authors of business histories from naming the many former and present employees who have contributed essential technical advice and recalled past events, as the list would have to be a very long one. This rule must, however, be broken so as to thank Michael Paxton, Public Relations Manager of Associated Biscuits, who as 'liaison officer' between company and author has cheerfully endured many calls on his time, as have his staff, particularly Mary Cottrell and Kathleen Hogg. The brilliant work of Frank Chapman, company photographer, in restoring to life many dingy old photographs and prints has considerably enhanced any value this book may have as a record of the past.

The author's final impressions at the end of this long pilgrimage are not of the abstract concepts that are the tools of his trade: production functions, profit ratios, technological change and the like, but of the people he has met in spirit along the way. Old Joseph Huntley, a cross between Mr. Turveydrop and Mr. Micawber, bowing customers in and out of his little shop; the apprentice George Palmer excitedly taking back to his master some of Huntley's biscuits he has just come across for the first time; Thomas Huntley suffering mentally, as well as bodily, when his partner's recklessness seems to foreshadow yet another bankruptcy in the family; the unsophisticated gaiety of the factory excursions on river launches and in special trains; the workpeople bringing up their families on a pound a week but indignantly rebutting outside charges that their labour was being exploited; and, finally, the hundreds of thousands of different men and women who filed into the factory, did their work and filed out again on some—or many—of the forty thousand-odd days of this period, and by their joint efforts helped to give Reading the fame in the world that it enjoys.

Reading   T. A. B. CORLEY

THE HUNTLEY AND

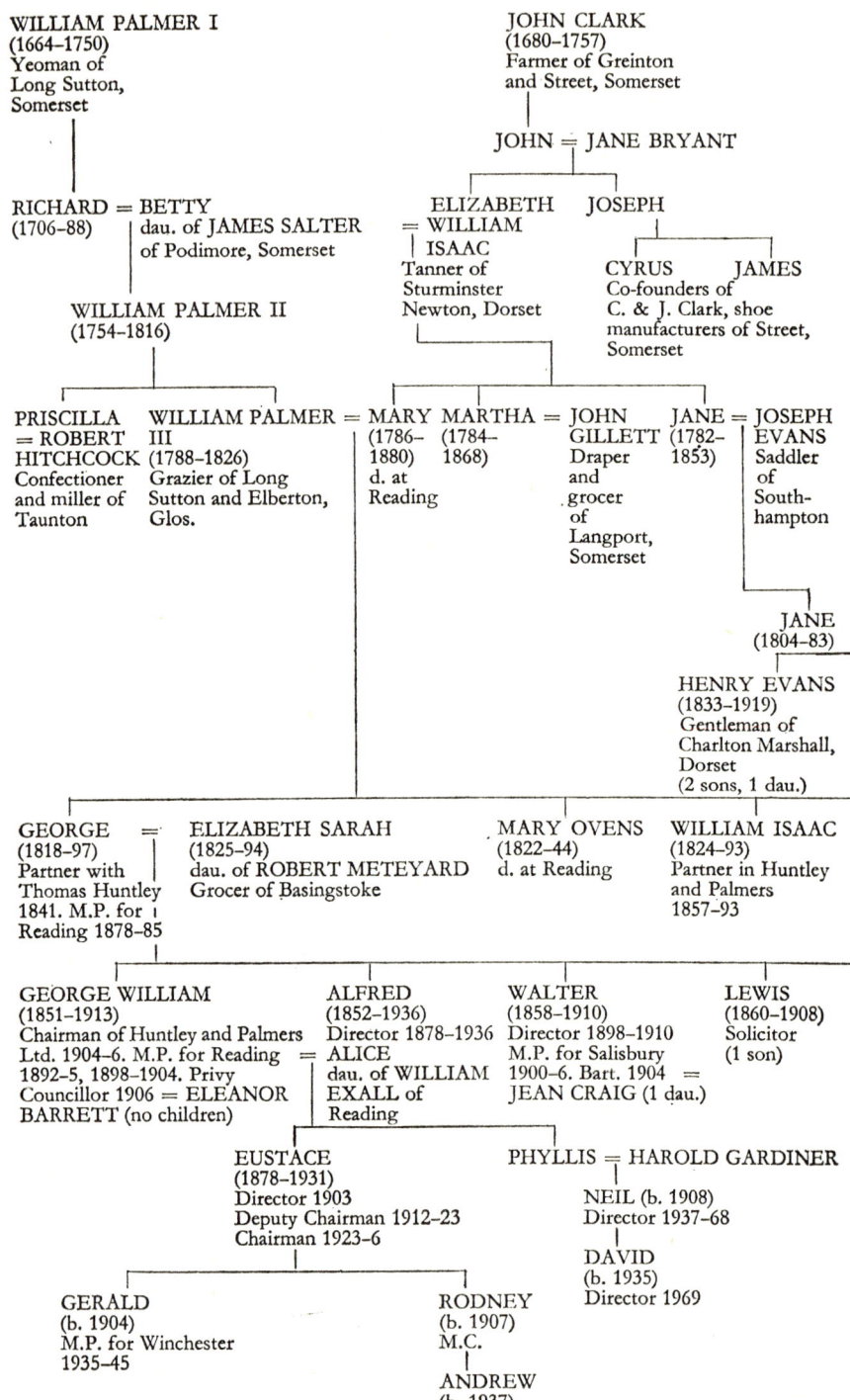

WILLIAM PALMER I (1664–1750) Yeoman of Long Sutton, Somerset

JOHN CLARK (1680–1757) Farmer of Greinton and Street, Somerset

JOHN = JANE BRYANT

RICHARD (1706–88) = BETTY dau. of JAMES SALTER of Podimore, Somerset

ELIZABETH = WILLIAM ISAAC Tanner of Sturminster Newton, Dorset

JOSEPH

CYRUS   JAMES
Co-founders of C. & J. Clark, shoe manufacturers of Street, Somerset

WILLIAM PALMER II (1754–1816)

PRISCILLA = ROBERT HITCHCOCK Confectioner and miller of Taunton

WILLIAM PALMER III (1788–1826) Grazier of Long Sutton and Elberton, Glos.

MARY (1786–1880) d. at Reading

MARTHA (1784–1868) = JOHN GILLETT Draper and grocer of Langport, Somerset

JANE (1782–1853) = JOSEPH EVANS Saddler of Southampton

JANE (1804–83)

HENRY EVANS (1833–1919) Gentleman of Charlton Marshall, Dorset (2 sons, 1 dau.)

GEORGE (1818–97) Partner with Thomas Huntley 1841. M.P. for Reading 1878–85
= ELIZABETH SARAH (1825–94) dau. of ROBERT METEYARD Grocer of Basingstoke

MARY OVENS (1822–44) d. at Reading

WILLIAM ISAAC (1824–93) Partner in Huntley and Palmers 1857–93

GEORGE WILLIAM (1851–1913) Chairman of Huntley and Palmers Ltd. 1904–6. M.P. for Reading 1892–5, 1898–1904. Privy Councillor 1906 = ELEANOR BARRETT (no children)

ALFRED (1852–1936) Director 1878–1936 = ALICE dau. of WILLIAM EXALL of Reading

WALTER (1858–1910) Director 1898–1910 M.P. for Salisbury 1900–6. Bart. 1904 = JEAN CRAIG (1 dau.)

LEWIS (1860–1908) Solicitor (1 son)

EUSTACE (1878–1931) Director 1903 Deputy Chairman 1912–23 Chairman 1923–6

PHYLLIS = HAROLD GARDINER

NEIL (b. 1908) Director 1937–68

DAVID (b. 1935) Director 1969

GERALD (b. 1904) M.P. for Winchester 1935–45

RODNEY (b. 1907) M.C.

ANDREW (b. 1937)

PALMER FAMILIES

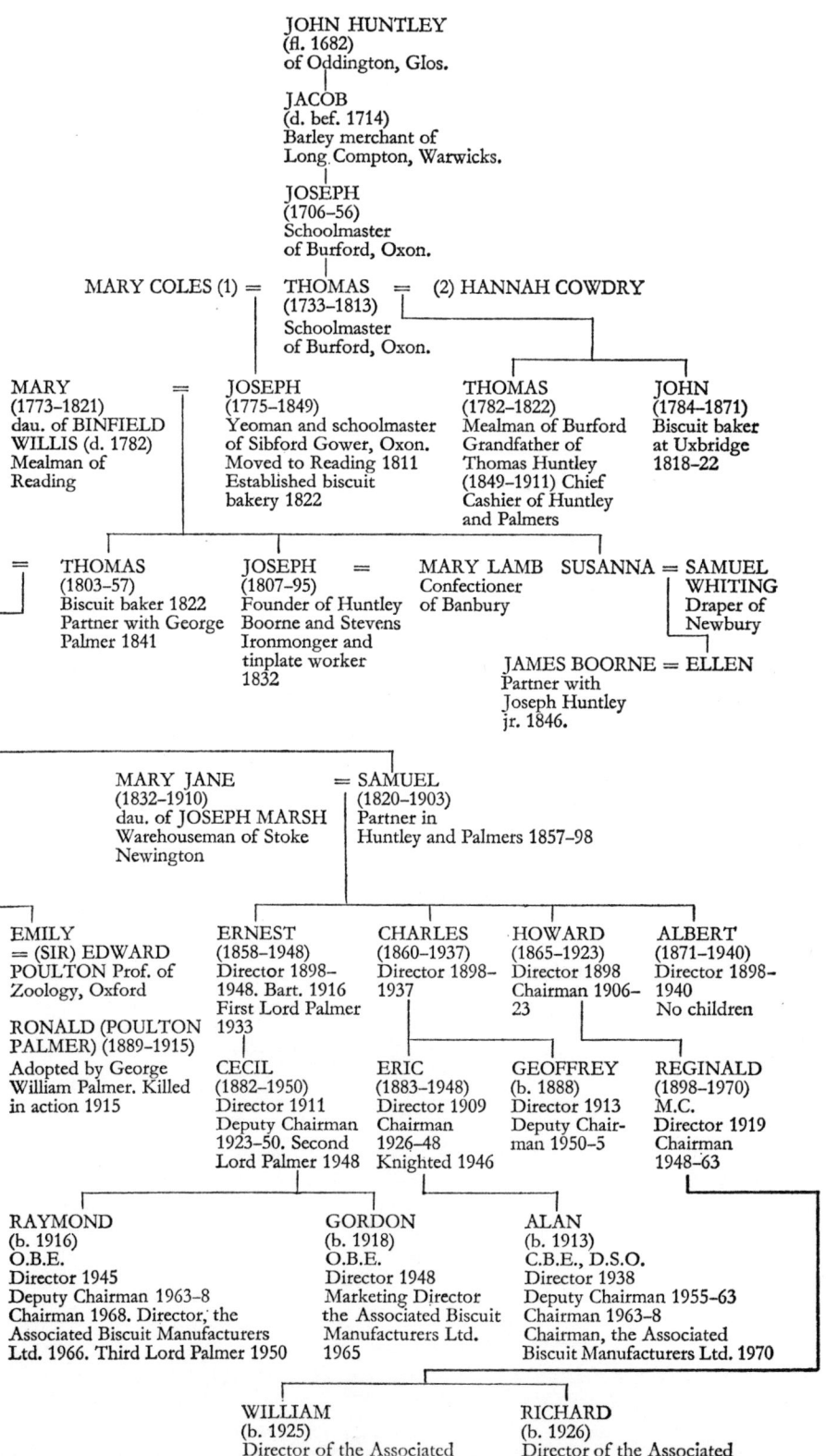

JOSEPH HUNTLEY
    Biscuit-baker   1822–1829

JOSEPH HUNTLEY & SON   1829–1838

THOMAS HUNTLEY   1838–1841

HUNTLEY AND PALMER   1841–1857
    Partnership: Thomas Huntley and
               George Palmer

HUNTLEY AND PALMERS   1857–1898
    Partnership: George, Samuel and
               William Isaac Palmer, and
               from 1874 their sons

HUNTLEY AND PALMERS LTD.   1898–1968
    Private Company: Subsidiary of
               the Associated Biscuit
               Manufacturers Ltd.
               since 1921

ASSOCIATED BISCUITS LTD.   1969 to date

PART I

The Origins

Introduction:
The Quaker Cousinhood[1]

Thomas Huntley and George Palmer, who in 1841 entered into partnership as confectioners and biscuit-bakers of Reading, were both members of the Society of Friends, and were also cousins by marriage. They thus belonged to the 'Quaker cousinhood', whose contribution to Britain's industrial development was out of all proportion to their limited numbers. Here we can do no more than list some of the fields in which Quakers were especially active: the basic industries of iron and other metal manufacture; mining and banking; the woollen and linen trades; and the homelier occupations, which included food processing. The part they played in the development of chocolate manufacture has been amply documented, but what they did for biscuit-making is less well known.

The two aspects of Quakerism which most greatly influenced the manner in which the Huntley and Palmer partnership was born were as follows. First was the highly individual method of discipline imposed by the Society: this drew them towards various specific fields of economic activity, such as those mentioned above. Second, there were the family and business relationships built up between Quakers, which very often helped their enterprises to prosper. These two aspects will now be considered in turn.

The Quaker system of discipline was partly self-discipline, and partly imposed from outside by the close scrutiny of members' actions by their fellow-members. As to self-discipline, Quakers fervently relied on the guidance of the Holy Spirit, and nourished and reinforced their faith from two sources, the Bible and the published writings of Friends, of which the collective injunctions were the most influential. The regular Yearly Meetings, held in London, drew up minutes and advices 'for establishing and conducting the discipline of the church'; books of extracts appeared at intervals from 1782 onwards.

These minutes and advices were not confined to general rules of personal conduct—for instance, urging plainness in dress and speech and temperance in eating and drinking—but included copious instructions on how members should behave in the conduct of trade. They enjoined Friends to keep regular accounts and pay debts as soon as they were due, and not to trade beyond one's capital or indulge in any dishonest practice 'which endangers peace of mind'.[2] Further advices were required to be read out at least once a year in the Quarterly and Monthly Meetings throughout the country. 'Maintain strict integrity in all your transactions in trade, and in your other outward concerns, remembering that you will have to account for the mode of acquiring, and the manner of using, your possessions', was one such rule. Moreover, Preparative Meetings had to answer in writing 'queries' on such topics as 'Are Friends just in their dealings, and punctual in fulfilling their engagements?' The answers, in digest form, went right up to the Yearly Meeting, which passed down any action which was felt to be necessary.[3]

These rules and queries have been described as unparalleled in spirit or general acceptance by any other religious group of the time.[4] Since each Quaker community was small enough for every adherent to know pretty well everybody else's business, the periodical repetition of such queries, and subsequently drawing attention to shortcomings, naturally exercised a powerful conditioning effect on members' behaviour.

The inward strength and corporate unity, which Quakers undoubtedly derived from their method of discipline, made them into some of the most uncompromising nonconformists—in the widest sense—of their times. Not unexpectedly, they were constantly at loggerheads with the official world outside. From the Society's establishment by George Fox in about 1650 until the Toleration Act of 1689 they were regarded as a direct threat to the safety of the State; occasionally with good reason. A Quaker great-great-great-grandfather of George Palmer's, Thomas Bryant, is said to have harboured in his Somerset home the rebel Duke of Monmouth after Sedgemoor in 1685, and later to have been sentenced to death by Judge Jeffreys during the Bloody Assizes.[5] They were persecuted with much vigour for not attending church or receiving the sacrament; we shall see in Chapter 1 how the first known ancestor of Thomas Huntley suffered in this way during the 1680s.

In the eighteenth and early nineteenth centuries Friends were harried mainly because they refused to support the Established Church, whether by tithes in the country or by church rates in the town parishes. The civil authorities thereupon distrained on their property. The Quakers in turn entered all distraints, as well as imprisonments, in Books of Sufferings, which were read aloud at each Quarterly Meeting as 'testimony'.

Introduction: The Quaker Cousinhood

These records of Sufferings, which at the time helped to strengthen the resolution of the hard-pressed Quaker communities, nowadays tell us much about life in the various parts of the country. Farmers of all religious persuasions, for instance, greatly resented the tithes, but only the Quakers among them consistently refused to pay.

Between 1794 and his death in 1816, William Palmer, George Palmer's grandfather and a tenant farmer of some substance, forfeited each year the equivalent of £16 on average for tithes, plus about £1 extra for 'charges' incurred by the parish officers. Included are two fines for refusal to serve in the militia. Normally, livestock or 'grains of divers sorts' were seized to pay the debt, and any excess accruing from a sale would be 'left in the house' of the victim. On rare occasions Providence took a hand, as when the officer driving away an ox from the Palmer homestead fell and broke his leg, and his successor, appointed by the magistrates, became 'in the Friends' debt', apparently by not pressing the distraint.

In Reading, too, as late as 1847 the still young firm of Huntley and Palmer had six tins of biscuits, worth 17s. seized for non-payment of church rates. Moreover, between 1816, when Thomas Huntley's father Joseph first became a householder in Reading, and 1847 the Huntleys' resistance to those rates cost Joseph seven tables, two chairs and 4 lb. of tea in all, while Thomas himself had a total of 136 lb. of sugar confiscated from his bakehouse; Thomas's brother Joseph the younger, in his ironmonger's shop opposite, had nine tea kettles and three complete sets of fire-irons seized. Even the women of the family were not exempt, for on one occasion Thomas's sisters, Mary and Hannah, had four yards of flannel and two shop stools taken. These distraints were to recover about £10 due for the church rates over the whole thirty years, plus an equivalent sum for charges.[6]

Since such losses were very small in relation to their means, the Palmers and the Huntleys thereby suffered inconvenience rather than disaster. Yet to many farming people these were reminders of the time when distraints and other penalties had been so brutally enforced as to drive Quakers off the land altogether. Such penalties may have helped to reduce the Huntley ancestors in Gloucestershire to virtual penury as husbandmen in the late seventeenth century, although (as we shall see) a general fall in agricultural prices may have been as effective. On the other hand, the Clark family of Street in Somerset, maternal ancestors of George Palmer, survived various severe periods of imprisonment in the penal era, but later developed into quite prosperous farmers.

The Palmers themselves probably did not become Quakers until early on in the eighteenth century, when the worst days were over. It was therefore on economic rather than religious grounds that George

Palmer and his brothers were apprenticed to trades in the 1830s, just about the time when their cousins in Street also abandoned agriculture in order to found the shoe-making firm of C. & J. Clark, which still remains in family hands. Agriculture was depressed following the end of the Napoleonic wars, and people of enterprise were starting up their own businesses in the wake of the industrial revolution.

What kinds of livelihood did the Quakers take up when they left the land? In fact, the opportunities were greatly restricted by their consciences. They refused to swear oaths, on the grounds that this practice encouraged double standards of morality: freedom to lie openly on all ordinary occasions, but constraint to tell the truth when swearing on the Bible. Although affirmation for most legal purposes was later permitted by law, until the mid-nineteenth century entry to most learned professions was conditional on swearing allegiance to the sovereign. Quakers were thus debarred from them.

The eldest Huntley sons therefore became schoolmasters, since this was one of the very few professions that required neither capital nor oath. The younger sons went into commerce, notably the food trades which were widespread in the small market towns where they settled. Corn-millers and mealmen, grocers and confectioners predominate in their family tree; in the Palmer family, whereas until the 1830s the sons almost invariably stayed on the land, the daughters tended to marry men engaged in similar ranges of food trades.

Here Friends were assisted by three of the Quaker virtues. First, their consciences would not allow them to sell, or use as ingredients, any but the best quality of goods. In an age when short weight and adulteration of foodstuffs was very common, the consuming public came to trust Quaker integrity. Second, they offered their products at fixed prices, instead of expecting each customer to bargain for some reduction; an agent could be told to buy a sack of flour from them or a child sent out to buy a loaf or some buns without running the risk of being cheated. Third, although millers had a traditional reputation for roguery, and notably for making vast profits from hoarding grain in times of shortage, Quaker millers were never guilty of these practices, although they were not forbidden to secure genuine profits when grain was scarce.

It is therefore understandable why Quaker families concentrated on certain food-processing industries. The Cadburys, Frys and Rowntrees all made their mark in the manufacture of chocolate; in the early days fancy biscuit manufacture also, at least outside London, was partly in the hands of Quakers. Besides Carr's of Carlisle and at least one Scottish

Introduction: The Quaker Cousinhood

biscuit firm, the three families which have brought their companies into the Associated Biscuit Manufacturers Ltd.—the Palmers of Huntley and Palmers, the Carrs of Peek Frean, and the original partners of Jacobs—were all Quakers by origin.

The second aspect of Quakerism to be described here is the type of relationships that grew up between Friends. These resulted from two factors: a belief in the equality of all their members, regardless of station in life, sex or social background, and their self-imposed isolation. The feeling of equality—a traditionally Christian virtue which tended to be at least overlooked in other denominations—was greatly helped by the broadly similar social groupings to which members tended to belong, namely the moderately prosperous commercial classes of the kinds which we have already met.

On the whole there were few rich men, except self-made ones, for it was well known in Quaker circles that 'a carriage and pair does not long continue to drive to a Meeting House';[7] and, indeed, neither Thomas Huntley's son nor any of the Palmer brothers' children died Quakers. Nor were there more than a handful of the poorest section of the community, such as labourers, menial servants or unskilled operatives. Of the teen-age female servants in Thomas and Joseph Huntley's households at the time of the 1841 Census, none was a Quaker; the reason for this was that Quaker writers urged employers to keep servants at work rather than let them indulge in 'unprofitable' uses of leisure, which by definition meant anything at all recreational. There were, of course, poor Friends, as a rule of the artisan type, who were continually being reminded of their duty to try to maintain themselves and their families by 'frugality and industry', notwithstanding the 'primary obligation' of other members to support them.[8] The paternalistic relationship of the Palmers with their workpeople, noted in Chapter 8, can in part be traced to this ambiguous Quaker attitude towards the poor.

Quakers' isolation from the outside world can be seen from their denying themselves such harmful pleasures of the senses as strong drink, tobacco and gambling, and also less directly harmful pastimes such as recreational card-playing, music and dancing. The fact that these are the kinds of pleasure that are in the ordinary way shared socially only tended to cut them off even further from contact with non-Quakers. Until 1859 a Friend was not allowed to marry a non-Friend in Meeting, and 'marriage before priests' carried immediate and normally permanent disownment. Their fellow-members brought very strong pressures to bear when they learnt, as happened very quickly in such small communities, that a member was contemplating marriage 'outside'. The Monthly Meetings of men or of women (as the case might be) used to appoint a small delegation to visit the member concerned and to make earnest remonstrations, which emphasised the threat of expulsion.

Young Quakers therefore possessed only very restricted opportunities for meeting people of other denominations. This did not necessarily lead to a high rate of intermarriage within each local community, however. For one thing, they were not allowed to marry their first cousins. Again, there was a good deal of journeying between meetings by ministers and elders, not all of whom were married or particularly old, and hospitality was freely given to young Quakers who had to travel on business or with other serious objects. One rule urged Friends to be generous with their hospitality in order to keep these young men out of trouble.[9]

Thomas Huntley's wife was the daughter of a Southampton saddler, while his brothers and sisters had spouses who came from Banbury, Guildford and Newbury and were confectioners, ironmongers and drapers respectively. On the Palmer side, George Palmer's wife came from Basingstoke: except for his mother—who had migrated from Dorset to his father's village—his immediate ancestors and uncles and aunts with one exception all found partners over a wide area of Somerset and just over the border in Wiltshire.

Hence, if these are a fair sample, partners were frequently drawn not from the same Monthly Meeting (say, Reading and its environs), but from roughly the area of the Quarterly Meeting, which comprised one county or several adjacent counties, say Bristol and Somerset or Berkshire and Oxfordshire. In consequence, Quakers tended to have a large number of cousins scattered over a fairly wide, but not too wide, geographical area.

The atmosphere of fellowship to be found within the Society thus comprehended a large element of close social and family links among its members. They inevitably used these links for business purposes, although not in the way that was common at the time. As Adam Smith stated in *The Wealth of Nations*, published in 1776, 'people of the same trade seldom meet together, even for merriment or diversion, but the conversation ends in a conspiracy against the public, or in some contrivance to raise prices'.[10] This remark did not apply to the Quakers; however, where a business man was 'travelling in the ministry' and was too far from home to return the same night, he would often be put up in the home of someone who was in the same line of business. Although the *Rules of Discipline* asked plainly of ministers and others 'Do any overcharge themselves with trade or other outward engagement to the hindrance of their service?', there was no bar to Quakers in similar

Introduction: The Quaker Cousinhood

occupations to the traveller joining his host after Meeting, for discussions on matters of common interest and to offer mutual help. Such discussions have been described as performing functions analogous to those of present-day trade associations, which was undoubtedly true in the iron industries where Quaker activity was so strong.[11]

However, in smaller and more fragmented trades, such as food processing, these meetings were probably more important in fostering vertical rather than horizontal relationships. Those invited would not be so much other Quakers in the same trade, as those who were either suppliers or customers. Thus in the food trades, confectioners and biscuit-bakers would have been glad to meet the corn-millers who provided their flour or who were the sources of information about price trends. They could also exchange news with grocers and druggists, some of whom bought their products, and with those (sometimes grocers themselves) who supplied sugar and other ingredients wholesale.

Thus Thomas Huntley's father Joseph (who was in fact the founder of the Reading firm) is described as having 'acted as his son's commercial traveller on a small scale, turning his visits to Monthly Meetings, Quarterly Meetings and other gatherings of the body to good account ... and as Friends welcomed Joseph to their homes, so they gave orders for fresh supplies of biscuits'.[12] There is no evidence that Friends believed that they had to buy from other Friends out of denominational loyalty, however. Joseph Huntley received orders for biscuits not because they were made by a Quaker but because they were good to eat.

In its early days the Reading business by no means relied entirely on Quaker sources for its supplies. The two local mills which provided the bulk of the wheat were owned by non-Quakers. At the same time, a Quaker grocer, John Smith—whose sister had married George Palmer's uncle—supplied many of the other ingredients, while some of the more fancy ones came from Batger's, a London Quaker firm. On the packing side, Thomas's brother Joseph Huntley junior, the ironmonger, turned to making tins when these were needed to carry biscuits well beyond the immediate locality, and one at least of the firms which printed biscuit-tin labels, White & Pike of Birmingham, was Quaker-owned.

Thus the opportunities created and the sanctions imposed by its discipline helped to build up within the Quaker community business connections that were closer—because based on a high degree of mutual trust—than was usual in most of industry and commerce at that date. More generally, it was Quaker convictions, and the way in which those convictions reflected themselves in everyday conduct, that gave Quaker enterprise its characteristic qualities.

The first part of this book will show how their Quaker faith impinged on the lives of both the Huntleys and the Palmers, and caused these qualities to persist in the Reading firm long after its principals had ceased to be practising Quakers: a disciplined orderliness in the factory, strong direction at the top, a paternalistic interest in employees and in their material and mental welfare, and less than complete generosity over wages, coupled with a readiness to help those in financial distress for any reason. Chapter 1 will deal with the background to the Huntley family and Chapter 2 with the Palmer family.

I
The Huntley Family 1638–1838

In 1841 George Palmer became a partner in what he later described as 'a comparatively small business, having already a good name'.[1] That business had been founded by Thomas Huntley's father Joseph almost twenty years before. By 1846 George Palmer had begun to transform it by inventing the first effective machinery for making fancy biscuits and by setting up a properly organised factory. Within fifty years, in conjunction with his brothers Samuel and William Isaac Palmer, he had built up the largest biscuit enterprise in the world, which was also among the forty most important industrial companies in Britain.[2] His products were by then a household word, while the tins, with their distinctive labels, had become familiar throughout the inhabited world.

By the standards of the Victorian era, this spectacular achievement in one lifetime was not all that uncommon; yet it is noteworthy enough to be related at some length. First of all, however, we need to ask some preliminary questions and to investigate them in the present and subsequent chapters. How was it that George Palmer, the eldest son of a line of yeoman farmers, and Thomas Huntley, the eldest son of a line of schoolmasters, took up the craft of biscuit-baking at all? Why did they come together in Reading when the one was born in Somerset and the other in Oxfordshire?

The Huntleys were originally from Gloucestershire and lived on the eastern fringes of the Cotswolds not far from the Oxfordshire border. One shadowy figure precedes their entry into nonconformity: John Huntley, a husbandman, was farming sheep at Oddington, near Stow-on-the-Wold, at the time of his death in 1638. He was a member of the Established Church, and having been described thirty years before as a labourer, was probably little more than a peasant farmer.[3] Another John Huntley of Oddington—presumably a son or grandson, but the first who was undoubtedly an ancestor of Thomas Huntley—was reported to the ecclesiastical authorities by a presentment in 1682 for not attending church or receiving the sacrament. He and his wife Sarah were described as 'very poor'.[4] That was a time of low agricultural prices, and many conforming farmers were also ruined and forced off the land. Thus it is improbable that his poverty sprang entirely from his religious views.

At any rate, John's son Jacob became a barley merchant, a few miles away in the Worcestershire village of Long Compton. His son Joseph, on the other hand, was a schoolmaster at Burford in Oxfordshire; in the Introduction it was explained how schoolmastering was one of the few professions open to Quakers, since no oath was required. They were leniently treated in that town, for in 1739 the vicar had to report at the time of the bishop's visitation that he had summoned the Quakers to appear before two Justices of the Peace for non-payment of church rates, but that he 'proceeded no further'; and, he added, 'I never received a farthing from them since I had the vicarage.'[5]

Joseph, being free from petty persecution, had full scope to concentrate on his pastoral work as well as teaching, for he was the first of four successive generations to become Quaker elders or ministers. In 1741, when only thirty-five, he composed a pamphlet about the True Gospel Ministry, which earned him widespread praise for his 'sound doctrine and verbatim and properly applied citations from scripture'. The following year he was elected to the highest office of the society, Clerk of the London Yearly Meeting. Unfortunately he died at the age of fifty from a painful internal disorder, perhaps of the kind which carried off his great-grandson Thomas—of Huntley and Palmer—also in his early fifties.[6]

Joseph's son Thomas (1733–1813) was even more widely known in Quaker circles. From 1751 to the early 1800s he was headmaster of a boarding school, named Hillside Academy, at the top of the long steep hill which is Burford's most noteworthy feature. His was one of the two most important Quaker schools in southern England,[7] and his house was regularly visited by important members going to and from meetings, especially the London Yearly Meeting, of which he in turn became clerk in 1792. Like his father he was a competent scholar, but in languages rather than divinity, for he compiled French, Latin and English grammars and wrote tolerable Latin verses as well as bad English ones on conventional themes.[8]

In addition to the basic subjects and languages the pupils were taught double-entry book-keeping, mensuration and trigonometry. His most celebrated pupil, the manufacturing chemist Luke Howard—who went on to become an entrepreneur of distinction—complained that he learnt at school 'too much Latin grammar and too little of anything else',[9] and undoubtedly that type of education was becoming outdated even during Thomas's professional lifetime. The strength of Quaker education generally was in giving commercial training, as well as some elementary science, at a time when the public and grammar schools were concentrating on the dead languages. By the last quarter of the eighteenth century Quakers were seeking new attitudes in education, which led to the establishment of more professionally run schools, where the headmaster was subject to a committee instead of being in sole charge of curriculum and finances alike. Ackworth school, for instance, had been founded in 1779 and was soon followed by others. In the end Hillside Academy declined either because of this outside competition or because of Thomas's age.

Thomas was a cautious as well as a pedantic man. He was approaching forty before he married for the first time, and it was not until he was fifty-seven that, as a later testimony put it, 'he first opened his mouth in the ministry'.[10] Although, like his namesake of Huntley and Palmer, he gained the affection of everyone who was associated with him, his personality lacks colour compared with that of his second wife, Hannah. She had shown much spirit—in the direction of religious zeal—from an early age; now, in addition to bearing him eight children and bringing up two stepchildren, she acted as the school's matron. For £20 a year (to cover 'Board, Teaching and Washing') she changed pupils' linen once a week, and for twenty guineas, twice a week. Connoisseurs of extravagant school-clothing lists will appreciate the reassurance given to an anxious parent that 'six or eight shirts, four night caps, six pocket handkerchieves and six pair stockings will be sufficient'.

As soon as her youngest child was old enough, she became a minister and made at least one journey outside the Monthly Meeting area to 'give testimony'. There was an occasion when she heard that a large party of the nobility and gentry were assembled at a Burford inn for the races, and, like some Salvation Army lass of later times, felt the urge to pay a religious call on them. Thomas accompanied her and had the thankless task of breaking the ice. She received a respectful and attentive hearing from the quality, and afterwards declared, 'Sweet is the reward of obedience to the Holy Spirit'; her husband's comments are not recorded. She has a place in this history because she found time amidst her other activities not only to rear pigs but also to bake biscuits in the school's large oven. The bacon went to feed her many charges, and very occasionally to be seized by the parish constable for non-payment of church rates. The biscuits she sold outside the school, where coaches had to stop in order to put on the drag when going downhill or to allow the horses to regain their wind at the end of the climb. She lived until 1835, so that some of her recipes may well have been handed down to the Reading business.[11]

Some of her enterprising spirit was transmitted to her elder stepchild Joseph.[12] He could not have been more different from the remainder of his family, trustworthy, honest and plodding as they were, for he never shrank from cutting corners, so to speak, to further his own interests. Above all, he was probably a man of large ideas, some good and some bad, but every one requiring a great deal of money to translate into reality. His father was not rich, so Joseph was astute enough to marry an heiress two years his senior, Mary Willis. Mary's grandfather, Binfield Willis, had been a wealthy Quaker maltster, at a time when Reading was one of the most important malting centres in England. He owned a freehold shop in Reading's market place, a large granary and malthouse by the river Kennet, and some property held on long lease in London Street and Church Street, Reading. As her own parents had died prematurely, he left his property in trust to her and her two younger sisters jointly. After his death she became a householder in her own right in London Street. Not only did she provide a home for her sisters but she also suffered inconvenience for her beliefs. Once she lost by distraint for church rates three pairs of ebony candlesticks, one coal-scoop, sixteen pairs of knives and forks and carving set to match, and a copper warming pan. By her marriage to Joseph in 1801, she forfeited this independence in exchange for a farm at Sibford Ferris, near Banbury, and an erratic husband.

Joseph was then serving his term in office as overseer of the parish, which he was affluent, or extravagant, enough to do by deputy. In the next few years he seems to have divided his attention between three main interests. First, since the early age of twenty he had been a Quaker minister, and this vocation took him on many religious visits into other counties. Second, he had a number of outside financial dealings—with his wife's money, of course—for in 1802 he was an investor in the Banbury and Shipston Turnpike, which ran near his home. Third, he had his mixed arable and sheep farm, which he must have neglected somewhat, judging by the casualties he incurred among his ewes. In 1806 he had to sell out his interest of £50 in the turnpike investment to his friend Joseph Lamb, and about the same time he became schoolmaster of the small Quaker school, with twenty-one pupils, at Sibford Ferris. His eldest son Thomas was born in 1803 and Joseph junior (who became an ironmonger and manufacturer of tin boxes) was born four years later.

However, his occupation as village schoolmaster clearly did not solve his money problems. In 1811, with four young children and another very evidently on the way, he and his wife moved to Reading. He may well have been drawn by the far more plentiful teaching opportunities there. In her thinly diguised account of the town, entitled

Belford Regis, the local author Mary Russell Mitford wrote that all its principal streets, especially on the outskirts, were furnished with 'classical, commercial and mathematical academies for young gentlemen, or polite seminaries for young ladies', in 'showy and spacious looking mansions'.[13]

Whatever post Joseph obtained, it must have given him an established position in Reading's Quaker community. On the strength of the customary certificate which Banbury Monthly Meeting despatched at the time of his move, and which testified that he was free of debt, he was straightway accepted at Reading as a minister. Then only a few years later he became the centre of a scandal which must have convulsed the highly respectable circle of the hundred-odd Reading Quakers.

In October 1814, shortly after his last child had been born, the Monthly Meeting learnt that he was 'at present placed in such a situation as to incapacitate him from bearing the expence [*sic*] of educating his children'; in short, as Mr. Micawber would have said, insolvent. To make matters worse, he had apparently been in this situation at the time of his move in 1811, notwithstanding the certificate from Banbury.

A series of acrimonious notes now flew backwards and forwards between Banbury and Reading Monthly Meetings. According to Quaker practice, since Banbury seemed to be at fault through having incorrectly forwarded a certificate of solvency, that Monthly Meeting should take the responsibility for educating the eleven-year-old Thomas and his sister, who (as Reading now pointedly stated) 'require immediate attention in this respect'. Whilst accepting this responsibility, Banbury refused to take back the offending certificate, on the grounds that it had been true to the best of their knowledge and that no satisfactory proof to the contrary had been produced.

As a rejoinder, two elders at Reading drew up a statement of Joseph's affairs at the time of his arrival in 1811. This very interesting document has unfortunately not been preserved, but scarcely had it been forwarded to Banbury than Joseph bounced back into solvency. The explanation given was that he had become possessed of 'considerable' property following the death of a relative; moreover (it was alleged), as he had had an interest in this property, which he could have sold earlier, technically speaking he had been quite solvent in 1811. The two Monthly Meetings were too relieved that the dispute had been resolved to enquire too deeply into this explanation, but it furnishes a possible reason why they should have returned to Reading.

Mary's property, it will be remembered, was locked up in her grandfather's trust, so that although Joseph was able to make free with her income, he could not touch the capital sum. Then one of her two sisters died early in 1811, a few months before their move, which may have been prompted by his determination to have the trust wound up and the capital divided. They came back to live in Broad Street with an aged aunt of Mary's, Elizabeth Speakman, who had a small competence derived from the liquor trade. Joseph's expectations in that direction were dashed when the old lady died in 1815 and was found to have left her whole property to a brother of hers, and poor Mary received no more than a keepsake, 'the secretary desk in the parlour'.

Whatever wrangles went on between Joseph and the trustees, they had not been resolved by the autumn of 1814, when a combination of economic misfortunes struck Reading. The year had begun badly when a prolonged frost brought communications between London and Reading, both by road and by water, to a halt for twelve weeks. Then the corn harvest was ruined by blight, and an abnormally dry autumn so lowered the levels of the canals and rivers that boats could not get to and from London.[14] Reading's trade was therefore so depressed that creditors there were forced to call in their debts, and fresh trouble followed three months later when Marsh Deane & Co.'s bank collapsed. Joseph, who must as well have been fending off an earlier bunch of creditors, dating back to before 1811, now found that plausible talk was no substitute for hard cash.

These uncommon visitations of nature, by destroying Joseph's creditworthiness, were ultimately to transform the future of Reading. Had they not occurred, his son Thomas might well have followed the eldest son's traditional calling into the fourth generation and become a schoolmaster. That would have suited his gentle and scholarly nature which took after that of his grandfather at Hillside Academy, and the town's subsequent industrial history could have been entirely different. Instead, as soon as he was fourteen years of age, he was sent away to be apprenticed. His master, Benjamin Doubleday, was a Quaker who had a grocer's business in High Street, Epping, near London.

Meanwhile Joseph became a householder by taking over one of Binfield Willis's small houses, with a rateable value of £8 a year, in Church Street, near the Meeting House. However lightly he was able to shrug off these financial ups and downs from his broad shoulders, their effect on Mary, who now had to return to a much inferior house in a part of Reading where she had once been a young householder of independent means, in a house rated at £18 a year, must have been profound. During 1815, when the fracas between the two Monthly Meetings was at its height, she felt called on to resign her office as overseer of the Women's Meeting, and six years later she died, aged only forty-seven. The inconsolable widower never married again: he inherited what was left of her capital; he had three daughters to look after him; and, besides, he was on the point of hatching out yet another of his large ideas.

After spending two years with Benjamin Doubleday, Thomas at the age of seventeen had moved to Uxbridge, then the centre of a very prosperous corn-growing and milling area. He lived with his uncle John Huntley, who is said to have had a bakery and biscuit shop just off Uxbridge's High Street. Two years later John Huntley returned abruptly to Burford; of the various traditional explanations that have survived, the most likely was that he ran into financial difficulties. Once again, it seems, Thomas saw at first hand the demoralising effects of insolvency.[15]

Nevertheless, when he came back to live in Reading in the middle of 1822, he was fully trained, and Joseph had decided to open a biscuit bakery and confectioner's shop, managing the business and keeping the books, while Thomas was doing the baking and one or more of the girls were serving at the counter or making themselves useful in other ways. As it happened, the tenant of a shop at the southern end of London Street, a few minutes' walk from the Church Street house, was about this time struck down by a runaway coach while crossing the street. The lease of his shop became vacant when he died early in November, and before the end of the year the Huntleys were in occupation.

Thus the business from which Huntley and Palmers developed was originally founded in 1822, and not in 1826 as is commonly stated, and under the proprietorship of Joseph, not of Thomas Huntley. The correct date was gradually lost sight of during the next fifty years; a directory of 1826 confirmed that the business had been in existence then, and the next step was to maintain that 1826 was the year of foundation. Huntley and Palmers' centenary was for that reason incorrectly celebrated in 1926.

The shop at 72 London Street was later remembered as a little old-fashioned shop, approached by steps. It was in fact only eighteen feet in width and hence less than half as wide as the shop which still exists. But the premises went back a long way; there was a large underground bakehouse, with a fanlight, in the cellar, and a covered alleyway at the side, through which Cocks's Court, with its outhouse and two cottages, could be reached.

Trade must have been on a very modest scale at the outset: it was one of three Reading shops which specialised in biscuit-baking, while most of the thirty other bakers in the town made at least some biscuits. Indeed the American Quaker Elihu Burritt, who visited Reading in 1864 and talked to the Huntleys' first employee—by then foreman of the factory—was told that initially a sack of biscuit flour had lasted for six months, and that no more than a quart of milk a day had been required for biscuit-making.[16]

If Joseph ever experienced any uncharacteristic moments of diffidence about his venture, they must soon have been stilled by the conviction that the town offered a good market for his products. At that period Reading contained three sorts of people: the poorest class who were huddled together in the insanitary courts and largely remained out of sight as well as mind; the tradesmen who flourished on the market activities which provided the town's *raison d'être*, and those who considered themselves to be the 'upper crust'. The latter were specified by the son of a Reading doctor, born in 1823, as follows: 'The clergyman, the doctor, the solicitor, the banker, the brewer, the retired general and admiral who has served under Nelson and Wellington, the widower and spinster with a good income, form a social circle the members of which meet in each other's houses, play whist ... and end with the temperate tray of sandwiches and negus.'[17]

A not dissimilar circle in the Knutsford of the day, immortalised in Mrs. Gaskell's *Cranford*, was finding plentiful opportunities for serving biscuits: ladies' finger biscuits with cowslip wine for mid-morning refreshment, currants and biscuits for dessert, and Savoy and sponge biscuits, again with wine, at evening parties.[18] Not surprisingly, therefore, as Mary Russell Mitford tells us, when Quaker biscuits came to Reading they were soon 'in the fashion', so that 'nothing could go down for luncheon in any family of gentility but Mrs. Purdy's biscuits'.[19] These were not in fact Huntley's biscuits but almost certainly those of Thomas Perry, who opened a shop in the market place a few years after 1822.

Thomas Perry's handiwork at one point evoked an almost lyrical passage in Miss Mitford's book. Yet he has now been completely forgotten, whereas the fame of the Huntley products soon progressed far beyond Reading, for Joseph Huntley had the makings of an entrepreneur in him. He saw an opportunity, and he grasped it.

The Huntley shop happened to be situated opposite the Crown Hotel, a posting inn on the main thoroughfare between London and Bath. Three coaches departed every day to the West Country, namely the 'Ship', the 'York House', and 'Franklands', which bore the landlord's surname, and there were other regular services. Many notables stayed at the hotel. King George III, for instance, used to break his journey there *en route* for his holiday resort of Weymouth, as did John Wesley as he preached around the country. However, the Crown is unlikely to have supplied any more palatable food than its fellows in coaching days. Their bills of fare are said to have consisted invariably of 'Chop, sir, steak, broiled fowl'.[20] Coaching inns were also in the habit of overcharging, since waiters used to delay presenting the bill until the passengers were being rounded up for departure.

Travellers halting at the Crown were therefore drawn to the little shop across the way in order to buy refreshments for the journey. The shop may also have dispensed non-alcoholic beverages, for later on it was to stock Jacob Schweppe's mineral waters, but we have no records for these very early days. The resourceful Joseph therefore conceived the idea of sending the delivery boy with his hand-basket to sell biscuits to passengers waiting round the inn yard while the horses were being changed. Perhaps the biscuits were wrapped up in twisted pieces of paper, for the paper bag as we know it did not come into general use until several decades later. Whatever wrapping was used, it could not have kept them fresh for more than a few hours. Nevertheless, travellers began to demand Huntley's biscuits from their grocers at home, and the potential market of the business suddenly ceased to be a purely local one.

Joseph therefore took two crucial steps. The first was to enlist the help of his younger son Joseph, who had already been apprenticed to a Reading ironmonger—probably Edwin Fardon, who was also a brazier, coppersmith and tinplate worker in London Street, and was married to the elder Joseph's niece by marriage. Joseph junior had then gone away to complete his training in the Black Country, the centre of the iron trade; on his return he had in 1832 opened an ironmonger's shop next door to the Crown Inn and therefore exactly opposite the biscuit shop. His father now persuaded him to make tins and tin-lined boxes, which solved the problem of keeping the biscuits fresh.

The other step taken by Joseph Huntley senior grew out of the fact that his own shop was rented from James Cocks. Cocks was a Reading fishmonger who in 1802 had invented a sauce that was soon popular enough to be sold throughout the United Kingdom. Between 1812 and 1819 he had increased the number of his retail agents in London from seventy to 250; in 1819 there were thirty retailers in Bath, twenty in Bristol and thirty as far afield as Edinburgh and Glasgow.[21] James Cocks in fact lived next door to the Huntley shop until his death in 1827, when his business was worth about £10,000. The receptive Joseph must have learnt a great deal from his neighbour about the methods of distributing household products.

Whether the Reading sauce was then sold through a single London agent (as it was later distributed by Crosse & Blackwell) or by a series of travellers in different parts of the country is not recorded. However, the first Huntley traveller was Thomas Worth, a Leicestershire man who for some years had been settled in the south of England, and since

1821 had lived in Reading very close to the shop. Being a 'traveller in grocery' he dealt in several different commodities, possibly including the Reading sauce. His labours were to some extent assisted by Joseph himself, who combined regular travel in the ministry with some canvassing for orders. Perhaps Joseph's canvassing was too open for Quaker susceptibilities, which may account for the equivocal tribute paid him after his death by Reading Monthly Meeting. 'We believe', they wrote in carefully chosen words, 'he was desirous of walking in the path of apprehended duty.'[22]

By the late 1830s the firm was selling about twenty different kinds of biscuit, ranging from the Captain's, Abernethy and Oliver varieties to the more choice Cracknels, Macaroons, Ratafias and Sponge Tea Cakes. In addition, it made four kinds of cake. Apart from 'Rich Bride Cakes', made to order, these were all produced in batches, according to demand. There were also one or two items of confectionery, including fancy bread rolls and some seasonal products such as Easter (hot cross) buns and Twelfth (Night) cakes. The business's growth is reflected in the increase that took place in its gross estimated rental, for rating purposes, from £12 in 1822 to £28 in 1838, plus an extra £4 from 1837 onwards when it took over the warehouse in Cocks's Court.

The first surviving account book, opened at the beginning of 1837, shows that turnover on credit accounts came to £1410 in that year; total turnover was therefore perhaps a little over £1600, including cash sales over the counter. Each customer's name is followed grandiloquently by the words 'To J. Huntley & Son' in Joseph's clerkly but somewhat shaky handwriting. There are 117 customers (chiefly grocers) seventy of whom can be identified as being situated in fifty-two different towns or villages scattered over a wide area of southern England. All these localities could be reached by the various canal and water routes, except for a small group like Stow-on-the-Wold and Chipping Norton in the Cotswolds, which were served by carrier from Banbury.

The Kennet and Avon canal, opened in 1810, transported his biscuits to Bath and Bristol, and along the Bristol Channel to such accessible towns as Bridgwater, Newport in Monmouthshire and Ross-on-Wye. Biscuits also went via the Thames to the Medway towns of Rochester and Aylesford, by the Grand Junction Canal to Hemel Hempstead, Aylesbury and Buckingham, and by the Oxford Canal as far north as Leamington Spa. Some south coast towns, including Bognor, Portsmouth and Poole, may have been reached through the Wey and Arun navigation. The canal system was used in preference to roads not merely for reasons of economy—since goods went from Reading for at least half the price of road transport—but also because on the water there was far less risk of damage by vibration than over the bad roads.

One of the problems which arise when a retail business becomes a wholesale one is that of finance. Very little working capital is needed when all sales are strictly for cash and suppliers provide ingredients on credit. Many of the Huntley wholesale customers were reliable ones, settling their accounts within a few days or weeks of presentation. The largest customer, who bought on average £100 worth annually between 1837 and 1839, was Samuel Beesley, the Quaker proprietor of the celebrated cake shop at Banbury. His own sales of Banbury cakes were not far short of the Huntley biscuit turnover, reaching £1160 in 1840, and some of these were sold in Huntley's shop at twopence apiece.[23] When Samuel died in 1843 his shop was taken over by Mary Lamb, who later married Joseph Huntley the younger. A non-Quaker customer was William Fortt of Bath, whose average trade in Huntley's biscuits was £30 worth a year in the late 1830s; his Bath buns, being far more perishable, do not seem to have been sold in Reading. However, many years later Huntley and Palmers were to make Bath Oliver biscuits under licence from Fortts.

On the other hand, among the very slow payers was James Busvine, a Bristol grocer who paid little heed to the admonition in the Quaker *Rules of Discipline* not to run up debts or trade beyond one's capital. Busvine owed about £75 at the beginning of each year; since this was not much short of his annual purchases, the Huntleys were undoubtedly restricting him to twelve months' credit. The grocers' own credit customers were often shamefully slow in paying their bills, and there is plenty of evidence as to tradespeople's bitter resentment at this tardiness. Yet indirectly, and quite unwittingly, Busvine was to be the instrument through which the next great leap forward in the Reading business was to be achieved, as Chapter 2 will show.

The total of debts owing to the Huntley shop rose more than proportionately to the increase in turnover. At the end of 1836 these debts came to £466, or a third of total credit sales; a year later, when credit sales do not appear greatly to have exceeded £1300, debts were as high as £590. In addition to the financial problems, however, was a growing managerial one. Joseph Huntley, although not much over sixty, was now badly afflicted by shaking paralysis, and in 1838 he retired.

Thomas, excellent craftsman as he was, did not really possess the capacity to run the business entirely on his own. His father had not even made him a partner until 1829, when he was twenty-six. Although three years later he had married Jane Evans, the daughter of a Quaker saddler at Southampton, and Joseph had moved to a nearby house with one of his unmarried daughters, Joseph had remained effectively in charge. There was a further difficulty: Thomas's own health was beginning to fail, for he was suffering from prostate trouble. He therefore had to find a partner to take his father's place, and to provide extra capital for expansion in the future. In fact, Joseph did not draw any capital out of the business on his retirement, but instead agreed to draw a pension of £80 a year, payable quarterly as a prior charge before profits were calculated.

It was three years before Thomas was joined by a new partner, who turned out to be quite as enterprising and forceful as Joseph Huntley had been.

2
The Palmer Background 1727–1841

The kind of business partner sought by Thomas Huntley after his father's retirement in 1838 needed four characteristics above all. First, he had to be a Quaker; and, second, he would have been thoroughly trained in biscuit-baking. Third, he would preferably be a former journeyman working for the first time on his own, since Thomas naturally wished to be the senior partner. On the other hand, Thomas's natural lack of entrepreneurial qualities and intermittent bouts of ill-health required the presence of a competent man who would tactfully assume full responsibility when required. Fourth, the partner must be able to bring into the partnership a reasonably large amount of capital, in the region of £500 for a half-share.

Such a combination of characteristics should not have been all that rare, as there seems to have been an ample supply of young Quaker confectioners at that time. The three years' delay before George Palmer joined him in partnership is puzzling; no correspondence of any kind earlier than 1849 has survived, and we have to rely on indirect evidence alone.

Not unexpectedly, the lack of written testimony has given rise to an oral tradition within the business. According to this tradition, George Palmer happened to be on his way from the west of England to seek his fortune in London. In his luggage, or his head, were plans for machinery of a kind that would revolutionise biscuit production. On alighting from the stage coach during a halt at the Crown Inn—the story continues—he caught sight of Thomas Huntley's shop just across the road, struck up an acquaintanceship with him, learnt that he was in need of a partner, and straightway offered himself for that situation.

Such evidence as we do have indicates that this traditional account is almost wholly incorrect. In any case, it would be straining coincidence too far to suggest that these two men—who complemented each other's qualities so remarkably—met purely as a result of chance. We have already seen how the origins of the Reading business had been influenced by certain chance happenings, such as the natural calamities of 1814 which uncovered Joseph Huntley's financial straits, and a fatality in a traffic accident that left vacant at precisely the right moment a shop facing the Crown Inn and next door to the manufacturer of a very well-known proprietary product of Reading. To the business historian, unlike the scholar disillusioned in his convictions about a steady progress towards enlightenment, the factor of chance is merely something that is given. What interests him is the entrepreneur's response to chance happenings: if bad, whether they are met half-way so as to minimise their harmful consequences, or if good, whether they are seized to further the business's interests, or alternatively, whether the opportunity of positive action is allowed to slip by.

The coming together of Thomas Huntley and George Palmer was influenced partly by chance factors and partly by responses to chance. Until the 1830s no connection existed between their two families, for the Palmers were entirely a West Country family. They made a living as yeomen—that is, men of some substance who were tenant farmers—at Long Sutton, a village of 900 inhabitants situated in the plain of mid-Somerset. There a branch of the Society of Friends had been established well before 1670, the date when the old thatched meeting house had been wrecked in the great persecution of that year, even the mats being stripped off the benches. A new meeting house, an austere but well-proportioned Queen Anne building with a high-pitched roof, was erected under the will of a rich benefactor in 1719.

By that date, a member of the Palmer family, William Palmer I, and his family were already Quakers. In 1727 William held on lease thirty-five acres of arable, pasture and meadow land, together with a farm-house, garden and orchard.[1] Twelve years later his son Richard married Betty Salter, from Podimore, a village five miles away. Her grandfather had been converted to Quakerism by Thomas Ellwood, a close friend of George Fox and John Milton, while her father James, who with the rest of his family endured severe persecution before 1689, subsequently built a meeting house in his village and was very active in Monthly and Quarterly Meetings throughout Somerset.

From the Quaker point of view, the union between Richard Palmer and Betty Salter was prolific in quantity rather than quality. During the next century and a half no less than eighteen of their descendants were interred in the burial ground by the Long Sutton meeting house, plus another twelve Palmers whose relationship is less certain. However, they did not take the active part in Quaker affairs that might have been

The Palmer Background 1727–1841

expected, bearing in mind their ancestry. Richard's son William Palmer II had nine children; yet none of them or their descendants, except for George Palmer himself, became a minister or elder.

Nevertheless, they prospered in a material sense. William Palmer II died in 1816 worth about £3000 and his holdings in the parish, although scattered in a truly medieval manner, amounted to 112 acres.[2] He had already distributed £1600 among his six sons, to allow them to take up farming on their own account, and the eldest—William Palmer III—was able to pay his widowed mother £170 a year for the use of the 112 acres in which she had a life interest. William Palmer III had the reputation of being a 'gay' Quaker; he rode to hounds and his own will shows that he brewed home beer and cider, which his 'plain' brethren must have deplored. Undoubtedly the most significant event of his life was his marriage to a remarkable woman, Mary Isaac.

Mary and her sister Martha had come to Long Sutton some years before, to help a relative of theirs to run the village shop in what had been the old meeting house at Long Sutton, a thatched cottage just opposite the new meeting house. The fair hair and brown eyes of the sisters attracted the attention of young Friends, and others, over a wide area. No doubt the Quaker householders of the village found their hospitality being sought by admirers who claimed that their business affairs happened to bring them in that direction.

Portraits of Martha and Mary in their old age, wearing the distinctive Quaker black dress partly covered with a shawl, cravat with bands and silk-edged bonnet, still survive. Martha, who enjoyed a relatively uneventful life married to a draper and grocer at Langport, the nearest town a few miles away, has a wistful and serene expression appropriate to one much admired in her youth. Mary's features, on the other hand, seem to have been set by misfortune and make it difficult for later generations to recapture her attractiveness. Yet she brought a new strain into the Palmer family which was far more important to them than mere good looks. Like Hannah Huntley, she was extremely devout as well as extremely energetic; she turned her hand to biscuit-making, and walked regularly the seven miles into Yeovil market, in order to sell her biscuits there.

Her ancestry is of some relevance to the unfolding of this story. The Isaac family had been tanners for many generations in the small Dorset town of Sturminster Newton, in the Vale of Blackmore, with its 1500-odd inhabitants. Their business was quite a thriving one, for when her father William Isaac died in 1814 his 'goods, chattels and credits' were worth £2000, a fair sum for such a country business. George Palmer's and his brothers' success at Reading was later claimed by the youngest brother, William Isaac Palmer, to have resulted from the combination of two elements in their blood, the 'producing' industry of farming and the 'manufacturing' one of tanning.³

In fact, the element of heredity was even more important than appears from this statement. For all their farming skill, the Palmer family was not particularly distinguishable from its neighbours until Mary Isaac brought into it, through her own mother, the inherited qualities of the Clark family of Street in Somerset. The Clarks were an extremely inventive family. The most noteworthy were the brothers Cyrus and James Clark, who in 1833 became partners in what is now the great shoemaking firm C. & J. Clark of Street; they were cousins of Mary Isaac.

Another cousin, John Clark, invented and patented a process of waterproofing cloth which proved to be uneconomic, owing to the expense of one ingredient. He therefore sold the patent to Charles Macintosh, a Scot who eventually found a cheaper ingredient for the process, and is therefore held to be the inventor of the raincoat which bears his name. John Clark also built a machine that would construct Latin hexameters; lest he should be regarded merely as an eccentric, a notable geologist of the day called him 'one of the few really gifted and clever men it has been my lot to know'.⁴ Mary Palmer and her children were soon to be called on to make full use of these hereditary gifts.

In 1826, when he was only thirty-seven, William Palmer III died of heart disease following rheumatic fever. George, his eldest son, was only eight, Samuel six, Mary Ovens (named after a childless aunt on her mother's side) not quite four and William Isaac just under two. After his mother's death and the formal division of the family estate between the eight children a few years before, he had moved away to Elberton, a very small village in Gloucestershire. He rented the largest farm there from one of the Goldney family, Quakers who were connected with Bristol Old Bank and with the Coalbrookdale iron works. The Manor House, where the Palmers lived, had additional Quaker associations, as the birthplace thirty years before of the corn merchant and philanthropist Joseph Sturge; he had been a nephew of Mary Palmer's aunt by marriage, but it is not known whether this relationship influenced the move to Elberton or not.⁵

The form of William Palmer III's will, and the idiosyncratic spellings (such as 'bead linning' for 'bed linen', and 'nateral'), were his own, but the ideas clearly came from Mary Palmer. She had seen at first hand the decline in agricultural values since the end of the Napoleonic wars, and decided that her sons should not try to make a living as tenant farmers but should be apprenticed to trades; not even the eldest son George was to remain on the land. The will therefore set up a trust, comprising their uncle Joseph Palmer and Aunt Martha's husband John Gillett (the

The Palmer Background 1727–1841

draper and grocer described in the will as 'drugest' [druggist] of Langport), to see to the children's upbringing, education and eventual apprenticeship.

All four children thus received a sound upbringing. Joseph Palmer himself and his brother Robert had been two of the earliest pupils at Sidcot, a Quaker boarding school near Weston-super-Mare. Sidcot was one of the new-type establishments of the kind which had superseded the older schools like Thomas Huntley's at Burford. Indeed, it had been established in 1808 as a counterpart in the south of England to Ackworth in the north.

Together with five Palmer cousins—four girls and a boy—who partly overlapped them, Mary Ovens and her brothers each spent five years, from the age of nine to fourteen, at Sidcot. Both the boys' and the girls' schools were in the same grounds, but not until 1838 were they under the same roof, even though in different wings. So complete was the segregation that the sexes were neither taught together nor allowed to mix out of school. The opportunities even for brothers and sisters to see one another were limited to half an hour once a week, under strict surveillance.

Other aspects of the school in its early days do not sound encouraging to present-day notions. Owing to the need for economy, the food was exceedingly gruesome: bullocks' hearts (one being, incredibly enough, considered sufficient for forty boys), liver and lungs, and quantities of herrings alternated on the menu, while those out of favour with the waiters received nothing more than stale bread for breakfast. Punishment, too, was harsh by any standards, let alone the normally humane standards of the Quakers. Boys were caned and strapped for very minor misdemeanours, and the 'refractory' ones were shut away for long periods in narrow cupboards nicknamed 'coffins'.[6]

By the time when George Palmer entered the school in 1827, some at least of the rigours of diet and punishment had been relaxed a little. He could not have been unhappy there, for as the very young head of a fatherless family, he was too purposeful to court any of the ruthless punishments of the day. Nor is there any reason to suppose that he ever noticed particularly what he was eating, except for biscuits. What matters here is how far this kind of education affected his subsequent development.

He found the practical nature of the curriculum quite stimulating. This consisted of grammar and geography in the initial years, and later on some experimental lessons in chemistry, electricity and acoustics. Such lessons would nowadays seem quite crude and elementary. Nevertheless, they were enough to awaken in him an interest in science which never left him, and which soon developed into a practical skill in engineering and a mechanical insight later recognised as exceptional in a layman.

At Sidcot no history or English literature was taught, nor did he master any foreign language, living or dead, so that at the age of fifty he had to admit his complete 'inability to speak either in French or German'. But he derived such enjoyment from the science that he did learn that he willingly continued his studies outside school hours. He worked hard to keep going a 'Juvenile Society for Mutual Improvement in Useful Knowledge'; indeed, his first recorded piece of organisation was to re-form that society after it had expired for lack of support. His plan, sensibly enough, was to restrict its scope to natural philosophy, including 'the nature of atoms, attraction, repulsion and inertia'. Countless boys of twelve or thirteen have found the laws of science going to their head, and have found to their cost, as George Palmer did when the society folded up once again after three meetings, that repulsion and inertia were not confined to inanimate beings. What was unusual was that this consuming interest persisted throughout his own career and those of three or four descendants.[7]

In 1832, when he was fourteen and a half, he left Sidcot. He was immediately apprenticed to an uncle in Taunton, to learn the trade of confectioner and miller. His master, Robert Hitchcock, had married in middle life William Palmer III's elder sister Priscilla. The Hitchcocks were a comfortable childless couple, who must have looked after their nephew with a little more warmth than most apprentices of the day enjoyed, although he still had to sleep under the counter like the rest of his breed.

There is no direct evidence as to why his guardians chose that particular trade for him. His parents' brothers on both sides were either farmers or tanners, but perhaps the decisive factor was that two of his aunts had married millers in Taunton, a town that was no more than twenty miles away from home.

His was by no means a solitary life as an apprentice, for his master encouraged his highly constructive outside interests. He was an active member of the Mechanics' Institution at Taunton; although none of its records are extant, he may well have given talks there on the engineering topics that were already beginning to absorb him. He made friends also: a fellow-apprentice there attended a commemorative occasion in Reading as late as the mid-1880s, and the Institution's secretary, Edward William Cox, was a young man who years later, when an eminent lawyer and journalist, recalled their association in a letter of congratulation on George Palmer's election to the House of Commons.

It was at Taunton also that he began to develop the other major interest of his life: politics and public affairs. He helped to organise, when only twenty, part of a grand trades procession to commemorate Queen Victoria's coronation in 1838. There were fifty-four representatives in the confectioners' and bakers' section of which he was the marshal: each carried a peel—the shovel they used for putting loaves into and removing them from the oven—and wore white and green rosettes garnished with bunches of roses and green ears of wheat. A banner at the head proclaimed their trade in gold letters, with a pineapple and wheatsheaf as their respective devices. No doubt he also assisted that same afternoon at the monster tea for 2700 children, who between them put away 1700 lb. of plum cake and (as the *Taunton Courier* described it) over 200 gallons of 'real good tea and coffee—not wash': three-quarters of a pint per child.[8]

However, the most far-reaching event of his apprenticeship occurred during a visit he paid one day to Bristol. His account of it was written in old age, as part of an affidavit for a court case against the Reading Biscuit Co., referred to in Chapter 11. While browsing in the shop of James Busvine—the grocer whose slow payments have already been mentioned—he bought some of Huntley's Reading biscuits, and took them back to his master. The fact that he recalled this happening so clearly sixty years later indicates his sense of excitement at this discovery, his desire to learn something about the Huntley business, and perhaps an aspiration to try his hand at making biscuits of such quality by machinery. From then onwards he could have been helped by the workings of the 'Quaker cousinhood', for his cousin Jane married Thomas Huntley the same year he went to Taunton, and his guardian and uncle Joseph Palmer married into the Smith family of Reading three years later.

At any rate, as soon as he was out of his indentures, in 1840, George Palmer went off to Cardiff. His mother assigned the lease of her Elberton farm to Joseph Palmer, and she and Mary Ovens joined George in Cardiff; from then onwards the fortunes of his mother and sister were to be linked with his own. As he only stayed at Cardiff for less than a year, he may have gone there to gain mechanical experience, perhaps in the manufacture of ship's biscuits. Then in mid-1841 the three of them moved to Reading.

All in all, George Palmer's preparative years must have been reasonably happy ones. He relished the plentiful opportunities to develop his various interests and to learn new facts. Likewise, his youngest brother William Isaac seems to have had a happy upbringing, for he was as much a favourite of his teacher as he was his mother's favourite child. While still at school he signed the pledge to abstain from alcohol and helped the teacher to set up the type for a periodical named *The Sidcot*

Teetotaller. In after life he used to relate how he was chosen to keep watch with a telescope from a window overlooking the British Channel for the *Great Western* on its maiden voyage in 1838: the first steamship to cross the Atlantic from east to west.[9]

The other two children, having inherited something of their father's less sombre character, found the life at Sidcot a little trying. Mary Ovens' schooldays comprised interminable afternoons of making and mending clothes and listening to a schoolmistress reading aloud from *Chambers' Journal* and similar literature that tried to combine interesting articles with improving ideas. Of these oppressive days she commented simply: 'I was often sensible of the goodness of the Lord; but the world and the things of it drew my heart from dedication to him.' The main problem was that her unformed but perceptive mind, when she was scarcely in her teens, found it hard to accept 'that the little things I then felt about, could be noticed by such a *great and gracious* Creator ... I *think* that I believed in Christ, and that I could only be saved by him'. Without being morbid or conventionally pious in any way, she was very like her brothers in taking nothing on trust and being entirely honest with herself.[10]

Samuel, too, being more vivacious and extrovert than the others, could have found little in the curriculum, the discipline or living conditions at Sidcot to commend themselves, although the cleverness with figures which he later displayed may have been developed there. After leaving the school in 1834 he became a clerk in the banking house of Dimsdale, Drewett, Fowler and Barnard, of Lombard Street in London. That house had strong Quaker connections, and eventually through successive amalgamations became part of what is now the National Westminster Bank. For many years it was to be the London bank of the Reading firm. In 1840 Samuel took a commercial post in Bristol.

Thus there were two interconnected elements in the background to the Palmer family. The first was the access of fresh blood, by marriage into the Clark and Isaac families, to the hitherto not very noteworthy stock of the Palmers. The second was the mother's decision to seek more promising and lucrative outlets than farming for her children's energies and abilities. Although George Palmer was at first the only member of his family concerned in the management of the Reading business, he later adopted the common practice in Victorian family firms, of bringing his two brothers into the organisation. From Thomas Huntley's death in 1857 until its amalgamation in a larger group of family firms, the Palmers were entirely in control of it. All the members of the family who have been partners or directors were descended either from George

Palmer or from his brother Samuel; William Isaac Palmer never married.

The earliest example of George Palmer's reliance on his brothers was in 1838, just about the time of Joseph Huntley's retirement, when Joseph junior took on William Isaac Palmer as an apprentice ironmonger; undoubtedly the trustees did this on George's suggestion. From then on William, of a quieter disposition but no less alert to events going on around him, must have kept his brother informed of events in Reading. He thus played a part in the genesis, as well as in the later growth, of the partnership.

PART II

*The Partnership Era
1841–98*

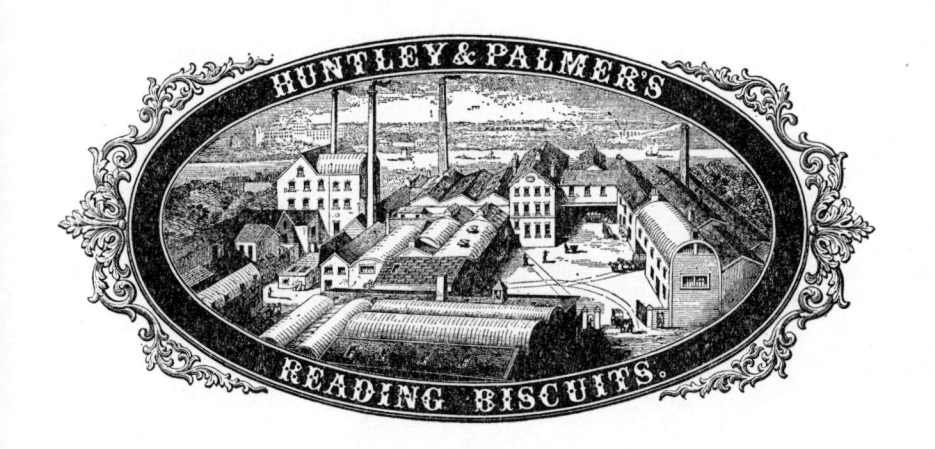

3
Commencement of the Partnership 1841–6

On 24th June—midsummer day—1841 Thomas Huntley and George Palmer concluded their partnership agreement. It was to run for a period of fourteen years, namely until midsummer day 1855; when that date arrived everyone had apparently forgotten about the provision, since the agreement was extended for a further twenty-one years, but not until several months later.

The gross value of the business was estimated at just over £1000, of which three-quarters, about £750, represented debts owed by customers. Stock-in-trade came to only £72, while valuation of the respective types of fixtures and fittings undertaken by Joseph Huntley the ironmonger (£75), a builder (£49) and a carpenter (£66) totalled no more than £190. The shop premises were, of course, rented. On the debit side £400 was owed by the business for ingredients and other supplies. After deducting one or two minor items such as bad debts, Thomas Huntley's financial interest in the business was computed as £550; to this George Palmer now added an equivalent sum, in three instalments paid by the end of the year, and his partner drew out £400 to liquidate the outstanding debts.

Thomas Huntley's status as senior partner was formally recognised in various ways. In the event of the partnership being dissolved, he had the option of repurchasing the business at a fair valuation of the 'capital stock and effects', plus a premium equal to the average of the final two years' profits. (In 1846 this provision was changed to allowing either partner to purchase the business if it were to be wound up.) He was to keep the accounts and ledgers as well as supervise the packing department, and spend seven hours a day on this work. Over and above this he was 'not obliged to attend any further than he shall think proper'.

George Palmer, on the other hand, was to manage the manufacturing department, where he would spend at least five hours a day. The remainder of his time he had to devote to the general duties of the business; these included sales and all the correspondence. He was now the one to live over the shop, at a net rent of £20 a year, while the Huntleys rented a house in a nearby street. He also had to provide a lodging for the shop assistant, who conveniently happened to be his sister Mary Ovens, already living in. Their mother was meanwhile in Reading as well. While preparing to take over the house as soon as the Huntleys moved out, she was staying with her husband's relative, John Smith the grocer further along London Street.

Despite appearances, however, George Palmer from the outset had effective control of the business. He insisted on a bank account being opened—for the business had managed without one until then—and on all the takings being deposited once a week. He also stopped the discount which Joseph Huntley junior had been receiving on the biscuits and cakes he bought. Thomas must have greatly regretted having to give up the biscuit-making side, where he had worked so diligently and contentedly for nearly twenty years, and take on the accounting work which he plainly disliked. He did not understand the crucial difference between a profit and loss account and a balance sheet: when drawing up the first year's balance sheet in June 1842, he included in it cash receipts and expenditure, which threw up an entirely incorrect balance of funds belonging to the partners. However, these errors were soon corrected, and George Palmer sought for ways to realise the potentialities of the business.

For all its 'good name', only eight people were engaged in the business, apart from the shop assistant and the traveller: namely the partners, two journeymen (Richard Brown and a former apprentice, William Bitmead), two apprentices and two boys, who presumably did the packing as well as making the local deliveries.[1] There was practically no machinery, except for a 'dough machine brake'—a rolling machine worked by hand, of a kind already used by bakers for at least four centuries—and a small hand-roller, through which strips of dough were fed in order to stamp the name HUNTLEY on Jamaica biscuits: this latter machine was still regularly used in the business up to 1939.

Output, and hence profits, could only be raised by building up, in co-ordination with each other, the business's productive capacity and also its market. The first had a special fascination for him, and he very soon took two short-term steps to that end. First, he enlarged the premises by renting the shop next door, and second, he introduced the first set of power-driven machinery.

Barely three months passed before, in September 1841, he secured the lease of 73 London Street, to the north of his own shop and forming the other half of the same frontage. The combined rent came to the substantial figure of £70 a year. The extra cellar gave greater baking space, but the supplementary bakehouse was still in the outbuildings at the rear, while the two cottages were rented to the senior employees until they were turned into storerooms in 1853. Above ground, the shop was now doubled in size, although its rear wall may have been brought forward in order to enlarge the ground-floor bakehouse.

The steam-powered machine, installed some time during the first year, was of no more than $1\frac{1}{2}$ h.p.[2] Presumably it was situated in the ground-floor bakehouse, and was intended to save labour in the dough mixing, the most arduous of all the processes. It clearly proved successful enough to encourage him to plan the machinery for the factory which he aimed to set up in due course. Although, as we have seen, he had until very recently been a journeyman biscuit-baker and was therefore no trained engineer, he had a practical aptitude and interest in mechanical matters. He was now fortunate enough to discover precisely the kind of man he needed as technical adviser on the spot in Reading.

At that time, such heavy industry as Reading possessed was along the river Kennet, where good wharfs already existed. One of the rapidly growing enterprises there was the iron foundry of Barrett Exall and Andrewes. The junior partner, William Exall, was a skilled inventor and improviser who relished all tasks involved in developing and perfecting mechanical ideas. Although many of his most noteworthy innovations were in the field of agricultural engineering, he willingly collaborated with George Palmer in mastering the technical problems of mechanising fancy-biscuit manufacture.[3] Some of these problems will be mentioned in Chapter 4, such as how to adapt an intermittent process—where steam power is connected and then disconnected as required—to continuous working. His friendship with William Exall developed so far that when his second son Alfred Palmer wished to marry William's daughter Alice Exall, he did nothing to hinder the marriage, even though it was held in a Congregational church, and led to the couple's later becoming members of the Church of England.

It was not good enough merely to increase the firm's productive capacity: an equally pressing need was to extend the scope of the market. One way was by selective advertising. Even though George Palmer had left school at the age of fourteen and a half the good feeling he had for grammar and style is reflected in his persuasive copywriting. In the 1842 *Reading Post Office Directory Advertiser* he shared a full-page advertisement with Joseph Huntley, 'Ironmonger and Tin Plate Worker'. There he proclaimed that his own firm's 'excellent' biscuits, which 'have attained such celebrity that they are now sold in nearly all the Towns near Reading, and in London, as well as in many distant parts of the Kingdom, need only a trial to prove their superior quality and secure their preference'.

Two years later he even rose to a small advertisement in *The Times* of London, which spoke of the firm's 'superior' biscuits being 'sold in London and the principal towns of the country by respectable grocers and Italian warehousemen'. These last then possessed some of the cachet nowadays enjoyed by Continental delicatessen shops, and sold Italian fruits and groceries, including olive oil. It was perhaps understandable for him to apply the epithet 'superior' to what was after all a high quality product. However, many consumers of the day felt that the word had been so overworked that it was 'getting to be shopkeepers' slang'.[4]

A further advertisement of the period showed one method by which such celebrity was achieved: 'the great satisfaction which these Biscuits have given in those fashionable Watering-places, and other towns where they have been introduced', it ran, had evoked 'inquiry for them in London by persons on their return to town'. The firm had therefore appointed five London agents to undertake wholesale as well as retail business.

Thus, as in the Huntley era, personal trial and personal recommendation were among the most cogent means of publicity, backed up with occasional nudges in the press. However, the development of the market would be impeded unless the goods were in the right shops, and George Palmer therefore made the most strenuous efforts to spread his outlets extensively throughout Britain. Thomas Worth had single handed, with a little help from the elder Joseph Huntley, built up the existing network of retailers over much of southern England; however, Worth was by now approaching seventy. After 1842 his name appears less and less frequently in the ledgers and vanishes entirely after 1847. He died of apoplexy four years later.

Instead George Palmer engaged seven or eight commission agents in different parts of the country. Like Worth, they were not salaried employees of the firm but combined their work for it with commission work for other firms. They were in fact not so much concerned with obtaining routine orders as in collecting unpaid accounts. John Cooper —apparently a Quaker—was responsible for the most extensive recruitment of retailers yet undertaken; between April and September 1842 he secured no less than eighty-two of them in the Midlands and North of England, from Birmingham to Sheffield. Many of these Midland accounts were taken over by Gawen Ball Kenway, a Birmingham Quaker whose son later became a full-time traveller for the firm.

John Fry Wilkey of Exeter was yet another Quaker commission agent. Having failed in his own retail business, he had begun to travel in the four western counties for a number of manufacturers.[5] A London firm, G. D. Myers & Co. (which also printed some of the earliest biscuit tin labels and wrappers), was responsible for East Anglia and Lincolnshire, and Samuel Neave of Totton for the Portsmouth area. The standard commission they earned was 7½ per cent. Thomas and William Fayle of Dublin (who were Quakers, like Samuel Neave) received from the firm 10 per cent and expenses; the higher remuneration was presumably to compensate them for the greater risks and expenses involved in a country during the throes of the potato famine. In fact, the amount of business they brought the firm was under £300 a year for the whole of Ireland. These rates of commission were onerous for the firm, but they had to be borne for the sake of allowing it to grow.

The upshot was a slow but steady increase in turnover. George Palmer never forgot the exact figure of his first year's sales, for 1841-2. Just forty years later he recalled it without difficulty to his Continental traveller, Joseph Leete, in—of all places—the tea-room of the House of Commons: namely £3200. In fact, he seems to have included in that year's cash receipts the capital sum of £550 he had brought in, and a more accurate total was a little over £2700. The next year turnover rose by almost a quarter, to £3360, of which about £400 comprised retail accounts. Thus the wholesale side of the business had more than doubled in value since the late 1830s. Then in 1843-4 turnover made a further jump, by nearly 40 per cent, to £4650.

However, profits showed far less satisfactory progress than did sales. Indeed, in the initial year of 1841-2 the firm made no profit at all, since the partners' drawings of £100 each were exactly offset by a loan of £200 made by William Golding, a Quaker ironfounder of Newbury. Actual profits for 1842-3 were only £215, and the firm had to incur two further loans. Thomas Terry, who owned Swallowfield Mill, a few miles from Reading, and provided the firm with practically all its flour, lent £200. This is quite an interesting example, found in many industries, of a supplier helping at a time of need the business it supplies.

Mary Palmer, now supervising the shop as well as keeping house for him and his sister, lent £150 that year and a further £66 during 1843-4, when profits amounted only to £323, and the Reading bankers Stephens Blandy & Co. made a loan of £100. In June 1844, therefore, the firm's outside loans amounted to £716, on capital and reserves not much greater than the original £1100. Not only would it be progressively risky to incur further loans, but since the existing ones all carried interest at 5 per cent, the prior charges of rent, rates, interest on these loans, insurance and Joseph Huntley's pension totalled £212 a year.

There was also the persistent problem of trade credit. Customers' debts to the firm were by 1843-4 nearly 37 per cent of the year's turnover, a higher proportion than in 1836. Similarly, net debts outstanding—namely, debts receivable from customers less debts payable, mainly to ingredients suppliers—had risen from £350 in June

1841 to £876 in June 1844. In order to economise on cash, therefore, until 1847-8 the partners never drew more than £200 a year each, except in 1845-6 when they ventured to draw out £220. Nor was Mary Palmer paid any interest at all until mid-1845. In short, during the first three years of the partnership true profits, of £538, were barely enough even to cover the increase in net credit given, let alone build up reserves against future expansion. Hence the partners' combined drawings had to be covered largely out of loans.

The initial three-year period therefore ended with a question mark. Had the business any chance at all of surviving in its present form, let alone of fulfilling the very ambitious aspirations which George Palmer cherished for it? Then in 1844-5 it experienced a minor, but distinct, turning point in its progress. Although turnover expanded only by $22\frac{1}{2}$ per cent compared with the previous year, to £5700, profits soared from £323 to no less than £969; these profits represented a very welcome rise from 6·7 per cent of turnover on average in the past two years to 17 per cent. By then the five or six employees at the outset had increased to sixteen; thus there had been little improvement in labour productivity. Some mechanisation had taken place, for the value of 'machinery and fixtures' had nearly trebled from £190 to £550, and two additional ovens had been installed during 1842-3 after the firm had taken 73, London Street. Stock-in-trade had risen even more sharply, from £72 to nearly £300. The firm therefore needed some product that it could conveniently, and profitably, manufacture under the existing cramped conditions. This product turned out to be a 'patent unfermented bread' produced by Henry Dodson, a Southwark baker, according to the recipe of John Whiting, a celebrated doctor of the day.

In March 1844 Huntley and Palmer paid £50 for the right to make and sell the bread within five and a half miles of Reading; the agreed royalty was the token one of a shilling a year. In place of yeast, the bread contained hydrochloric acid and carbonate of soda, which generated carbonic acid gas for lightening the dough. A leaflet issued by the firm contained a number of testimonials from well-canvassed doctors in Reading as well as in London and also specified that luncheon cakes, milk biscuits and biscuit powder were made from the same recipe. Biscuit powder was then widely used as an easily assimilable food for invalids and infants, being made up into a pudding of pappy composition.

Until then, the only bread which the firm produced had been fancy rolls. However, the new type of bread proved an immediate success. Over the next year Mary Russell Mitford, living within the five-and-a half-mile radius from Reading at Three Mile Cross, bought a brown loaf regularly twice a week, and only an occasional Banbury cake or pound of Thin Captain biscuits. The firm apparently ceased to make the patent bread after the factory was opened in 1846; five years later, when Miss Mitford had reached a dyspeptic time of life when she subsisted on boiled sole or whiting and fruit, she plaintively asked a correspondent regarding the food in his locality: 'Is there good brown bread?'[6]

The bread clearly made a substantial contribution to the gratifying rise in profits, which in 1845–6 exceeded £1000 for the first time, while turnover that year showed a further 20 per cent rise, to just under £6900. Profits on turnover were therefore still at the encouraging level of 15 per cent. The partnership had weathered the first crisis of its existence, although the greater risks that would arise if George Palmer persisted in his determination to set up a new factory, remained ahead of it.

Only a single misfortune, and that an irreparable personal one, damped his sense of exhilaration and of dedicated optimism during the first golden days at Reading. Amid all the recent commotion and house-moving, it was not discovered until 1842 that his young sister Mary Ovens, only just out of her teens, was in an advanced and incurable stage of consumption. On the threshold of life, she shrank from death, for life had too much to offer her, and during the two remaining years of her life she was often reduced to blank despair.

As the disease progressed, the rather gloomy house over the London Street shop, which caught only the evening sun and lacked a garden, was no place for a sick girl, and at the beginning of 1844 she was sent off to pass the spring and early summer on her uncle's farm in Long Sutton. Any physical easement she may have derived from the purer Somerset air was outweighed by the severe mental conflicts that now assailed her. She later told two of her brothers how one evening, while sitting alone in her bedroom at the farm, she had suddenly become convinced that she could not even look forward to salvation, from which she felt herself 'shut out' because she could not subjugate herself entirely to God's will.

About a month before she died she returned home. Increasing debility had much reduced her mental struggles, but her over-active mind became more and more preoccupied with her brothers, who were clearly on the route towards spectacularly successful careers. She believed that they were too materialist at heart, and feared lest in their progress to the top, they might become corrupted by the 'things of the world'.

On the last Sunday of her life they all gathered round her bedside, and after prayers had been said she proceeded to give them some good sisterly advice. They must give up their entire hearts to serving God in the days of their youth: 'no half measures will do: it must be the whole heart ... I want you all to come to me in heaven: you will endeavour to come to me, won't you?' was her final moving appeal to them. There was a pause while she rallied her strength; then she asked one of them to read out the thirtieth chapter of Isaiah to her, that powerful attack on the 'rebellious children' who refused to listen to God's word, and plea for repentance.[7]

When she died in September 1844 some virtue seems to have passed out of the family. An only sister among several brothers all dedicated to serious ends can often lighten their gravity, and the Palmers, in particularly now that Samuel no longer lived regularly at home, became that much more withdrawn and abrasive than before.

Meanwhile life had to continue, and George Palmer at least was able to take refuge in his strenuous work of preparing for the next step forward: the move to a properly equipped factory. At that time the firm made only a small contribution to the economy of Reading. The partners' own incomes were very meagre, while the sixteen people employed at the end of 1844 earned between them no more than £10 a week: the total wages bill for the twenty-six employees as late as mid-1846, shortly before they took over the factory, was only £14.10s. a week. Indirectly the firm gave regular work to only a handful of Reading suppliers. Naturally enough, Thomas Terry of Swallowfield was the largest supplier of ingredients; in 1845 he received £1208 for flour delivered; the Berkshire farmers who had grown the wheat did not necessarily spend much of their incomes in Reading. John Smith the London Street grocer sold the firm £325 worth of butter and a little sugar, but a London firm provided the bulk—over £500 worth—of the sugar supplies. The firm paid much smaller amounts to Reading traders for lesser items such as coal and milk.

The other major materials were the tins and tin-lined boxes; even here, as late as 1846–7, the output of tins for the firm was no more than £1100, or a third of the turnover of Joseph Huntley and his newly acquired partner, his nephew by marriage Joseph Boorne; the remainder of Huntley and Boorne's trade comprised retail sales of ironmongery and contracting. Almost all the wooden cases were made inside the factory.

The firm must have created some additional work within the town by the organisation there for transporting the biscuits and cakes over increasingly wide areas of the British Isles. Carriers had to convey the goods to the canal wharves and to outlying districts of Reading, and also bring back the returned tins and tin-lined boxes. Nevertheless, when all these items were added together, a single sitting of the Assizes brought in net purchasing power to the town—estimated to be about

£2000—which was not much lower than the purchasing power generated by Huntley and Palmer in the course of a whole year.[8]

Where was this new factory to be situated? The creation of King's Road, to connect Broad Street with the intersection of the London and the Wokingham roads (later Cemetery Junction), had recently opened up a hitherto undeveloped area to the north-east of Reading. It was mentioned earlier how the large-scale industry in Reading tended to be concentrated to the west, along the banks of the River Kennet. Further downriver, between the town centre and the point where it flowed into the Thames, a small section of canal, known as the New Cut, had been constructed. By the early 1840s the wedge-shaped island site between the canal and the river already had a number of factories standing on it, including the Cannon Brewery, the Gas Works and a tobacco factory.

Another of these buildings, Messrs. Baylis's silk crape factory had been opened with a great flourish in 1841,[9] but had never paid its way. It had been closed down a year or two later and was still vacant. Its floor space was 5000 square feet on a half-acre site, and it was joined by a party wall with the tobacco factory to the west. By mid-1846 George Palmer's plans were far enough advanced for him and Thomas Huntley to negotiate for the purchase of the silk factory. The vendor was John Weedon, a prominent Reading solicitor and property owner. In September they bought it for £1800, which Weedon immediately lent them on mortgage at 5 per cent. The burden of an extra £90 in interest, coupled with the obligation to repay at a—fortunately unspecified—future period, could only be the first instalment of a massive burden for the firm. Thomas Huntley had had too much experience of his father's pet schemes, requiring as they did ever more funds, to feel at all easy about the way in which George Palmer's scheme was now developing.

One problem was that the only access to the factory from the nearest thoroughfare, namely King's Road, was along a narrow right of way used in common with the Gas Company. Nevertheless, George Palmer was convinced that the site offered substantial advantages. It was a level one, but there was little risk of flooding: as it happened, only twice, in 1894 and in 1947, did floods interrupt even a minor part of the factory's working. There was a good wharf to take care of the river-borne traffic, both to bring in the ingredients and other supplies coming from any distance, and to carry away the finished products. For more local freight, the London Road was very close to King's Road. Moreover, the Great Western Railway was only a few hundred yards off; this now connected Reading not only with London and Bristol but also with Taunton, Oxford and Gloucester.

At the same time, the long-term prospects for future expansion seemed very good, at least to George Palmer. His bold and imaginative mind must at least have contemplated the possibility that one day his firm might own and make use of the whole island site, up to the boundary with the Gas Company, and also all the land northwards across the river as far as the railway line. In the early 1840s the firm used the railways for only a small proportion of its freight traffic: although they had the advantage of speed, they were more expensive and as yet less far-ranging than the canal system. However, he could well have dreamt of the day when sidings would bring goods trains right into the factory for the purpose of loading and unloading. He was to see all these developments made reality during his working life.

This point of time, when the firm was on the brink of introducing new techniques into biscuit manufacture, seems a convenient one to break off the narrative, in order to study the way in which that manufacture originated.

4
Origins of Biscuit Manufacture

The opening of the King's Road factory in 1846 was a landmark not only for Huntley and Palmer but also for the biscuit industry as a whole. The firm now had its opportunity to achieve a spectacular growth rate, of which it duly took full advantage. More important in the long run, by pioneering the first continuously running and integrated machinery for biscuit manufacture, it went far towards creating the industry we know today, and very soon established itself as the dominant firm.

Thus the crucial step was the mechanisation that accompanied the move to the factory. An invention—such as George Palmer's—has been defined as 'the novel combination of pre-existing knowledge to satisfy some want better';[1] the want may be either an actual one, of needing to overcome a physical shortage or reduce costs, or a potential one, which requires the creation of a market in order to exploit the invention. The biscuit machinery clearly fell into the second category.

In order to put George Palmer's achievements into perspective, it is necessary to look closely at the state of the 'pre-existing knowledge' available to him. The present-day type of British fancy biscuit tends to be crisper and more brittle than the continental equivalent, which owed much to the techniques of the pastrycook. In all probability, therefore, the ship's biscuit, and the process of its mechanisation, contributed towards the innovations in Reading, and these topics, as well as the early organisation of fancy biscuit making, need to be discussed.

The history of the biscuit is said to go far back into antiquity. However, since manufacturing techniques made virtually no progress before the early nineteenth century, it seems unprofitable to enquire whether or not it is basically similar to certain foodstuffs of Old Testament and Roman times. The primary definition of 'biscuit' given by Dr. Samuel Johnson in his great dictionary published in 1755, was 'a kind of hard dry bread, made to be carried to sea'. It was in fact a convenient method for travellers to take about a basic foodstuff. Seafarers on long voyages, in particular, needed a substitute for bread that was both nutritious and possessed of reasonably good keeping qualities. According to the greatest of British naval surgeons and 'the father of nautical medicine', Dr. James Lind, a pound of biscuit a day—the normal ration in the mid-eighteenth century—was a more solid and substantial food than two pounds of ordinary well-baked bread on land.[2]

However, being much tougher in consistency, biscuit was more difficult to digest, since it comprised merely a flour-and-water paste which, unlike bread, was not lightened in any way by fermentation. The seaman of the day, being extremely robust, was able to endure for a number of years the combination of 'hard tack', pickled salt meat, spirits and infrequent vegetables, although predictably enough his expectation of life was not high. Shakespeare drew attention to one of its unappetising qualities, in the telling phrase 'as dry as the remainder biscuit After a voyage'.[3]

A further shortcoming of the ship's biscuit has often been documented in lurid detail, namely infestation with insects.[4] Even within the lifetime of Huntley and Palmer's founders, a former officer in Nelson's fleet contrasted weevilly and maggoty biscuits in the following terms. Weevils were bitter and inedible, whereas maggots were fat and cold to the taste, proving that the biscuit was merely in the first stage of decay, and could be eaten very well.[5] Thus sailors, when offered a biscuit, would always rap it on the table to dislodge some of the dust and insects. The Reading firm never made ship's biscuits as such, but in the 1830s and 1840s, while a number of military men, from general to sergeant, were buying its fancy varieties, not one naval officer—rare as he may have been in this inland town—is recorded among its customers.

Being thoroughly baked—according to Dr. Johnson, no less than four separate times for long voyages—ship's biscuits could only have become contaminated as the result of inadequate storage. They were supposed to be kept in watertight casks, but in fact were often left loose in the storeroom or put into canvas bags. Even the wooden casks normally used as containers were either badly made or not properly cleaned out between uses. (By contrast, the returnable airtight tins and tin-lined boxes used by the Huntleys from the early 1830s onwards were thoroughly scoured before being refilled.) Indeed, ship's biscuits, when subjected to intelligent care, could be kept quite free of insects. Captain Cook, for instance, during his voyage round the world, succeeded in keeping his biscuit 'sound in every respect' for upwards of three years, even re-baking it in the ship's oven once during each voyage.[6] Hence such infestation was very largely avoidable.

The earliest ship's biscuit-bakers were small men, whose premises were within easy reach of the wharves where provisions were loaded. At the beginning of the eighteenth century, for instance, William Marshal was a 'sea-biscake baker' near the Nag's Head on Rotherhithe Wharf, and Caleb Claggett—whose biscuits were probably as hard on the mouth as was his name—operated in Parish Street, Horsley Down, close to the present Tower Bridge.[7] At that time, production was still on such a limited scale that a team of two men, namely a master baker and his mate, sufficed. These shared between them the tasks of kneading in a trough, cutting the dough into small pieces, flattening them into shape and baking them in the oven for half an hour. Sometimes an idleman kept the oven supplied with wood and undertook the most strenuous part of the kneading.[8]

However, these small bakers were quite unfitted to cope successfully with the widely fluctuating demands of the Royal Navy. Naval contracts for all they could supply in time of war afforded the quickest route to bankruptcy when the war terminated and demand shrank to peacetime levels. During the eighteenth century, therefore, the victualling officers at each main naval dockyard, namely Deptford, Portsmouth and Plymouth, began to set up their own bakeries;[9] this helped to speed up technological change in a manner scarcely predictable in government establishments of the day. By the end of the century, one such establishment had carried the division of labour process so far as to create what was essentially a human assembly line, in which each worker's movements were integrated with those of the others.

At the Royal Clarence Victualling Yard at Gosport, near Portsmouth, there were nine ovens, each with a team of five or six men.[10] The *idleman* was now responsible for mixing the flour and water into a dough, by kneading it for half an hour with his bare arms up to the elbows; to 'finish it off', he jumped into the trough and trod it with his bare feet. (Well into the twentieth century, small coastal bakeries placed the biscuit dough under canvas, and used 'heavy boots on large feet' to knead it).[11] The dough was then removed and put in a wooden platform called the brake. Here the *brakeman* rolled it with the aid of a brake-staff, a lever loosely attached to the wall; he sat astride the other end, and performed his task by shuffling to and fro in what was described as a 'most uncouth' motion.

The next stage was for the dough to be taken, again by hand, to a moulding board, where the *moulder* cut it into squares and worked them by hand into rough circles. His assistant then stamped each biscuit with the King's mark and the number of the oven, and 'docked' it by perforating it with small holes. Docking introduced air into the mixture and prevented it from swelling up into blisters while being baked. The *furner* stood by the open door of the oven, holding the handle of the long shovel named a peel, the blade of which was lying flat on the oven floor. The *pitcher* threw each biscuit on to the peel; then by agitating the shovel, the furner arranged the biscuits over the whole floor of the oven.

The members of each gang developed such a remarkable deftness and skill in co-ordinating their joint efforts that they were capable of producing about $12\frac{1}{2}$ cwt of biscuits a day; two 'charges', that is, oven-loads, of 450 biscuits or about a hundredweight a time, could be completed every hour. Yet the strain on them must have been intense. The pitcher for instance, was throwing at the rate of over a hundred a minute, and could not look away for even one moment. Moreover, the quality and sizes of the biscuits were extremely uneven. Too much water made them 'flinty', with very hard splinters inside, while the variations in the times actually in the oven caused some of them to be overbaked and some underbaked.

A further disadvantage arose when demand soared, as it did during the Napoleonic wars. The dockyard employed double gangs of workmen, presumably one day and one night shift respectively, and they also made use of contractors. Even so, waggon loads from the contractors sometimes had to be unpacked in the streets of the dockyard towns and hoisted without delay on board warships that were already under sailing orders, instead of being taken into stock first in the victualling yards. It was not consideration for either workers or the consumer, but a fear of shortages in the event of a future war that led to the introduction of machinery for ship's biscuits, however. This took place about seventeen years after Waterloo, in 1832.

Before such machinery is described, some account of fancy biscuit manufacture up to that date needs to be given. The second definition of 'biscuit' in Dr. Johnson's dictionary is as follows: 'A composition of fine flour, almonds and sugar, made by the confectioners'. In fact, confectioners used many additional ingredients, including such delicacies as rose and orange flower water, aniseed, carraway seeds and preserved orange and lemon peel.[12] Certain bakers also made biscuits like their other fancy items, as a profitable side-line.

Although some biscuits' names, such as Captain, Cracknel, Ginger Wafer and Presburg, were fairly standard throughout the trade, the main proprietary brands were those named after Dr. John Abernethy and Dr. William Oliver: a reminder that the curative properties of biscuits had been recognised at least from Stuart days onwards.[13] Although by the mid-twentieth century chemists tended to stock only slimming and medicinal biscuits, druggists were quite common a century earlier among the Reading firm's ordinary retailers.

Origins of Biscuit Manufacture

Production was on the whole as unspecialised as the naming of biscuits. In small establishments the process involved was little more than 'to mix a handful of flour and water with your fingers, to divide it and bake it and call it a biscuit';[14] in one small bakery—Meaby's at Reading—for instance, as late as the 1890s three men worked three hours on making fifty-six lbs. of biscuits every six weeks or so, and hand-worked machines, such as those in the Huntley establishment were rare.

The reputable or 'full-price' bakers need to be distinguished from the 'subsistence' ones, who concentrated on bread alone.[15] The latter were often journeymen employed by millers who supplied them with inferior flour; they cut their prices drastically and survived only by using sweated—often foreign—labour and by further adulterating the flour. Both types of baker relied on night work, so that the operatives had to come on duty about eleven o'clock at night. Sometimes they took a short rest in the bakehouse; they then worked through until the morning, when they were sent out to deliver the bread. George Squire of Jermyn Street, who supplied Buckingham Palace, had to make sure that the bread—fancy for the royal family and plain for the staff—arrived by 7.45 a.m. at the latest since the Queen's breakfast was served punctually at eight.

In the 'full-price' establishments the biscuit bakers began their shift at 7.30 a.m. and continued sometimes as late as eight at night; thus the bakehouses as well as the ovens, were in use night and day.[16] In the cramped, overheated and unventilated conditions that prevailed, it is not surprising that many operatives kept going only by heavy drinking. Nor is it to be wondered that the baking and confectionery trades enjoyed a bad name, which did not help the reputation of fancy biscuits.

Charles Dickens, who had a very highly developed sense of social distinctions among working people, used bakers and confectioners as butts in some of his broadest farce. In *Nicholas Nickleby* the pretentious barber declines to shave a coal-heaver with the retort, 'If we was to get any lower than bakers, our customers would desert us, and we might (as well) shut up shop'. Similarly, in *Great Expectations*, the crooked witness whom the attorney Mr. Jaggers rejects with extreme disgust was a 'murderous-looking' confectioner 'in a short suit of white linen and a paper cap', who 'was not by any means sober, and had a black eye in the green stage of recovery, which was painted over'.

In Dickens's eyes even the master bakers bore some of the taint of their humbler colleagues. Herbert Pocket, also in *Great Expectations*, told Pip, 'I don't know why it should be a crack thing to be a brewer; but it is indisputable that while you cannot possibly be genteel and bake, you may be as genteel as never was and brew. You see it every day.' A sound economic reason existed for such a distinction, as a witness revealed to a Government enquiry a year or so after that book was written. Before 1815 the master baker 'moved in the upper ranks of his class, was generally a man of substance, was able to support his family and educate his children liberally, while at the present time [1862], in the majority of instances, he is a bare remove in position from the man he employs'.[17]

Even in 1886, when George Palmer was the senior partner in a gigantic enterprise, a former Member of Parliament and almost a millionaire, he felt called on to apologise for his trade and to declare that 'bakers need not be ashamed of their business'. Moreover, he continued, 'they could stand as firm on their feet as some others who might be disposed to look down on the journeyman baker'; nor was he personally ashamed of having at one time had his 'sleeves tucked up at the business'. This was well after some of the worst features of baking had been eradicated by legislation on hours and conditions of work and by the mechanisation of bread manufacture, which had proved much slower to carry out than the mechanisation of biscuits.[18]

It is possible that these poor conditions were confined mainly to London and the large cities. In the rural areas the grosser examples of cut-throat competition were absent: there were fewer bakeries per head of population, and each was able to make at least a living without overt adulteration. Indeed, the better confectioners in market towns, such as Reading, were able to sell their fancy goods wholesale to the more primitive bakeries in the outlying villages.[19]

An infallible guide to the status of any trade at that time was the Quakers' attitude towards it. As early as the 1760s Daniel Perry—who happened to be the father of Thomas Perry, the Reading biscuit-baker mentioned in Chapter 1—was unable to make the business of baking pay in London; he therefore migrated to Suffolk, where he prospered.[20] This was over half a century before the influx of 'subsistence' bakers led to the further deterioration in conditions referred to above. Although plentiful enough in country districts, Quakers in the baking and confectionery trades tended to keep clear of the metropolis.

Even those firms in London which specialised in biscuit manufacture, and thus avoided night work, were almost wholly non-Quakers; they included F. Lemann, Hill & Jones and (from 1857 onwards) Peek Frean. Nor were the cramped sites in the City of London conducive to large-scale manufacture, for not until 1862 had Hill & Jones as many as seven ovens, and no other manufacturer in the City was reported as having above four.[21]

Thus fancy-biscuit manufacture in the early nineteenth century was at a truly pre-industrial stage, with primitive production methods and

Origins of Biscuit Manufacture

very localised markets. Jane Austen tells us much about the social life of her day and class: yet in the whole of her novels, there is only one mention of biscuits. The events in *Mansfield Park* are usually held to have occurred in 1808–9: the heroine Fanny Price, during a brief and joyless stay with her own improvident family at Portsmouth, is depicted as sending out her brothers to purchase some biscuits and buns when she found the food more than usually intolerable.[22] Thirty years later there is fictional evidence of a more persistent demand among the kind of society to which she belonged, in towns as far apart as Reading and Knutsford in Cheshire. By that time one or two Quakers of the day had turned their attention to biscuit-making and to the problems of its mechanisation.

They had before them the precedent of (Sir) Thomas Grant who, when storekeeper at the Clarence Victualling Yard at Gosport, had invented a form of machinery for ship's biscuits in 1829. This was installed three years later under the direction of Sir John Rennie, the civil engineer; it proved so effective that Grant was awarded £2000 by Parliament, as well as a Gold Medal by the Society of Arts. Presumably the parliamentary award was in lieu of patent rights, for one private contractor, at Wapping, is known to have adopted his basic designs shortly afterwards. Steam provided the driving power, and a central furnace heated all nine ovens. The main items of machinery comprised a mixer, a roller and a cutter.

The flour for the mixing machine was weighed out in the store above, and was then shot down by means of a chute. A small cistern, for feeding in the required amount of water, was attached to the top of the mixer, which was cylindrical in shape and held fast in a horizontal position by brackets. A shaft through the centre could be connected up to the steam engine as required; this rotated the eighteen blades inside the cylinder so as to mix the dough thoroughly. The dough was then removed by hand through a trap-door underneath the cylinder, and deposited on to a board, over which a mechanical roller ran to and fro, until it had reduced the dough to a uniform thickness of two inches.

The board was then pushed on friction rollers to the next stage, where the dough was cut into pieces, to be made into the correct thickness for biscuits by a second roller. Each piece was then slid under the cutting machine, which docked and stamped out the biscuits into hexagonal shapes; thus no waste occurred. The machine did not cut the biscuits right through, so that the complete piece could be moved on to an iron plate, which was then placed in the oven. Once baked, the sheet could be broken up into individual hexagons.

Undoubtedly here was an example of technological progress, for it carried production on to a new plane altogether. The nine ovens at Gosport had previously required forty-five men to produce about 1500 lb. of biscuit an hour, at a cost—including wages, materials and wear and tear of capital—of 1s. 6d. a hundredweight. Following mechanisation, sixteen men and boys could produce almost 50 per cent more, namely a ton an hour, at a cost of fivepence a hundredweight; this represented an enormous saving.[23]

What is not known is how far the fancy-biscuit bakers were familiar with Grant's invention. To be sure, some of them were soon advertising the manufacture of biscuits 'by machine instead of by hand', as James Turner of Bishopsgate Street, London, did in 1842. However, he could not have had genuine steam-powered machinery for by 1851 he was employing no more than six men.

Much is known, on the other hand, about Jonathan Dodgson Carr, a Quaker who in 1831 founded a milling and biscuit-making business at Carlisle, now Carr's of Carlisle Ltd. About seven years later he designed a machine for cutting and stamping biscuits, for which he received technical help from a member of the Scott family, of Hudson Scott & Son the printing firm. They borrowed their basic idea from the hand-operated fly-press, itself dating back to William Caxton's printing machine of the late fifteenth century. Here the sheet of kneaded dough was placed on a sliding table that was covered with a woollen cloth, so that the biscuits could be picked up easily. The table was then wound under the hinged cutters, which in the same process closed up and cut out the biscuits. Being rectangular, they left behind no waste, and they were arranged by hand on to a tray before baking.

Carr's process was clearly quicker than stamping out manually, but it was in no sense automatic. Even so, in May 1841, by canvassing his local Member of Parliament, Carr succeeded in being granted a Royal Warrant of appointment to Queen Victoria; curiously enough, this did not entitle his firm to an entry either in the *Court Kalendar* or after 1885 in the *London Gazette*. On the strength of the cutting machine, Carr's of Carlisle has ever since strongly upheld that city's claim to have been the birthplace of the biscuit industry.[24]

George Palmer's comments on this claim may be of some interest. In his submission to the jury of the Amsterdam Exhibition in 1869, he stated categorically that his own firm had 'introduced an industry'. As early as 1841, 'the first steps were taken for introducing machinery in [Huntley and Palmer's] biscuit trade'—clearly a reference to his first steam engine of $1\frac{1}{2}$ h.p. He admitted that biscuits were then being made by machine at Carlisle, but those machines were 'unfitted for the purpose', for they produced two kinds of biscuit only, as against the two dozen or more at Reading, and Carr's biscuits 'have not held their ground'.

Thus he did not feel that an 'industry' was created simply by installing a single type of machine never put into general use, for a network of machinery suppliers had not grown up; indeed, at that time 'there was no engineering establishment in England where machines for the manufacture of fancy biscuits could be purchased'. By contrast, all his competitors, 'though not entirely are in degree indebted to us for the type of biscuit and very largely for the distinguishing names of their biscuits': for instance, the Ginger Nut, Osborne and Pic-Nic. Even more conclusively, he referred to his own introduction of the travelling oven, which will be described in Chapter 5, and which by 1869 was being 'used very commonly by biscuit-bakers for baking fancy biscuits in large quantities'.

As a result of these submissions, the Amsterdam jury, which had as its aim 'to make known articles in which food is included, invented and produced by various nations or by individuals, which had tended to the general prosperity and comfort of the people', accepted his claim and granted Huntley and Palmers a medal 'for Progress'.

What was so epoch-making about his own machinery? He must have been familiar with that in use at Gosport, but there were two problems peculiar to his branch of manufacture that he had to overcome. The first was that, whereas there was only one kind of ship's biscuit, which required no more than an indefinite quantity of a standard dough, fancy biscuits came in many varieties, with differing ingredients and times for mixing, rolling and baking. The second problem was how, in spite of all these varieties, to make the machinery run continuously rather than intermittently.

He dealt with the first problem by treating separately two basic types of dough: hard doughs for the plainer types of biscuit, and soft for the fancier varieties. It is not quite certain how mixing was carried out during the earlier years in the factory, but later on the dough for plain biscuits, which required only a few basic ingredients, was mixed in reduced versions of the Gosport drums: the latter mixed five hundredweight in two minutes, whereas the Reading ones took a 280 lb sack of flour and mixed it in fifteen minutes. Since Reading biscuits were made in batches according to the demand for each variety, smaller and less powerful drums were more economical.

The other mixer, which was first made by Barrett Exall and Andrewes to George Palmer's design from 1851 onwards, was an open circular pan, which rotated one way, while a grooved wheel inside the pan moved in the opposite direction. As all the manufacturing processes at King's Road took place on the ground floor, the storeroom above was used for weighing out ingredients, and the flour was dropped down into the mixers by the same kinds of chute as were used for ship's biscuits. The storeman above could communicate with the mixing machine attendant through a metal speaking-tube, and rang a bell when he was about to send ingredients down the chute. The attendant probably added by hand all the other ingredients, such as eggs, sugar, milk and (for Ginger Nuts) treacle, and used a large wooden peel for stirring the mixture together.

It took some time before the second problem, of connecting up the machinery into a continuous whole, was solved. The dough, once mixed, still had to be taken by hand in wooden tubs to the rolling machine: and indeed, a century or more later, a similar gap existed in the sequence, although by then it was bridged by fork-lift trucks. However, there was in George Palmer's system a lever for putting the polished rollers into reverse. Instead of having to be cut twice into various lengths, therefore, the dough went backwards and forwards under the rollers as many as six times. Being then in sheets twenty to thirty feet long, it was carried along a canvas moving band through the cutters.

Again, two different types of cutter were needed, depending on the type of dough. Hard doughs were stamped out by an up-and-down motion, similar to that used for ship's biscuits, but the softer types went under cylindrical cutting machines. These had the added advantage that the whole range of some assorted biscuits (such as the Fancy Nic-Nac, introduced in the late 1850s, which had six different shapes) could be stamped out in one process. The spare dough was carried on over the machine into a trough, where it was collected and used again. One boy, standing in a hole below floor-level—to save him from having to stoop continuously—kept the moving band supplied with trays, on to which the biscuits fell in regular order. Another team of boys collected the trays as they reached the end of the band, stacked them twelve deep on specially made trolleys, and wheeled them off to the ovens.

Other biscuits required certain modifications to the basic manufacturing process. Thus cracknels, after being rolled and stamped out, had to be dropped into a cauldron of boiling water, where they immediately sank and rose to the surface again when cooked. They were then fished out with a net and plunged into a cold bath, before being conveyed to the oven. For some of the rectangular patterned varieties the dough, once mixed, was extruded from slits in a cylinder, to form continuous strips that were cut to the right size before baking. Macaroons were produced by means of a squirt gun; the operative pushed the piston of the gun against his chest just hard enough to force out the required quantity, which he then cut off and dropped on to an iron plate for baking.

The hand ovens were from sixteen to forty feet in depth, and were heated underneath to minimise dust. When baked, the trays of biscuits were taken by a lift, called by the nautical name of Jacob's ladder, to the second storey of the factory, where boys sorted through them and removed the damaged or overcooked ones. A special machine broke up the imperfect biscuits, a pound of which was given to each employee every week, and the remainder sold as broken biscuits. The whole ones were put into store casks, to await packing.

They were packed mainly into tins or tin-lined boxes, although some biscuits for destinations within Britain travelled in airtight barrels. Later on, assortments were packed by putting casks containing each variety in succession on a long counter. This was alongside a railway track, which ran extensively throughout much of the factory, to facilitate the pushing of heavy loads. A boy pushed a trolley, bearing a large pair of scales, along the track, took a handful of biscuits from each cask and put it in the scales. At the end of the counter, when he had reached the correct weight, he handed the pan to a packer, collected another pan and started again.[25]

Owing to a dearth of information, at the moment we have only vague ideas as to what causes technological change. A commonly held view is that a man invents something because his ideas have been stimulated by an earlier scientific discovery.[26] However, this view overlooks the fact that inventors themselves, at least in the nineteenth century, have tended to be highly practical men who have concentrated on the ultimate goal: for instance, a completely new market to be exploited, or substantial savings in production or other costs. Many inventors, indeed, have used no scientific knowledge at all, or knowledge that was far from new at the time.

This is what happened in the biscuit industry. If we take the three pioneers Thomas Grant, Jonathan Carr and George Palmer, each was a non-scientist in charge of a factory and was faced with a 'want'. Each then found a scientifically minded collaborator, who furnished technical help that went some way towards satisfying that want. Yet George Palmer's was clearly the most successful because his vision was the most complete, and took in production, marketing and finance as well as innovation and therefore minimised the risk of adverse factors wrecking his scheme during its critical early stages. He can thus claim to be an entrepreneur of superior calibre to the other two.

5
The Last Years of Thomas Huntley 1846–57

The move into the new factory at King's Road, Reading, did not involve a clean break with the primitive production methods of the past. On the contrary, the evidence suggests a long drawn out period of settling in, and an even more gradual process of mechanisation. During the settling-in period, the value of the firm's total output rose gradually rather than dramatically, from a weekly average of below £120 in July 1846 to just under £140 in October, £157 in November and £175 in the first three weeks of December. As November was the month in which the labour force grew from twenty-seven to forty-five, the main removal may have taken place then.

From mid-September onwards, parties of men were regularly at the factory, no doubt trying to clean up at the same time as the first seven ovens, the machinery and the gas for lighting were being installed. The only two machines proper to be put in at first were one for rolling and stamping out the hard dough, and known generically as a 'Captain's biscuit machine', and one for the softer kinds, a 'Cracknal [sic] machine'. The general mess and discomfort can be deduced from the heavy expenditure on candles, the delivery during three days towards the end of October of no less than 105 sacks of sawdust, and the need to provide beer as well as other refreshments for the men. Although George Palmer never tired of warning his hands that beer 'does sometimes touch the head without making it more sensible', he was enough of a countryman to recall the reinvigorating effects of cider or beer during energetic times such as the harvest, and its value—in small quantities—here also.[1]

Some of the more specialised confectionery items still continued to be made in the London Street bakery, which was not finally given up until 1861. However, as the factory's production began to soar, the share contributed by the bakery declined from 6 per cent—£164 out of £2796—between February and June 1847 (when the ledgers began to separate work in the two units) to about 2 per cent—£759 out of £33,300—in the financial year of 1849–50.

The expenses of fitting out the factory were necessarily heavy, and George Palmer himself itemised them in the ledger so as to keep a running check on them. His purchases of plant and machinery totalled just over £1000. The two machines, as well as the iron work for the ovens, the rollers and various minor items, were all made by Barrett Exall and Andrewes. A 25 h.p. steam engine provided the motive power; this had apparently been taken over from the silk mill, as the iron works charged £220 for altering, removing and refixing it. This expense may have included the installation of overhead shafting, which connected up the engine with the various machines, by means of endless bands.

A further account in the ledger, headed 'Getting into the Factory', came to £230, of which the largest item was £136 for legal fees and stamp duties. Joseph Huntley installed the gas supply, from the Gas Company next door, at a cost of £18, and no less than £10 worth of coal—roughly ten tons—was need to dry out the seven ovens. Although the partners actually paid off only £400 of the £1000 capital cost in the financial year 1846–7, during the whole of that year they were constantly in one difficulty after another.

A key problem was that of finance. The mortgage cost £90 a year in interest charges alone, and although repayments on the £1800 borrowed did not have to start immediately, they could not be delayed for too long; in fact they began in 1849. The rent of the London Street shop was £70 a year, and the combined rateable value of the two premises was £105. Moreover, the physically feeble but mentally irrepressible Joseph Huntley senior was still enjoying his pension of £80 a year; he went off to live with a brother at Stoke-on-Trent, where he died of paralysis in July 1849.

The confusion in Joseph's financial affairs did not end with his death. No will was ever proved or grant of administration made, and a legacy of £100 he had apparently promised to the Reading Dispensary was still 'receivable' more than seven years later.[2] The old meeting house at Stoke-on-Trent has now become a Red Cross headquarters; the burial ground next door is closed off and neglected, and a mass of weeds and nettles covers the unmarked grave of the original founder of one of Britain's more noteworthy enterprises.

Meanwhile, Thomas Huntley was becoming exceedingly alarmed at the prospect that capital expenditure was sure to rise even further. Declared profits for income tax purposes in 1846–7 were only £1500 and the actual profits were lower still: £1143, or only £80 up on the previous year. The need to conserve funds was so pressing that the partners drew only £190 each: the lowest drawings since 1843–4. Thomas—no doubt egged on by his wife—must have considered seriously how much of his stake in the business he would ever see back. Restricted as he was to bookkeeping and packing duties, he was impotent to affect policy in his own business. 'George will ruin us!' he lamented, and to the dynamic young man who was not yet twenty-nine he pleaded, in the Quaker speech that was already falling out of use, 'George, thee let well alone.'[3] But George showed no intention whatever of letting well alone.

In addition to these financial difficulties, there were technical problems as well. In any firm the combination of new premises and untried machinery offers a double set of hostages to fortune. Whether the machines themselves functioned from the outset without serious breakdowns we do not know, but the seven new ovens certainly gave much trouble. A circumstantial account written much later (which George Palmer preserved among his papers, unfortunately without expressing an opinion as to its accuracy) declares that when the first steam coil oven was started up, the coil exploded, wrecking the oven and nearly killing him and other bystanders. If this is so, it helps to explain why a circular of 1st January 1847 needed to apologise for 'the delays in executing all the orders recently received'.

In fact, no value at all was entered in the ledger for output during the fourth week in December, which included Christmas. In the first two weeks of January output was not much higher than it had been in October, and sagged even further in the succeeding week, when one and a half days were lost. It must have been an exceptionally gloomy new year for Thomas Huntley in the counting house. Worse still, George Palmer had been planning a promotion campaign to take effect shortly after the move; he now had to explain in the same circular that 'our trade had outgrown our premises, but having now new premises, and machinery for a much larger business, in future we shall be more expeditious in getting off orders'.

On the supply side at least, his promises were to be fulfilled. On three separate occasions before the following June the factory managed to turn out over £200 worth of goods a week, although it was not until August that weekly output was regularly in the £220 to £250 range. For the year ended June 1847 output totalled £8260 in value, compared with £6890 for the previous year, a marked increase of just 20 per cent.

Apparently unperturbed by these difficulties, George Palmer pressed forward with the next stage of the factory's development. In 1847–8 he did have to meet the £600 bill for the remaining initial items, but he felt able to repay Thomas Terry's £200 loan, and met all other commitments out of current earnings, so that profits rose to £1549. The following year he paid off his mother's £216 as well as £300 of the £1800 owing to John Weedon, and profits shot ahead to £3369.

By then turnover, at just under £18,000, was over double what it had been in 1846–7. It is instructive that in August 1847, following a satisfactory harvest, he was able to reduce the prices of many biscuits. Throughout the nineteenth century at least, the firm adjusted prices almost entirely according to changes in the cost of ingredients, mainly that of flour, which accounted for over a third of total costs; wages, by contrast, represented less than 10 per cent. Since demand remained almost embarrassingly buoyant, the economic justification for the price cuts was limited, but as a good Quaker, he felt bound to pass savings in costs on to the customer.

However, to make sure of being able to meet this inexorably soaring demand without encountering periodical crises like the one at the beginning of 1847, he recognised that the baking process would have to be overhauled. Biscuits were still put into and removed from the ovens by hand, and at the end of a mechanised production line, this represented a serious bottleneck. He therefore sought a travelling oven, in which products could pass through at a speed regulated according to the baking period required.

As long before as 1810, a native of Boston in the United States who became a British admiral, Sir Isaac Coffin, had patented a 'perpetual oven' some fifty feet long for baking ship's biscuits. A moving belt of wire mesh ran through its centre, but it was never brought into service because the cast-iron rollers at each end, which moved the belt, were well outside the oven and therefore caused undue dispersal of heat.[4]

George Palmer's search for a more practicable version of this was long and exhaustive. In the closing months of 1849, when the surviving correspondence begins, he was following up two ideas. One was a revolving oven which had been patented by a London firm improbably called the Patent Desiccating Co., and the other a patent hot air oven which was offered for sale by Thomas Harrison's of Liverpool. He was clearly impressed by both ideas, but he felt that the cost of buying the patents was too great. Although he couched his replies to the firms in such a way as to encourage negotiations, he met with no response.

Then early in 1851 he heard of a revolving oven for baking ship's biscuits, directly heated by fire, and made by William and Maxwell Scott of Tranmere, near Liverpool. This oven was 20 ft. long and 4 ft. 6 in. wide, and contained a feeding web on which boys placed the biscuits. The shafting moved the web intermittently so that the cycle would take the five to fifteen minutes needed to complete the baking. Teams of boys would be standing by; a screen left a gap just wide enough to let the biscuits through, while minimising the heat loss.

As George Palmer pointed out in his submission to the 1869 exhibition, this innovation was to benefit the whole industry as well as to his own business. Another Liverpool firm, T. &. T. Vicars, had been established in 1849 to make machinery for bread- and biscuit-bakers, and following George Palmer's development of this oven, was soon offering similar types both to existing and to new firms. The heating engineers A. M. Perkins & Son of London began to manufacture baking ovens in 1851 and together with Joseph Baker & Son, founded in 1876, provided equipment for Huntley and Palmers. These two suppliers amalgamated as Baker Perkins in 1920; Vicars and Baker Perkins have continued to be the leading specialists for biscuit-making and allied machinery ever since.[5]

Despite his preoccupation with financial and technical matters within the factory, George Palmer did not neglect marketing, or relations with customers generally. We have seen how the new commission agents had since 1841 established a comprehensive network of retailers; by the beginning of 1847 these retailers numbered no less than 717, in 382 different towns throughout the British Isles. Just over 630 were situated in England, sixty-two in Scotland, sixteen in Wales and eight in Ireland. According to his circular of 1st January 1847 (already quoted), there had taken place 'a rapid extension in our Trade, without any particular effort'; although what seemed effortless to the energetic George Palmer might have felled a lesser man.

So as to make these retailers known as widely as possible, he prepared a small sixteen-page booklet, illustrated on the cover with a woodcut of the factory and listing their names under the respective towns. Over the next year or two, these booklets were placed in each tin of biscuits sent out: to indicate the ephemeral nature of such ephemera, of the several thousands printed, only two are known to have survived, one beneath the roof of a Cambridge house until it was discovered in 1936. Meanwhile, he coaxingly informed each retailer, 'we believe that the collateral advantage of having your Name in our list of Agents will make it quite worth your while to push [our biscuits]'.

What products did these retailers mainly deal in? The vast majority were of course grocers and tea dealers, with a handful of bakers and confectioners. As mentioned earlier, chemists and druggists were well represented, but less predictably, one or more came from each of the following trades; ironmonger, soda-water maker, seedsman, stationer, greengrocer and linen draper. Several small-town post offices and some circulating libraries—haunts of those with both money and time to spare—in 'watering places' also sold Reading biscuits. In the London area the seventy-seven agents ranged from Fortnum & Mason in Piccadilly, which bought £127 worth in 1846, and Crosse & Blackwell, which did only £2 worth of trade between 1846 and 1848—for its great days of biscuit distribution were still to come—to two small provision shops in Hoxton.

In its relations with distributors, the firm insisted on four requirements. The first was that satisfactory references as to creditworthiness must be forthcoming before trading could begin. Second, there should be only one distributor in each locality. In 1856 the firm's chief traveller Henry Lea reported of its Carlisle rivals that 'Carr's trade has been shattered ... in consequence of the article not being first rate and their calling on everybody': in other words, not restricting outlets to a limited number of what George Palmer called 'good family traders'.

The third requirement was that distributors should sell at a recommended price. In 1849 the firm warned a Southampton grocer who had been selling a new brand, Pic-Nic biscuits, at 6½d. instead of 7d. a pound: 'We are quite aware that it is unusual to interfere with the retailer's price; nevertheless it has been our practice to do so to some extent, with such success as justifies our so doing in your case.' In fact, the travellers when opening an account specified the retail prices that were expected. Not until sixty years later, when competition was far more severe both among manufacturers and from the multiple shops that were springing up, did the firm express the opinion that in general 'the good business sense of our friends'—the grocers—would lead them to sell its biscuits at such a price that was 'likely to secure success'.[6]

Most agents in the 1840s accepted this arrangement, since at the time their gross margins, as a discount from the recommended price, varied from 28 per cent on Pic-Nics and 20 per cent on Ginger Nuts and Albert biscuits (all at 8d. per pound) to 14 or 17 per cent on the shilling varieties *for those buying most cheaply*: namely loose by the hundredweight in 80 lb. casks or 28 or 40 lb. wooden boxes. Out of this margin, the retailer had to meet all his selling expenses, as well as carriage outwards beyond London or an equivalent distance and the loss on the broken ones that had to be sold off cheaply. Retailers who bought in, say, 5lb. tins received a much smaller margin. Only wholesale agents, and a few favoured customers such as Fortnum & Mason, received a discount in addition, of 7½ per cent in London and 5 per cent outside.

The terms were net cash if the account were settled within three months, which happened to be the interval between the traveller's calls. Such a marked growth in the number of outlets, however, caused the problem of debt collection to rise dramatically. Quarterly accounts were sent out by post; if they were not settled by cheque or Post Office draft, they were collected in cash by travellers on their three-month visits. Sometimes more pressing measures were required: in an effort to bring in cash before the end of the financial year, George Palmer collected in no less than £450 in the course of various special trips between March and May 1848.

Debts which remained unsettled despite personal calls were sometimes put into the hands of debt-collecting agencies, such as the London Association for the Protection of Trade. Normally then a sharp letter from that source produced immediate payment. One debtor, at College Green, Bristol, who employed alternative tactics, in 1850 sent 'a most pitiable appeal' to George Palmer, offering to pay 'in *stuffed birds*'. When his offer was accepted, he backed out, and George Palmer, with the sharp comment that 'he tells fibs without scruple', instructed the Association to 'have no mercy, but settle the account'. In fact, the dealer combined selling biscuits with selling stuffed animals, a normally lucrative trade in Victorian times.

To help with debt-collection, as in other ways, George Palmer made use of his brothers when he could. William Isaac Palmer, having completed his apprenticeship with Joseph Huntley, the ironmonger, had joined a commercial house in Liverpool. There he showed a different side of his capabilities by being asked to straighten out some complicated books of the business.[7] He occasionally took orders and collected accounts for Huntley and Palmer. Samuel, who was working in Bristol until 1847, also acted as a collector, but on a much more regular basis. As his handwriting appears in the firm's books for a few months that summer, he must have helped in the counting house at Reading while *en route* to London. He set up there on his own as a general commission agent in St. Benet's Lane, off Gracechurch Street.

Despite this help from his brothers, George Palmer judged that the time had arrived to establish a full-time traveller at Reading. The man he chose was Henry Lea, who joined the firm at the end of 1849. Lea was a Quaker, who had shared lodgings with William Isaac Palmer when they were both working at the Liverpool house, and who therefore came with a very strong personal recommendation. He did not disappoint his new employers. A genial man of great personality and drive, he was perfectly capable of holding his own against the cocky young commercial travellers who made fun of his Quaker gear: the traditional coat without lapels and a stiff turn-down collar and boiled shirt with dress studs but no tie. His laundry problems in an age of grimy trains and air polluted cities must have been immense.

Partly because the fairly narrow range of occupations, into which they were impelled by their consciences, often involved them in much business travelling, Quakers have always taken a lively interest in the welfare of commercial travellers. Lea, like the firm's West Country agent J. F. Wilkey, strove hard to improve working conditions for them, so that gradually they became the 'aristocrats' of business employees in

Victorian England, earning £4 a week. Lea therefore well deserved the title by which he was often known: King of Commercial Travellers.[8]

Although for the time being Huntley and Palmer's commission agents remained responsible for their own areas, Lea was able to co-ordinate their efforts, and in time, as the agents dropped out, he was able to create his own team of wholly salaried travellers. Perhaps the first to join his team was Charles Williams, from a family which had been coach proprietors in Reading for several generations, but whose livelihood had been destroyed by the railways. Charles and his younger brother William Bullivant Williams were both working for the firm as clerks: the one went on to succeed Lea as senior traveller when Lea died suddenly in 1890, aged sixty-seven, while the other eventually took charge of the firm's general administration and became the first non-Palmer director when the firm became a limited company in 1898.

Meanwhile, the physical distribution of the firm's biscuits was being transformed by the development of the railway system. Not only was rail traffic speedier and more convenient than older means of transport, but it could better cope with the steadily increasing demands of the factory. In 1849–50, when output was just four times as great as in 1846–7, at £33,300, carriage inwards—of returned tins, charged to the firm—came to £54 for railway and £17 for canal traffic. Carriage outwards, comprising consignments of biscuits and cakes, on the other hand, amounted to only £18 paid directly to the Great Western Railway and £1038 to Pickford's the carriers. How far Pickford's at that time shipped goods on the railways is not known, but a Warehouse Day Book of 1852 suggests that by then all but purely local deliveries from the factory were made by rail, at least on their departure from Reading. The firm itself paid rail charges outwards as far as, say, London or Bristol, and the retailer had to bear the rest. As George Palmer informed an enquirer at Liverpool, 'beyond London we cannot deliver'. From the railway termini much freight was transhipped by sea: thus hoys sailed from Hambro's wharf in London to Faversham, the Kent coast and the Medway towns, while steamers departing from Bristol served ports as far apart as Hayle and Penzance in Cornwall and Neath in South Wales.

For some years after 1846 George Palmer's time was still fully committed with day-to-day problems as well as planning further investment. The years 1849–51, for instance, saw not merely the first travelling oven but also the first pan-type mixing machine and new types of cutters for Pic-Nic and other biscuits; moreover, a new counting house and warehouses were added on to the original silk mill. Thus the 'machinery and fixtures' item rose from £1680 in 1847 to over £9000 ten years later, when the factory buildings (not included in the balance sheet until

1849, presumably because their value was cancelled out by the outstanding mortgage) were valued at £6600.

Nevertheless, with the gradual development of routine operations in the factory, he was able to take up some outside public duties. However, of more personal significance was his marriage in January 1850, on the day before his thirty-second birthday. His wife was Elizabeth Meteyard, the daughter of a Quaker druggist who was Huntley and Palmer's agent in Basingstoke. She was aged just twenty-four. In appearance she was homely rather than good-looking, but like his own mother, she came of an interesting family.

Her father had sailed at the age of fourteen to Newfoundland as apprentice to a storekeeper there. He endured his master's tyrannical treatment for four years, which included being compelled to start work at 3 a.m.; he then returned to England, where he learnt the chemist's trade, and later opened the first photographer's studio in Basingstoke.[9] George Palmer would have appreciated his dogged and outspoken nature, as well as Elizabeth's equally persevering capacity for self-education, which made her fill whole notebooks with information about philosophy and natural history.

During the next fifteen years she was to bear him ten children; four sons and three daughters survived infancy, and three of the sons in due course entered the firm. In his married life he displayed the same qualities which friends observed in his religious faith: simplicity of outlook, absolute devotion and absolute reticence.[10] One or two of his letters written to her while she was away from Reading are extant. The formal but affectionate letters of a busy Victorian paterfamilias, they speak naturally of children and household pets, and by implication show how he regarded his home as a secure base for his business and official life.

On the day of the marriage Richard Brown, now officially the factory's foreman, appeared to be 'scheming' for a short day in order to mark the occasion. However, the clerk in the counting house, the Quaker John Horsfall, knew where and in what condition most of the men would end up; he therefore vetoed the scheme, and 'all passed off apparently as usual'. So the bridegroom was informed on his brief honeymoon by letter, which kept him posted about the latest batches of correspondence and events within the factory.

The hands were in fact granted their celebration soon afterwards. Factory suppers had already become annual occasions, usually in April, but that year the event was brought forward to early in February. Long tables were set out in the main factory building and 'tastefully' decorated with evergreen and flowers. All the male and female employees, wives and sweethearts were invited, as well as numerous guests. In a supremely tactful gesture, Richard Brown made presentations not only to the bridegroom but also to Thomas Huntley: each received a handsome cream jug, to which all the workpeople had secretly subscribed. The latter's, which his descendants still hold, bears an inscription expressing 'the esteem and best wishes' of the Biscuit Factory employees. After the supper, a local worthy delivered a lecture on electricity, and amid general excitement gave some of the boys mild electric shocks; a magic lantern display rounded off the evening.[11]

George Palmer's life now agreeably combined the elements of domestic felicity, a thriving business and numerous absorbing outside interests; yet an undercurrent of discord existed between himself and his partner. A few months after his marriage he complained in writing to Thomas Huntley about being obliged 'to take an unfair responsibility in the business, arising from thy not fulfilling thy contract to keep the books and superintend that part of the business as agreed' in the 1841 articles of partnership. Indeed, the number of business trips George Palmer had to undertake, often far afield, and the considerable volume of correspondence, written usually in his own hand, confirm how hard pressed he was in carrying out his own side of the business alone. The root cause of his partner's lack of diligence, he believed, was a suspicion that he was not acting fairly towards Thomas's son, Henry Evans Huntley.

Henry was now seventeen, and when George Palmer had raised the question of his own brother Samuel's being brought into the business as manager, with the prospect of a partnership after four or five years, Thomas refused to consider the proposal unless Henry were given a similar opportunity to be taken into partnership at a future date. George Palmer was close enough to the family to know that the youth, being an only child, was having his character sapped by a mother who alternately indulged him and rowed with him. He therefore gave no encouragement to this expectation, and in the same letter finally requested that their differences, according to normal practice within the society, should be referred to three Quakers as arbitrators.

That Thomas Huntley had neglected the accounts seems to have been entirely true. Although the customers' account books, which came under George Palmer's department, were always scrupulously well kept, the ledgers were in a sorry state: columns were not totalled, and errors remained uncorrected. George Palmer not merely entered certain outlays himself when it was vital to keep track of them, but once or twice even annotated a page with the words: 'This account is confused', and brought forward the correct balance to a new page.

Nor do the annual balance sheets give an accurate picture of loans by outside individuals. As it happened, these were gradually being liquidated. William Golding's £200 was paid off early in 1850, just about the time when John Weedon the solicitor died, and the remainder of the mortgage was repaid to the executors by the end of the year: as the profits in 1850-1, of just under £7500, were on a turnover of £41,100, this was done without undue difficulty. That year the partners drew over £1800 each, and the gross value of the business was not far short of £25,000. From then on, as long as the business remained an independent unit, it financed the whole of its growth from retained earnings.

As a result of the arbitration, some necessary reforms took place. A full-time bookkeeper was appointed to relieve Thomas Huntley. His son Henry was packed off to Colchester to receive a professional training, while Samuel Palmer was offered a salary equal to 1½ per cent of the turnover, entirely free of risk, if he would take charge of sales from the Reading office.

According to family tradition, Samuel told his brother in quite unquakerlike language that he was damned if he was going to live in Reading. He preferred to remain in London and be paid by results. He was given his way; on the whole to the firm's ultimate advantage. He handled with rare ability the London and Export trade, and the purchasing of ingredients. In Reading there might well have been serious friction between himself and his brother, but he succeeded in combining a busy life in the City with some gratification of his country tastes. A photograph of 1855 shows one side of him: as a dandy in clothes of the most costly materials and cut. His dark masculine good looks and large nose gave rise to the rumour that the Palmers had Jewish blood in them. No trace whatever of this supposed ancestry is to be found in their genealogy; the speculation probably arose from the common confusion between the name of Isaac, a West Country Quaker one, and the undoubtedly Semitic name of Isaacs.

He did accept a cut in his commission to 6 per cent, for George Palmer felt that the existing 7½ per cent was too high now that the firm's products were firmly established. Perhaps because of Samuel's refusal to settle in Reading, in the middle of 1851 William Isaac Palmer was brought into the firm, at a starting salary of £200 a year, the same as Henry Lea's. His position was that of factory manager, for Richard Brown, although a good foreman, was clearly not capable of the kind of responsibility now required with a labour force of 150. William Isaac was utterly dependable, and not given to challenging the authority of the head of the family. Besides, he would be company for his mother, now living over the shop in lonely state with a Quaker companion.

This managerial reorganisation took place none too soon. The first expansion into adjoining sites began in 1852, when the firm bought for

£700 six houses facing King's Road, and shortly afterwards for £240 a small piece of land, also on King's Road, for use as a stable yard. The following year George Palmer told a London commission broker that he hoped he would soon reach the limits of expansion—a few months before the tobacco factory next door came on the market after the owner's mortgage had had to be foreclosed. The purchase of two other small pieces of land in 1855 left the firm holding all the island site as far east as the gasworks, with the sole exception of the Cannon Brewery, at the corner of King's Road and Watlington Lane.

Output in 1855–6 was over £105,000, and net profit was £12,050; the 11 per cent ratio of profit to turnover happened to be below the average of recent years, for this was the concluding year of the Crimean war; besides, after a poor season ingredients, especially flour and butter, were dear. The summer, with the return of peace and a more satisfactory harvest, fortunately led to a general improvement in conditions. Then the winter of 1856–7 turned out to be a very trying one, with alternate spells of very chilly and very mild weather. Only the post-war budget of February 1857 brought some cheer, with some welcome reductions in the duties on tea, coffee and sugar, and in the rate of income tax.

Very early in the new year Thomas Huntley, confined to bed with a severe cold, wrote a poignant letter to his partner, with news that his cold had worsened markedly and had thrown him 'sadly' back again. Two months later he was dead. The untreated prostate complaint had inflicted constant pain on him, with the added regular torment of the catheter. As his obituary in the Quaker *Annual Monitor* indicated, death was a merciful release from all his sufferings, which he had borne throughout with complete patience and resignation.[12]

The local newspaper commented on his 'remarkably quiet and retiring manners' and his kindly and benevolent disposition: which is, however, not incompatible with his occasional outbursts of petulance towards a business partner whose rough and autocratic manners had often given offence to him.[13] In the last resort he was a man to whom events happened, rather than one who directly influenced the course of events. His only surviving portrait shows a large-featured man with kindly eyes, and strong fingers that would have preferred holding a pen—for he was after all a frustrated schoolmaster—to kneading dough. His generosity was shown in the £1550 of charitable bequests he made out of an estate valued at £35,000: £500 went to the Royal Berkshire Hospital, £100 to the dispensary and £50 each to the firm's Sick Fund and Library, of which he had been treasurer.

His funeral, in the Friends' Burial Ground at Reading, was held the following Sunday; as an eyewitness remembered it, 'such a rough day—snowed enough to blind you'.[14] Eight carriages followed the hearse from his villa in the suburb of Whitley: the 400-odd workpeople, shivering in their cheap clothes along the route, must have deeply regretted the passing of such a well-loved man, and wondered what the future was likely to bring, now that the headstrong George Palmer would presumably take full charge. They would have worried even more, had they known that he too would all but succumb in the next few weeks.

6
The Second Partnership 1857–74

The first Huntley and Palmer partnership was automatically dissolved by Thomas Huntley's death in March 1857. The second comprised the three Palmer brothers on their own account; it continued until the next generation of the family began to be taken into partnership in 1874.

Under the agreement of 1841, as amended in 1846, the surviving partner had the option of buying the business. Naturally enough, George Palmer fully intended to take up this option; however, for the moment he was in no condition to do so. He had a severe chill, no doubt contracted in the blizzard on the day of the funeral. Having effectively carried the whole burden for a number of years, he was unable to fight off the chill, which developed into a general debility—the nearest he came in his whole working life to a breakdown. His doctors must have made it very clear that unless he were to take a prolonged rest well away from Reading, they could not answer for the consequences.

That April he therefore went away for a month to drink the waters and sample the bracing air of Great Malvern. The doctors' ban did not extend to postal correspondence, of which he must have had shoals. William Isaac Palmer, perhaps a little diffident at being left in charge of the factory, sent lengthy progress reports and sought instructions on quite minor points. As an executor of Thomas's will, Joseph Huntley the ironmonger looked in from time to time at King's Road to keep an eye on the Huntley interests: 'although I do not think I have the talent for much usefulness in this way', he wrote to George Palmer, 'I have often felt a satisfaction in taking the little part that has seemed to fall to my share'.

Samuel, regularly shuttling between his City office and Reading, also kept in touch with Malvern. In his sophisticated London way he could not resist teasing his spare and strict teetotal brother. 'I really have no faith in the waters doing you any good', he wrote jauntily. 'If you were [of] a full habit with gout and heated with high living and brandy it would do, but you require nothing taken out, but blood put in. Enjoy the air: that is the medicine for you.' Fortified by regular bulletins, therefore, George Palmer had leisure to think out the future organisation of the firm.

In the past the chief managerial weakness had been at the top: too much responsibility placed on the dominant partner. To help overcome that weakness, only the previous October Samuel and William Isaac Palmer had been given their promised partnerships, but on a limited basis. They brought in no capital nor did they acquire any claim over the firm's assets; however, in return for their full-time labours they received three and two twenty-fifths of the profits respectively. The senior partners' shares were each reduced to two-fifths each, out of which they paid the one twenty-fifth to which their traveller, Henry Lea, was entitled, although not a partner.

Henry Evans Huntley, now of age, had not been brought in at the same time. A few years earlier, in 1855, he had undergone a trial period within the firm: this lasted only twenty months and clearly did not prove a success. In the words of another regular correspondent with Malvern, William Slocombe the firm's Reading solicitor, Thomas Huntley's judgement—if not his heart—had led him to the conclusion that his son lacked both the competence and the interest to earn him a place in the business: to that extent he had died a disappointed man. If the survivors had any apprehensions that Henry might now claim a partnership, their fears were soon set at rest. When tackled by Samuel on this matter during the interregnum, he declared that neither his health nor his inclination drew him towards 'the conditions of punctual application to the business'. All he desired was his share of the capital in cash, which would allow him to buy a mill or a landed estate.

So matters worked out conveniently. The old partnership was wound up as from 31st March 1857 and its value calculated. Henry Huntley's 'moiety' of the total net assets, subject to a small life interest for his mother, came to £23,743, plus £10,049 premium representing the average of the past two years' profits less partners' drawings. Over a third of this sum was paid over to him in cash within the year and the remaining £20,000 secured on the assets of the business. It was finally paid off in two equal instalments towards the end of 1858 and 1859 respectively. To illustrate the public's consistent tendency to overvalue this very lucrative firm at a time when its affairs were completely hidden from the outside gaze, his share was widely reported to be £60,000.[1]

In the meantime Henry had married, in the Church of England, Augusta Ainsworth, the daughter of a Dorset landowner. Those who have followed thus far the ramifications of the Quaker cousinhood will not be surprised to learn that she was directly descended from the James Salter whose daughter Betty had married Richard Palmer of Long

Sutton. Augusta's mother had in fact been born a Quaker, to be subsequently disowned for marrying an Anglican.

Shortly after his own marriage, Henry bought an estate at Charlton Marshall, near Blandford in Dorset, and settled down to the life of a country gentleman, served—ironically enough—by a head gardener named George Palmer. He took his seat on the board of Blandford workhouse and on the governing body of a school in the next village, and maintained some tenuous links with the firm: he used to receive a Christmas cake annually until he died, aged eighty-five, in 1919, and from time to time he would make a tour of the factory while staying with his daughter Ada Frances Wright in Reading. However, unlike George and Samuel Palmer, he founded no dynasty. His elder son Henry Ainsworth Huntley, also of independent means, and the younger son Frederick, a solicitor at Boscombe, both died childless, and the three children of his daughter never married.

As part of the general settlement he readily covenanted not to allow his name to be associated with any other biscuit firm. That pledge he appears to have carried beyond the grave. After his death Charlton House became a preparatory school and the housekeeper occupied the room where he had died. Although she had only the sketchiest knowledge of the previous owner's connection with the firm, she always loyally ordered its biscuits. One time, however, the wholesalers induced her to order those of another maker. As she told the firm's representative, most earnestly insisting that what she said was true, she was thereafter disturbed each night by his ghost until she bought Reading biscuits once again.[2]

Under the new agreement, dated 19th October 1857, the business was given its present name of Huntley and Palmers. Samuel and William Isaac Palmer were brought into full partnership as from the previous 31st March: each would henceforth be entitled to a quarter of the profits, and had in return to contribute an equivalent proportion of the capital, namely £11,871. Their obligations included taking over jointly the £20,000 mortgage at 5 per cent owed to Henry Huntley; as long as the debt remained outstanding, they were not allowed to draw more than £1000 annually. The burden they thus assumed was not so onerous as might appear. The total profit for the initial year, ending on 31st March 1858, came to £18,019, of which Samuel and William Isaac received £4505 each as their quarter shares. Samuel removed the London office from St. Benet's Lane to Philpot Lane, off Fenchurch Street in 1861, and four years later to Rood Lane, also off Fenchurch Street. These ground-floor premises, leased at a rent of £300 a year, consisted only of two rooms and a passage-way and were considered large enough until the mid-1880s. George Palmer himself took the opportunity to withdraw a little from the day-to-day running of the business. In the new partnership agreement, he waived the initial premiums of £5000 each that his brothers should strictly have paid, in return for being granted 'liberty to decline taking an active part and absent himself partly or entirely as he thinks fit'. He wanted time for pursuing his interest in public affairs. His first important step in this direction was to offer himself for election as Mayor of Reading from November 1857.

The period of the second partnership was especially noteworthy, for throughout it, the firm maintained the highest continuous growth rate in its history. Only the few years at the close of the 1840s had seen a greater momentum, when output had doubled and redoubled in each of the two biennial periods 1846–8 and 1848–50. From 1857–8 to 1873–4 the average growth rate in the value of turnover was no less than 13 per cent compared with the previous year; in 1865–6 it reached nearly 19 per cent. Turnover in 1873–4 was almost six times—more precisely 5·9 times—what it had been in 1857–8.

Physical output was scarcely less buoyant, at nearly 12,600 tons in 1873–4, or 5·4 times the level of 1857–8. Capital and reserves rose from £50,000 to £320,000, while the value of the fixed capital, plant and machinery, and factory buildings rose from £27,000 to £113,000, with stock in trade up from £10,500 to £58,000. The fire insurance value of the factory was by 1874 over £210,000. Net profit rose from £18,000 to more than £84,000. Since the total profits over the whole period came to £715,000, the partners were able to put aside all the funds needed for expansion while themselves enjoying great personal wealth; it is only after this period that they began to live up to their affluence. So far from requiring outside loans any more, George and William Isaac Palmer each lent their cousins Cyrus and James Clark £500 when the shoe manufacturing firm fell into severe financial difficulties in 1863.[3]

This sustained growth rate can be attributed to two factors, one internal and the other external. We have traced how from 1841 onwards the Huntley craftsmanship and insistence on the highest standards were fruitfully combined with the Palmer flair for business. After 1857, the three brothers worked together as an harmonious and integrated team for upwards of thirty years, each contributing his particular gifts to the enterprise: George's imaginative vision and mechanical insight, William Isaac's soundness and reliability on the manufacturing side, and Samuel's sure judgement over marketing, the purchasing of ingredients and financial matters generally.

Moreover, all the Palmer brothers were served by able, or at least faithful, lieutenants. Richard Brown remained as head of manufacturing

The Second Partnership 1857–74

until his premature death, aged fifty-seven, in 1866, and had three sons who themselves were all in due course to hold high positions within the firm, as did a grandson and great-grandson. His eldest son, Charles, succeeded as factory manager, and by 1874, with a salary of £325 a year, was the most generously paid of the factory employees: those with higher salaries were all office or travelling staff. In charge of the offices was William Bullivant Williams, at forty earning £1000 a year, plus an annual gratuity of £100 for balancing the books, sometimes supplemented by an extra gift for 'holidays etc'. He was already the firm's 'confidential manager' in every respect except having charge of the Private Ledger, which housed the most intimate details of partners' income and drawings.

The home travelling staff had by the end of the period, with one exception, become entirely salaried employees instead of commission agents. Henry Lea, the still very energetic chief representative, earned £750 by 1873–4; since 1857 his percentage share in the profits had been commuted in an augmented salary. Charles Williams, his deputy, had just moved to Richmond in Surrey, as a suitable base for the lucrative territory of the Home Counties: his salary was £500, half that of his brother W. B. Williams. Other representatives were based at Manchester, York and Dublin: the three who operated from Reading were responsible for the eastern counties, Gloucestershire and Wales, and the south-west respectively. The last, John H. Day, had taken over in 1872 from the septuagenarian J. F. Wilkey. All these belonged to the 'aristocratic' class referred to in Chapter 5, earning over £4 a week: their salaries varied between £160 and £350 a year.

Apart from a traveller in the Isle of Man with an exiguous turnover, only Gawen B. Kenway of Birmingham continued to be paid on commission at 5 per cent. Although he collected fewer accounts than any of the principal travellers, his earnings were far greater, more than £1500 in 1873–4. That this anomaly would in the course of nature be abolished was clear from George Palmer's reply when the cocoa and chocolate firm Cadbury Bros. offered in 1851 to act as the firm's agent in the Birmingham area. 'We find that business done by ourselves is so much more satisfying than by commission', he told Cadbury's, 'that if we make any alteration at Birmingham, we are at present inclined to take the ground into our own hands.' In fact, G. B. Kenway did not die until 1883, aged eighty, when his son, G. Kenway, took over with a salary.

The travellers' ledger reveals that in 1873–4 just under 25 per cent of all sales were made in London and 48 per cent in the rest of the British Isles: about 28 per cent were exported. Since 1865 Joseph Leete, the Continental representative, had been rapidly building up a substantial volume of trade in Europe.

Yet this combination of entrepreneurial and managerial talent could never have been so fruitful but for certain contemporary developments outside the firm: namely, changes in people's consumption habits.[4] Many English families were now beginning to eat different kinds of food, and at different times of day, from their parents. To be sure, at that time the changes affected only a small percentage of the whole population. The real national income rose by 54 per cent between 1857 and 1874, but the poor had little opportunity to alter their diet. As late as 1904 working-class families earning less than 25s. a week spent on average 1¾d. a week on biscuits and cakes, but only ¼d. in London and its suburbs, while those earning the good wage of over 40s. a week spent only 7½d., and 5½d. in London.[5] Similarly, middle-class people with modest incomes looked on fancy biscuits as something that rarely came their way. Not until after 1940, with the combination of full employment and subsidised food subject to general rationing, did first-quality biscuits of the Huntley and Palmers kind become articles of general consumption.

Before the 1860s, the principal meals of the well-to-do tended to consist of a large breakfast, say at 9 or 10 a.m., and dinner in the early evening—six o'clock or earlier—with sometimes, but not invariably, a cold collation at lunch-time. The chief times for consuming fancy biscuits were the late evening, as a substitute for cakes or sandwiches, and at mid-morning, when the ladies might regale visitors with a glass of wine and a biscuit: this was usually a Captain's biscuit, of the kind that made merry the stony heart of Mr. Pecksniff. In 1849 the Reading firm had introduced an improvement on this variety, the Pic-Nic, which proved such a winner that well into the following year the factory was working virtually non-stop to keep up with demand, until such time as new machinery could be bought into service. By the 1850s the Pic-Nic was accounting for a fifth of all the firm's sales by value, and (since it was less expensive than the sweet varieties) about a quarter by weight.

However, once the prosperous classes adopted the practice of having less ample breakfasts, hot lunches and dinner at seven or even eight o'clock, the peculiarly English custom of afternoon tea grew up. By the late 1860s, then, the firm's hundred or so varieties catered for all tastes of those who could afford them. At the really luxurious end of the scale came the fancy rout cakes, for the fashionable evening parties bearing the suitably old-fashioned name of 'routs'; these cost 2s. per lb.—a day's wages for an unskilled hand in the factory. Lemon and orange dessert and raspberry biscuits, Queen's drops and ratafias all sold for over a shilling a pound. More modestly priced biscuits—particularly suitable for afternoon tea—included the Ginger Nut, Osborne, Abernethy, Digestive, Excursion, Gem, Nic-Nac and Tourist. The firm also made a series of dry biscuits with a nautical ring, namely the Britannia, Cabin, Captain, Cuddy, and Water.

In changing their eating habits and buying machine-made biscuits, the comfortably-off were only following the example of their superiors. Members of the peerage with retail accounts included William Cobbett's friend the Earl of Radnor; William Pitt's friend and rival Addington, later Viscount Sidmouth, who until his death in 1844 had a home at Erleigh, near Reading; the celebrated astronomer the Earl of Rosse; and that magnificent nobody the Joint Hereditary Lord Great Chamberlain of England, Lord Willoughby de Eresby. History does not record whether the great Duke himself sampled Reading biscuits, although his country house at Stratfield Saye was only a few miles distant. However, he used to keep on his desk a small packet of Abernethy biscuits, from which he would break small pieces to nibble in preference to eating proper meals.[6]

Many intellectual figures of the day were also faithful customers; the firm dealt directly with Mrs. Hawtrey, the Headmaster of Eton's wife, and the manciples of King's College, Cambridge, and Exeter College, Oxford, for instance. The biscuit habit was therefore strong in affluent rectories and cathedral closes. The Bishop of Carlisle had as a child in the Huntley days waited eagerly for the carrier to make a weekly delivery of Reading biscuits to the local shop at High Wycombe, while a small boy of the 1870s who frequently visited the palace of Christopher Wordsworth, Bishop of Lincoln and son of a prelate, remembered above all 'a housekeeper with ringlets and an inexhaustible mine of Osborne biscuits'.[7] The firm had introduced that variety as recently as 1860, and it was to prove one of the most enduring successes.

When the royal family (after whose holiday residence in the Isle of Wight the Osborne was named) began to purchase Huntley and Palmers' biscuits is not known. As early as 1844 the Hon. George Anson, private secretary and privy purse to Prince Albert, bought a few tins of biscuits. With the usual aristocratic offhandedness of the day, he left his bills unpaid for the best part of a year, but he may have introduced his master to them. At some stage in the next decade the firm began to make regular deliveries to Windsor Castle. Since no direct ledger entries were made, perhaps the private office kept a special account book which has now disappeared; so have the archives of the Lord Steward, which might have shed some light on this matter.[8]

At any rate, when in 1867 Joseph Leete secured royal warrants from Napoleon III and Leopold II of the Belgians, in a letter of congratulations that September Samuel Palmer remarked: 'We hope to report similar success on this side, when we will at once take steps to make the best of it'. His hopes must have been fulfilled, for the following month the price lists began to assume the royal arms and describe the firm as 'By Appointment to the Queen'. Then in 1883 a clause was added to an Act of Parliament to do with patents, designs and trade marks, prohibiting unauthorised use of the warrant by tradesmen. Huntley and Palmers straightway applied for a royal warrant and was granted it in 1884.[9]

Not only in the palace, college, club or home did biscuits fill a genuine need. An article written for the *Morning Star* in 1860 purports to describe how Church of England and nonconformist divines alike were adopting the habit of taking a few biscuits to fortify themselves before entering the pulpit for the three-decker sermons that their congregation then expected of them. In addition, people on both sides of the platform at the philanthropic and political meetings at Exeter Hall in London, which then lasted for five or six hours at a time with no break for lunch, would bring out their biscuits at the luncheon hour with little attempt at concealment. Despite its brand of wordy facetiousness, this article is in other respects too well informed to be dismissed as merely a surrealist fantasy.[10]

We are on surer ground when we examine such developments as the growth of tea-shops and of long-distance travel. Until about the eighties, it was said, 'there was not a place where a woman could get a cup of tea in all London town'; only men were allowed into chop houses, and ladies had to be satisfied with a glass of sherry and a Bath Bun in confectioners' shops.[11] As restaurants and tea-shops began to spring up, so their customers demanded sweet biscuits and shop cake with their cups or pots of tea.

Likewise the biscuit was a convenient substitute for formal meals during long journeys; passengers in the stage coaches who halted at the Crown Inn had made this discovery, to the advantage of the business, some forty years since. Now as people began increasingly to go on long-distance train journeys, so their discomfort at the lack of any dining facilities on the journey grew apparent. On the Great Western Railway, restaurant cars did not become available for first-class passengers until the 1890s and for others until well into the twentieth century. Anthony Trollope portrays the notorious Lady Eustace as keeping herself going with sherry, biscuits and chocolate on the twelve-hour journey from London to Scotland in the late 1860s; she did not get out, as did her male companion, during a twenty-minute stop for dinner at Carlisle.[12]

There were additional hazards on the railways for the famished traveller. The writer in the *Morning Star* relates the classic story (which loses little in the telling) of an alleged acquaintance of his who, during a five-minute halt at a station alighted and ordered a plate of soup from the platform buffet. No sooner was it handed to him than the whistle blew: he made a dash for the train, plate in hand and pursued by an irate attendant, who telegraphed to the next station, where the offender was taken in charge. After lengthy explanations he was released, but not before the 'pert' boy in the bookstall had forwarded full details of the incident to the newspapers. Thereafter the acquaintance never undertook a journey without a pocketful of biscuits.

The Palmer brothers, who in aggregate travelled many thousands of miles by train, were very well aware of the inadequate refreshment facilities. They therefore devised about this time a simple but most effective means of advertising their products. Every first-class passenger departing from Paddington was handed a small packet of biscuits in a neat wrapper, with instruction to look out for Huntley and Palmers' works at Reading. Indeed, to this day the red-brick factory is perhaps the most conspicuous feature of the town which through passengers on the trains are able to identify. Thus although they could only imperfectly have understood such long-term social changes, the Palmers tried every means of exploiting the steady expansion in demand for biscuits that was the consequence.

By 1860, with 500 employees in a factory covering an acre and a half of land, and with ovens that enclosed a baking surface of no less than 4180 square feet, Huntley and Palmers was already the largest biscuit firm in England, producing 3200 tons of biscuits a year, valued at £180,000—this was thirteen years before it put forward its claim to be the largest in the whole world.

It had long since outstripped its competitors in size and was in all respects acknowledged to be the leader. What had only a few decades previously been a collection of scattered biscuit-making units had rapidly acquired the recognisable shape of an industry. Firms were already exchanging information about their own and competitors' prices and voicing complaints to one another about the failure of third parties to follow conventional behaviour. George Palmer was a frequent confidant from all sides. In 1849–50, for instance, he received a series of anxious enquiries from Carr's of Carlisle about prices and discounts granted to customers, as well as complaints about Hill & Jones' undercutting of both firms' prices. However, he merely told Carr's that if it felt so strongly it should itself try to induce Hill & Jones to 'play fair and not cut up the trade'.

George Palmer soon changed his tune when he discovered that Hill & Jones was trying to poach labour from him, and his letter of remonstrance is a fine example of his reproachful (rather than irate) style. 'We think ourselves fortunate in having some in our employ having too true a sense of honour to be bribed by your offer. . . . Our mode of acquiring our business and conducting it has not been by unfairly enticing away the men employed by other houses, which in this case has produced you no good and has only done us the harm of a trifling advance in wages.' He then pressed home his advantage by suggesting a personal talk with the proprietor William Hill about prices; with what result is not known. A dozen years later Hill's firm had only eight ovens and a little machinery, so that his tactics had scarcely paid off.

However, these established rivals represented a less serious challenge than a new entrant of this period. In 1857, George H. Frean, a West Country miller and ship's-biscuit maker, joined forces with James Peek, his uncle by marriage and a retired tea merchant, to start up the firm of Peek Frean & Co. in London. Five years later they took into partnership the Quaker John Carr, younger brother of the Jonathan Carr who had founded the Carlisle firm. Peek Frean closely concerns Huntley and Palmers' history, for two reasons. In the twentieth century they were to establish business links with one another, under a holding company the Associated Biscuit Manufacturers Ltd., in which descendants of John Carr are still fellow-directors of the Palmers. More important for the period 1857–74, Peek Frean affords a standard of comparison for Huntley and Palmers' achievements. Its initial production at Bermondsey, in London, was mainly of ship's biscuits, as well as a form of aerated bread like the unfermented bread made in Reading during the 1840s. After 1870, however, Peek Frean decided to confine production to fancy biscuits.

Here Peek Frean appeared to enjoy some initial advantages. On the production side, it was able to equip its factory with the latest biscuit-making plant and travelling ovens made by Vicars of Liverpool. As to marketing, it benefited from the taste for biscuits which Huntley and Palmers was building up, and from the willingness of family grocers and others to become retail agents. As we shall see, it achieved progress by some very successful individual lines rather than by trying to match the sheer range of Huntley and Palmers' varieties, which numbered 100 in 1865, 150 ten years later, and no less than 400 by 1898.

Nevertheless, between 1863 and 1897 Peek Frean's sales of fancy biscuits averaged less than 45 per cent of Huntley and Palmers' value; its profits figures for 1862–7 and 1880–97 (the only years available) were 5·5 per cent of turnover, compared with Huntley and Palmer's 13·3 per cent. One reason for this difference was that Peek Frean had twelve partners for varying periods up to 1901, who as a whole lacked the united drive and expertise of the Palmer family.

Indeed, the main problems which then faced Huntley and Palmers were caused by the steady and apparently unbounded growth in its sales. Above all, it needed to safeguard adequate supplies of high-quality ingredients. In 1856-7, for instance, the flour required cost just under £25,000 for the nine-month period; more than half came from Swallowfield, Hurley and Whitchurch Mills, all within a few miles of Reading. From the earliest days, George Palmer had been prepared in bad seasons to help local farmers with advances of cash, to allow them to buy their seed-corn and manure.[13] The firm was thus helping to support British farming at a time when it was being slowly stifled by imports. For other products, some sources of supply were far afield: much butter was imported from Ostend, while Ireland—then a very important source of agricultural products for the English market—provided the bulk of the eggs that the firm required.

By 1873-4, the firm's annual requirements of flour were more than 10,000 tons, costing just over £195,000; this now came from East Anglia as well as Berkshire, while imported flour was used only for some types of cake. It also bought annually 10,000 tons of coal and coke, nearly 2350 tons of sugar, 1100 tons of butter and lard, 8·2 million eggs, 270,000 gallons of ordinary milk and 22,000 gallons of skimmed milk, from any source that could guarantee the first-rate qualities required. Samuel Palmer's presence as buyer in the London produce markets was thus vital to the firm.

The problems of how to forestall ingredients shortages were paralleled by the need to provide adequate productive capacity. A few months after his partner's death in 1857 George Palmer had planned a substantial building programme to make the best use of the limited site. He not only extended the original silk mill southwards, but also put up a large four-storey building—the South Factory—on the site of the old tobacco factory. These works, costing about £7000 in all, would hopefully take care of production growth for a number of years, but he still had the long-term anxiety of whether, and how, he could eventually break out of the island site.

To be sure, a few adjacent parcels of land did become available at different dates, notably some on the eastern side of Gasworks Road, nowadays occupied by the Recreation Club. Yet the valuable Cannon Brewery site did not fall in until 1872; the purchase price was the fairly heavy one of £3000. This acquisition allowed the firm to enlarge the South Factory, and also extend the offices on the King's Road frontage as far as the junction with Forbury Road. The Cannon public house, on the same frontage, had constituted a grievous source of temptation to the home-going workpeople, and the teetotal partners were very glad to see it closed down.

Yet the only direction in which the firm could expand on a large scale, without having to open up a new site altogether, was to the north. The further bank of the river Kennet, known as Blake's Wharf, was owned by John Jackson Blandy, a former Mayor and Town Clerk of Reading. He had steadfastly refused to sell, but immediately after his death in 1866, William Isaac Palmer asked his nephew and heir, William Frank Blandy, for the first refusal of the site. Mr. Blandy promised to consult the executors, but then entirely forgot.

Since other would-be purchasers were showing active interest in the site, the Palmers were naturally enough on edge, for much of their future prosperity depended on securing the land. At this tense moment George Palmer encountered William Blandy—whether by chance or design is not clear—and had words with him, attacking his behaviour and, for good measure, that of the whole Blandy family as well. The outcome was a hurt and somewhat incoherent letter from William Blandy, which contrasted the kind of feelings which the mild William Isaac Palmer had always shown him with the 'wholesale condemantion' that 'escaped from you this morning'.

However, no permanent rupture took place. The tactful William Isaac Palmer soothed William Blandy's feelings, and almost unobtrusively acquired the land for £6600 on behalf of the partnership. George Palmer was soon pressing on with a survey, not only for building what became known as the North Manufacturing Department, with its own packing rooms on the upper stories, but also to construct railway sidings that would run into the heart of the factory. Both the north and the south departments were to have their own loading sheds, into which cases of biscuits for despatch were projected from the upstairs packing rooms down inclined planes. The firm had its own locomotives, which hauled the waggons to and from the main railway lines to which the sidings were connected.

Although this survey was made in mid-1868, it was five years before the buildings and works on Blake's Wharf were complete. The cost was just short of £50,000, with an extra £25,000 for 'fixtures and machinery'. The manager of the North Manufacturing Department was J. R. Moore, who as a boy had given much trouble to the Sick Club committee (see Chapter 8) for his persistent flouting of the regulations, but had since put his energies to more constructive ends.

The partners ceremonially declared the new buildings open one Saturday evening in November 1873. The number of employees was then in the region of 2500, over six times as many as the 400-odd in 1857 and nearly three times the 920 employed as recently as 1867. About 4000 were invited to the opening, the maximum number that the buildings could accommodate. The hosts laid down very precise instructions as to who should be admitted. Married men were allowed to bring their wives, but exceptionally, those who had worked in the factory for more than five years and whose wives were ill, could bring another member

The Second Partnership 1857-74

of the family instead. Unmarried men with over five years' service could also apply for another ticket, but as a rule only for 'some female member of his family'. We do not know how many young men were detected passing off their girl-friends as sisters, but perhaps official vigilance was for once exercised leniently.

At 5.30 p.m. the guests were served with tea, bread and butter and cake and afterwards diverted with a choice of eight entertainments from 7 to 10 p.m. These entertainments had been specially arranged by the Royal Polytechnic Institute; they were carefully graded from weighty scientific and travel lectures to displays of clairvoyance and juggling and those comical sketches (with titles such as 'Pussy's Road to Ruin') so beloved of the Victorians. The huge top room of the new factory was, according to a contemporary account, 'devoted to the votaries of Terpsichore, who found more than enough to satisfy their appetites in the shape of quadrilles, waltzes and polkas'. At five minutes to ten, an electric signal, transmitted to every room, was the cue for the proceedings to close with the singing of the National Anthem.[14]

This ceremonial occasion in a sense marked the close of this memorable period, for only four months later the first two representatives of the new generation, George Palmer's sons George William and Alfred, were admitted to partnership.

7
Exports and International Exhibitions

Huntley and Palmers' overseas trade apparently began soon after George Palmer, on becoming a partner in 1841, extended the home market from a limited area of southern England to the whole of Britain. The opportunities for selling perishable foodstuffs abroad were far more promising than might have appeared; consignments of Banbury cakes, for instance, were by 1840 going to the United States, India, and even as far as Australia.[1] Since these probably travelled in wooden boxes, they must have become rather stale during the many weeks' journeys, but for fancy biscuits the introduction of tins overcame this difficulty.

In 1844 Huntley and Palmer was therefore advertising 'biscuits packed in tin cases (of all sizes) for Families residing in the Country and for Exportation', and at least two London fancy biscuit firms also were by then exporting in tins.[2] Five years later George Palmer informed an enquirer that his firm's soldered tins, being completely airtight, had been found good even after voyages of some years.

Military men, who had from a very early date been regular customers at home, naturally sent back for Reading biscuits once they were posted abroad. We find in 1849 a Quaker agent at Gibraltar, John Stewart, submitting orders on behalf of the garrison there, and grappling with such problems as officers' dishonoured cheques drawn on Cox & Co., the army bankers, and damage to cases and barrels during the often tempestuous voyage from Southampton across the Bay of Biscay. Civilian consignments were by that date going to India; these were arranged through commission agents in England with merchants in such ports as Bombay, and were not invoiced direct. The first overseas account proper was with a Brussels firm in 1850.

Huntley and Palmer did no active marketing overseas, but just waited for orders to come in. Not unexpectedly, therefore, export figures totalled only some £8000 in 1852–3. Moreover, the firm went practically unnoticed at the two international exhibitions of the decade: the Great Exhibition of 1851 and the one at Paris in 1855. At the Crystal Palace in 1851 Huntley and Palmer was one of the seventeen entrants from Reading—which included Barrett Exall and Andrewes, and Cocks's of Reading Sauce fame—but was the only fancy biscuit manufacturer; its products were relegated to the highly residual category of Class 29, 'Miscellaneous Manufactures and Small Wares' and tucked away in the North Transept Gallery, where only the most indefatigable sightseers ever penetrated.[3] It therefore received only the bronze medal and certificate given to all exhibitors, while at Napoleon III's *exposition internationale* it secured no more than an honourable mention. In a memorandum to a later exhibition, the firm explained away these disappointing results as the consequence of the fancy biscuit trade being in 1851 'small and only partially developed', and so little understood at Paris 'that our biscuits were called sea biscuits', which it had in fact never made.[4]

It was only when the firm's general marketing effort came into the hands of very capable men with a personal stake in its growth, such as Samuel Palmer and Henry Lea, that exports began to grow. Henry Lea had brought from his commercial house at Liverpool in 1849 a conviction that the Reading firm could build up a large export business in biscuits, a view heartily reciprocated by the Palmer brothers; however, for some years he had to give almost his entire attention to the home market.

Lea opened his first United States account in 1854, and a brief but acrimonious quarrel with George Palmer the next year—all because he had slightly overdrawn his Journey and Export accounts—shows that he had correspondents as far afield as China, Brazil, the River Plate area and the west coast of Africa. However, by 1855–6 he was reponsible for booking only 12½ per cent of total export orders, compared with Samuel Palmer's 60 per cent; the remainder were arranged with the factory direct. The value of exports that year was just under £16,000, equal to 15 per cent of turnover.

Export figures had in fact scarcely increased since 1853–4, owing to some chance happenings. The Crimean War had caused disruptions in world trade as well as a shortage of sea transport, and the Reading biscuit had not yet become the recognised 'comfort' for those on active service, that it became in later wars; one looks in vain for stacks of Huntley and Palmer boxes or tins among the stores illustrated in Roger Fenton's evocative photographs of the Crimean front. At the same time, the bad harvests of 1854 and 1855 severely curtailed the supply of suitable biscuit flour; George Palmer therefore decreed that home order must take precedence of exports.

Henry Lea, while not challenging this decision, urged that with peace in prospect and a more abundant harvest promised for 1856, the firm should stand ready to fulfil a 'heavy export trade to all quarters'. His advice was heeded, although during 1858 a troublesome shortage of tins led to many overseas consignments missing their sailing dates. By 1859–60 exports were about double those of 1855–6, being valued at some £30,000, or nearly two-thirds of total exports from the United Kingdom of 'bread and biscuit'. The firm was greatly encouraged by the bronze medal 'Honoris Causa' which it won for excellence of quality at the London Exhibition of 1862. Peek Frean, exhibiting for the first time, won a bronze medal, without citation.

According to family tradition, it was Samuel Palmer who opened up the trade with France by crossing the channel with a sample biscuit box under his arm. Yet this trade languished for some years. The firm's appointment in 1859 of H. Cuvillier, of the Rue de la Paix in Paris, as its commission agent for France, proved largely unfruitful, despite the backing of annual trips until 1863 made by Bullivant Williams, from the Reading office. Then in 1865 the firm found its solution: the appointment of a very able representative for the Continent, whose territory eventually stretched as far as Russia, Turkey and the north coast of Africa, from Morocco to Egypt.

A young man in his early thirties, Joseph Leete, who for the past twelve years had run his own agency to handle 'shipping and custom house matters', had often in the course of business visited Huntley and Palmers' London Office. That year he proposed to Samuel Palmer that he should seek orders for biscuits on the Continent while travelling for other household names of the age, such as Crosse & Blackwell's food products, Allsopp's ales and Horniman's tea. According to Leete's recollections, Samuel Palmer replied that the previous day he had remarked to his partners that he knew of only one man who could sell their biscuits on the Continent: Leete himself. He therefore gratefully accepted the offer.

Once again the Palmer luck, or good judgement, in finding the right salesman at the right time, was to bring dramatic results. Joseph Leete set to work in Europe with as much determination and efficiency as Henry Lea was showing at home. In his first full year, 1866, Leete brought to Huntley and Palmers over £10,000 worth of custom. Some of his coups were spectacular: that year he succeeded in cutting out Peek Frean and capturing the biggest single order for biscuits in the whole of the Continent by the simple expedient of what is nowadays called 'the blindfold test'. He invited the proprietor of F. Potin, the celebrated Parisian food emporium in the Boulevard Malesherbes, to taste six of each firm's biscuits in pairs while blindfolded. The proprietor unhesitatingly chose five of Huntley and Palmers' and F. Potin remained the firm's largest Paris and Continental customer until the First World War. In 1867, as related in Chapter 6, Leete secured for the firm Royal Warrants as suppliers of biscuits to Napoleon III and to Leopold II of the Belgians.

Despite these rare triumphs, most of Joseph Leete's work for the firm inevitably consisted of protracted and incessant slogging. With an imposing presence and unusual linguistic gifts, he possessed what a member of the family recalled as 'a florid manner, a river of talk, part of the equipment of a successful man in that profession'. He was the first traveller in biscuits to visit Spain, Portugal, Scandinavia, Russia and Turkey, and even to penetrate into the remoter parts of western Europe. Moreover, he had to spend much of his time with cabinet ministers and customs officials in each country haggling over tariff rates and the contents of fancy biscuits, notably the percentage of sugar, as well as attempting to dispel misconceptions about their nature. Not unexpectedly, 'since he could make no difference between his business manner and his domestic manner, there came a time when everyone to whom he talked felt like a recalcitrant grocer or the proprietor of a new hotel *de luxe*'.

His first real test came in 1867, with the opening of the Universal Exhibition in Paris, which marked Napoleon III's last great display of grandeur before his downfall at Sedan. Leete's persuasion, and Samuel Palmer's support, allowed the firm to spend as much as £1350 on the expenses of the exhibition; previously it had limited its outlays to trifling amounts. The celebrated industrial designer Owen Jones prepared (for a fee of £52.10s.) a perspective drawing of the Reading factory, which was greatly admired but can hardly be classed among his best works. Nor did the firm's showcase match up to Peek Frean's solid oak one nearby. However, De La Rue's, the London printing firm responsible for many of the firm's biscuit tin labels, set a new fashion by breaking away from the old stereotyped designs, and producing some striking labels for Huntley and Palmers' Napoleon and Leopold biscuits: these had backgrounds of the French and Belgian tricolours on the front side, and for the first time had bold designs on all the other sides and the top. Owen Jones also designed labels for smaller tins, which were among the most pleasing ones ever used by the firm.

The biscuits themselves were much in demand at the exhibition; Leete arranged for them to figure on the bill of fare in many of its restaurants; and while inspecting the firm's stand, the jury spent many happy minutes sampling them. Rival biscuit-makers were hard put to it to compete against these efforts. The French already enjoyed a reputation second to none as a nation of pastrycooks and confectioners—their *petits fours* were especially noteworthy—yet they could not produce goods that had keeping qualities. As a commentator wrote 'French biscuits are sweet, showy and succulent; but after a day or two . . . they lose their gloss, their flavour, and their crispness, and become limp, sour, dry, and tasteless. The English biscuit, scrupulously prepared and as scrupulously packed, will defy time and climate.'[5] However, the jury concerned with biscuit exhibits chose as its adviser M. Guillout, the largest biscuit manufacturer in France. He induced the jury to award the gold medal to himself, and later on boasted openly to Leete that he had thereby deprived Huntley and Palmers of it. The firm had to be content with the Silver Medal; once again Peek Frean was placed in the same class.

From the Paris Exhibition of 1867 until that of 1878 the firm won on average a medal a year, mainly in Europe but also as far afield as Lima and Santiago. At the Vienna Exhibition of 1873 George Palmer's sons George William and Alfred superintended the work of fitting out the firm's display. Their father throughout his life felt himself handicapped by a lack of foreign languages, and therefore encouraged his sons to acquire them; that particular occasion gave them an opportunity to practise their German as well as exercise their skill at organising. The rectangular show case was designed by Owen Jones: one of the last pieces of work he did for the firm before his death in 1874. The case was situated in the centre of the room set aside for British agricultural exhibits, and housed a collection of conspicuously labelled tins. The firm earned a bronze medal 'for progress in new inventions and the introduction of new materials and contrivances'.[6]

By that time Leete's sales on the continent had topped the £100,000 mark—and the firm had had to scale down his commission from 5 per cent on the full amount to 2½ per cent on all except the first £5000. The outbreak of the Franco-Prussian War in 1870 temporarily halted the growth of his trade; it was Peek Frean which was commissioned by the French government to provide, with the aid of other British firms, over 16,300 tons of ship's biscuits to save Paris from starvation after the siege was raised at the end of the war. On his side, Leete did what he could by dispatching one of his travellers, Macnamara, to the capital with a large consignment of the firm's biscuits, as well as Crosse & Blackwell's provisions, ham, cheese and cornflour. At Dieppe Macnamara persuaded a German military guard to let him have a soldier's cap and uniform. In this transparent disguise he travelled as a railway servant to Paris, where he disposed of the consignment at cost price.

The Paris Exhibition of 1878 gave the firm its first major success, and established its name internationally as one of the great exhibition winners of all time.[7] In 1867 it had been cheated out of what it had felt to be its rightful honour. Now when M. Guillout's name appeared once more on the panel of jurors, Samuel Palmer, who happened to be passing through Paris, exclaimed to Leete: 'We are done again!' He reckoned without Leete's quick presence of mind. Leete straightway organised a joint petition from Huntley and Palmers, Peek Frean, and an American manufacturer; this prevailed on the authorities to add another member, an Englishman, to the panel.

In the event Huntley and Palmers was awarded the *grand prix*, a gold medal. Moreover, it was praised in the first eulogy ever made at an international exhibition, as follows: 'Unrivalled house, known throughout the world for its enormous output and for the excellent quality of its products.' Placed second in the list was Peek Frean, which also won a gold medal.

The firm had clearly learnt two essential lessons about international exhibitions. First, it now made the show case as conspicuous as possible, just like those of Guillout and other French entrants. The firm's case was no longer a plain rectangular one, but was deeply recessed at the sides so as to increase the amount of space for the contents. It was splendidly decorated, of ebonised wood picked out in gold, with rich mosaic panels modelled on the Alhambra in Spain. The display inside was far more imaginative than before. Some of the 150 different varieties of biscuits arranged, like so many anatomical specimens, in plain glass bottles, may have had a rather clinical appearance, but other jars were more decorative, as were the many gaily labelled tins and the two-tiered wedding cake in the centre. An illustrated catalogue, produced specially for the exhibition, showed off in full colours the entire range of 228 biscuits.

The second lesson that had now been mastered was the considerable publicity to be gained from giving away plenty of free samples of biscuits. At Vienna in 1873, the firm had left open its tins for visitors to help themselves: its stand had soon acquired the reputation of being the only spot in the entire exhibition where one could get something for nothing. In Paris, where Leete had secured for the firm the exclusive right to supply biscuits to the twenty-one most important restaurants, a 'gentlemanly attendant' at its stand coaxed all bystanders, however diffident, into sampling the contents. The whole impact of the multicoloured display and lavish free biscuits must have been somewhat overpowering, but they paid off, and George Palmer travelled to Paris in order to receive his prize in person.

William Isaac Palmer, another visitor at the exhibition, commented with justice that 'Leete has the energy of a hundred men', and that no one else could have achieved what he had at the Exhibition. Inevitably in a period when Henry Stanley's voyages into darkest Africa and his rendezvous with David Livingstone had made his name a household word as the explorer *par excellence*, the press, taking its cue from the jury's official report, dubbed Leete 'a very Stanley of commerce', as well as 'a polyglot dictionary in himself'.[8] Yet, as Henry Lea pointed out during his visit, the only cloud that hung over this triumph was the enhanced competition that it was likely to provoke. This turned out to be true. In 1878 about £169,000 worth of business was done on the continent, over three and a half times as much as in 1869; this was to rise to £278,000 by 1883. However, it never topped the last figure again during the remainder of the century, although the sustained efforts of Leete and of his assistants—ten by 1900—saved it from falling below £220,000.

Much of this decline was due to Continental countries increasing their tariffs. The era of free trade in Europe had come to an end with the fall of Napoleon III: France itself reimposed protection in 1873 and intensified it after 1882, to be followed by other European countries later in the seventies. The French Customs authorities in particular pursued their restrictive policies with great vigour; they even exacted a duty for each tin that was temporarily admitted and later returned to Reading once it was empty. Leete managed to get this provision relaxed slightly, but France was a crucial area since it happened to account for between 50 and 55 per cent of all his trade. Belgium and Holland, also high tariff countries, together contributed another 21 to 25 per cent.

Because of these difficulties, after 1878 Huntley and Palmers withdrew from the field of international exhibitions, apart from one or two outside main tariff areas, such as Havana in 1892. By then the firm was regularly exchanging information with Peek Frean about prices and discounts in overseas markets; this practice both helped to avoid cut-throat competition, and prevented unscrupulous agents abroad from playing off one firm against the other.

Before the Paris Exhibition of 1889, therefore, Peek Frean reminded Huntley and Palmers of the 'determined hostility' towards British goods of the French tariff, and thought that it would be rather agreeable if 'the leading English Biscuit Manufacturers were conspicuous by their absence', since they could not possibly reap any direct benefit at all commensurate with the heavy expenses involved. Huntley and Palmers agreed, and Leete contented himself with persuading all the French *restaurateurs* in the exhibition precincts to advertise the firm's biscuits on their bills of fare and wine lists. Then by 1900 the two firms felt themselves ready to exhibit again.

At Paris that year Huntley and Palmers was awarded no less than two *grands prix*.[9] In the one class, devoted to biscuits for home consumption, the jury stated: 'The firm has not ceased to progress, either in the expansion of its business or in the excellence of its products'; a very accurate judgement, none the less so for having been drafted by Leete himself. He had as usual been lobbying energetically behind the scenes;

this eulogy was unprecedented in international exhibitions, with the single exception of the one awarded to the firm in 1878.

In the other class, for products specially prepared for exportation to the colonies, the firm won a *grand prix unique*. These two awards indeed constituted a resounding victory, but unhappily Charles Palmer—who had taken over responsibility for Continental business in the London office from his father Samuel—in his congratulatory letter to Leete twice used the word 'disappointment', all because a *grand prix* had gone also to Lefèvre-Utile, biscuit manufacturers of Nantes. Like Guillout, that firm was only a fraction of the size of Huntley and Palmers, but it was a very strong competitor on *petits fours* and sugar wafers. To be sure, only a year or so had elapsed since the Fashoda crisis had brought the two nations to the edge of war, and Charles Palmer's letter referred also to 'the exceptional feeling' on the part of the French people towards Britain. Leete, however, throve on unstinted praise. The first generation of Palmers had always laid it on with a trowel; now even a cheque for a thousand guineas did not entirely efface the impression of qualified approval in Reading.

The rest of the world, not covered by Leete's territory, belonged to the export department; this was administered quite separately from the Continental department, right down to the packing and invoicing arrangements. Over this vast area, one man could scarcely have exercised the close control that Leete did over the Continent. Samuel Palmer tried his best, but he had responsibility for the London trade and ingredients purchasing as well; he therefore had to rely on whatever arrangements he could make.

These arrangements are largely unknown to us. We know of Leete's organisation from the two typescript volumes which he compiled for the firm's directors after his retirement, but our information about the export department's business is very fragmentary. Even annual figures of its sales were not kept until 1906; these therefore have had to be estimated by other means.[10] By the turn of the century the firm had resident representatives in North and South America, South Africa, India, China and Japan.[11] Nearly a third of the export department's trade was done through two large London houses, C. & E. Morton and Crosse & Blackwell; other British and colonial shipping houses did 60 per cent, while foreign merchants having direct accounts with the firm accounted for less than an eighth.

Only for North America can we piece together a fairly coherent story. In 1870 Charles S. Belcher, who claimed to be the largest biscuit manufacturer in the United States, sought from George Palmer the exclusive agency of the firm's biscuits; he pointed out how Peek Frean was flooding the American market with its goods and thereby gaining much ground. George Palmer not very cordially rejected the offer, saying that he had just made an arrangement with a traveller who represented several other English houses, and who was to make his headquarters in New York.

This arrangement, whatever it was, must have fallen through, as in 1871 J. G. Nall, a London commission agent, made a prolonged trip through South America and the following year to the north and south of the continent; his expenses were shared between two or three firms. He was responsible for £1850 worth of business for the firm in North America during 1873—about 10 per cent of total exports of 'bread and biscuits' from the United Kingdom there—but does not seem to have repeated his trip. By 1887 the firm was selling only £1280 worth of biscuits in the United States and £25 worth in Canada.

It appointed its first representative there in 1888: William S. Kennedy, a Quaker already established in the United States as traveller for Rowntree's of York. He was to receive £300 a year for two years, plus 5 per cent on any sales over £6000, whether made by himself or directly with the firm. Huntley and Palmers impressed on him that it dealt only with 'the very best houses' and, while giving him a free hand, urged him to concentrate initially on the highly populated eastern seaboard, where fewer problems regarding inland transport existed.

Kennedy began on the wrong foot, for the London office was soon informing him: 'We should have preferred to get our goods into the American cities and watering places first instead of the Wild West.' (The unruly localities presumably objected to included Chicago, Detroit and Kansas City.) It further chided him for being 'under the wrong impression' by treating the firm's biscuits solely as Christmas goods when they were in practice 'everyday necessities'. Even so, he succeeded in opening 608 accounts in Philadelphia and 118 in New York, and more than doubled sales to over £4000. These were well below the £6000 at which he would start to earn commission, and as Rowntree's also paid him £300, he had to write and explain that he could not possibly manage on £600 a year all in; as he put it rather sadly, 'it is dreadfully expensive travelling in the West'.

Huntley and Palmers thereupon granted him another £200 a year, and complained to Rowntree's, which had now decided to remunerate him on a 'commission only' basis, for 'venturing nothing' while deriving every benefit from Kennedy's journeys. Rowntrees' response is not known, but by the end of 1891, when he had not increased the firm's turnover even to £5000, and his proportion of British export trade in biscuits was under 40 per cent, no higher than in 1888, Kennedy threw in his hand. He took the London office 'entirely by surprise' by going into partnership with a merchant in Philadelphia. The firm cut its losses and appointed in his place Edward Valpy, from the celebrated family of Reading schoolmasters.

Valpy was an entirely different type from the querulous Kennedy, being elegant, detached, without illusions but full of charm. He was also a far more effective salesman. By 1894 the firm's trade with North America reached £7000, in 1896, £14,300, and in 1902 (his final year) nearly £22,500. He virtually routed the competition of rival British firms, particularly of Peek Frean; in 1894 his share of biscuit exports to the United States was 75 per cent; by 1902 it had risen to 86 per cent, and was to reach 94 per cent in 1906. For Canada the same percentage rose from 50 to 69 per cent.

This achievement was in spite of having to contend not only with high tariffs—between 15 and 50 per cent in 1902—but also with an American combine, the National Biscuit Co., which had now overtaken Huntley and Palmers as the largest biscuit firm in the world. By a series of mergers it now held 70 per cent of the American market, with sales of over $37 million in 1900 (over five times as great as Huntley and Palmers' total sales), and thus was able to exploit considerable economies of production and distribution.[12]

Huntley and Palmers' progress in South and Central America was less eventful. In the early 1870s J. G. Nall had secured £6200 worth of

VALUE OF HUNTLEY AND PALMERS' OVERSEAS TRADE*

	Continental Dept.	Export Dept. (including U.S. and Canada)	Total H. & P.	U.K. Exports of Biscuits and Cake	% of U.K. Trade
	£000s				
1852–3	—	—	8	42	19·0
1858–9	—	—	25	48	52·1
1868–9	28	62	90	162	55·5
1874–5	118	161	279	368	75·8
1878–9	174	204	378	455	83·1
1888–9	241	235	476	551	86·4
1898–9	236	221	457	609	75·0
1908–9	303	392	695	1032	67·3
1913–14	366	592	958	1622	59·1

*Gross figures (including value of tins, etc.) to permit comparability with Customs and Excise figures.

business there, four times as high as in North America; by 1906 its trade—just under £40,000, or 55 per cent of British biscuit exports to the area—was below the £43,000 in the north. Even so, those living in hot, and particularly humid, climates such as Venezuela appreciated the fact that Huntley and Palmers' varieties kept 'well and in a sound state' for many years in their tins, whereas those from the United States would not keep, even for a year, and the low-priced German ones could be stored only for six months.[13]

What of the firm's activities elsewhere in the world? As the table on p. 91 shows, the export department tended to grow more slowly than the Continental department to 1898–9, but thereafter went ahead of it. Indeed, owing to the increases in unit prices, the total physical volume of the Continental department's trade cannot have been much greater in 1908–9 than ten years earlier: tariffs on the Continent were then very high, and Joseph Leete, who was approaching eighty, had lost much of his early vigour.

Not until 1906 do we know the main destinations of the export trade, which may be compared with the Continental trade, as follows:

Continental Trade			*Export Trade*		
	Value (£000s)	% of Total H. and P. Overseas Trade		Value (£000s)	% of Total H. and P. Overseas Trade
France	139	21.8	India	64	10.0
Belgium	25	3.9	Dutch East Indies	61	9.5
Holland	18	2.8	Burma	44	6.9
Egypt	14	2.3	South Africa	43	6.8
			U.S.A.	36	5.3
			(Far East: India to China	224	35.0)
			(Africa	81	11.7)
Total	266	40.6	*Total*	375	59.4

If we assume that the growth in the firm's exports to India between 1868 and 1906 was comparable with that for biscuit exports from Britain as a whole, then India was consistently the export department's most important single customer, with 11 per cent of the firm's overseas trade in 1868–9; it was thus second only to France. We have seen how in the early days, merchants in India were importing through British commission agents; when General Roberts's troops entered Kandahar in 1879, Adam Jee, merchant of Bombay, had a placard advertising

Huntley and Palmers' biscuits prominently displayed on the walls of the town bazaar.[14]

Although two countries, France and India, may therefore have been jointly responsible for a third of the firm's overseas trade throughout this period, the other two-thirds was spread over a surprisingly wide range of countries. In 1864 the firm was already claiming that its products went as far afield as from Greenland to Cochin China, from Nova Zembla to New Zealand.[15] Ten years later it boasted: 'Seldom a ship sails from England that does not bear within his [sic] ribs a Reading biscuit', *en route* for virtually every port around the globe.[16] About the same time Samuel Palmer told a gathering that gentlemen in London often expressed surprise to him that his firm's biscuits should find their way to obscure parts of the world. His reply, he added, was invariably to ask that if ever they should encounter any obscure place where Reading biscuits were unobtainable, he would be glad to know, 'as it is our intention that they should be found there'.[17]

The Palmer brothers themselves were thus seeking every possible opportunity of publicising their products throughout the world. In 1862 they despatched biscuits valued at £2.4s. to the King of Madagascar on the occasion of his coronation, in the wake of gifts sent by Queen Victoria, Napoleon III and Pope Pius IX. Ten years later, George Palmer was responsible for a civic reception being held for a delegation from Japan, which was visiting Britain in search of new ideas to advance its country's welfare and interests.[18]

The approbation of monarchs, too, helped the firm in many overseas countries. The king of the Barotse tribe was fond of rounding off his midday meal with tea, native beer and Huntley and Palmers' biscuits.[19] Nearer home, in 1867 the Empress Eugénie was reported to demand constant supplies at each of the royal palaces where she happened to be in residence; forty years later, when France was once more a republic, President Fallières entertained Edward VII—one of the foremost gourmets of his age—to a superb luncheon at the Elysée Palace, which concluded with *petits Palmers*, as the firm's sugar wafers were called.[20] By then the firm held royal appointments to the courts of Belgium, Holland, Italy, Denmark, Japan and Siam.

Not far behind were the explorers. Henry Stanley, in central Africa, from time to time had to subsist entirely on Reading biscuits, while he once pacified a very warlike tribe at Suna, now in central Tanzania, with some tins of them as presents.[21] Once natives came to recognise them, the tins enjoyed an importance in their own right. From 1851 onwards they bore the highly distinctive trade mark of a garter and buckle, which the firm jealously protected from imitators in every part of the world. Thus tins began to travel along ancient and mysterious routes, outwards from the commercial centres where the firm's agents were situated, to emerge in quite unexpected places. The following examples all refer specifically to Huntley and Palmers' tins or biscuits.

In 1904, when the officer in command of the Tibet expedition arrived at the holy city of Lhasa, until that moment prohibited to Europeans, he was immediately offered tea, small cigars and biscuits.[22] Himalayan shepherds were reported to be willing to trade an empty tin for a week's supply of sheep's milk.[23] In the late 1860s a Mongolian chieftainess had, as an 'outward and visible sign of her high position', a large tin in which to grow some heads of garlic for flavouring a mutton stew. Lord Redesdale, who witnessed that scene, was reminded of it thirty years later when he saw two tins as ornaments on each side of the altar in a tiny Catholic chapel in Ceylon.[24]

The tins thus possessed a happy combination of intrinsic and sentimental value. The ten-pound size was large and sturdy enough to be used as an article of furniture. The rich kept their valuables in them; hunters their cartridges, and bereaved persons the cremated ashes of the deceased. The Queen's son-in-law Prince Henry of Battenberg, having died in the tropics, was brought back to England in a rum-filled tank made out of biscuit tins. In Switzerland they were used as ballot boxes in a local referendum, while in the Pyrenees they formed one of the props in a Basque pastoral play.[25] In Uganda native bibles and prayer books had to measure three inches broad by three inches thick so as to fit into the two-pound tins, which were about the only containers that would protect them against the ravages of white ants. The tins with their sacred contents were proudly conveyed to church every Sunday; it must have been interesting to hear the clatter which followed the minister's injunction: 'Let us pray'.[26]

Sometimes the tins were employed for less benign purposes. During the war against the Mahdi that culminated in the battle of Omdurman, some captured Sudanese swords were found to have scabbards with metal bands cut from tins, so that the firm's name (stamped on the base of each tin) was prominently displayed. The fictional 'amateur cracksman' Raffles, when anonymously returning to Queen Victoria a gold cup he had stolen from the British Museum for a prank, sent out for the largest available Huntley and Palmers' tin as a container, since it was both extremely robust, and in such common use as to furnish little indication of its origin.[27] The notorious swindler and train-wrecker of the Boer War, Jack Hinton, is alleged to have bought in 1874 twelve gross of five-pound tins, extracted the guarantee vouchers (which happened to be the same size as colonial £5 notes) and used those vouchers to 'buy' farm produce from Boer farmers, who were at that time mostly illiterate. Since the story was first promulgated in 1900, it is almost certainly a piece of crude anti-Boer propaganda, designed to show off the farmers' stupidity and greed.[28]

What is better authenticated is the occasion when Huntley and Palmers' products fell victim to piracy on the high seas. In 1862 the Confederate privateer *Alabama*, while prowling in the South Atlantic during the American Civil War, discovered that its ship's biscuit had been contaminated by vermin. Seamen were no longer prepared to tolerate weevils and maggots as normal hazards of life at sea; its captain therefore sought a prize that would rectify this deficiency. A long and exciting chase ended in the capture of a vessel, which yielded not only plentiful casks of ship's biscuit but also a liberal supply of export tins.[29]

Perhaps the most poignant reminder of the truly world-wide coverage of the firm's market is the fact that when a landing party of the Royal Navy went ashore at the remote islands of Juan Fernandez, in the Pacific off Chile—Robinson Crusoe's island—during the early 1900s, all it found there was a few goats and—an empty Reading biscuit tin.[30]

8
Life in the Factory 1846–98

'In the history of business, as in other kinds of history', it has been stated, 'biography is a powerful element.'[1] The history of Huntley and Palmers so far has been largely concerned with the business activities of certain key individuals, notably George Palmer and his brothers, and with the implications of these activities for the firm's development. In order to deepen our understanding of the Palmer brothers, it will be necessary to look more specifically at their characters and outside interests: this will be done in Chapter 9. As a preliminary, however, we need to explore an equally vital question: what were they like as employers? The present chapter will therefore seek to examine life from the employees' point of view.

Regrettably, the evidence is far from complete. Moreover, conditions changed very markedly as the factory expanded, and what was true at one period of time may well have been quite different at another. The rate of expansion can best be illustrated from the growth in the number of factory employees, as follows:

	Men and Boys	*Women*	*Total*		*Men and Boys*	*Women*	*Total*
1846	41	—	41	1867	910	10	920
1851	137	6	143	1873	2430	70	2500
1855	(340)	(10)	350	1878	(2900)	(75–100)	nearly 3000
1859	(460)	(10)	470	1889	3855	198	4053
1861	525	10	535	1898	4638	419	5057

Whereas until 1846 there was a single factory on roughly half-an-acre site, as well as the tiny London Street bakery, by 1898 there were no less than five separate manufacturing units: the South Factory, originally built in 1857; the North Factory, dating from 1872; H Factory, then in process of being built; the Cake and Rusk Factory; and the Sugar Wafer Factory. In addition to the manufacturing and packing operatives, there were tin washers and platers in the tin department, box carpenters and coopers in the carpenters' department, fitters, smiths and pattern makers in the engineering department, painters, plumbers, bricklayers and carpenters in the building department, as well as yardmen, engine drivers, shunters and oilmen for the railway sidings. Huntley and Palmers had in fact grown into a small town in its own right.

For the firm's employees, the transfer to King's Road in 1846 involved some costs as well as benefits. The main benefit was to move from very cramped, and partly underground, premises to a light and fairly spacious factory. At the same time, the hands must have found it difficult to become accustomed to what have been called the 'regularity, routine and monotony'[2] of factory conditions after the largely hand processes of the shop.

Perhaps for this reason, the original employees were mostly young men. An outsider who visited the factory in the late 1840s looked round and commented: 'Why, you have all boys except your foreman.' In fact, the foreman Richard Brown was still under forty, but appeared older because he had been grey since the age of thirty.[3] Of the 143 employed in 1851, 99 can be identified from that year's census; 42 of these were boys under eighteen, 30 men between eighteen and twenty-five, and only 27 over that age. But 11 in the last category were over forty, including the pastrycooks, storekeeper and a clerk in the counting house; the timekeeper and the engineer were in their early thirties, roughly the same age as George Palmer. In 1861, when 177—or a third—of the 535 employees are identifiable from the census, the proportion of those under eighteen had apprently declined to 35 per cent, while 27 per cent were between eighteen and twenty-five and 38 were over twenty-five; 14 per cent were over forty.

Thus the mainly youthful operatives had to be reinforced by some older and more experienced men. At Carr's of Carlisle in the same period, all except three of the bakers were under thirty; indeed, that firm was reluctant to employ older men, as they would have come chiefly from Scotland and often proved 'intractable' because of their drunken habits and refusal to comply with the factory rules.[4] No Scotsman was then employed by Huntley and Palmer. The ninety-nine identifiable employees of 1851, mentioned above, included one who was born in Lancashire and one in Nottinghamshire; the remainder, by some mysterious attractive force, had migrated from various southern counties which stretched from Devon and Wiltshire to Essex and Kent; forty-four were natives of Reading itself, nineteen came from elsewhere in Berkshire and twelve from Hampshire and Oxfordshire combined.

In 1861—bearing in mind the less satisfactory sample—a slightly higher proportion had been born in Reading itself, and there were one or two from as far away as Wales, Ireland and Australia. Yet almost 80 per cent had come from Berkshire, Oxfordshire and Hampshire combined; this process of 'short distance migration from the surrounding country' seems to fit in with the general pattern of labour movement throughout Britain at this time. People were apparently more concerned with finding jobs fairly near their birthplaces than with following their skills at a greater distance, and boys often had to support their unemployed or underemployed fathers; perhaps the young Charles and William Bullivant Williams were the breadwinners when the family coach business collapsed after the coming of the railways. Indeed, the railways themselves encouraged more migration over short distances rather than the same amount of migration much further afield.

By the standards of the twentieth century, the machines did not run very fast and therefore did not impose too great a strain on the workers, except for a few whose duties depended on keeping in step with the machines, such as the boy who put the trays at the end of the moving band, to receive the biscuits as they dropped. Most boys, however, had fairly mobile jobs, for instance carrying the loaded trays from the cutters to the ovens. To cater for their energies during break times, a yard was set aside as a playground; for a time in the early 1860s the firm appointed a schoolmaster, J. Clarke, at £40 a year, but his precise duties are unknown.

In the early days, a fairly informal atmosphere existed in the factory. For the payment of wages, employees were from 1847 onwards known by numbers as well as surnames, but their fellows used familiar names when one might have been confused with another. The foreman, one of five Browns, was invariably known as Richard, while the timekeeper, one of four Smiths, was called Betsey, perhaps because he came from Bexley. One of the two Henry Wellers was known as 'Nuts'.

As to clothing, each employee had to provide his own white apron, which was worn inside or outside the waistcoat, at choice: he could indulge in a wide variety of headgear, from the remote ancestors of trilby and bowler hats to versions, without tassels, of the peaked caps worn by all middle-class boys. By the turn of the century, hands were wearing a cloth cap or no hat at all. Some time later the foreman began to wear white overalls, but in the 1950s, for reasons of hygiene, peaked white hats and overalls were adopted by all factory employees.

What was arduous, above all, was the length of the working day. An employee who joined in 1850 recalled that he worked from 6.30 a.m. to 6.30 p.m. with forty minutes for breakfast and an hour for dinner, and finished on Saturdays at 2 p.m.[5] This 58½-hour week was the same as that adopted by Peek Frean on its establishment in 1857, and a little shorter than the 63½ hours worked at Carr's of Carlisle, which did not close on Saturdays until 5 p.m. In busy periods, notably the Pic-Nic crisis of 1849 when George Palmer reported that the factory was working 'night and day', there was much overtime, on occasions until 11 p.m.

Not until 1872 did Huntley and Palmers reduce its working week to 54 hours: the same as that for the girls, which unlike the men's hours were limited by the Factory Acts. The previous year George Palmer had responded coolly to an enquiry from Carr's about the possibility of shortening hours. There was no demand for it among the Reading workpeople, he asserted, and even if there had been, 56 hours would be preferable to 54, since a considerable loss of income would follow.

When shortly after that correspondence Peek Frean voluntarily introduced a 54-hour week, its employees clubbed together to present each partner with a silver-gilt inkstand. No doubt because of their cautious attitude, the Palmer brothers received no such presentation. The working week at Reading remained unaltered until 1918, when it was further reduced to 48 hours. When overtime was worked, half an hour's break was allowed for tea, from 6 to 6.30 p.m. More than single time was then paid, on a sliding scale, and double time after 11 p.m. Continuous night work earned 15 hours' time for a 12-hour shift.

Regular days off were given from the outset. In the 1860s they varied between 5½ and 7½ days a year: Good Friday, Whit Monday and three or four days at Christmas were allowed, as well as the occasion when the factory was shut for end-of-year stocktaking. Such events as the Reading races, Henley regatta and the Agricultural Show qualified for half-days off, sometimes at the employees' request.

The partners paid no wages for these lost days. That was the current practice at the time, and they would have argued—had anyone ventured to challenge them—that before Christmas at least, every employee could earn ample overtime payments. Not until 1873 did they pay wages for Christmas day; before then, their only tangible recognition of Christmas had been the customary gifts to sick hands and to other deserving cases, and they may have felt some moral pressure being exercised by the newly passed Bank Holidays Act. In later years employees were allowed to take extra days off either before or at the end of the holidays: unpaid, of course, and by arrangement with the foreman, so that if a week-end intervened, they might obtain a complete week's rest at Christmas time. By law they were also given a few hours off to vote at general elections.

As vital for employees as the length of the working day was the question of wage rates. Not until 1914—under the threat of a Trades Board—did Huntley and Palmers lay down a standard wage of 24s. a week for men and 12s. for women over eighteen. Since most of the work was unskilled and the firm was the largest single employer of labour in the town, the partners could in theory pay the lowest wages necessary to recruit and hold the required number of hands. They had no difficulty in general about recruitment: ever since the onset of the agricultural depression after the 1840s, the low wages and shrinking employment in the surrounding countryside had created an inexhaustible reservoir of labour.

According to the economic theorists of the day, the firm might have been expected to pay a uniform wage to all unskilled workers, closely related to subsistence levels. In fact, individual wage rates for many years reflected the firm's notion of each employee's usefulness, and the management reviewed them every half-year. Good employees, unskilled as well as skilled, had their wages raised at intervals. Richard Brown's son Charles, for instance, was earning 24s. a week in 1857, when he was twenty-five, but 75s. by 1868; he then joined the salaried staff, presumably when confirmed as Factory Manager. Richard Brown's own salary had increased slowly, from £2 a week in 1844 to £140 a year in 1859, but he was awarded occasional gratuities to mark his greatly increased responsibilities as foreman. Both he and the burly, white-bearded engineer William Ruddock had the rent of their houses paid by the firm. Like his close friend Thomas Huntley—who left him £20 in his will—Richard Brown was afflicted for some years with a very painful bladder disease, and his final salary of £250, which remained unaltered from mid-1863 until his death three years later, may have been a generous one in the circumstances.

Among the operatives, John Moss rose from 16s. a week in 1844 to 49s. in 1868 when he was over sixty. However, Thomas Drane, who joined as a pastry-cook in 1846 at 22s. a week, was reduced from 28s. to 24s. in 1862 and not restored to 26s. until 1869, at the age of sixty-eight. There was a regular practice in the factory whereby, when a deserving employee became 'past his job', he was offered light work at a reduced wage. Yet two much younger employees, paid 26s. in 1857, were reduced to 25s. in 1860 and did not revert to their former wages until 1865 and 1868 respectively: we have no idea how they had offended their superiors.

The whole system of calculating wage rates was changed in the 1870s, when the workforce trebled from 1000 to 3000 in a decade; this will be dealt with in Chapter 10, and a survey of nineteenth-century wages in the firm is given in Appendix I. However, it should be noted that the flexible wage system was arbitrary from the employee's point of view, since he could never be certain if his wages would be changed up or down, or left unaltered. Nor were the partners, normally willing as they were to see an employee at any time, amenable to negotiations over wages. Once, it is claimed, a deputation of two employees waited on George Palmer to suggest with some trepidation that they should be granted a wage rise: he routed them with a command to be off, before he kicked them downstairs.[6] As late as 1901, when the hands in the fruit department (which dealt with dried fruit, such as currants) made a similar request, the departmental manager, with the directors' sanction, told them firmly that it would not be granted.

Employees could look forward to non-contributory pensions, paid out of the firm's profits, when they had completed fifty years' service; although no one therefore became fully eligible until the 1890s, some allowances were made even after much shorter periods of employment. In addition, a few widows of senior managers were given pensions, such as the £52 a year granted to Richard Brown's widow in 1866; when she died, an unmarried daughter received £20 a year until her own death in 1895. Henry Lea's widow received £500 a year: seven pensioners, including another widow, were receiving gifts of Christmas cakes in 1891. In 1898–9 the firm was paying out £2750 a year in pensions; by 1913–14 the sum had risen to £6350, of which almost half was to former operatives and the rest to foremen and staff.

The amount of labour turnover was probably far smaller than in many other firms, for to change very often meant leaving the town since so little alternative work was available. In 1899 the equivalent of an eighth of the men and boys and a seventh of the girls voluntarily left the factory, not counting the 250 temporary workers, engaged to help with the Christmas rush, and then discharged again. However, many others settled down to a career in the firm; as early as 1881 outside people were surprised that perhaps one in twelve had served in the factory for more than twenty years; the corresponding figure in 1898 was roughly one in ten and in 1913 as high as one in three.[7]

Very early on the firm laid down its 'Rules and Regulations, for the purpose of preserving good order'. At that stage it punished no non-criminal offence, however grave, with dismissal; Quakers have never had much faith in the ultimate deterrent. Not until 1853 is anyone noted as having been discharged for such 'improper conduct' as fighting or stealing ingredients. Forty years later suspension or dismissal were the normal penalties for serious infringements of the rules.

Fines were levied at various rates. Using profane language, striking anyone on the premises and injuring any machine through 'wantonness and neglect' (on top of the cost of repairs) cost 1s. Absence without leave (plus loss of time), smoking in the factory and bringing in liquor cost 6d.; wasting time or being at work with hands and face unwashed —since this was a food factory—cost 2d. For men earning three to four shillings a day these fines were severe, but they were mitigated for boys with low wages. All fines were paid into the Sick Fund Box, of which more will be heard later.

There was much more to life in the factory than the routine and rules alone, for a number of amenities were also to be found. From 1846 to the early 1850s the partners provided at their own expense factory suppers, until increasing numbers made them no longer practicable. The one shortly after George Palmer's wedding may have been the last. There was then a gap until September 1857, when the Palmer brothers paid for a special train to the Crystal Palace, still a great novelty three years after it had been re-erected at Sydenham.[8] The outing was entirely free (including tea for 450), except that railway tickets had to be bought for 'men's friends', including wives.

Thereafter, the Palmers arranged some event or other virtually every alternate year during the next decade. They repeated the Crystal Palace outing in 1859, 1866 and 1868, the numbers invited rising from 830 to 1530. In 1862, to commemorate its award, a special visit was arranged in September 1862 to let employees see the firm's display at the London Exhibition. The partners stood the 1s. admission ticket as well as the special train at 2s. a head, and 1084 sat down to tea.[9] A single mishap was recorded on that occasion: one Cook, a young man in the packing department earning 16s. a week, was reimbursed out of the firm's Trade Charges the sum of 30s. for damage to his girl's dress at the exhibition.

Two years later, on the completion of the new offices and warehouses on the King's Road frontage, the Palmers invited employees and a guest apiece, totalling between 1200 and 1300, to a tea in the new warehouse. They provided lavish quantities of tea, bread and butter, and cake, after which some listened to a programme of songs and others took part in dancing, accompanied by the Temperance Band. At 10 p.m. the company feasted on 600 quarts of strawberries and 600 lb. of cherries, after which the entertainment closed at 10.45 p.m.[10] Two points about such meals call for comment. First, the generous provision of two ounces of sugar a head—say, eight teaspoonfuls—illustrates the craving for sugar at that time, when average weekly consumption was no more than half a pound a head. Second, fruit—and frequently oranges—formed a regular item on the menu from factory supper days onwards.

The partners helped in other ways also to cater for welfare needs. They set aside a Breakfast Room for employees to take their meals in.

This was initially a cottage by the river, where behaviour 'in such a way as to be a just cause of complaint by another' was punishable by a 6d. fine. When the factory was enlarged in 1872, a new Breakfast Room was built, at a cost of £360. Most employees in fact went home during the breakfast and dinner breaks: during the 1860s Newtown sprang up as a dormitory area, to the east of the factory as far as the mouth of the Kennet. At break times all employees had to be out of the factory, or else be subject to a 6d. fine. Women workers were by the 1870s being provided with an afternoon cup of tea daily, on the principle that they worked more efficiently on it.[11]

However, the most important amenity was the Sick Fund, set up in 1849, with George Palmer as its president, Thomas Huntley as treasurer and Henry Lea as secretary. Later on William Isaac Palmer took over as president; being the factory manager and exceptionally open-handed besides, he found it helpful to know the state of the fund's finances and the names of those who were sick. Initially all adult employees contributed 6d. a week and received a not ungenerous sickness pay of 12s. a week; boys' contributions were 1d. and benefits 2s. a week. Later on a sliding scale of both contributions and benefits was substituted. Although a compulsory scheme, anyone belonging to another benefit society could contract out of it altogether.

George Palmer was too much of a realist to believe that all employees put aside money for rainy days, although for the thrifty ones he did establish a Penny Bank in 1868, which continued until 1903 and was affiliated to the Reading Savings Bank. Instead, he recognised that in practice when they fell ill, many had either to fall back on public assistance or to beg from their fellow-workpeople—including himself. Moreover, when they left the firm, they lost all claim to benefit. He therefore actively supported such organisations as the Christian Mutual Provident Society for every workman, as 'standing him in need wherever he might be employed'.[12]

A committee of six employees administered the firm's Sick Fund, and took great pains to make sure that it was not wasted. Employees had to be medically examined before becoming members. The factory doctor provided services, at an honorarium of £25 a year, that were almost medieval in their scope—cupping, bleeding, tooth-drawing and applying leeches; but a sick member had to pay 1s. for each initial visit. Nor was anyone receiving benefit allowed to travel more than two miles from home. To see that he was complying with the rules, the employee living nearest to him had to call on him once a week.

Although the fund was supposed to be self-supporting, the partners provided £5 to launch it, and in various ways mitigated the stringency of some of the provisions. Anyone unable to afford the 1s. doctor's charge could go to the counting house and ask for a voucher. On one occasion, in 1852, the partners so violently disapproved of the committee's decision to reduce three employees' benefit (to a quarter of the usual rate) that they made a further donation of £10 to the fund. Two years later they gave £20 which helped to keep the fund solvent (as reported to the Annual General Meeting in 1855), thanks also to the 'large amount of good health' enjoyed by members 'whilst disease and pestilence has been raging round us'.

In 1857 Thomas Huntley bequeathed £50 to the fund, and the firm subsequently made regular donations, of about £50 a year; these enabled the fund to give members annual rebates, averaging a third of total contributions in the 1870s. Some slight difficulty arose when the Truck Act of 1892 forbade employers to deduct sick fund payments from wages. The Palmers overcame this problem by paying wages in two separate envelopes; the one containing the contributions had to be given back immediately. Otherwise the scheme worked uneventfully until it was superseded by the official National Health Insurance scheme in 1912–13.

In 1854 the Sick Fund was augmented by what was known (at least outside the factory) as the Mutual Improvement Society. That winter, some employees asked if a reading room and a library could be provided.[13] George Palmer, having a lively enthusiasm for what he had earlier called 'feeding the mind', immediately set one up and stocked it with books and periodicals. The latter included *The Times*, *Sunday at Home* and *Good Words*; the partners also defrayed half the cost of *Chambers' Journal*, *All the Year Round*, *Once a Week* and *London Society*. Much later, *Punch* was taken as well. All employees over sixteen were allowed to use it, on payment of 1d. a week.

The Mutual Improvement Society seems to have catered for a variety of interests. At the more serious end, the Library was made a separate unit with the aid of a £50 legacy from Thomas Huntley in 1857. It bought some books locally (from Golders, the Reading booksellers), and had others supplied from Mudies, the circulating library. The partners let it be known that they did not at all object to replacing damaged books as long as they were actually read; they also undertook to meet the annual deficit out of the firm's profits. Weekly lectures were organised during the winter months.

A less intellectual side centred round the piano, probably donated by William Isaac Palmer. Members helped at intervals to arrange musical soirées, which always attracted large audiences. In addition, Saturday-evening entertainments were held regularly from 1855 onwards; their object was avowedly to keep workpeople and their families out of the public houses. In February 1855 a tea party was held, for which 208 were tickets sold at 6d. a head. The partners donated 4 lb. of tea and sold 128 lb. of currant cake at wholesale prices. The remaining foodstuffs required were 60 lb. of bread, 6 gallons of milk and 25 lb. of sugar.

However, the most spectacular events of the year were the excursions. These were quite separate from the ones organised from time to time by the partners; although paid for by the Reading Room, they were probably subsidised by the firm and by William Isaac Palmer. The first 'annual aquatic excursion' was held in July 1855, when about 200 employees, wives, children and 'female friends' travelled by river to Park Place, near Henley. This was repeated a year later; in the summers of 1857 and 1858 similar trips were made to Coombe Lodge, between Pangbourne and Basildon. The arrangements did not vary much: three 'pleasure boats' *Queen of the Thames, Prince of Wales* and *Princess Royal* (in the victory year 1856, dressed overall with the flags of the Crimean allies) were hired; Captain Codd and his band of the Royal Berkshire Militia, together with a Quadrille band, were in attendance; archery contests and cricket matches took place in the grounds, and the livelier ones—since the average age of employees was still low—diverted themselves with boisterous games of the 'He' variety and practically non-stop dancing.

At tea-time George Palmer, with some of his friends, appeared among them, and on the return trip the indefatigable bands, primed only with non-alcoholic beverages, accompanied choruses and solo performances. The noise carried far in the darkness over the still pastures on either bank, and at each riverside village groups of well-wishers turned out to wave their greetings. Then at their destination in Reading, the company gave three cheers and sang the National Anthem before dispersing.[14]

The Reading Room organised a trip to Wokingham Cricket Ground by special train in 1863. There were the makings of a very enjoyable day: tents, benches, tables and food, cricket to watch and a band for dancing, and the partners and their families looking on benevolently. However, a very heavy rainstorm brought the outing to a premature end; everyone was relieved when the stationmaster ordered up the special train ahead of time.[15] In 1864 and 1865—the latter year at Bulmershe—a tea and sports replaced the excursion, no doubt on the Palmers' suggestion.

From 1866 to 1871 the Reading Room held regular excursions by rail, to Hampton Court, Brighton (twice), Portsmouth, Southampton and Hastings. Only those who subscribed 1d. a week were given the opportunity to go; all their expenses were then met apart from meals, although dependants usually had to buy their own tickets. In addition, a winter entertainment—with the inevitable band—was put on, usually in the Town Hall, about the only building in Reading large enough to accommodate all those who came. However, the numbers going on the Reading Room trips were relatively small: normally around the 300 mark, only rising to 450 by 1871. The following year, therefore, the firm sensibly proposed to employees that it should henceforth provide one day's paid holiday, normally late in June when the days were longest, and that a proper Excursion Fund should be set up, to which interested employees could subscribe regularly. The cost to the firm of the subsidised trips had risen from £76 in 1857 to £325 in 1868, and once numbers had trebled to over 3000, further such trips were out of the question.

This proposal was accepted, for it left non-participants free to go elsewhere or stay at home if they preferred. Membership of the Reading Room predictably declined to between 30 and 40 in the mid-1870s, and recovered only to 80 by the end of the decade. Employees duly organised the Excursion Fund, to which everyone over sixteen could contribute 1d. a week or more according to the size of his family. The destination was to be decided by ballot each year. Not unexpectedly, the majority view favoured the seaside resorts that could conveniently be reached on the two railway networks nowadays forming part of the Southern Region. In 1873 499½ tickets were required for the trip to Portsmouth, but by the twentieth century the numbers had risen to 7000, which required up to ten special trains and the excursion being split between two or more resorts. The excursions were held annually until the 1914–18 War; they were never resumed afterwards, as statutory holidays were introduced in 1919.

Seaside towns seem to have regarded with equanimity the descent of the firm's excursion parties, even when each numbered several thousands;[16] by contrast, Peek Frean's outings had had to be discontinued altogether after 1875 because of rowdyism. The only untoward incident recorded at Reading occurred in June 1898, and moved the Excursion Committee to commission large posters, proclaiming in blood-red letters an inch high that 'A GLASS BOTTLE WAS THROWN FROM ONE OF THE CARRIAGES, during the JOURNEY TO RAMSGATE, nearly hitting a plate layer', and urging members to refrain in future from jettisoning any articles through the carriage windows.

Occasionally in later years, employees benefited when joyful events, or the opposite, involved the management. When George Palmer was married, it will be remembered, no time off was given, although a supper was held a little later. Thomas Huntley was providently buried on a Sunday, so that the factory did not have to be closed on full wages. However, in 1872, when his eldest son George William came of age, George Palmer paid an extra day's wages and gave a tea party for employees and guests in the grounds of his house, the Acacias. Nine years later, Samuel Palmer celebrated the marriage of his eldest son Ernest, by entertaining 260 employees to a dinner in one of the girls' packing rooms at Reading. The guests comprised the heads of department, and also all others employed for at least twenty-three years, namely ever since Ernest Palmer's birth. The factory closed that day at twelve noon, so that those not invited at least received a paid half-holiday. The press commented on the fact that some of the guests had been with the firm ever since, or even before, the factory was opened in 1846: clearly an unusual length of service for those days.[17]

Employees were given the day off for the funeral of each Palmer brother and also on Jubilee Day 1897, as well as half-days when certain departmental heads, such as J. R. Moore, died in harness. Again, when the firm won two prizes at the Paris Exhibition of 1900, it gave a bonus of an additional day's wages. The value of production lost, running to £700–£800 for a full day, was entered not as a charge on the Manufacturing Account, but an overhead included in the Profit and Loss Account.

During the 1870s and 1880s the leisure activities of the British people began to change markedly, with the growth of organised sports of all kinds. The earliest recorded cricket match had been held during the 1855 excursion, when a team of married men played, and defeated, one consisting of single men.[18] In the following decade the Factory Cricket Club undertook regular outside fixtures each summer, and the firm made donations to help it.

Yet the Cricket Club's great days did not really begin until the 1880s, when Samuel Palmer's son Howard joined the firm. Although he never played for the county, he was a keen and experienced player, and when the Club was re-founded, proposed William Isaac Palmer as its first president, thus securing a generous source of funds. Howard Palmer was able to play only infrequently in the Factory Club's matches: four times in 1892 and nine in 1893, for instance. His batting averages were eighteen and thirty-four respectively, or double those of his younger brother Albert, who played more regularly as his factory duties were less onerous.

Howard Palmer used to hold a cricket week at his estate near Wokingham, where he collected a strong eleven composed of the principal players of the county.[19] He also became president of Reading Athletic Club a few years later. The firm had already given twelve acres of King's Meadow for a cricket ground after the old Reading Racecourse had closed down, and had also agreed to undertake its maintenance; athletic sports were held annually there from 1892 onwards. That same year the firm gave a challenge bowl to the Reading Working Men's Regatta for four-oar races between crews representing the factory's different departments.

In 1898, immediately after the limited company was set up, the directors canvassed the idea of forming a Recreation Club, and the many signatures of potential members demonstrated the widespread support for it. Directors stressed that the new club should cater for other sports besides cricket; the first annual report showed that 2430 employees were members, or just under a third of the total workforce, and that the company had provided all the equipment for four cricket elevens, a football team, hockey, quoits, bowls, tennis and athletics, as well as a horticultural show. Even the firm of Cadbury Bros., which had opened its model factory at Bournville in 1879, did not have a properly constituted recreation club until 1896;[20] thus Huntley and Palmers' must have been one of the earliest clubs of its kind in Britain. In January 1899 the directors gave a smoking concert in the large Town Hall to celebrate its inauguration. Later on the club catered for other recreations, including choral and dramatic entertainments; the firm's share of the total cost was £225 in 1898-9 and over £400 by 1913-14. The Reading Temperance Band, composed almost entirely of factory employees, was greatly in demand for all these fixtures.

We do not know the extent of the partners' private generosity to individual employees, but personal items of this kind appear in the 'Trade Charges' account from an early date; in 1876-7 they totalled £150. After 1869 'Donations and Subscriptions' were entered in a separate account, and include contributions to every conceivable good cause, from colliery disaster funds to ragged schools, from the Pure Literature Society to Eisteddfods. Averaging £300 to £500 in the following decade, they may have helped the firm's reputation in the localities concerned; but rarely if ever benefited the hands directly.

In an era when working people insisted on costly funerals as 'a traditional tribute to the dead and a communal reaffirmation of the living',[21] the firm provided one to every employee dying in its service. That same year of 1876-7 Ruddock the engineer's burial cost the firm £17 and Drane the pastrycook's just under £7. The faithful Richard Brown had ten years previously been given a grand funeral costing £38, which perhaps included the headstone in the Municipal Cemetery.

Although some needy employees thus received small sums from Trade Charges (which were also debited with loans to employees that were never repaid), the principal source of them was the Sick Fund Box. The box's income (£1 to £2 a week) arose from donations, fines and unclaimed wages. An operative whose wife had just died in childbirth, a destitute widow or an employee with a small child to bury, for instance, could count on a small sum from the box, in the region of 10s. or £1, and very rarely as much as £2.

A more obvious item affecting employees in Trade Charges was compensation following industrial accidents. In the 1880s the accidents reported to the Factory Inspector (usually to do with lifts or machines) averaged between one and three a year, and involved lengthy correspondence as to the exact circumstances. Earlier, in 1867, the firm had given a workman an artificial arm at a cost of fifteen guineas; he may have suffered an accident in the manufacturing department (where he had previously worked) as he was found a job in packing.

Apart from Sick Fund payments, these benefits were entirely at the partners' discretion and were in no sense granted of right to the employee. Nevertheless, the element of paternalism is very frequently a keynote of the Victorian family firm. The partners felt keenly the need to maintain the firm's good name in the town. Males and females had to enter and leave the factory by different routes and at different times; they were all instructed by printed notice to follow the rule 'of always GOING TO THE RIGHT'. When a heavy fall of snow occurred one December, a notice about 'SNOW BALLING in the Streets' proclaimed: 'It will be a kind and MANLY act for everyone to discountenance it, and help to make it known in the Office when any serious offence occurs.'

After a teen-age brush with the police one Saturday evening in 1886, the management warned the factory lads (again by notice) that 'although mischief may be done by boys not working here, a large number of our boys being present, the Factory get the credit of it'. About the same time, an allegation was made that theatres were out of bounds to the firm's employees. A society journal reported, on the authority of 'Lady T.' that any transgression of this rule involved instant dismissal.[22] This report is almost certainly untrue, but helped to nourish the general supposition that a killjoy atmosphere existed in Quaker firms.

Clerks in the offices seem to have been as prone to high jinks as their fellows elsewhere at that time. Since the firm sought to build up a managerial structure that afforded reasonable pay and prospects, it attracted many men of good background. For instance, in 1859 a son of the governor of Reading Gaol joined as a clerk in the Invoice Office. Being more than usually exuberant, he must have found the work there somewhat oppressive, since it involved examining orders on arrival, passing them on to the warehouse to be executed, and on their return pricing them and entering them in a day book, from which the Ledger Office posted each customer's account. At any rate, he had to be given notice by William Isaac Palmer, who was astonished to see him still at his desk after the notice expired. When asked for an explanation, he replied that he did not find it convenient to leave. He remained for sixty years in all, and his familiar remark became part of the office lore: over the years it was transmuted into the words of Dean Ramsay's celebrated Scottish retainer, who had retorted (in translation) when his laird tried to dismiss him: 'If you don't know when you've got a good servant, *I* know when I've got a good place.'

Other offices spent much time in 'calling over' entries from one ledger to another, as the firm prided itself on its accuracy, which customers very rarely ventured to challenge. The Sales Office had to complete its work after the other departments had gone home, and the hours therefore tended to be very long; this did not deter the more energetic clerks from getting up early and doing some gardening or swimming in the river before they started work. Their pranks ranged from having elaborate warning systems for allowing them to congregate round the coal fire during chilly days, and yet be back at their desks when higher authority appeared, to indulging in weightlifting exercises with the very heavy ledgers.[23]

Yet if opportunities for diversion during working hours existed in the offices, few were available in the factory itself, which was dictated by the incessant activity of ever more powerful machinery. One whose working life spanned the years 1850 to 1913 put it as follows:

> My occupation? I was in the manufacturing department. Had to drive the horizontal machine, which cuts the dough to the required size before it drops into tins and runs along to the ovens to be baked. That was my daily task for well nigh fifty years.
>
> Monotonous? Rather.[24]

9
The First Generation: George, Samuel and William Isaac Palmer

Regrettably enough, the subject-matter of the present chapter has in many people's eyes been pre-empted by the view, expressed in connection with another celebrated British firm: 'We have read so often before of Victorian middle-class entrepreneurs, whose success was built on the exploitation of new technology and the underprivileged work force, who found their justification in a cloud of moral humbug, and who aspired to the status of landed gentry.'[1] At a very superficial level such remarks could perhaps be applied to the Palmers of the founding generation. However, there was far more to them than that, and they seem to have kept singularly free of the less attractive Victorian charactcristics, as the following account of them will show.

The quality that bound the three brothers most closely together was undoubtedly their very strong sense of duty, which George Palmer at least had shown from his schooldays onwards. Like their superior intelligence and habits of hard work, they inherited this trait from their strong-minded mother Mary Palmer, who lived until 1880. Yet they were not all stamped in exactly the same mould: two of them, George and William Isaac Palmer, had the sombre tinge of their mother's character, while Samuel, as their dead sister had, possessed much of his father's geniality which lightened an almost compulsive dedication to his work. The brothers will now be considered in turn.

George Palmer was the first to make his mark outside the factory. Until the late 1840s he was absorbed in planning and moving into the King's Road factory and in gradually evolving the mechanical operations there. His only outside interest at that time was to sit on the committee of the Mechanics' Institution, which took up little time or energy. However, once the pressure of organisation in the factory eased, while still being intermittently busy with improvements in technology, he felt able to turn his abundant energies towards his main outside interest, namely service to the community. Unlike many, he never seems to have suffered discomfort from the enervating climate of the Thames Valley.

As might be expected, his first public office was to do with education, as secretary of the Boys' School on the British System. The school, in Southampton Street, had been founded in 1810 on the pattern laid down by the great Quaker educationalist Joseph Lancaster, to teach boys of all classes and religious sects. George Palmer's office, to which he later added the duties of Treasurer, was no sinecure, for the school was then at a very low ebb. He immediately recruited a strong committee of management and went on to build up both the numbers and the efficiency of the school.[2]

He followed up this work with a long letter to the *Reading Mercury* in 1847, which pointed out that in the town there existed plenty of schools side by side with a great number of children roaming the streets who were untaught and little cared for. A 'hungry barrier' in these children frustrated all 'efforts to feed the mind'. He therefore suggested that a 'ragged school' should be set up for the very poor, similar to those already established in Aberdeen. The children could be provided with one or two good but plain meals of oatmeal porridge and soup each day, as well as facilities for bathing themselves. This letter was directly responsible for the town's first ragged school being founded about a year later.[3]

Shortly afterwards, he became actively involved in politics. One of the interesting aspects of Victorian political life was the tendency, revealed in the poll books, of butchers to vote Tory and grocers to vote Liberal.[4] Certainly Quakers, many of whom became grocers but few butchers, tended to espouse Liberalism, with its strong nonconformist and temperance element, in opposition to the 'loyalty' of the Conservatives. One of the members for Reading, both Liberals, was Serjeant Talfourd, to whom his great friend Charles Dickens dedicated *Pickwick*, and who all but induced Dickens to stand for Reading in 1841. When Talfourd resigned in 1849 and Liberal headquarters in London put up a candidate with no regard to local feelings, certain party members in Reading violently objected and formed a breakaway Radical party.

At a Radical protest meeting, George Palmer sat on the platform and delivered a strong speech which was—unlike those of some of his fellow speakers—also full of good sense. Together with Thomas and Joseph Huntley, he voted for the Radical candidate whom the dissidents had nominated in opposition to the official one. The split only led to the return of the Conservative candidate, but it helped to make George Palmer well known in the town. Next year he was elected to Reading council.

There he became a conscientious and effective councillor, during a decade of unprecedented change for the town. Until lately, the built-up part of Reading had been confined to a limited space, less than one seventh of the borough's total area. Except for some of the main thoroughfares, such as London Street itself, the roads were extremely narrow, off which ran courts where the poor were herded together in deplorable conditions. The overcrowded courts were not the only hazard to health. Even London Street as late as 1846 was often disagreeably filthy. The romanticised toffee-box portrayal, freely drawn upon in certain twentieth-century advertisements, of the Huntley and Palmer shop as an elegant bow-window establishment, with Regency ladies trailing their long skirts over spotless paving stones, does not stand up to the facts. George Palmer's indignation boiled over that September in a letter to the *Reading Mercury*.

Down nearly the whole street, he protested, ran a 'black open gutter', fed by little gutters which traversed the asphalt pavement. In this respect the street was 'only a fair specimen of the whole town'. The gutter was not merely offensive, notably in the summer time, but also injurious to people's health. Moreover, if he set the water running so as to wash away some of the filth in front of his shop, the officials of the Reading Water Company, who took 'so much care of their property', frequently complained to him about the waste of water. Sometimes they even invaded the yard, the former Cocks's (now renamed Huntley's) Court, in order to turn off his water-tap.[5]

Rightly, he and his partner had a scrupulous regard for cleanliness, in spite of very great difficulties as long as they remained in London Street. But he knew well that without radical measures to safeguard health, further increases in the town's rapidly rising population would only lead to disastrous epidemics. In the same letter he referred with approval to the General Drainage Bill which Reading Corporation had presented to Parliament. For various trivial reasons it was never passed into law; a consequence was that between 1841 and 1849 the death rate in the town nearly doubled, as successive epidemics of cholera and typhus swept the town.

Then in 1848 Parliament passed a general Public Health Act, which at last gave local authorities the powers to sweep away the 'black open gutters'. George Palmer joined the council just as a new Board of Health had been set up in Reading, and he was rapidly co-opted to that board. It planned a comprehensive main drainage system for the whole town without delay; it also arranged for the council to buy up, with the owners' full co-operation, the Reading Water Works, which were enlarged so as to safeguard future supplies of fresh water. The council also undertook a massive clearance scheme of many of the ancient courts and closely packed slum tenements.

As a persistent advocate of public recreation grounds, he vigorously supported the council's purchase of the Abbey ruins, when their surviving rubble walls were in danger of final destruction. He took an active part in having the adjacent Forbury Gardens enclosed and 12 acres of King's Meadow, to the west of Caversham Bridge on the banks of the Thames, bought as additional recreation space. In 1876 he himself presented to the people of Reading 14 acres of adjoining land on King's Meadow.

Several times after 1850 he was pressed to accept the office of Mayor. This remained out of the question while the ailing Thomas Huntley was his only partner. However, once he had solved the problem of the firm's direction by accepting his two brothers as full partners after Thomas Huntley's death—with the right to please himself as to the amount of time he should henceforth devote to the business—he allowed his name to go forward as mayor, for the year beginning November 1857. His term of office literally started with a bang. The day after his election, some over-enthusiastic supporters incautiously fired off the ceremonial gun that stood on the mound in the Forbury; being primed with stones and nails, the charge blew out most of the windows in the vicinity and scorched the cornfields in rural Caversham on the opposite bank of the river.[6] Apart from this loud report, the year seems to have passed, like most mayoralties, without any unduly memorable incident.

He was able to avoid certain irksome civic duties on the grounds of health, for he did not regard himself as fully recovered from the effects of his breakdown in the previous spring. However, he did present an address of congratulation to the Queen and Prince Consort in London on the occasion of the Princess Royal's marriage. Later that year his wife accompanied him to Birmingham in order to see the Queen open a public park there. These particularly meaningless acts of civic duty gave him no urge to alter his way of life or seek more elevated social contacts.

When in 1865, after several moves, he found a permanent home, it proved to be a fairly modest villa of Bath stone, the Acacias in London Road. Until he later bought the freehold, it was on lease from the corporation for ninety-nine years at a ground rent of £20 and (as the agreement put it) 'one couple of good fat and well-fed pullets on Xmas day annually'. It had been built in 1818 by a local coal and salt merchant; the original owner's trade and its rectangular shape caused it to be nicknamed Salt Box Hall.[7] A remote consequence of his choice of house was that in the twentieth century, through the generosity of his sons, it was to form the nucleus of the University College, and later still the University, of Reading.

His critics were moved to derision over the fact that this wealthy man, who in the 'new Domesday Book' for 1873 was recorded as owning just under 2000 acres of land in Berkshire, Hampshire, Oxford and Surrey with a gross estimated rental of £2360 a year[8], should live in this middle-class way rather than in a manner befitting a captain of industry. Yet the house was comfortable, spacious enough for his seven living children, and centrally situated. He used to walk to the factory every day along Watlington Street; sometimes he would encounter Martin Hope Sutton, an almost exact contemporary whose transformation of the Reading seed business to one of a national and world-wide fame closely paralleled his own achievement. In the way of commercial men, their talk often consisted of banter about the rival merits of their respective products: but Sutton invariably had the last word. 'There'll never be a time when people won't require seeds', was his parting shot as they went their separate ways at King's Road.

George Palmer performed his most lasting service to education in Reading just after W. E. Forster—himself a Quaker until he was disowned for marrying outside—had piloted through the Education Act of 1870. He threw himself with his customary vigour into this work, by proposing formally to Reading Council that the Act, which like the Public Health measure was an enabling act, should be put into operation there. A local School Board was set up and he was elected as vice-chairman. However, he served for only three years, as he had so many outside calls on his time, and he always disapproved of taking on commitments which he could not really honour. He had already given £500, and his brothers £300 between them, to the building fund of Reading School, newly refounded after years of neglect and about to be transferred from the centre of the town to its present site.

In the 1870s he did partly emerge from the middle-class background which his critics felt to be somewhat incongruous. He became a more important landowner in Berkshire, and he entered Parliament. His first really large-scale acquisition of land in the county was of two adjoining estates at Bothampstead and Eling, near Hermitage, in 1877 for just under £60,000. These measured about 1650 acres, over four times what he already owned in the county. He farmed Eling for himself through a manager; both there and at his Surrey estate of West Park, near East Grinstead, he tried out various experiments which involved leasing allotments and smallholdings to deserving tenants. That was a bad time to institute such a venture, as it coincided with a cycle of bad seasons, culminating in those of 1879 and 1880 which ruined so many farmers and landowners. He had to learn the hard way that the successful cultivation of a smallholding was not so different from the successful running of a business, in that it requires both expertise and constant attention, and cannot be undertaken by men with full-time outside work. Unlike his son George William, he was not always as cautious as he should have been in matters outside his professional competence.

Ten years later he added another 1170 acres to his estates by acquiring Marlston for £22,260. Although he made Marlston House his country retreat it was then quite as modest a residence as the Acacias, but when in 1896 he transferred it to George William Palmer, his son had it rebuilt as a mansion in the Elizabethan style.

He was elected to Parliament in 1878. Reading then returned two members to Westminster, and following the sudden death of one member, he was asked to stand as a Liberal. He had strong reservations about taking up a 'new life' at the age of sixty, but with the shift of political power from the old landed proprietors to business men, it was increasingly common for great entrepreneurs to become M.P.s. Nor was religion any longer a barrier, for the first Quaker, Joseph Pease, had been elected in 1832, only three years after the Test Act had substituted affirmation for swearing oaths of allegiance. Indeed, what influenced George Palmer above all was a personal appeal from John Bright, the former cabinet minister who was now the *doyen* of Quakers in Parliament.

The two of them had earlier jointly opposed practically all their fellow-representatives at the Quakers' Yearly Meeting of 1875, over a delicate and highly charged social question. For some years Friends had been campaigning for the repeal of the Contagious Diseases Acts, which licensed prostitutes in dockyard and garrison towns. So stubborn was the pair's resistance to this campaign that the clerk of the meeting had to minute that in the absence of unanimity, no further action should be taken. They certainly had no urge to hinder the cause of women's rights, for which Josephine Butler and other reformers were working. Since they received no hearing in the Quaker journals, we can only guess at their motives. No doubt they recognised more clearly than most that the root of the problem was the inadequate recreational and domestic amenities then provided for the common soldier and sailor.[9]

Bright now wrote pungently from Rochdale to 'Dear Friend George Palmer' as follows. 'Don't allow the seat of Reading to be in danger—at this moment it is of first importance that no seat should be allowed to go over to the Government. Make some sacrifices for this if necessary.' Possibly the sacrifice proved greater than the new member expected. He was already well known for his reticence at Meeting, although when he did speak, it was with good sense and great conviction. In the seven years he spent in the House of Commons, he made only very few contributions to debate.

Interestingly enough, his maiden speech was in support of another emotive topic, a private member's bill to grant women the vote. 'What is the best thing to be done in the interests of the country?' he asked, and in answer cited the case of a widow left to rear a large family. The occupier of a considerable portion of an agricultural parish, she acted as its overseer and was probably its most intelligent parishioner. Yet she was disqualified from voting simply because she happened to be a woman.[10] This widow was no oratorical fiction, but his mother during her last years at Elberton. Seven years later he changed his opinion regarding women's suffrage, for reasons which his wife confided to her sister, but which were apparently too personal to be handed down to posterity. At any rate, he did not neglect his daughters' education. One of them took the first part of the M.B. examination at Bedford College, London, and another mixed well enough in intellectual circles to marry an Oxford don; both their husbands became Fellows of the Royal Society.

His slender contributions to debate earned him the title of 'silent member'; it is likely that parliamentary life never really appealed to him. However, political leaders and fellow back-benchers thought well enough of his judgement to seek his advice on all commercial matters. Surprisingly enough, in an age when there were very few representatives of the working man, apart from the trade union M.P.s Henry Broadhurst and Thomas Burt, he was recognised as a 'labour representative', although his interests did not exactly coincide with those of the worker. In 1885 he stood down when the number of Reading seats was reduced to one; he was defeated when he contested the freshly created Newbury division of Berkshire, and did not seek election again.

So far, his life appears to have differed very little from those of provincial worthies up and down the country, who crowned their careers with a seat in Parliament and a landed estate close (but not too close) to the locality where they had made their fortunes. What separated him from the majority of these was a rugged refusal to seek personal or social advancement. He took a town house in Grosvenor Street, not because it was a very fashionable area—as indeed it was—but because it was equidistant between Paddington station and the House of Commons. The hostile critics, mentioned above, could not understand why, with such wealth and such a good London address, he should have held himself aloof from Society and from the artistic and literary worlds; they concluded that he must be the type of Quaker who 'form a clique of their own, despising and being despised'.[11]

In fact, he was not much given to despising anyone, and tried to be as honest as he could both with himself and with others. He told an audience of commercial travellers without hypocrisy: 'I have not escaped either the effects of temptation, or the unpleasantness of meeting men who could tempt me to sin.' As a Quaker and a member of the Peace Society, he deplored Disraeli's warlike posturings, yet he admitted that there may be times when war becomes inevitable. In later life he even modified his strict teetotal principles, and could attend the weddings of his younger children in the most fashionable London churches without scruples.

He had occasional lapses, for instance over his ambiguous attitude to music. In the Quaker *Book of Discipline*, music was condemned as a 'vain or frivolous pursuit', calculated to gratify the senses and distract listeners from 'the sober realities of life and the duties of religion'. As he had no ear for it, in 1857 he told the accomplished musician and former resident of Reading, Mr. Venua, who had sought his patronage, that he could do nothing personally without compromising his religious principles, but he would willingly grant the *Mayor's* patronage. William Isaac Palmer, on the other hand, knew from a lifetime's experience of temperance work that bright and tuneful music was a far better means than strong drink of helping the poor to escape from their hard and monotonous existences. He therefore openly encouraged the dancing and community singing that were important features of the firm's outings as well as the concerts at other times of the year. Himself liking music, he often paid for musically gifted young people to receive an Academy training. Again in contrast to his elder brother, he collected paintings: mainly innocuous but pleasing local views, which as one of its earliest benefactors he later bequeathed to the Reading Art Gallery.

George Palmer was as good as most public men in delivering congratulatory speeches that meant very little; yet he would suddenly bring up the listener short with some extremely provocative remark. In 1883, for instance, he attended the consecration of St. Luke's Church, Reading—to which he subscribed handsomely—and made soothing remarks about a fashionable sermon by Archdeacon Farrar at St. Margaret's, Westminster, the previous Sunday, which had convinced him, occupying a 'privileged seat' as a special guest, of the 'true spiritual unity' of the different denominations. He then launched into an unexpected attack on the Church for not leading thought as much as it should, for instance, in the fields of temperance, education and the emancipation of the slaves; he proceeded to rub it well in by declaring that 'he had sometimes heard prayers offered which seemed to ignore the fact that the God whom we worshipped in England was the God of the people of other countries'. The Bishop of Oxford mildly expostulated that these strictures were unfounded in the case of education, but was not deterred from making a few months later the celebrated 'Reading biscuit' speech, quoted in Chapter 10.[12]

Indeed, the bishop knew George Palmer well, and himself did not hesitate to make disquieting remarks when he felt that they were needed. Four years previously, when the foundation stone of Reading Town Hall was laid in 1879, he called the rapid increase in the town's population a 'source of anxiety', because spiritual and recreational opportunities were falling well behind that increase.[13] Perhaps George Palmer privately commended that remark after the ceremony, for the very next day the bishop wrote to him, asking for help in establishing a church in the west of Reading. This help was immediately forthcoming—in the shape of half an acre of land—but the bishop's other statement at the same time, that he had looked in vain for a recreation ground in the east end of the town, did not bear fruit until some years later; in 1891.

George Palmer's appearance in later life resembled less that of an entrepreneur than of a retired sea-captain, with his shaggy white beard, florid complexion and light grey-blue eyes with a faraway look. He had been born in Regency times, and seemed to carry into the middle and late Victorian scene some of the full-blooded vigour of the Regency. His contemporary William Morris, the artist and manufacturer, prided himself on being mistaken for a ship's captain by tars ashore, and was capable of hurling down on to the head of his unfortunate domestic below stairs a plum pudding that he claimed to be too small, with the scornful words 'D'ye call that a pudding?'[14] No doubt the diplomatic but firm-minded Elizabeth Palmer forestalled any outbursts by her husband at the Acacias, but in the factory his authority was as supreme as that of any captain afloat. As he had shown by his routing of the two employees who sought a wage rise, collective action by workers was as unthinkable as mutiny.

His quarterdeck manner, whether directed at Thomas Huntley, Henry Lea or William Blandy, was apt to give deep offence at the time, but never seems to have inflicted a lasting breach. With disarming innocence, he neither bore a grudge against others nor expected others to bear any grudge against himself. He had, and could afford to maintain, the rough unpolished exterior of one who never needed to ingratiate himself with more complex if thinner-skinned people. He was in fact a shy man who was very fond of children and others who are underprivileged in any way.

The first Lord Shaftesbury once said that since every man of capacity holds within himself two men, the wise and the foolish, each of them ought freely to be allowed his turn. George Palmer had this streak of irresponsibility in him. As a man who had made a fortune, he just could not resist helping those less well endowed than himself. Very properly he supported numerous charitable organisations—although he would give only when asked—and private individuals also. Often his generosity was amply justified: he helped those who genuinely needed funds to set themselves up in business, provided that they could convince him that they were not 'fanatical fools' and that their projects were 'commonsense' ones.[15] Yet frequently enough he allowed himself to be put upon by spongers, to whom he handed out half-crowns indiscriminately. Reading in his lifetime was said to have become the haunt of beggars from all over the kingdom.[16]

William Isaac Palmer on the whole enjoyed an easier life than his elder brother. He was the youngest and favourite son, who never married, and took his sister's place as their mother's companion, in the way that his sister had prophesied on her deathbed in 1844. His basic philosophy was contained in his remark: 'I have a wonderful opinion of oil. It makes machinery work easier, and it is because the oil of human kindness is often forgotten that we hear of unpleasantness between masters and men'. He declared at the same time that he liked to hear of any grievance within the factory first-hand, whereupon he would try his best to remedy it.[17] To be truthful, it was lack of bargaining power on the part of labour that averted any serious trouble in the biscuit factory during the nineteenth century. Even so, his tact and geniality must often have restored calm at critical moments. His men had a deep respect for George Palmer; but it was Thomas Huntley, and later William Isaac Palmer, who won their real devotion.

He was a more successful landowner than his brothers, for at his summer home at Grazeley Court, near Reading, he concentrated on the rearing of cattle: a sensible choice, as he had inherited a marked aptitude here from his farming ancestors. His shorthorn herd was one of the finest in the country, and he carried off many prizes. However, his celebrity did not arise from these talents, but from his many other outside activities. These were listed in a remarkable letter which a Reading butcher named William Dorchester sent to the Prime Minister, Lord Salisbury, in 1885.[18] This letter sought a 'well merited honour' for William Isaac Palmer as one of the greatest philanthropists in England, who 'quietly, unceasingly and without thought of reward on this earth' spent perhaps as much as £10,000 a year on good works.

For the past twenty-five years he had been the 'life and soul' of the temperance movement in England, and had made that movement respectable long before the Church of England had taken it up. As to his public philanthropy, he had supported at his own cost a free library in Reading for some years, and when a municipal library and reading room were planned in an extension to the town hall, he donated a total of £25,000 as well as handing over all the books in the old free library. His private benefactions were no less noteworthy: 'In the morning when at home you will find inside and outside his house *every* day at 9 *a.m.* from fifteen to twenty people all wanting advice, money or aid of some kind; one and all leave with lighter hearts than they previously had. He assists widows, orphans, tradesmen etc. etc.'

Admittedly, Mr. Dorchester's object in drawing attention to his fellow-citizen's public-spiritedness was not entirely disinterested. 'I am a Churchman, Freemason, Knight of the Primrose League etc.' he declared, and alleged that the offer of an honour to the staunchly Liberal William Isaac Palmer, even if (as seemed all too likely) it were refused, would mean a hundred extra votes to the Conservatives in Reading at the next election, and indirectly all over the country would 'carry great weight in our favour among the working classes and nonconformists where his name is a household word'.

Despite this well-meaning advice, William Isaac Palmer was not offered any honour, and was therefore spared the embarrassment of having to decline it. He appreciated far more such local acts of recognition as being presented with an illuminated address by the Reading Temperance Society in 1877. His main wish then was to hang the address in his mother's room now that she was bedridden, so that she could 'see that the honour that is paid to her son is paid to her'.[19] In the testy way of old ladies, Mary Palmer retorted that she sincerely hoped William would not 'grow uplifted with all this praise'.

Three years later, at the age of ninety-five she finally succumbed to her infirmities, and he subsequently revealed that the two happiest months of his life had been spent in his dying mother's bedroom, with his head sometimes resting beside hers on the pillow, while he read sacred texts and hymns aloud to her. To later generations this may seem an odd way for a bachelor of fifty-five to conduct himself; however, he was doing no more than indulging in the common Victorian preoccupation with death.

There had always been an impulsive, if not unstable, streak in him, and after losing his mother, he became even more prodigal of his time and fortune in the service of others. He had already founded the Help-Myself Society, which organised regular social tea-parties to assist the lonely. He also became a member of the executive committee of the National Temperance League, in addition to promoting the Blue Ribbon temperance movement in Reading. His life was described as one of 'rushing hither and thither on the railway and across country in all sorts of conveyances', and it is not very surprising that in January 1893 he should have died suddenly of a ruptured artery in his abdomen. He was only sixty-eight.

Like his brother, he knew that he was often cheated by people who took advantage of his open-handedness. 'Do you know that —— is deceiving you?' a friend once asked him. 'Yes', he replied. 'I know it. The responsibility rests with him. It pays to be robbed sometimes.'[20] He also had the disconcerting habit of confronting people with sides of their characters that they wished to keep hidden. When a fellow-clerk at Liverpool, many years before, had complained that his social superiors took no notice of him, he said quietly: 'How much notice do *you* take of the people below you?' This worldly wisdom was an integral part of his deep spiritual life. He would often retire for a few minutes of prayer before going out or making an important decision; according to family tradition, he held that if he had not been born a Quaker he would have chosen to be a Roman Catholic. He had only recently promised to Reading council £30,000 so that the town hall and the adjoining public library and museum could be enlarged. On his death his benefactions and promises of funds were found to exceed his assets, which were valued at £123,000. His brothers therefore had to help out from their own resources.

In contrast with the relatively well documented lives of George and William Isaac Palmer, little is known about Samuel Palmer the man. His private papers and letters were entirely destroyed after his youngest daughter died in 1948. Moreover, as he consistently declined all invitations to enter public life, we lack the usual contemporary accounts written to satisfy general curiosity about men of affairs. He lived almost wholly for his work and his family.

As to his work, the genial and sometimes jaunty approach which he adopted towards life concealed a thoroughgoing professionalism. He created the London office single-handed: this was responsible for sales not only in the London area but also overseas. Just as George Palmer had from 1841 onwards built up the business into a nation-wide one, so Samuel gave it an international standing. Whereas his brothers were provincials at heart, he was a true cosmopolitan.

Under his direction, the London office also undertook the arduous task of purchasing ingredients. Once the firm could no longer meet from local sources—that is, from the Berkshire region—its ever growing requirements of flour, he became a very well known figure at the Corn Exchange in Mark Lane. In 1867 alone he had to buy no less than 5000 tons of flour, as well as over 3,350,000 eggs from France, Belgium,

Spain and Ireland; the flour had to be of the right quality and consistency for biscuit-making. Indeed, his expertise became so widely recognised that in 1884 he was asked by the committee of the London International Health Exhibition to adjudicate on the best samples of flour.[21]

He did not marry until 1856 when he was thirty-six. His wife, then aged twenty-four, was Mary Jane Marsh, daughter of a Quaker commission agent of Stoke Newington. Mary Jane's mother had been a Clark of Taunton, and may have been related to the talented Clark family of Street. Like many women of her kind, having been merely pretty as a girl, she became a handsome woman, with plenty of character, by the time she was forty. By then she had had eleven pregnancies in fifteen years, which she sailed through without undue strain—admittedly with the assistance of a growing domestic staff and later on of her elder daughters.

Although married in Meeting, Samuel and his wife very soon afterwards became members of the Church of England. For much of their subsequent life at least, they maintained the Quaker practice of living in a comfortable but unostentatious way. They began in Marlborough Hill, St. John's Wood, and then as their family grew, in 1864 moved to a larger house, with a reasonably ample garden, in the Finchley Road.

In those early days, he spent as much of his leisure time as he could at home. A breakfast of bacon and eggs was served punctually at 8 a.m., and he seems to have practised the sherry and biscuit habit at lunch-time, for a three-course dinner was served between 6 and 7 p.m. as soon as he returned from the City. His wife and those of his children who stayed up to dinner, having partaken of a sustaining lunch, often found it hard to match his hearty appetite in the evenings. When dinner parties were held at home, these were usually for 7 and never later than 7.30 p.m.

His eldest child remembered Sunday as 'a great day'. To give the breadwinner a brief lie-in, breakfast was not served until 8.45. A hot dinner at 1.30 p.m. followed the family's return from church, and consisted of roast joint, fruit tart and custard, rounded off by dessert as a treat for the children. At 4.30 came afternoon tea laid in the dining room, and at 8 a cold supper.[22] The children were given reasonable scope for enjoying themselves on Sundays: a freedom that was not universal in the Palmer family. George's son Walter, for instance, forbade both games and any running about on Sundays, according to a frequent guest, Oscar Wilde's son; the only books allowed for reading were the Bible and—of all unsuitable choices, even in the expurgated version—*Gulliver's Travels*.[23]

Whether Samuel Palmer was seen much at the play or at musical concerts is not known, although he may well have been a concert-goer as his son Ernest later became an accomplished musician. Although from 1847 onwards he lived continuously in London, he was paradoxically enough the most countrified of the three brothers. He owned two farms, one at Burton Hole in Mill Hill, and in the early days he used to ride over from Hampstead across the open fields. However, he was really too busy a man, and his bailiff was too unreliable, for the farm ever to pay. He also used to hunt regularly with John Hargreaves's hounds, later known as the South Berkshire Hunt, with which many other members of the family were later associated. His main recreation with the children was Continental holidays, which for himself always involved an element of work: to see personally how biscuit sales were shaping in the countries they visited. The outward and homeward journeys must always have been spoilt for him by his chronic seasickness.

His way of life seems to have changed markedly as his family grew up. In 1881 his eldest son Ernest married the daughter of an Alderman, and future Lord Mayor, of London, which must have involved him in much social entertainment. The following year he moved into his last home at Northcourt, Hampstead, where early in 1883 he gave what Joseph Leete, one of the 135 guests, described as a 'Grand Ball'.[24] The opportunities for a quiet dinner and a restful evening with his family had greatly diminished. He was now approaching his middle sixties, a man of distinguished appearance who was the reverse of pompous and who enjoyed a well-earned reputation throughout the City. Then towards the end of 1887 he fell sick, and the doctors diagnosed an attack of rheumatism. He never fully resumed work.

Attended by his two unmarried daughters, he travelled round from one English spa to another, and when visited by Leete the following summer confided to him sadly: 'We have known each other for a long time, but I think in future you will have to steer without me.' He had in fact contracted Parkinson's disease, and within a few years was reduced to a wasted invalid, subject to periods of intense weakness and depression. When his grandchildren called to see him before returning to school, their regular half-crown tip had to be placed in his shaking hand before he could present it to each of them. In this distressing state he outlived his two brothers and died in 1903, aged eighty-two.

10
The Second Generation 1874–98
(i) *The Seventies and Eighties*

For an independent firm manufacturing a foodstuff that was then not a very important part of the average family's diet, Huntley and Palmers during the last quarter of the nineteenth century made a far from modest contribution to the country's overall industrial activity. At that time it was providing almost a five hundredth part by value of all exports from Britain. As far as our very approximate estimates of aggregate industrial trends allow, the proportion of output was significant as well.

In 1874 this single firm appears to have been responsible for a little under one thousandth—0·095 per cent, to be precise—of total industrial production in the United Kingdom by value, or £919,000 out of an estimated £968 millions. In 1898 the proportion was marginally less, at 0·092 per cent, namely £1,311,000 out of £1,428 millions. At the beginning of this period the firm was employing about 3000 out of an industrial population in Great Britain of up to $6\frac{1}{2}$ millions, and at the end nearly 6000 when the industrial population was some 9 millions, many of whom must have been making a far smaller contribution per head to output than the firm's employees did.[1] Since Huntley and Palmers thus had such a stake in the nation's production and exports, it was inevitably sensitive to general economic trends.

The main cycles in the later nineteenth century happen to coincide with definite phases in the firm's history. Chapter 6 showed how the firm achieved an exceptionally rapid rate of progress during the great mid-Victorian boom of 1850 to 1873. In 1858 the firm's contribution to the value of Britain's aggregate industrial output—again bearing in mind the very high margins of error implicit in such estimates so far back in history—had been only about 0·025 per cent, but by 1874 had climbed to the 0·095 per cent referred to above. In absolute terms, during those seventeen years from 1858 onwards the physical volume of its output, namely the tonnage produced, expanded by nearly 600 per cent, or over 30 per cent a year.

From 1874 to 1896 the British economy was in the long cycle known —ironically enough to later generations who were to learn what a genuine depression was like—as the Great Depression. Over the same period the firm's tonnage increased by no more than 57 per cent, or less than 2½ per cent a year. More significantly, as the figures quoted at the beginning of this chapter show, the growth of its output by value barely kept pace with aggregate industrial growth.

The Great Depression was caused partly by an overall decline in the growth of export business.[2] Other countries, notably the United States and Germany, were by the 1870s beginning to match Britain's early industrialisation and take advantage of mechanical improvements. As these countries developed into serious competitors of Britain, the physical volume, but more especially the unit value, of British exports were falling markedly, as can be seen in the following tabulation.

percentage changes

	UNITED KINGDOM				HUNTLEY & PALMERS
	All Goods Exported		Bread and Biscuits Exported		Exports
	Volume	Value	Volume	Value	Value
1874 over 1850	+162	+236	+350[1]	+777[1]	+3388[1]
(1874 over 1857)	+ 72	+ 96	+611	+695	+1644
1898 over 1874	+ 63	− 3	+ 91	+ 65	+ 45
	Wheat Prices		Wholesale Prices	Import Unit Values	Retail Prices
1874 over 1850	+36		+30	+24	+17
(1874 over 1857)	− 9		− 4	−12	− 2
1898 over 1874	−44		−37	−38	−26

Note 1 = 1853 instead of 1850.

Estimates of Huntley and Palmers' exports indicate that their value rose by about 36 per cent annually between 1855–6 and 1868–9. From that year until 1898–9 the average annual rise in them was only 11½ per cent. Deliveries to the Continent rose by about 61 per cent annually between 1866—Leete's first complete year—and 1872. From that year until 1882 the average annual rise was only 10 per cent, and thereafter the trend was broadly a static one. The firm's sales to the United States and Canada from 1873 onwards varied largely according to the effectiveness of its representation there and to tariff charges; therefore they do not really conform to the general pattern. Nevertheless, we have already seen how in the United States, as on the Continent and elsewhere, local firms were now making their own biscuits, protected by high tariff barriers.

A noteworthy characteristic of the Great Depression was a steady decline in the general price level, which was due partly to a fall in the cost of primary products, especially wheat, but also sugar when it was admitted duty-free after 1874. Wholesale prices and unit values of imports declined on average by well over a third during this period. No reliable general index of retail prices exists for the United Kingdom, but in aggregate these must have fallen by just over a quarter. As to the firm's own selling prices, that of Ginger Nuts, which always remained one of its most popular varieties, was only 4 per cent dearer in 1873–5 than it had been in 1858–60, namely 20s. 4d. for a dozen 2 lb. tins compared with 19s. 5d., but by 1897–9 had fallen by 15 per cent to 17s. 3d. The price of Osborne biscuits rose from 18s. in 1860–2 (the first three years of its production) to 19s. in 1873–5, but fell to 16s. 1d. in 1897–9; a decline of 15 per cent.[4]

Moreover, the average price per hundredweight of biscuit and cake exports from the United Kingdom rose by 11·8 per cent between 1857 and 1874, but thereafter fell again by 13·7 per cent by 1898. The earlier rise may well reflect the growth in importance of fancy-biscuit exports, compared with the far cheaper ship's biscuits, but from 1874 onwards fancy biscuits predominated in this category.

At the same time, manufacturing wages did not follow prices downwards. Average *money* wages for all occupations in Britain are estimated to have risen by 6 per cent between 1874 and 1898, even when allowance is made for the higher number of unemployed. In *real* terms, taking into account the price decline, they increased by almost 30 per cent. The precise changes in Huntley and Palmers' wage rates are not very easy to summarise. During the 1870s, when the workforce trebled from 1000 to 3000 in a decade, the individual wage rates, based on supposed efficiency in the job, were giving way to rates for specific ages and jobs. Thus in 1872 girls of fourteen were paid 5s. a week, on a scale rising to 11s. at the age of twenty.

As the wages books were no longer kept in the old form, there is a gap in our knowledge for the next twenty years, but from 1895 onwards at least, the personnel manager's black book noted all the basic rates. By then girls' wages ranged from 4s. at fourteen to 10s. at twenty, with the 'top girl' for each room getting no more than 12s. Boys were being paid 5s. at thirteen, rising to 13s. at eighteen, but were dismissed when they reached that age unless there happened to be men's jobs available for them: a practice repugnant to several members of the Palmer family in the twentieth century. Those who stayed on as men had wage scales that went up to 19s. at twenty-one; they could earn up to 2s. extra on various kinds of unskilled jobs.

According to the little black book, in most rooms of each factory the foreman earned between 36s. and 40s. and his deputy about 26s. The spread of the operatives' wages can be seen from the example of the machines for rolling the dough and cutting out the biscuits, where it specifies: 'square up (the dough) 20s., roll down 22s., put under and guide out 10s. and 18s., altering 14s., feed ovens 19s., run away goods 20s.' The firm paid those working on the long travelling ovens which by now measured sixty feet '1s. extra all round', perhaps as a productivity bonus.

Certain workers were now entitled to piece-rates, for instance those working on various hand-made biscuits, and especially on icing them. Some rates were reduced in the mid-1880s, about the same time as the ones for pasting labels on tins were increased, when an improved system of numbering returnable tins—to identify them when they came back—was introduced. Before then, the worker had had to pencil the date on one coloured strip of each tin.

Those making cakes were also on piece work; bakers received basic skilled rates, 24s. on wires and 25s. on tins, and in addition a premium of 1s. to 2s. for each oven's worth but lost $\frac{1}{2}$d. for every pound of biscuits spoilt in the baking, or $\frac{1}{4}$d. if the burnt part could be scraped off. The penalty kept bakers alert: one reported spoiling biscuits 'to the extent of sixpence' in a week, a very modest proportion of the total premium earned.[5]

Appendix I sums up our knowledge of the firm's wage rates in the nineteenth century. While our old source of data—the wages books specifying changes in individual workers' rates—finishes after 1867, we do have a count of employees in March 1894, with average wages in each department; this unfortunately does not specify boys' and men's wages separately. However, if we multiply the average wages paid in each department for 1867 by the numbers in the department in 1894, and compare the product with the actual wages paid in 1894, the overall increase turns out to be 19 per cent: nearly 21 per cent in manufacturing, 18 per cent in packing, and just under 17 per cent among the fitters, carpenters and other tradesmen. The firm's insatiable demand for labour, at a time when the supply from the countryside was beginning to dry up, helped to keep wages buoyant. The number of females employed rose from a handful to nearly 200 and boys from 300 to nearly 550.

The course of wage rates after 1894 can be touched on briefly here. In September 1900 the lower paid workers had their wages raised. Boys up to the age of fifteen were paid 6d. a week more, but their numbers continued to fall sharply, from the peak of 804 in 1896 to 440 in 1904, and to 315 in 1913. No doubt more were staying on at school, particularly after the Education Act of 1902 came into operation: the total

The Second Generation 1874-98: (i) The Seventies and Eighties

of boys and girls over thirteen at local authority schools in Reading rose from 264 in 1896 to 666 in 1904.[6]

The management's reaction to the poaching of their potential labour by the educational authorities was to raise boys' wages two months, or on the half-year, before their birthday: 'this is the rule. Boys are scarce', the managers were told. Probably fewer girls than boys were staying on at school, for their numbers in the factory went up from 49 in 1895 to 407 in 1904, but women over eighteen rose from 155 to 665 over the same period. Despite the dramatic increase in female labour, men still predominated in the factory. By 1904 they represented 73 per cent of the total work-force, compared with over 82 per cent ten years previously, but by 1913 they were down to 68 per cent, only a few points above the 66 per cent of 1867.

How did Huntley and Palmers' management respond to these less euphoric conditions for trade generally? From 1874 onwards it chanced that the new generation of the Palmer family was coming into harness, after undergoing suitable apprenticeships. The first to do so were George Palmer's elder sons George William and Alfred, who joined as unpaid clerks at the age of sixteen as soon as they left school, the one in 1868 and the other a year later.

Whatever favouritism Henry Evans Huntley had received as the son of a partner was not extended to the Palmer boys. They were given a thorough grounding in every part of the factory. To judge from subsequent speeches made by themselves and by departmental heads on commemorative occasions, they seem genuinely to have made plenty of friends among all ranks while learning the business.[7] Indeed, at that time a truly personal spirit still existed within the firm, while the number of employees was still below the thousand mark.

Their father showed no unseemly haste in promoting them to partnership status, and incidentally to financial independence—for in the meantime they had to be content with a modest allowance from him. In mid-1873, a full year after George William had attained his majority, George Palmer raised the question of a partnership with the firm's elderly and devoted solicitor in Reading, William Slocombe. However, before any conclusion was reached, he decided to send both sons to Vienna for the International Exhibition; their work on the firm's display there was clearly to be treated as a kind of passing-out examination. The Prince of Wales's personal congratulations to them were convincing proof that they had passed with commendation, and they were both admitted as partners from the beginning of the financial year 1874-5.

Then in 1879 and 1880 respectively Ernest Palmer, Samuel's eldest son, and George's third son, Walter, became partners, to be followed by Samuel's younger sons Charles in 1883, Howard in 1887 and Albert in 1892. All were then twenty-one or twenty-two years old, and had served about three years' apprenticeship, except for Walter Palmer, whose training was shorter because of his B.Sc. degree from London University. Samuel Palmer personally trained Ernest and Charles in the work of the London office, which was now increasing so rapidly that in 1883 the office was transferred from Rood Lane to much larger premises at 162 Fenchurch Street; these were to be occupied by the firm for over seventy years. Howard and Albert Palmer concentrated on work at Reading. George Palmer's youngest son, Lewis, did not choose to enter the business; he took a degree at Cambridge and was later called to the Bar.

The exact transfers of shares involved in these new partnerships are of no great interest, and can be outlined very briefly. From 1878 onwards the amount of partnership capital, which had been just under £50,000 in March 1858, stood at £350,000 but was not further increased before the partnership was dissolved in 1898. Of this George Palmer had a half share, namely £175,000, but after successive transfers to his sons he held only £65,625 on his death in 1897. William Isaac reduced his share from £87,500 to £43,750, almost entirely by transfers to Samuel's sons, and under his will the residue was divided equally between those four sons; Samuel Palmer adopted the same practice. From 1893 onwards, therefore, the total capital was divided equally, George Palmer and his three sons owning one half and Samuel and his four sons the other half.

Informed observers are not agreed among themselves as to whether in general the transfer of power to the second generation necessarily tends to slow up a firm's development or not. Some writers have detected in the creators of great businesses a 'founder mentality', which inhibits them from making the effort of consolidating those businesses; by implication, that work falls to younger men.[8] On the other hand, the economist Alfred Marshall, who had an extensive personal knowledge of British industry at this time, held contrary views about founders' descendants. While 'the son of a man already established in business starts with very great advantages over others', because he can learn both the technical side of the business and also the best way of negotiating with suppliers and customers, he seldom makes full use of these advantages.

He will, according to Marshall, tend to lack strong fibre—because he may have been 'left a good deal to the care of domestic servants'—and may also be more interested in social or other outside distinction.

Therefore 'the business almost invariably falls to pieces unless it is practically handed over to the management of new men who have meanwhile risen to partnership in the firm'; alternatively, it becomes a limited company no longer controlled by the family.[9]

George Bernard Shaw made a similar point more pithily, if not brutally, in *Major Barbara*, where the armaments king Undershaft (who adhered to a long-standing tradition of adopting a successor) stated that in big business houses, each son tended to 'learn the office routine without understanding the business', so that 'the firm would go on by its own momentum' until a rival should 'invent something new, and cut him out'.[10]

How far do these statements apply to Huntley and Palmers? Undoubtedly, the founding generation's energy and interest had declined by 1874. George Palmer had devoted only part of his time to the business since 1857, and his two brothers in turn began to rely heavily on members of the new generation as they proved themselves. But the basic outlook of that generation was quite different from its forbears': in particular, it tended to be more conformist. As is well known, much enterprise in England has owed its development to 'outsiders'—those in some way or another excluded from the normal sphere of society, such as Jews, Quakers, Scotsmen and foreign immigrants.[11] Some reasons for this phenomenon, in so far as they applied to Quakers, were discussed in the Introduction.

George Palmer was a good example of the kind of cross-grained entrepreneur who refused to be assimilated into what later generations were to call the Establishment. So to a lesser, but still marked, extent, were his brothers. He refused honours from royalty; two of his sons and two nephews accepted them. He remained a Quaker and a Liberal, but all the second generation joined the Church of England and—except for George William Palmer alone—became Conservatives.

George and Samuel Palmer had gone to a Quaker school that prepared boys for commercial careers; they sent their sons to middle-class schools where prospective entry into trade was not looked down on. Those sons sent theirs to Eton or to Harrow, and usually on to Oxford as well. The first generation had lived fairly modestly in proportion to their wealth; all but one of their sons had their country estates and their country pursuits.

This—fairly typical—social transformation inevitably coloured their attitude to the business. They understood its 'routine' very well indeed; Marshall commended the kind of rigorous training they had undergone as 'almost the only perfect apprenticeships of modern times',[12] and having been made partners, they showed no lack of diligence or energy. Nothing was too much trouble to investigate. They were constantly trying out new lines and introducing them, so that the number of varieties increased from 130 in 1870 to over 400 by 1898. These evolved not merely from experiments within the firm, but also from regular searches in trade papers as far afield as the United States for fresh recipes and ideas. In 1877, for instance, the firm bought for £2500 the exclusive British rights of an American Soft Cake and Jumble machine, which allowed a man and two boys to do more efficiently what had formerly required thirty employees working by hand.

As the scientific partner, Walter Palmer was indefatigable in studying all the biscuit displays at both the 1878 and 1900 Exhibitions. He was convinced that 'some kind of register should be kept to show how our foreign trade is being influenced by opposition'. No register was in fact ever compiled, but having inspected most carefully all the biscuit exhibits (including two from Russia and one from the United States) at the 1900 Exhibition, he was convinced that the exhibition was 'wanting in interest', especially compared with that of 1878 when many more biscuits had been shown.

In fact, what was missing was a strong guiding hand, to give the firm a sense of direction and pilot it towards the next stage of its growth. The natural choice for such a steersman would have been George William Palmer, but he never consciously exercised control of this kind. The reasons for his failure to do so are not clear, for he was in many ways a man of strength and initiative. Perhaps as a reaction to his autocratic father, he saw his role as one among equals. Not until 1906, when Howard Palmer became Chairman of the limited company, did it begin to regain its sense of direction.

Meanwhile, the business seemed healthy enough. Profits as a proportion of turnover were 13·9 per cent on average between 1874 and 1898, as against 12·4 per cent in the previous seventeen boom years: an unexpected result in a period when business profits generally were being squeezed. Ingredients in the 1890s represented 40 per cent of the cost of goods produced by the firm; as their prices fell, so the firm was able progressively to bring down its retail prices without impairing these generous profit margins. Labour, although its cost was rising, was still on the whole cheap and plentiful. It is not unfair to surmise that life may have been a little too comfortable for the Palmers during the closing decades of the Victorian era.

One important innovation at this time was in packaging. While it was still a novelty, the fancy biscuit had sold largely on its merits alone. We do not know what kinds of label the tins of Huntley biscuits had borne before 1841, but Joseph Huntley did have as a pattern the very distinctive orange label of Cocks's Reading Sauce. By the late 1840s, George Palmer was ordering from White & Pike of Birmingham and De La Rue of London labels that were decorative rather than strictly utilitarian. Then in 1851 White & Pike devised the garter and buckle label; these, together with ceramic plaques depicting the factory, must have helped to brighten up the rather sombre grocers' shops of the day. As early as 1863 Huntley and Palmers introduced display tins with hinged lids, to catch the customer's eye.

However, the innovation which proved quite revolutionary for the firm was the discovery of offset-litho printing on tin. Since it then became possible to print on curved surfaces, tins could be made of all shapes and patterns. The story of how Barclay & Fry of London invented the process, and Bryant & May acquired the patent and appointed Huntley Boorne and Stevens to undertake the actual printing, must be left until another occasion. From the 1880s onwards Huntley and Palmers was able to market novelty Christmas tins; these continued to come out practically every autumn during the next sixty years, until the Second World War.

These tins fell into two categories. The first were of abstract shapes, whether in the basic form of rectangles, circles, squares or triangles, modified by curves. The illustrations printed on them often rang the changes on scenes of what was supposed to be traditional British life of the hunting, Yuletide and doggy varieties. Others reflected events and talking-points of the day. Japanese designs appeared after the Knightsbridge exhibition of 1885 and Gilbert and Sullivan's *The Mikado* of the same year had aroused public interest in Japan. Moroccan scenes recall the crises at the turn of the century, while some *art nouveau* motifs begin to creep in during the 1900s. By then, the second category of tin appears: one that imitated material objects. Bells, sundials, easels, pagodas, piles of dinner plates, sets of bound volumes, globes, and cannons were some of them. Although on the whole of little artistic merit and not always very serviceable as biscuit containers, these tins make a minor but interesting contribution to social history. Their peculiar shapes and the limited number of each that was produced, involved assembling them by hand, but the ratio of profit to selling price was high enough—often over 30 per cent—to constitute useful additions to revenue.

However, the advent of these new and lucrative Christmas tins could not hide the unmistakable signs of inefficiency within the firm. The number of factory employees expanded to 5500 by 1898, but the office staff rose even more rapidly: their exact numbers at this time are not known, but salaries grew from the equivalent of an eighth of the total wages bill in 1874-5 to a fifth in 1898-9. The increase in the number of varieties to 400, already mentioned, both caused production and marketing costs to rise, and precipitated a noticeable decline in labour productivity. In 1857 each factory employee had been producing close on 75 tons a year, and in 1867 roughly 71½ tons. Admittedly after a small cut in working hours, the tonnage per employee had fallen to 49 by 1889 and to between 45 and 47 tons in the mid-1890s.

Since they did not directly affect the partners' incomes, these worries were felt to be incidental and were therefore largely disregarded. To be more precise, the partners continued to rely on flair in making decisions, rather than attempting to cost alternative policies being considered or even the ones actually in question; the first Wages and Tonnages book was not introduced until mid-1903. Yet this was a period when the firm's successes were provoking far more widespread competition than in the past.

A number of rival firms became active in the 1880s. The Imperial London Biscuit Co. Ltd. was founded in 1881 with a share capital of £100,000, and the A.1 Biscuit Company, of Battersea, seven years later with £50,000 capital. Both were to have managers who had been enticed away from Peek Frean; in their prospectuses they claimed that the quality biscuit market was at that moment 'almost monopolised by two leading firms' which had realised 'enormous fortunes' in the trade during the previous twenty years. The A.1 Biscuit Co. was wound up in 1897. A successor company was one of the cheap manufacturers connected with the Association of Biscuit Manufacturers in 1911 and expired in about 1955, but the other firm was apparently stillborn. Hill & Jones assumed the royal arms in about 1879 but did not succeed in being granted a royal warrant when appointments to the Queen were put on a regular footing in 1884. Francis Lemann's did receive a royal warrant that year, and in the next reign was proud to describe its products as being 'by special appointment to Edward VII, the royal families of Europe and the Nobility and Gentry of the United Kingdom'. None of these businesses had an output that was particularly large.

Outside London, the firm of Jacob's, which had been manufacturing fancy biscuits in Dublin since 1851, was by the 1880s making inroads into the English market. In 1885 it introduced the variety by which it is perhaps best known to this day, the Cream Cracker. This proved such an immediate success that within a few years Huntley and Palmers had brought out its own version. Shortly afterwards one of the Jacob family moved to Liverpool in order to develop the marketing of his firm's biscuits in Great Britain; in 1914 it established a branch factory in that locality, at Aintree.[13]

The Second Generation 1874–98: (i) The Seventies and Eighties

In Scotland, too, there were signs that a regular trade was being developed. In 1885 Robert McVitie, a baker of some forty years' standing, began making biscuits by machine in his Edinburgh bakery and four years later took into partnership C. E. Price, a Quaker who had previously been employed by Cadbury Bros. In 1886 Macfarlane Lang, a Glasgow firm, opened a fancy biscuit department. R. Middlemass & Son and Mackenzie & Mackenzie had entered the trade somewhat earlier, in the 1860s.

However, the company which Huntley and Palmers had to watch most closely was Peek Frean, which in 1865 had caused a stir by introducing the Pearl biscuit. Being of a small, oval and globular shape, it was something new in biscuit-making since it did not require 'docking' or punching with holes; it had the further rare distinction of being used regularly in the sacrament service of one particular church for decades before it was dropped from the list in 1907.

Peek Frean's turnover rose in 1865 to over half that of Huntley and Palmers, and remained so until 1871, despite the latter's retaliation with its own Pearl biscuit within a month. The Garibaldi biscuit, which Peek Frean introduced in 1861, does not appear in Huntley and Palmers' list until 1872. In 1875 Peek Frean brought out the Marie biscuit to commemorate the Duke of Edinburgh's Russian bride, and Huntley and Palmers very quickly followed suit. However, neither firm was prepared to let this brand rivalry develop into an all-out war. They both clearly belonged to the same class of business—in a way that, for instance, Carr's of Carlisle did not—and with the onset of a chillier economic climate, felt that collaboration was more sensible than conflict.

Thus from the mid-1870s onwards, the two firms worked closely together, not only on list prices but also on the rates of discount to retailers and the categories of customer to whom these discounts could be given. When in 1883, for instance, both happened to be on the point of introducing a Toast biscuit at the same time, Peek Frean sought precise information on Huntley and Palmers' intended selling price, and thereupon adjusted its own price to match. Again and again, Peek Frean recognised Huntley and Palmers as a price leader by acquiescing, often against its better judgement, in either price changes or in keeping prices unaltered when ingredient costs changed. The office staffs of each firm soon reached the stage where they could predict almost exactly the price that the other would charge even for a new variety.

The two firms had no wish to extend such close collaboration to outside firms in the rest of the industry; where they did, they usually discussed less immediate matters. In 1877 their representatives, together with those of Jacob's, Carr's of Carlisle, Serpell's and Gray Dunn's of Glasgow, met the Home Secretary to urge on him various amendments to the Factories and Workshops Bill then before Parliament, which for the first time brought bakehouses within the scope of the Act. They pressed for more flexibility over hours, as theirs was a continuous process like paper-making, and thus involved night-work; it was also a highly seasonal trade, so that the amount of permitted overtime should be extended. Twenty years later, after consultation with Reading, Peek Frean canvassed eleven other manufacturers to decide what to do when the retailers, through the Grocers' Federation, tried to resist a proposal to raise the price of returnable tins.

This was by no means the sum of the competition which Huntley and Palmers had to face. Most of its rivals at that time were to a greater or lesser extent selling quality biscuits at quality prices—although few exercised such stringent control over ingredients and production as the firm did. But now there was a growing demand for biscuits of a far lower standard altogether. Average real wages for the country as a whole, like those in Huntley and Palmers, seem to have doubled between 1857-8 and 1899-1900. Perhaps the first pioneer of cheap biscuit manufacture on a large scale was the Co-operative Wholesale Society in its own factory at Crumpsall, Manchester, from 1873 onwards. Seven years later there were over 900 Co-operative Societies, chiefly in the North of England, with half a million members; by 1903 Crumpsall was producing over 2700 tons of biscuits a year, valued at nearly £100,000.[14]

Perhaps a less welcome development was that certain multiple groceries, now springing up in urban areas, were setting up their own biscuit-making plant, encouraged by the low price of wheat and the ease of buying such plant from Vicars and other suppliers. J. Sainsbury, David Greig and Thomas Lipton all opened their first shops between 1869 and 1871; the first two went on to become good customers of Huntley and Palmers, but Lipton was soon establishing a biscuit factory of its own. During the 1880s multiples like the Home and Colonial Stores and the Maypole Dairy made arrangements for their own biscuit supplies. One multiple baker, Bilsland Bros. of Glasgow, which had pioneered bread baking by gas and steam ovens, bought its technical know-how in biscuit manufacture by acquiring an interest in Gray Dunn's, the Queen's biscuit-makers in Scotland.[15]

Had Huntley and Palmers vigorously combated these trends by itself bringing out a wide range of inexpensive biscuits, it would undoubtedly have forestalled much of the competition. Yet there were a number of reasons why it could not do so. One was the question of space on the factory site. The extensions of the early 1870s had used up only four out of the twenty-six acres of Blake's Wharf earlier bought by William Isaac Palmer, and in 1876 the firm acquired another four acres, on which it erected the Central Warehouse and some extra factories. But four years later the Reading Gas Company, having secured the passage of the Reading Gas Act, compelled William Isaac Palmer to sell to it the large eastern wedge of this plot, covering thirteen acres in all. This left only five acres in the centre, which Huntley and Palmers bought in 1882 to build store rooms and workshops for making wooden cases.

Thus expansion to meet the threat of cheap biscuits would have meant opening a branch factory elsewhere, and hence required a far more complex management structure and much greater financial resources than the family could itself comfortably provide. An unacceptable loss of family control might have followed. On the distribution side, an army of extra travellers and a network of regional depots would have had to be set up, to supply the thousands of retail outlets in these urban markets.

The firm also had to consider a loss of goodwill if its name—or even a different one that was known to be connected with the firm—was used for cheap biscuits. But above all, such changes would have conflicted with all that it stood for. In later years the only way in which the firm could supply any part of the lower-income market without jeopardising its own goodwill was by deliberately breaking up good stock and selling it as broken biscuits. Thus Huntley and Palmers stood aloof from these far-reaching developments in the industry it had done so much to create.

The harmful effects of all this competition can be illustrated as follows. The firm's overseas trade seems to have risen in value by about 60 per cent, from £280,000 to £450,000 between 1874–5 and 1889–90. Yet concurrently the physical volume of tonnage which it produced rose only by 52 per cent. Since the official returns show the unit prices of biscuit and cake exports as on the decline, in real terms its home trade must have been shrinking.

Just at a moment when it was encountering some of the problems of maturity, the firm began to acquire the status of a British institution. In true national style its origins, including the date of its foundation, had already become lost in the mists of antiquity. Since 1884 its Royal Warrant had been confirmed in the *London Gazette*, which gave rise to various commemorative articles. It was visited by many distinguished people, including ex-President Grant of the United States in 1877, the Prince of Wales in 1882, and the Empress Eugénie, who dropped in unannounced one Thursday in 1885. Their example was followed by many minor royalties, both British and foreign, and by overseas politicians and diplomats.

Parties of humbler visitors in their thousands had also been passing through the factory from the early days onwards. In the final uncomfortable year of Thomas Huntley's life the partners had had to suspend visits, explaining that while they regretted 'being obliged to withhold from any a gratification', the 'hindrance and loss arising from the admission of so many' imposed 'a sacrifice on us that is too great for continuance'. However, the thirty-nine surviving visitors' books show that regular factory visits began again in 1869 and continued, with wartime interruptions, until 1964.

Yet the firm's full acceptance as an institution was sealed by the unusual tribute—for a Quaker firm—of an episcopal commendation, which gave rise both to a *Times* leader and to a *Punch* cartoon. When the Church Congress met at Reading in 1883, the Bishop of Oxford was moved in his address of welcome to speak as follows:

> In this diocese we have no great masses of population, no imposing displays of national power, no hives of manufacturing industry. The busy swarm of toilers to which Reading owes its modern prosperity is scarcely an exception; its staple has a savour of the quiet fireside and of the social board.

The Times, having nothing of greater moment to comment on next day, devoted a leading article to the bishop's address, and asserted with some hyperbole that the last phrase 'almost deserves to be quoted by the side of COWPER's poetical equivalent of a cup of tea [*sic*]': '*the cups that cheer but not inebriate*'. 'In future', continued the Thunderer in its blandest vein, 'it will be difficult to think of MESSRS. HUNTLEY AND PALMER without associating them with "the savour of the quiet fireside and of the social board".' Not to be outdone, *Punch* in its next issue portrayed 'the "Reading Biscuit" Bishop' as a jack-in-the-box holding a biscuit and emerging from a Huntley and Palmers tin.[16]

Exactly two years later Edward Lear, in his villa at San Remo in Italy, was concocting some nonsense rhymes for a small girl correspondent in England, and wrote to her:

> Huntley and Palmer arose
> With the earlyful beams of the morning sun;
> Huntley a chop for his breakfast chose
> Palmer preferred a bun.

To people in well-appointed English homes, as to him, the biscuit tin was so much a part of the furniture that in the next generation a candid friend could remark idly to a more than usually schizophrenic young woman in the Bloomsbury set: 'You are like a tin of mixed biscuits. Your parents were Huntley and Palmer.'[17]

Even more remarkably, the slang equivalent of 'take the biscuit' (carry off the prize), namely 'take the Huntley and Palmer' came into use about this time; it was first recorded in print in 1895. Similarly, Reading Gaol became in thieves' slang the Biscuit Factory, since the two establishments were next door to one another. Although beyond the reach of the average purse, therefore, Reading biscuits and their manufacturers had passed into the language of the people.[18]

11

The Second Generation 1874–98
(ii) The Nineties

The economic background to the events of the 1890s can soon be recounted. During that decade the British economy moved through a complete cycle from boom to slump and back to boom again, in the course of which the general price level declined from a so-called 'peak' in 1890 to its lowest ever point—at least since 1860—in 1895. The 'peak' was of course merely an upward spur in a falling trend which had persisted for twenty—some would say for nearly forty—years. The economy then recovered to beyond the 1890 level in 1900.[1]

In money terms, Huntley and Palmers' own turnover followed a similar cyclical path during the course of the 1890s. The value of its overseas trade declined from a high point in 1889–90, which was not exceeded until 1900–1; at the same time, turnover at home revived concurrently with trade in general. Of more immediate concern to the partners, the firm's average net profit on turnover in the nine years 1889–90 to 1897–8 proved to be at the rate of 14·5 per cent, nearly a whole point higher than the 13·6 per cent averaged over the fifteen previous years from 1874–5 onwards; as shown in Chapter 10, this compared very favourably with the 12·4 per cent of between 1857–8 and 1873–4.

By weight the weekly average of 'goods turned out' exceeded for the first time 400 tons in 1890. The firm had passed the 100-ton mark in 1866, 200 tons in 1873, and 300 tons as recently as 1880. Yet it dipped thereafter to 370 tons on average for the years 1893 to 1895, and did not achieve 400 tons a week again until 1896–7. From that year onwards, as the Great Depression at long last worked itself out, the firm's output went on rising until the early 1900s.

Apart from these vicissitudes in output and profits, the main managerial event of the decade was the disappearance of the first generation. In 1887 Samuel Palmer's health began to break down, and his two elder sons, who had for some years been assisting him, took over completely the London office. During the following years George and William Isaac Palmer, by then in or approaching their seventies, also ceased through death or infirmity to be connected with it. In all but the formal sense, they had handed over the watch to the younger generation.

Like his father, who for so many years had managed the correspondence work, George William Palmer was responsible for the offices. Alfred Palmer was in charge of the engineering department, which made nearly all the biscuit machinery and some of the dynamos and boilers. Between 1882 and 1908 he installed three very large generating engines, which he touchingly named after his wife Alice, his daughter Phyllis and his granddaughter Betty respectively.[2] Had it not been for Alfred Palmer's mechanical inventiveness, the firm would have been quite unable to turn out so many different kinds of biscuit of such varying shapes and textures.

However, these biscuits had to be invented first, and many of them were due to Walter Palmer, the able working scientist who created the firm's scientific department. He was tireless in travelling round international exhibitions and scrutinising very carefully the products and ideas of rival exhibitors. His greatest triumph was his discovery of the Breakfast biscuit, quite by chance while carrying out some experiments of another kind. (His daughter has claimed that it was invented on purpose to relieve the dyspepsia of the author George Meredith, a family friend, but this claim is not otherwise substantiated.)[3] That biscuit was put on the market in 1891. It was perhaps the most impressive result of the close collaboration between Alfred Palmer and himself, for there were both scientific and mechanical problems to be overcome in using yeast in a biscuit. It proved an immediate success as a palatable substitute for the baker's roll that in high circles was usually consumed with early morning tea or coffee.

The next year Joseph Leete introduced the Breakfast biscuit into France. He persuaded the customs authorities there to charge the very low rate of duty levied on *pain d'épice*, instead of the rate on ordinary biscuits, which came to close on half their wholesale value. He also by a well-thought-out plan obtained the approbation of a number of French doctors, without having to incur the exorbitant fees which the doctors usually charged for their testimonials. The consequent demand for this biscuit in France helped to arrest the decline in Huntley and Palmers' sales there. Within two years the general market for it, both at home and overseas was so great that a new Breakfast factory had to be built.[4]

Of Samuel Palmer's sons, the third, Howard, held a key position in overall charge of the manufacturing and packing departments, while the youngest, Albert Palmer, who seems to have been of a more artistic bent, was responsible for tins, labels, showcards and miscellaneous matters.[5]

It was not merely the social characteristics discussed in the previous chapter—notably an inclination for conforming to the upper middle-class way of life—that dictated the partners' attitude towards the firm and its activities. They were probably rich enough by now to have been able to sell out to strangers, as many of their contemporaries in other businesses were doing, but this did not appeal to them. Above all, they had great interest and pride in biscuit-making; with one exception—namely, Ernest Palmer's directorship of the Great Western Railway, which indirectly benefited the firm—they kept free of outside business commitments; clannish and inward looking, they were anxious to maintain entire control in their own hands, as well as to resist change of a revolutionary (as opposed to an evolutionary) kind.

However, while they were at that time numerous enough to supervise between them all sides of the business, the prospects of doing so for the remoter future seemed less sure. In 1898, when the eight sons of George and Samuel Palmer had completed their families, they had produced no more than seven sons altogether, so completely had the fashion of patriarchal families declined. George William and Albert Palmer had no children and Walter Palmer one daughter only. Alfred, Howard and Lewis had one son each, and Ernest and Charles two sons apiece. Of these seven grandsons only five were to enter the business, dangerously few to preserve family influence. After trying out one young candidate in the family, whom he found wanting, George William decided to adopt his sister's younger son, Ronald Poulton. The young man's career is described in Chapter 14.

Closely connected with the problem of future management was that of maintaining financial control of the firm. Under the partnership structure, Huntley and Palmers was owned entirely by the three brothers of the first generation and the seven of the second generation; until the previous decade the partnership had been the predominant form of business organisation in British commerce generally. The solid mid-Victorian world had commended the idea of families staking the whole of their private fortunes in their own businesses, which was what the unlimited liability of partnerships entailed. Although the various Acts of 1856–62 had authorised the setting up of joint-stock companies, for several decades afterwards such companies remained under suspicion because they were thought—often with some justice—to lack stability and probity.

However, by the 1880s the joint-stock company was beginning to make headway. Shareholders as a body benefited by incurring only limited liability in the company, while those wanting to control policy-making—as, for instance, the Palmers did—needed to hold no more than 50 per cent of the ordinary shares. The nominal capital of new companies registered therefore rose from £152 millions in 1873 to £353 millions in 1888.[6] Moreover, the increasing taxes on inherited wealth, and death duties in particular, encouraged family firms to seek incorporation. In the 1894 Budget the Liberal Sir William Harcourt introduced a graduated estate duty which rose to 8 per cent where an estate exceeded £1 million. From then on, the convenience to the partner of maintaining unrestricted ownership was outweighed by the inconvenience of full liability to duty on his death. In this period, therefore, many biscuit firms became limited companies.

Jacob's of Dublin had 'gone public' in 1883, and Carr and Co. Ltd. was registered at Carlisle, with a capital of £253,000, in 1894. Among others following the same trend during the decade were Meredith & Drew in 1891, R. Middlemass of Edinburgh in 1896 and Mackenzie & Mackenzie in 1898. A little later they were followed by Peek Frean in 1901 and Macfarlane Lang in 1904. Hill & Jones, which became a limited company with £15,000 capital in 1893, was wound up in 1901.

Following these developments, in 1896 the financial press began to drop hints that Huntley and Palmers was shortly to 'go public' with a share capital of £6 millions. The wild exaggeration in the figure (which later turned out to be £2·4 millions) shows how completely the firm's true profits were hidden from the outside world. More sensationally, a few months later the *Liverpool Journal of Commerce* spread a report, said to have been current for some years past, that the firm was about to amalgamate with Peek Frean, and that a prospectus of a limited company would shortly be placed before the public.[7]

Huntley and Palmers for its part straightway denied the rumours; in fact neither firm's records reveal that any written negotiations actually took place. There may have been some verbal discussion, but it could not have gone very far: when in 1912 Peek Frean sounded out Huntley and Palmers and four other competitors as to a possible merger Huntley and Palmers' directors categorically refused to discuss the matter as they opposed any form of association.

One company whose incorporation in 1893, with a capital of no more than £25,000, was of some concern to the firm was the Reading Biscuit Co. Ltd. Having built up such a massive reputation both at home and abroad, Huntley and Palmers not unexpectedly attracted many would-be imitators. Such imitations might have seriously jeopardised its trade, particularly in the remoter parts of the world where very slight differences in design would have passed unnoticed. Shortly after the official Register of Trade Marks was set up, it had in 1876 registered the Garter and Buckle device, which it had used as a trade mark ever since 1851. A black tin box in the firm's archives, filled with dossiers, reveals the vigour with which the firm pursued the various imitators overseas.

Of the far less common cases at home, perhaps the most bizarre arose in 1910. An ex-publican named Palmer had married a Miss Huntley (both being quite unrelated to the biscuit families) and had set up a grocery business at Raynes Park, Wimbledon, in his sons' name G. & H. Huntley Palmer Bros. Here he retailed the company's biscuits to a very modest extent. He was incensed one day to receive a letter from the company, stating: 'We have the strongest objection to any other firm in the grocery or provision trade adopting as their Trading Name a combination of the words "Huntley" and "Palmer", and shall be glad to learn without delay that you are arranging to alter the style of your firm'.

Like the British tar in *H.M.S. Pinafore*, resisting a 'dictatorial word', Mr. Palmer defiantly forwarded a photograph of himself, sons and assistants posed outside the grocery, and declared his intention to trade under whatever names he happened to choose. He also expressed pain and astonishment that a firm of Huntley and Palmers' standing should concern itself with such absurd trifles.

The firm was in fact trying to guard against the—admittedly improbable—eventuality of Mr. Palmer's starting to manufacture biscuits on his own account. Before deciding on the next move, the London office therefore reconnoitred the enemy position carefully by despatching a succession of clerks who, pretending to be ordinary customers, made small purchases in the grocery and brought back intelligence gleaned from artful questioning. This operation completed, the firm imposed sanctions by refusing to supply the few pounds' worth of biscuits he had ordered, and then sought Counsel's opinion.

Counsel somewhat predictably stressed the impossibility of securing a legal injunction, as there was no evidence of any wish to deceive or confuse. On his recommendation, therefore, the firm's solicitors wrote a strong letter to Mr. Palmer, warning him not to use the names Huntley Palmer in connection with any kinds of goods made by the firm. Mr. Palmer, left in possession of the field, did not deign to reply.

The Reading Biscuit Co. Ltd., presented an altogether more serious and immediate problem. Since 1840 a baker named Thomas Shepherd had been operating in Queen's Road, Reading; at one time it had supplied bread to the biscuit factory nearby, but it also made a few biscuits of its own by hand. On his retirement in 1885, Shepherd sold out to Albert Meaby, who collaborated with a miller named Farnworth in producing a special kind of wholemeal flour with the fancy name of Triticumina. In 1892 they and some associates decided to go in for biscuit-making on a large scale, with the most modern machinery, and announced the formation of the limited company.

Huntley and Palmers retaliated in May 1893 by seeking an injunction

The biscuit shop, 72 London Street, Reading—the original premises occupied from 1822 to 1861: an imaginative reconstruction (see p. 113), but the upper storeys are correctly represented

Thomas Huntley, 1853

George Palmer, *c.* 1860

Mary Palmer, mother of George, Samuel and William Isaac Palmer

Samuel Palmer, aged thirty-five, 1855

The factory, 1851

Entrance to the factory, 1867

Above: George Palmer among his men, 1872
Inset left to right: Alfred Palmer (*in bowler hat*), William Isaac Palmer, George Palmer, Charles Brown (*all in top hats*)

Opposite above:
A PARTY AT THE ACACIAS, 1870
Mary Palmer in bath chair, George and Elizabeth Palmer to her right, George William Palmer standing between them in second row, Robert Meteyard (*with white beard*) far left, Samuel (*with check rug*) and Mary Ann Palmer far right, Alfred Palmer (*with top hat*) sitting down, behind him William Isaac Palmer (*holding lapel*) and Charles Brown (*bareheaded*). Joseph Leete and Henry Lea are directly behind the bath chair

Below: A PARTY AT MARLSTON HOUSE, 1906
George William Palmer (*sitting inside canopy*), Eleanor Palmer far left; the young women are her nieces on the Barrett side

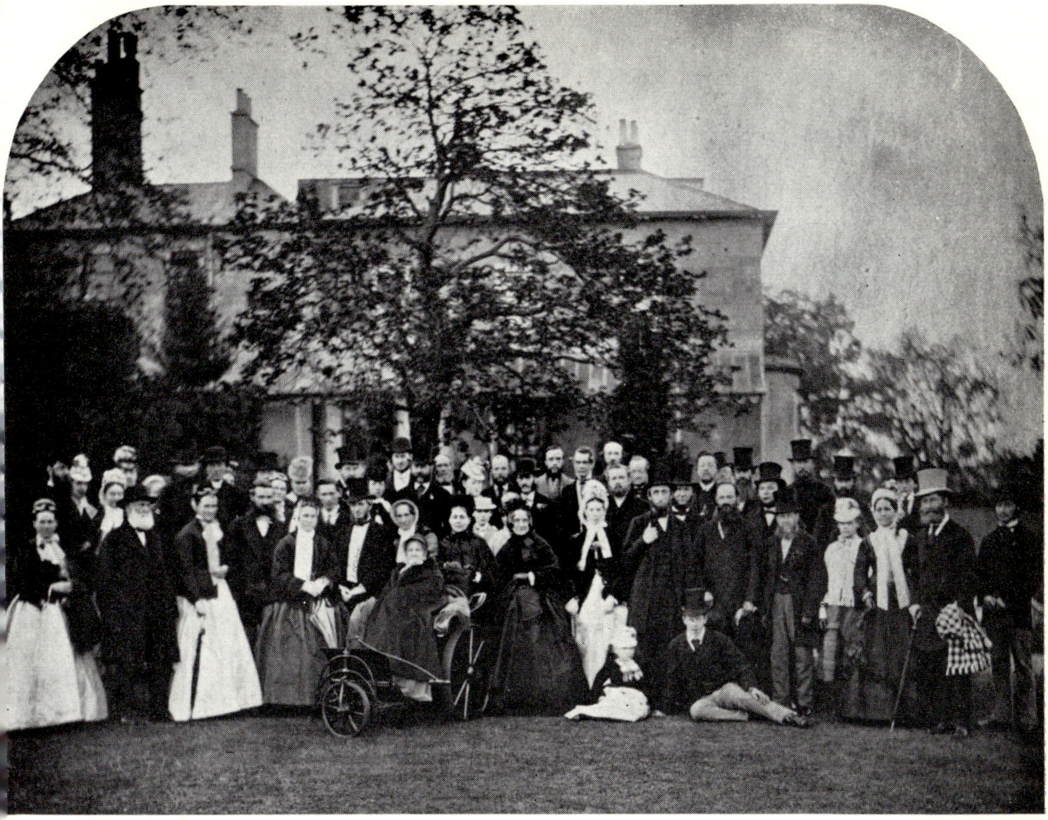

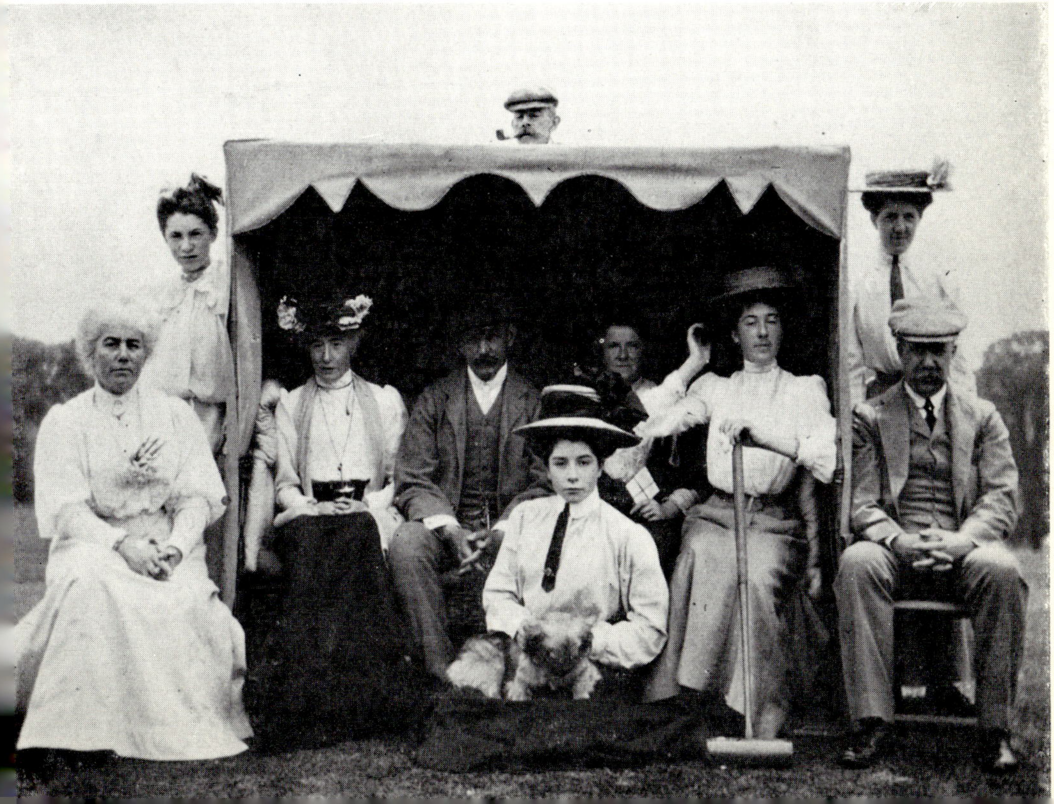

George Palmer in later life

THE GENTLEMEN IN THE BOARD ROOM, 1933

Left to right: Front row: Herbert Pretty, Cecil Palmer, Eric Palmer (Chairman), Lord Palmer, Charles Palmer. Second row: Bennet Palmer, Clement Williams, Reginald Palmer, E. A. Wrottesley, Albert Palmer, Geoffrey Palmer

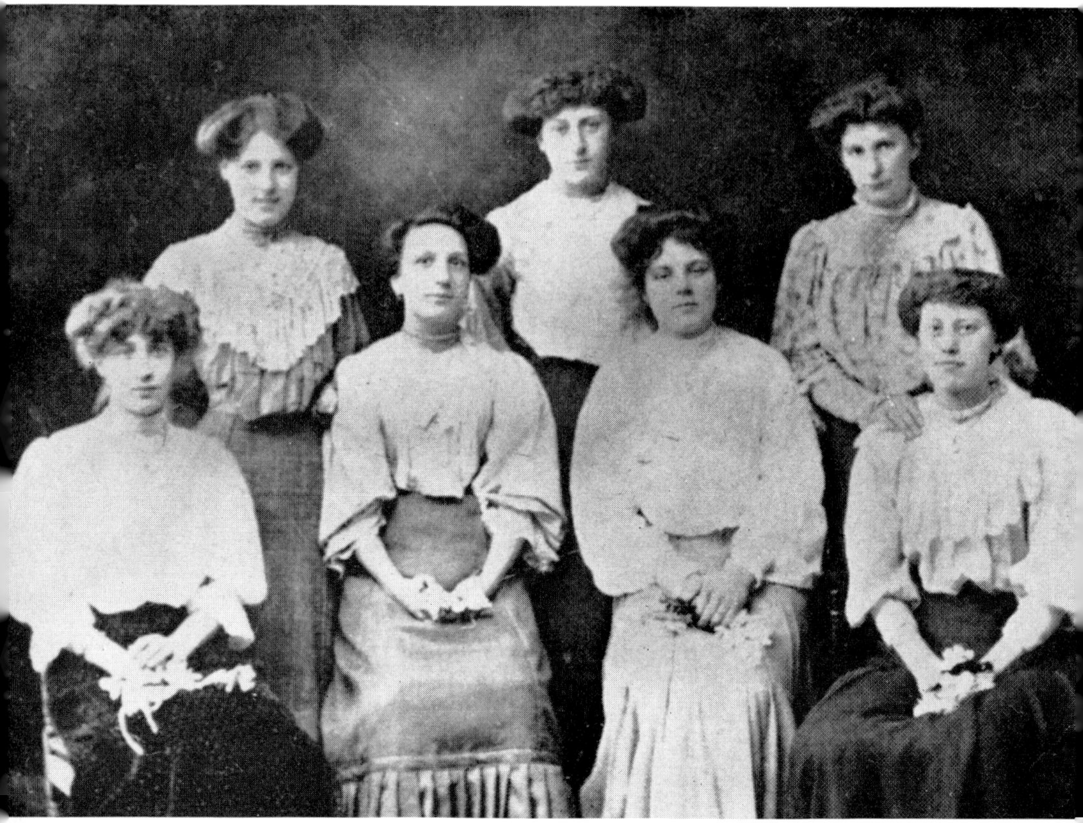

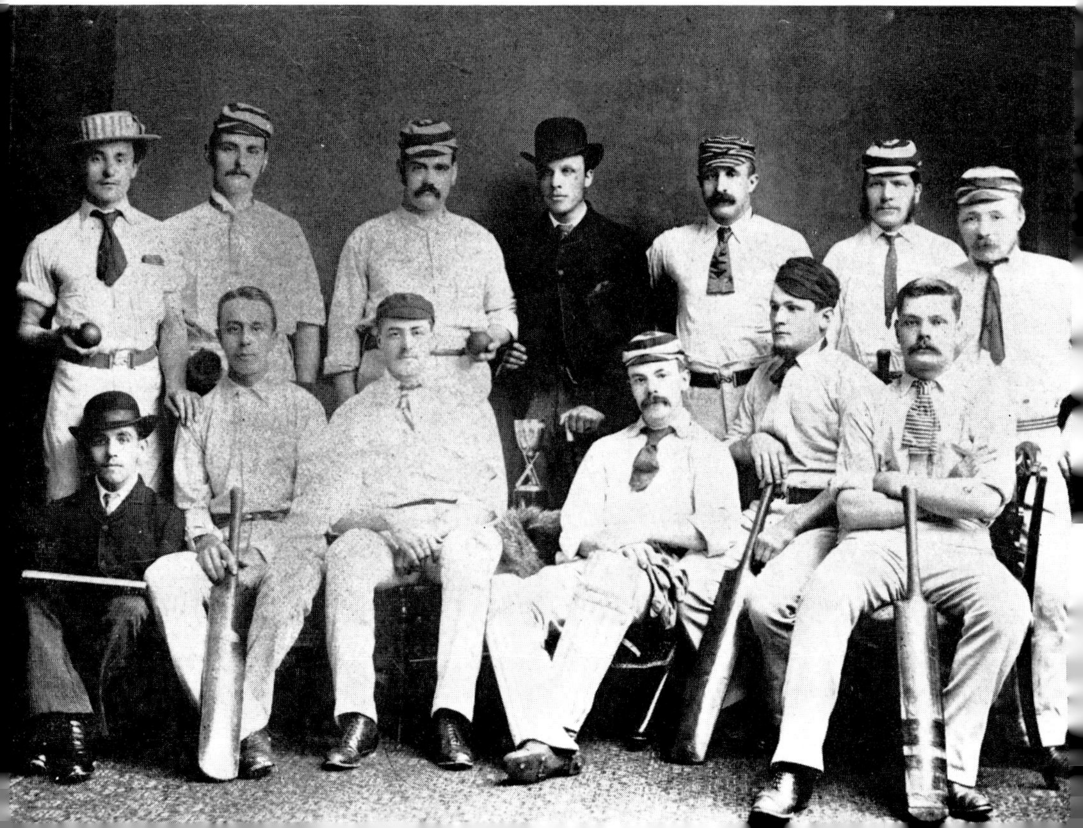

Above: Huntley and Palmers' new offices, built in 1936

Opposite above: The ladies in the sugar-wafer department, 1906

Below: Huntley and Palmers' First XI, 1886. Howard Palmer seated second from left

Above: Men cutting out biscuits, 1900
Below: One of the seven 200 ft. gas fired, thermostatically controlled ovens each capable of producing 1½ million biscuits per hour, 1970

Decorated biscuit tins, 1898

THE BOARD, 1968

Left to right: C. D. van Namen, Richard Palmer, Neil Gardiner, Lord Palmer, Alan Palmer (Chairman), Hector Hanford, Gordon Palmer, William Palmer (portrait of George Palmer, on wall)

to restrain the new company from using 'Reading' as a description of its biscuits. The firm collected a large number of affidavits from customers, ranging from such London stores as Harrods, Whiteleys and Spiers & Ponds, and export firms like C. & E. Morton, to provincial grocers: all submitted that Huntley and Palmers' were known universally as Reading biscuits.

Perhaps the most interesting of the other affidavits was one from George Palmer, which recalled the fateful day, nearly sixty years previously, when as an apprentice he had bought some of Huntley's biscuits at James Busvine's shop in Bristol. It also stated that Thomas Worth had in the Huntley era 'regularly visited the University towns of Oxford and Cambridge, at both of which Huntley's biscuits had a great reputation as Reading biscuits and were jocularly known as read-ing biscuits'. The account books show that George Palmer's memory was playing him false about Cambridge, which was apparently not canvassed before 1842, but his evidence in general is most valuable.

Huntley and Palmers duly secured its injunction, and the case attracted some attention because of two interesting features. First, the firm had won without having had to prove actual damage to its trade, for the defendants had not yet even begun to produce biscuits. Second, a trade name, which was not itself a trade mark, could acquire valuable rights if it were used exclusively over a long enough period: the judge had accepted the argument that, apart from Huntley and Palmers, Reading by itself had no reputation in the biscuit trade. The trade *mark*, mentioned above, was the Garter and Buckle device, which had been fully registered, but the trade *name* (of Reading biscuits) must have been invented by old Joseph Huntley, on the analogy of his next door neighbour's Reading Sauce.

The Reading Biscuit Co. straightway changed its name to Meaby & Co. Ltd., but even without the loss of its prestigious name it was unlikely ever to have prospered. The two principal shareholders were a dentist and a veterinary surgeon; discord soon broke out among the top management, no dividend was ever paid, and in 1897 Huntley and Palmers was asked to purchase the business as a going concern. The offer was courteously declined, and the same year Meaby & Co. Ltd. went into liquidation. The biscuit industry was too competitive for unprofessional management of this kind to make much headway.[8]

By contrast, the managerial organisation at Huntley and Palmers was working so smoothly that George William Palmer, a member of Reading Council since 1882, had accepted the office of Mayor for 1889–90. Then in 1892 he was returned as Member of Parliament for

Reading. With a break of three years from 1895 to 1898, he continued to sit as member until he had to resign through increasing deafness in 1904. Like his father, he was very largely a 'silent member', asking parliamentary questions from time to time, but never contributing to set-piece debates.

That other partners might also be free to pursue parliamentary careers was surmised by the Conservative *Berkshire Chronicle*. Just after George William Palmer's election in 1892 a letter in that newspaper rather quixotically suggested that one of the other partners, all of whom happened to be Unionists, should stand against him in order to 'win back Reading' for the party.[9] In fact the only one of them to enter parliament was Walter Palmer who had been converted to protectionism by Joseph Chamberlain, and was elected Conservative member for Salisbury in the so-called Khaki election during the Boer War in 1900; he held that seat until 1906.

Towards the end of George William Palmer's term of office as Mayor, in October 1889, George Palmer unexpectedly announced that he would present to the people of Reading twenty-one acres of land to the east of Cemetery Junction for a recreation ground. A few months later he increased the area to forty-nine acres, so as to provide sports facilities, including cricket and football grounds and tennis courts. His only condition was that no intoxicating liquor should be sold in the park. To acknowledge this truly munificent gift, a body representing all kinds of Reading citizens collected no less than 4000 subscriptions of money to pay for the erection of a statue and to present him with an illuminated address. At the same time Reading Council voted to make him an Honorary Freeman of the borough, the first one to be conferred.

On the same day in November 1891 he was given the freedom of Reading in the Town Hall, his statue was unveiled at the east end of Broad Street, and he assisted in the opening of Palmer Park. The procession from Broad Street to the park was said to be the largest and most imposing ever seen in Reading, and took three-quarters of an hour to pass any given point.[10] The statue, which was removed to Palmer Park in 1928 when motor traffic in the centre of Reading became a problem, is of bronze, and was designed by George Simonds, a local sculptor. As a contemporary account put it, the subject is 'standing in an attitude of repose, as though about to address an audience; he is holding his hat and umbrella in the right hand, and the left has a restful hold of the coat near the collar in accordance with a familiar English habit'. Although his biographer in the *Dictionary of National Biography*, William Childs of Reading University College, dismissed it as 'inartistic', it is on the whole a good example of civic art, and represents more clearly than any other portrait of him the large Palmer nose and slightly stooping posture.

This occasion would scarcely have been complete without an explosion of wrath from the subject himself. The agent who had been acting for him was Dryland Haslam, of the well-known Reading firm of estate agents. In order to bring home to his fellow-townsmen the magnitude of the donation, he wrote a letter to the *Reading Observer* in April 1890, without his principal's knowledge, estimating that the forty-nine acres would have fetched up to £100,000 if they had been sold in the open market for development as building plots. George Palmer, who hated publicity in personal matters, protested vehemently to Mr. Haslam. 'I am astonished that you should have seen yourself at liberty to publish a statement of value of the land without my consent', a statement that was in any case 'purely speculative', he wrote, and insisted on its being immediately withdrawn.[11]

The golden jubilee of the partnership—which was not in any way celebrated within the factory[12]—happened also to fall in 1891, which thus represented the zenith of George Palmer's life in terms of public recognition. No doubt he could have pointed to other events of greater moment to him, such as the successful establishment of the King's Road factory in 1846 or the completion of the factories across the river Kennet in 1873. Yet before the year was out, he encountered a further attempt to thrust public honours on him. In mid-December he received a 'Private and Confidential' letter from the Reverend George Brown, Chaplain of Brixton Military Prison, seeking an interview in London a few days later. At the interview it turned out that an 'unknown friend' was offering him a baronetcy in the New Year's honours list.

The unlikely choice of intermediary is probably explained by the fact that Mr. Brown had at one time been an embassy chaplain, and was thus known to the Prime Minister of the day, Lord Salisbury, who was also Foreign Secretary. Lord Salisbury had been responsible for ennobling a number of influential business men, including brewers, bankers, engineers and representatives of other 'genteel' occupations, so that it seemed reasonable for a relatively minor industrialist such as a biscuit manufacturer to be rewarded with a baronetcy. Nor was it unheard-of for a Quaker to be offered an honour, for Mr. Gladstone had created the first Quaker baronet in 1882.

The increased distribution of honours had whetted the appetites of many prominent men, or at least their wives, as the Salisbury papers for those years reveal. Indeed, hopeful aspirants were directly or indirectly offering large sums of money, which the Conservative party sorely needed both to fight the forthcoming general election and to finance the rapidly growing expenditure of its headquarters. No financial *quid pro quo* was expected from the Liberal George Palmer, but as Mr. Dorchester, the eloquent pleader of William Isaac Palmer's cause, had earlier asserted, an honour bestowed on the Palmers might be very popular in Reading after the recent conferment of the town's freedom and the unveiling of the statue.

In fact George Palmer made up his mind instantly about the baronetcy, although he delayed for a week before he replied, no doubt in order to consult his family. 'I could not sustain the position it entails with comfort and satisfaction to myself', he then wrote. Although well qualified from the financial point of view—for he was practically a millionaire and had over 3000 acres of landed estates—he was just not interested in acquiring a handle to his name, and saw no good reason for pretending otherwise.

Yet the matter was not to rest there. Barely a fortnight later, a Mr. J. B. Chalmers, of the Elms, Highgate Road, London, wrote to ask for a meeting with George William Palmer on a subject of a 'complimentary character', which once again was too highly confidential to be committed to paper. This also turned out to be the offer of a baronetcy, and the would-be recipient must have been more than puzzled at the offer. His amazement would have grown had he learnt that Mr. Chalmers was in fact an honours tout, whose crooked activities came to the attention of the Director of Public Prosecutions a few years later. A dossier on the Chalmers Gang revealed how its members persuaded likely victims to part with large sums for charity, on which they reckoned to net a handsome 'commission'.

The three members of the gang were Chalmers himself, a knighted ink manufacturer, and the step-nephew of John Morley. Among the accomplices was a lady of doubtful virtue who lived in Greek Street, Soho. Their aim was to lure the prospective victim into the Café Royal —the rendezvous *par excellence* in the nineties—where Chalmers passed himself off as a most important official from 'headquarters'. Big names were freely bandied about, including those of the Grand Duke of Hesse-Darmstadt, Princess Louis of Battenberg, Lady Churchill and Lord Charles James Ker. Fact and fantasy become so intermingled that it would not be surprising to read that a distraught Patronage Secretary of the Treasury had sought the aid of Sherlock Holmes, who had then impersonated a gullible victim and unmasked the gang in the Café Royal, thereby earning another piece of personal jewellery from a grateful sovereign during a private trip to Windsor Castle. But Sherlock Holmes was otherwise engaged that year. Instead a policeman was detailed to shadow Chalmers, and proved so unbelievably incompetent that the Director of Public Prosecutions had to send a very inconclusive dossier to the Prime Minister, who commented tritely: 'The stories are very mysterious—but I agree there is nothing to be done.'[13]

Since the gang's aim was to choose victims whose vanity outweighed their judgement, they went after quite the wrong man in George William Palmer. His reply to Mr. Chalmers was that he had done nothing personally to merit such a marked distinction—for he was not yet even a Member of Parliament—and that he regarded the offer as arising entirely from the position which his father had gained during his many years of public life. He therefore declined the offer.

Not until the twentieth century did any member of the family receive an honour. George William Palmer himself was given the far rarer distinction (for a back-bencher) of a privy councillorship in 1906, and Walter Palmer became a baronet while an M.P. in 1904, but this became extinct on his death in 1910. Samuel Palmer's eldest son Ernest was also created a baronet in 1916 and a peer as Lord Palmer in 1933; however, his honours were not for political work but for distinguished services to music.

The freedom of the borough and the erection of a statue may have been the honorific climax of George Palmer's career, but it also marked the end of his active life. When the Duke and Duchess of Teck and their two children, who afterwards became Queen Mary and the Earl of Athlone, visited the factory in September 1892, it was William Isaac Palmer and George William Palmer who showed them round. The latter immediately afterwards wrote a full account to his father, informing him with boyish enthusiasm that the corpulent but zestful duchess 'was particularly jolly—we got on fine', while 'H.R.H.', the duke, 'was most considerate about my cold and made me keep my hat on'.

This royal visit happened to coincide with an interesting house-party at Walter Palmer's house at Norcot, on the western outskirts of Reading. His wife, Jean Palmer, was a young woman of great charm who had the gift—and the financial means—of attracting to herself men and women of widely contrasting creative abilities. She is said to have been one of the first to break away from the ponderous dinners of mid-Victorian times and to have invented the artistic London dinner-party and evening entertainment of the nineties.

An important innovation of hers was to discourage the men from lingering over their port, and to hustle them out for coffee and cigarettes with the ladies. Since she encouraged her guests to express their opinions freely, and to air their wit, she became very adept at averting the clashes of temperament that were bound to occur. Her daughter related, with a fine flourish of Victorian name-dropping, how Lord Randolph Churchill had once told her that she was the only hostess who could have Ruskin and Oscar Wilde and Gladstone round the same dinner-table, without their sitting silently and rather suspiciously eyeing each other.

Whether she did ever muster such a distinguished party is to be doubted, but she did bring Jan Kubelik the violinist to England; the young Isadora Duncan danced, barefoot but decently garbed in a long chiffon tunic, on the Palmers' terrace; they took a box at Bayreuth for the Wagner season; and in Paris she once had to endure a rather overpowering *tête-à-tête* on the sofa with Marcel Proust, who interrogated her on Oscar Wilde's private life and compulsively outlined to her a long work he was contemplating on sex abnormality.[14] It is difficult to imagine a group of people further removed from George Palmer's austere domestic environment.

None of their uninhibited ways brushed off on Jean Palmer, however, for her friendships, although intense, were entirely platonic. George Meredith, for example, idealised her as 'Queen Jean', and treated her with what has been called 'an affectionate make-believe of feudal devotion and ornate flattery'.[15] Her relations with Oscar Wilde were equally close, and he, his wife and two sons used to stay regularly at her house. That September when the Tecks visited Reading, she brought together Wilde and Meredith for the first time. These two, with their hard-earned reputations as *raconteurs*, did not much take to one another, although in deference to their hostess they played out their parts without overt hostility.[16] But they were conducted round the biscuit factory separately, Meredith with H. B. Irving, the actor son of Sir Henry Irving, and Wilde next day with the actor-manager Johnston Forbes-Robertson. There Wilde entered his occupation in the visitors' book as 'poet'.

By a horrible coincidence, Wilde returned to within a few yards of the factory little more than three years later, this time handcuffed and in convict dress. At the time of his trial, he had asked Walter Palmer to lend him £400, but this loan was refused. In 1862 the Quaker Elihu Burritt had numbered Reading Gaol among the four establishments in the town which had 'given it an honourable status and reputation at home and abroad', the others being Huntley and Palmers, the Iron Works and Sutton's Seeds. Burritt went on to describe the gaol as 'a very extensive institution for repairing the breaches of society, by punishing criminals and turning them out safer men and women'.[17]

In the 1890s these fanciful aspirations were nowhere near being achieved; and while someone in the factory was annotating his description in the visitors' book with three question marks in blue pencil and was coyly pasting over his name in the roll of distinguished visitors, Wilde himself was enduring the degradations of the prison routine of the day. Very occasionally, when the prison food proved too much for his digestion, a faithful warder, at the risk of dismissal, smuggled in some Ginger Nuts for him.[18] The firm escaped the embarrassment of having to discontinue the Oscar biscuit, for that variety had been intro-

The Second Generation 1874-98: (ii) The Nineties 151

duced in honour of Oscar II of Sweden but never put in the general list.

By then the elder members of the Palmer family were failing rapidly. About a year after William Isaac Palmer's sudden death George Palmer's wife died of bronchitis, in March 1894. It has been said that the outstanding Victorian woman was a blend of the great lady and the intellectual woman.[19] Elizabeth Palmer was not, to the external world at least, an outstanding woman, but merely the wife of an outstanding man; yet she played her unassuming part as governor of the British Schools and of the Kendrick Schools in Reading, and regularly attended their annual outings. She also tried to keep her well-stocked mind active, even though much of her life was taken up with her large household and family and with such charitable works as taking round coal tickets to the poor. If her husband paid more tributes in his public speeches to his mother than to his wife, it should be remembered that he was exceedingly reticent over those matters about which he felt most strongly.

After this last bereavement, George Palmer was never quite the same man again. A cousin of his, Miss Isaac, acted as his companion, and he saw a great deal of his children and the rapidly increasing tribe of grandchildren—for if his daughters-in-law presented him with no more than four grandchildren, his three daughters bore thirteen children between them. Yet as his eyesight began to deteriorate, he gave way to periods of depression. From time to time he went down to the factory, but there was little for him to do there, and he seems to have raised no objection when in August 1894 the firm's London accountants, Price Waterhouse, at the request of the active partners investigated the possibility of converting the business into a joint-stock company.

The accountants' memorandum set out objectively the pros and cons of such a step. The main advantage was that the capital remained unaltered no matter how many deaths or retirements took place. A possible drawback was that the company might 'have thrust upon it persons whom they don't want', although this could happen even in private partnership. However, the matter was taken no further, and next year he had a slight stroke while walking on his Marlston estate; a child of one of the estate workers, Harry Chamberlain, was given sixpence for summoning the carriage to take him back to the house.

At the beginning of 1896 George Palmer therefore proposed to retire as from 31st March, the end of the financial year, and asked George William to see that Samuel was consulted. Samuel immediately wrote to deplore the proposal. Even the effort of writing and the difficulty he now encountered in expressing his ideas did not dim his judgement. The whole family should, he said, 'present a united front to the world'; moreover, he and his brother could well 'have allowed Nature to end our connections and thus have met the views of the numerous critical circle—who will be surprised with your action after waiting so long'.

George Palmer therefore waited for Nature to take its course. In June of the same year he suffered a severe stroke, but his robust constitution helped him to rally, and he was soon able to go out again for short periods. The following May he associated himself with the firm's benefactions to mark Queen Victoria's Diamond Jubilee: a gift of £7000 to the Royal Berkshire Hospital in order to endow a special ward, and the presentation of a day's pay to all employees as well as fifty guineas towards the civic festivities. On 21st August 1897 he died, only a few months short of his eightieth birthday. He was buried in the simple grave which had been prepared for Elizabeth Palmer, in the Friends' Burial Ground at Reading, only a few feet from where Thomas Huntley and his wife, and his own mother, sister and youngest brother lay.

The funeral was an impressive rather than particularly sad occasion. Sixty-five carriages followed the cortège, as well as the 500 men who had been employed in the firm for more than twenty years. The other 5000 employees lined the route along London Road. A large meal followed at the Acacias for the family and certain guests; among the latter was Henry Evans Huntley, now a landowner in Dorset, whom George William Palmer had with characteristic kindness invited to stay with him over the period. The children of the party had such a rumbustious time that their scandalised nurses had to call them to order: one grandchild remembered having fallen out of the mulberry tree on top of a distinguished mourner.

With George Palmer's death, the surviving partners immediately went ahead with preparations for creating a limited company. These preparations did not take long, for on 29th March 1898 Huntley and Palmers Ltd. was formally incorporated. Samuel Palmer took the opportunity of the major reorganisation to make his formal retirement: it was to be fifty years before the last survivor of the second generation —in very different economic and trading conditions—finally severed his connections with the firm.

PART III

The Twentieth Century
1898–1972

'May you live in interesting times'
ANCIENT CHINESE CURSE

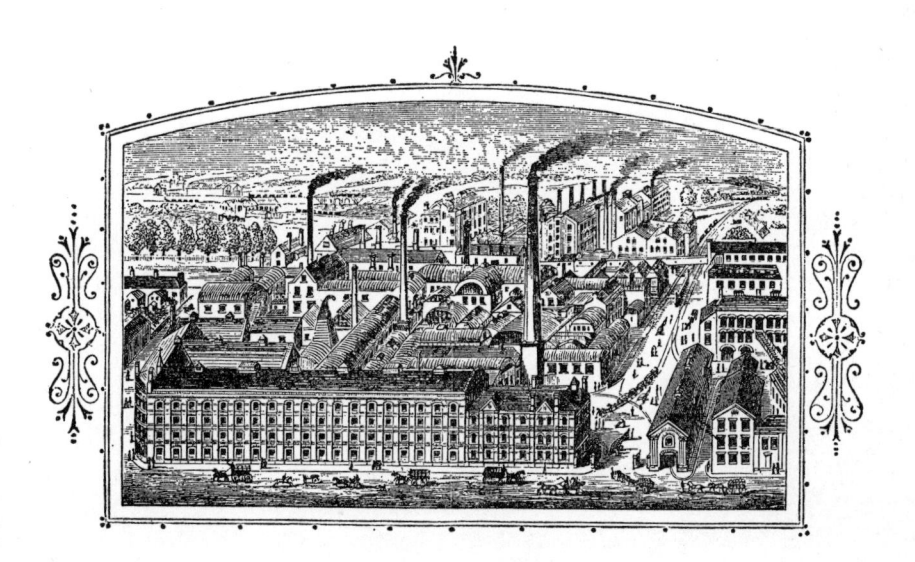

12
Turn of the Century 1898–1906

The relative tranquillity which had prevailed in Huntley and Palmers' affairs during much of the nineteenth century did not continue in the years that followed. On the marketing side the company was to be assailed by unprecedentedly sharp depressions of general demand, shifts in consumers' tastes, the relentless competition of rivals in the home market and overseas, export tariffs and prohibitions, and wars and the aftermath of wars; and on the production side by government intervention, or its threat, over wage rates and working conditions, trade union pressures, shortages of female labour and surpluses of male labour, and difficulties over supplies of materials.

However, this switch from tranquillity to turbulence did not take place all at once in 1898. Until 1914 the company's Chairman reckoned to be hunting, shooting or cricketing (according to the season) three days a week throughout the year, while the senior director was absent for six months at a time on four different occasions. The company's organisation remained unchanged: the working partners merely became working directors. They were joined by William Bullivant Williams, the firm's indispensable 'Confidential Manager' who dealt with financial affairs; his election to the Board was a formality, as he had no doubt sat in on partners' meetings for many years.

They all maintained the same functions. In Chapter 11 it was explained how five of the partners were at Reading: George William Palmer in charge of the offices, Howard Palmer of manufacturing and packing, Alfred Palmer of engineering, Walter Palmer of the scientific department, and Albert Palmer of tins and labels. Ernest and Charles Palmer were in the London office, the one being responsible for the London trade and export business and the other for the Continental business and ingredients purchasing. William Lea, a son of the former chief traveller Henry Lea, was company secretary but never became a member of the Board. The Chief Cashier was Thomas Huntley, a great-grandson of his namesake the Burford schoolmaster: having joined the firm in 1864, he retired in 1910. The last two officials were very little concerned with policy matters.

Similarly, the financial changes following the company's establishment were largely consequential. The assets and the net profits still accrued to the family: paradoxically, far more was now to be taken out of the firm in dividends than had been through partners' drawings. As with most Victorian partnerships of high standing, the partners' capital of £350,000, and the undrawn profits amounting to an equivalent sum, had represented only a fraction of the business's true value, and hence a substantial hidden reserve: in 1891–2 net profit, of over £200,000, had been equivalent to nearly 60 per cent of capital.

The new company's share capital was now fixed at a more realistic figure of £2,400,000, by the addition on the assets side of a massive goodwill figure of £1,650,000. This was slightly larger than the capital employed by the wonder firm of the age, Lever Bros. Ltd., whose turnover of about £1,300,000 in 1898, must have been almost exactly the same as that of Huntley and Palmers. Even in 1905, when Lever Bros.' turnover had risen to nearly £1,600,000—compared with Huntley and Palmers' £1,400,000—on a capital of £4 millions, Huntley and Palmers still ranked (in terms of capital) as 38th among British manufacturing companies, while Lever Bros. came 23rd.[1]

The bachelor William Isaac Palmer had disposed of his shareholdings in such a way that the limited company's capital—of £1 million in ordinary shares (and also) £1,400,000 in 4 per cent preference shares—was now divided equally between the two branches of the family: George Palmer's three sons on the one side and Samuel Palmer's four sons on the other. The Articles of Association specifically referred to 'George Palmer' and 'Samuel Palmer' shares: each type was to be offered for sale to the same branch before being offered to the other.

It thus resembled a large, and apparently growing, number of British companies of the day which were essentially partnerships (for the most part family ones) under another name. So declared a committee set up to look into company law in 1906, which in its report cited Huntley and Palmers and Crosse & Blackwell as examples. The committee felt that firms of this type should be clearly defined as 'private companies' by law and be forbidden to offer their shares and debentures for sale to the public. After these proposals became law in the Companies Act of 1907, Huntley and Palmers amended its Articles of Association so as to become a private company.[2]

The directors, for all their ability, undoubtedly suffered from knowing too little of how other firms worked. For several years they did not even elect a Chairman from among themselves, but simply took the chair by turns, in apparently random order. Not until early in 1904 did Ernest Palmer bring this matter before the Board. Himself a director of the Great Western Railway, and thus possessing a greater knowledge of outside commercial practice than his Reading colleagues, he proposed the appointment of a Chairman and a Deputy Chairman, to allow the company to 'adopt a more continuous and comprehensive line of policy', such as 'every other business, private and public, without exception has found to be both desirable and essential'.

The only possible candidate for the chairmanship, the senior director George William Palmer, was absent on one of his six-month voyages round the world, but in October he was elected to the post, with Ernest Palmer as Vice-Chairman and Howard Palmer as Deputy Chairman. Still a Member of Parliament, he resigned his Reading seat about the same time because of his deafness. No doubt for the same reason, he remained as Chairman only until the middle of 1906.

Below Board level, the directors did not establish an entirely satisfactory managerial structure. True, they appointed a Committee of Managers, to make recommendations to the Board and to comment on all memoranda sent up to the Board from below. They also engaged several well-qualified men from outside to strengthen the top management. The most noteworthy was Herbert Pretty, who joined in 1901 as Managing Director. As a young man he had worked for Joseph Leete, and had revealed his powers as a brilliant linguist and a highly capable traveller; later he had departed to manage his father-in-law's salt-mines in Cheshire. Now in his mid-forties, he was to put his experience and capacity to good use within the company. Three of the existing senior managers, concerned with manufacturing and packing, engineering, and the London Office respectively, were simultaneously made Managing Directors.

Despite their titles, none of the four had a seat on the Board; at first they attended regularly after the directors had concluded their private business, but after a time were summoned only when required. The company's solicitors immediately vetoed the arrangement, which infringed the Articles of Association since Managing Directors could be appointed only from among members of the Board. These four were thereupon re-named Assistant Directors.

All the same, neither the Committee of Managers nor the Assistant Directors were given the full responsibility that was their due. Collectively, they were consulted on many matters but made few important decisions. Individually, too, each tended to look to his departmental director rather than act on his own initiative. This practice helped to perpetuate the division of departments into self-contained units. It also tended to slow up decision-making, since apart from William Bullivant Williams, directors did not attend every day. No more than two of them were expected to be in at any given time, including Saturdays, except for the Board meetings once a fortnight.

These organisational weaknesses were really subordinate to the principal shortcoming of this period: that many of the underlying production and marketing problems went largely unresolved. For the company had no effective standard of comparison. On the production side many of the machines and buildings were patently obsolescent. In 1902 an *ad hoc* committee of managers, with the Chief Engineer Cyril Byham as chairman, did investigate the possibility of overhauling the existing plant, so as to speed up output; one or two minor improvements followed. About the same time the company introduced a Wages and Tonnages Book, to keep costs under monthly review, and laid down 'standard' wages per ton. These measures were only of limited effectiveness.

Then three years later, in 1905, it called in a firm of valuers, Wheatley Kirk Price & Co., to put a valuation on all its assets. That firm concluded that the assets were at the moment over-valued, and would therefore have to be written down by over £100,000. It then went on to lecture the company on the folly of keeping its machines in such condition as to prolong their lives unduly; there was thus no incentive to discard ones that were obsolescent. Moreover (it continued) even when machines had to be replaced, instead of introducing new and improved patterns the company merely copied the old ones, because they were known to be durable and reliable. These old machines would therefore become progressively uneconomic as time went on.

As to the ovens, 'it is incredible that the last word of invention should date thirty years back', when the factories north of the river had been erected: 'in no other trade can this policy hold'. Worse still, the South Factory, which dated from 1857, was now in such a ramshackle state as to be hopelessly inefficient, so that its demolition would realise considerable savings in costs. 'We look forward', declared the valuers prophetically, 'to seeing a new complete factory in which, for all ordinary biscuits, the operations will be automatic from the flour mixing, through cutting, baking and delivery into the packing room, ready for packing.'

The directors, although not unmindful of these strictures, refused to undertake the massive reorganisation that would have been involved. Consequently, the book value of plant and buildings actually fell from £486,500 in 1905 to £428,000 in 1914 because depreciation exceeded new investment. Even in 1910 they were still hesitating whether to rebuild the South Factory, since a new building would cost up to £100,000 and the present one was felt to be useful for making the large number of slow-selling biscuits on the list, in small batches. In fact, they could have discontinued with advantage many of the 400 varieties they were making. Peek Frean at that time was operating a 'black list' of slow sellers, which travellers and customers were discouraged from ordering so as to hasten their disappearance.

Thus although several manufacturers of biscuit machinery, notably Vicars and Joseph Baker (afterwards Baker Perkins), were supplying competitors with up-to-date machines, Huntley and Palmers persisted in adhering to the homespun policy of making and reconditioning its own machinery in the engineering department, which Alfred Palmer managed with conspicuous technical success. It therefore made only marginal improvements: in 1911, for instance, the cutting machines were speeded up by being adapted to the 'skip' motion and by the introduction of an automatic dough cleaner. This was the sum of innovations during the first quarter of the twentieth century. Not until 1925 was the South Factory closed, and the first automatic machines for standard types of biscuits had to wait until 1939.

As to the packing, biscuits were normally packed in tins or in wooden boxes lined with tin: however convenient to the company, the arrangement was wasteful for the retailer who had to weigh out quantities and suffer some loss on the broken biscuits invariably left in the bottom. Between 1901 and 1903 the Board twice considered, and rejected, proposals to wrap certain biscuits in paper packets. Only when the company was clearly shown to be losing to its rivals a substantial volume of trade did it permit the 'experiment'—but for overseas trade alone—of offering ½ lb. and 1 lb. packets, packing in 14 lb. tins, at 4s. 8d. (23½p.) a hundredweight extra: the same price as that charged by competitors.

Early in 1905 for the first time it offered Breakfast biscuits—a leading variety—to home customers in packets, with startling results. Whereas only 460,000 packets were put up in 1904–5, the number in 1905–6 was over 1,675,000; by 1913–14 the number topped the 5½ million mark. Further dramatic increases were held back only by shortage of space for packing. This demonstrated a fundamental paradox: the undoubtedly obsolete South Factory was maintained in existence because it was useful for making minute runs of quite unimportant biscuits, while the public demand for the fastest-selling types in packets remained unsatisfied because no space was available.

Again, the public were beginning to demand assortments rather than single varieties, not only in the Christmas decorated tins, but also all the year round. Yet a shilling tin of Choice Assorted biscuits was not put on the market until 1907. Public taste was also moving away from the hard semi-sweet biscuits, on which Huntley and Palmers had built their reputation, towards softer 'short-eating' varieties, like the shortbreads in which the Scottish firms held the market. In 1903 it introduced a shortbread-type Monarch biscuit, which did not prove much of a success. Chocolate biscuits, too, were becoming generally so popular that in 1906 Joseph Baker's, when canvassing for machinery orders, had to remind the company of the large turnover which rival firms were building up in this line. The company delayed until 1909 before even arranging for some of its own biscuits to be coated with chocolate at Fry's Bristol factory; although of superb quality, they sold only in minute quantities, as they cost 2s. 6d. ($12\frac{1}{2}$p.) a pound compared with rivals' 1s. (5p.). From 1912 onwards, therefore, the firm was compelled to begin manufacture itself, with plant from Joseph Baker's and a manager who had learnt his trade at Cadbury's.

These new demands for packets, assortments and chocolate biscuits, were irksome because they did not fit into Huntley and Palmers' traditional methods of production. Instead of altering their production methods, however, the company chose to side-step the issue by putting more and more effort into the overseas trade, where tastes on the whole were slower to change. Net sales overseas more than doubled between 1898–9 and 1913–14 from £372,000 to £771,000: a sharp increase from 28 per cent of aggregate turnover to 48 per cent. In these years the company gave absolute priority to export orders, everything else being sacrificed to the need for catching steamers.

Such a policy seemed vindicated by a calculation made in 1906, which showed that the export department's trade was earning 14·3 per cent profit on turnover, and the Continental trade 8·3 per cent, compared with 7·1 per cent at home. (Only in the United States, where the New York agents F. D. Moulton & Co. had taken over in 1902 from Edward Valpy, was there a net loss, of 9·8 per cent.) It was further gratifying that the whole of the £400,000 increase in trade occurred in the highly lucrative export department, since the modest increase on the Continent —achieved against great odds by the veteran Joseph Leete and his eleven travellers—was no more than balancing the decline of trade at home.

That these overseas markets might soon begin to evaporate through a collapse of the international monetary system was quite unthinkable: yet the fact remained that the company, by neglecting the home trade, was giving rival firms a foothold in its markets that it could never dislodge. McVitie & Price and Macfarlane Lang were by the early 1900s establishing factories on the outskirts of London, and Peek Frean, after some decades of torpor, was once again coming to life.

During those decades it had come under the domination of the co-founder James Peek's son-in-law Thomas Stone and Thomas's two sons: an unknown genius dubbed the unprepossessing trio Gravestone, Grindstone and Cod's Head and Shoulders, and their era as the Stone Age. They had in truth helped to ossify Peek Frean's growth by a combination of poor judgement and an overbearing attitude to those inside and outside the firm alike. For instance, they rather short-sightedly insisted on going after quantity rather than quality in production. Meanwhile John Carr (whom we met in Chapter 6) remained quietly in the background, but by the time that Peek Frean became a limited company in 1901 he and his two sons Ellis and Arthur were in full control. Having recruited some junior directors as able as themselves, they were soon energetically rebuilding their position in the quality biscuit market.

As a result, whereas in 1901 the value of Huntley and Palmers' home trade was between two and a half and three times as great as Peek Frean's, by 1912 the two firms were equal and the next year Peek Frean was 10 per cent ahead. In the provinces that firm had forty-nine salesmen; not until 1906 did Huntley and Palmers increase the number of its country travellers from twenty-three to thirty. However, when these extra travellers began to cover neglected areas of the country, trade began to improve, in Scotland by as much as 22 per cent.

Peek Frean became also a pace-setter in advertising. Since the 1890s popular daily and weekly periodicals and poster hoardings had sprung up, to create vast opportunities for the widespread advertising of consumer goods. Pears' and Sunlight soap and certain brands of tea, for example, became household words throughout the country. Huntley and Palmers declined to follow this trend. The opulent buyers of high-quality biscuits were, in the company's view, unlikely to be greatly swayed by advertising, for (metaphorically speaking) if the wine was good enough, the bush was superfluous. Herbert Foxwell, then Professor of Political Economy at University College, London, and the son of a wealthy provincial tradesman, remembered with pride in the 1920s that as a child he was taught never to buy a product that was advertised. 'Most of our best people never, or very rarely, advertise', he informed an American correspondent.[3]

To be sure, the company did indulge in a few discreet notices from time to time, no longer in *The Times* or *The Friend*, but in even less strident organs, like the *London School Board Gazette*. As early as 1902 Peek Frean was launching its outstandingly successful Pat-a-Cake biscuit with some very effective advertising in the halfpenny newspapers and elsewhere. 'For goodness' sake, eat Pat-a-Cake', prominently displayed on the manufacturers' delivery vans, became the catchword of the times, and for a while even superseded the immortal rhyme about the Pickwick, the Owl and the Waverley Pen. Huntley and Palmers hurredly brought out a rival, the Cinderella, once again giving priority to the overseas trade. The name was singularly ill-chosen, for the Cinderella, after a brief moment in the limelight, soon retired among the waifs and strays at the bottom of the list; for years it was preserved from extinction only because it was included in various assortments.

The Board did not lightly embark on defensive advertising, in spite of strong pressure from departmental managers. It had already rejected a proposal to advertise in newspapers throughout India and the Far East, even though nearly 60 per cent of the export department's lucrative trade was to that area. However, in the aftermath of the Cinderella débâcle, it did agree to a campaign at home and was more fortunate than it deserved. Its advertising agents, Mather & Crowther, were adept in securing favourable 'position spaces' opposite interesting articles in the quality press. They began by concentrating on the Breakfast biscuit, now seventh in popularity (after Petit Beurre, Fancy and Thin Lunch, Marie, Osborne, and Ginger Nut) and still without a rival; sales increased by over 40 per cent in the first year of the campaign. By 1905 the company's advertising expenditure was beginning to match that of Peek Frean, and six years later had doubled to £25,000.

The company did not attempt to copy the ingenuity of some of Peek Frean's sales stunts. In May 1904 that firm treated some 20,000 London retailers to a free outing at the Crystal Palace; there the varied programme of events included a moving picture showing biscuit-making in all its stages—perhaps the earliest film ever of an industrial process. Yet as the *Daily Mail* pointed out dryly the next day, it seemed curious that the Crystal Palace's luncheon rooms should sell Huntley and Palmers' biscuits exclusively. Two years later Peek Frean sent out nearly 200,000 picture postcards to housewives up and down the country. These contained mysterious propositions—sometimes misinterpreted by touchy husbands—which turned out to be free offers to anyone buying a packet of assortments.[4] However, even Fortnum & Mason's and other West End stores now felt obliged to stock Peek Frean's and other rivals' biscuits because of the demand which their publicity generated.

Huntley and Palmers' marketing problems at home were not confined to inadequate sales forces and advertising allocations. In 1907 the Home Trade Manager, H. J. Morton, reported how the old-fashioned family grocer was for the most part giving way to the 'company shop', such as Lipton's or the Home and Colonial, or to the 'pushing' independent or multiple grocer. Those were primarily interested in high profits, rapid turnover and cash sales. As they bought once a fortnight and sold out quickly, they were not worried if the contents of some biscuit tins deteriorated after a few months: McVitie & Price's biscuits were said to emit a peculiar smell when the tins were not opened for some time. Here the fact that the contents of Huntley and Palmers' tins kept good indefinitely was irrelevant. The company in fact had to rely increasingly on wholesalers, who did not have the same personal interest in pushing the sales of any one firm's biscuits.

By their failure to move with the times in the ways described above, the company was really concentrating on its short-term profits at the expense of the long term. In the thirteen years 1901–2 to 1913–14 it made £2,300,000 profit, nearly three times as much as Peek Frean, but the latter was creating a springboard for further growth denied to the former. Huntley and Palmers appeared as solid as the Bank of England, at a time of crisis for many family firms, protected as they were from public scrutiny by law. Of these making labels for the company, White & Pike went into liquidation in 1905, while the de la Rue brothers brought their firm to the edge of bankruptcy by highly irresponsible behaviour.[5]

Sir John Clapham, the economic historian, has suggested that 'the average attitude of British business about the turn of the century was rather too defensive'. A later economist has sought to break down this attitude into such characteristics as undue caution, inertia, excessive stubborn self-confidence, complacency, a desire for a quiet life, a deliberate cult of amateurism, and a sceptical mistrust of science.[6]

The Palmer family undoubtedly possessed some of these characteristics, but their worst fault was to mortgage the future by drawing all the profits. In 1898 they had had £388,000 undrawn partnership profits retained in the business and earning interest at 5 per cent: these had been converted into share capital. Since then the whole of the profits, down to the nearest round sum, were distributed annually as dividends. In 1904 Charles Palmer was sufficiently alarmed by this practice to propose that a Reserve Fund should be set up forthwith. He was outvoted, and no General Reserve was set up until the 1920s, all capital expenditure—such as H factory, built in 1897–1900 at the cost of £48,000—being borne out of current earnings.

Each of the family directors, except for Ernest Palmer, who lived in Grosvenor Crescent, London, owned a country estate, mainly in Berkshire. These estates had been bought with money drawn out years before and bequeathed to them by the first generation, and running costs were not so high as to make it essential for the profits to be distributed to the limit. They were not consciously milking the company in order to keep up their status as country gentlemen; they simply saw no need to set money aside for expensive and perhaps risky investment. Yet this possession of landed property inevitably invites comparison with the Forsytes.

True, the generations of John Galsworthy's fictitious dynasty more or less spanned those of the Palmers, and some at least of the second generation underwent the same conflict between self-centred provincialism and more outward-looking attitudes. Galsworthy would have made much of the idiosyncracies which contemporaries noted about certain Palmers: A, for instance, who used to rap the table at Board meetings so violently that his fellow-directors were alarmed for the safety of his signet ring, or B, delicate when a child, who was so encouraged to 'look after himself' in a robust adulthood that he never asserted himself in the firm. C was feared for his bitter tongue, while D was described by an associate—not in the firm—as 'difficult, intolerant, snobbish'.

What the author might have overlooked was that these characteristics were irrelevant by the side of the powerful family stability which existed. It was no paradox that any serious difference of opinion in the Board was ended in the firm's becoming stronger and not weaker; disputes were never pressed to the point of no return. Besides, technically they knew their jobs and the attitudes they struck while carrying them out could be forgiven. A director regularly visited Huntley Boorne and Stevens in order to inspect the design of new Christmas tins for the coming season. One year the star tin was in the shape of a vase; to show this off to best advantage, the designer had constructed a pedestal that had been roughly decorated. The director looked for a moment at the display; with the flat of his hand he sent the vase flying. Pointing at the pedestal he said tersely: 'We'll have that one.' He saw what no one else had seen: that the vase might have been moderately popular, but the pedestal, suitably worked up, proved a winner, selling out rapidly in each of the four years or so it was kept in production. And the Christmas trade was the one area where the firm had a definite competitive advantage at home.

Yet beneath the whiskers, frock-coats and little displays of self-assertiveness there was little in common between the two clans. The Palmers were of far greater affluence and distinction than the dogged and unimaginative Forsytes, who were solely 'middlemen' of wealth rather than its creators. Moreover, having come of genuine yeoman stock—which the Forsytes, for all their pretentiousness, had not—they merged naturally into the countryside as they followed their country pursuits.

Their refusal to establish a Reserve Fund in the early years of the new century can therefore be viewed as a symptom rather than a cause both of the failure to undertake new investment, and of the apparent reluctance to discard nineteenth-century attitudes. As Chapter 13 will show, in the second half of the sixteen-year period between 1898 and 1914, under the joint pressures of an economic recession and greatly intensified competition, the company did move a little way towards more progressive policies than in the first half to 1906.

13
Pre-War 1906–14

In June 1906 George William Palmer retired from the chairmanship. The Board took the opportunity to pay him some handsome tributes, singling out for praise his 'intimate knowledge of the necessities of the business', as well as his 'conspicuous courtesy, tact and ability'. With the recent coming into power of a Liberal government, he had been offered a peerage; having declined it, he had accepted the far rarer distinction, for a back-bencher, of a Privy Councillorship.[1] Thus public honours, combined with his emeritus position in the company, turned him at fifty-five into an elder statesman, a role which he played to perfection.

He exercised a strong unifying influence not merely in the Board room, but throughout the family as well. To him the family owed much of the close-knit feeling which characterised its succeeding generations. Every new year after it was rebuilt in 1898 he peopled his large house at Marlston with a week-long house party of up to seventeen nephews, nieces and young second cousins, on the female as well as the male sides.

They all enjoyed themselves greatly playing billiards, hockey and hide-and-seek, having a formal party and acting in plays such as Thackeray's *The Rose and the Ring*. Yet the enjoyment was not quite unalloyed, for each had to take turns at sitting next to him for meals. Somewhat peppery by disposition, very deaf and not a parent himself, he never became resigned to the unpredictable ways of children, and the mealtime sessions proved to be equally difficult for both sides. Perhaps it was the same feeling of strain that led a niece by marriage to leave behind, at the end of a short visit, a written list of breakages caused by her three young children.

In his place as Chairman the Board elected Howard Palmer, with Charles Palmer as his deputy. For many years Howard Palmer had been centrally placed at Reading in overall control of manufacturing and packing, and since 1904 he had been Deputy Chairman. He rapidly introduced certain reforms. For the first time he arranged for a full report on the company's progress to be presented at the shareholders' annual meeting. Since the shareholders were also the directors, in previous years George William Palmer as Chairman had contented himself with a few general remarks before formally moving the acceptance of the accounts. To compile his report the new Chairman called for regular reports from each of his managers; those of the Home Trade Manager and the Export Manager (which have survived) are particularly informative on every side of their work.

Howard Palmer also called for comprehensive monthly statistics of overseas trade to be kept. These specified not only the actual figures for each country but also the percentage they represented of total biscuit and cake exports from the United Kingdom. It was he who instructed the auditors to calculate the relative profitability of each market, as described in the previous chapter. Office methods were by then cumbersome and outdated, so he had loose cards substituted for bound ledgers and introduced addressograph machines.

He also overhauled part of the company's administration. He obtained authority from the Board for himself to sanction on its behalf at any time items of expenditure 'necessary for the prompt and proper conduct of the company's business'. He had Herbert Pretty appointed as the first General Manager, and made the Assistant Directors keep formal minutes of their meetings. These were chaired by Alfred Palmer's son Eustace, who had become an apprentice on coming down from Oxford in 1900 and had been elected to the Board in 1903; other directors attended from time to time. A few years later he decided to take the chair himself, and renamed the meeting the Chairman's Committee. He thereby helped to speed up decisions and give the Assistant Directors greater authority.

These reforms, useful as they were, did not basically alter the direction in which the company was moving. The value of home sales continued to fall at roughly the same rate, and that of overseas sales to rise. Whether Howard Palmer with unrestricted power would have wished for a wholesale recasting of production and marketing policies is not clear, but in any case, as the youngest director but two, he was still subject to his colleagues' overall control. Most of them let him go his own way. George William, Walter and Albert Palmer were preoccupied by their outside interests, and Alfred Palmer, left to his own devices in the engineering department, did not interfere much outside it. The pair most likely to press their views on policy matters were his two London-based brothers Ernest and Charles, and as he consolidated his hold on the company, Howard Palmer seems to have found their presence on the Board somewhat cramping.

'There goes the London contingent!' he would mutter as they departed for the metropolis, with satisfaction at his release from serious outside intervention until the next Board meeting. Yet the London contingent could have made a more effective contribution than it did towards dispelling the atmosphere of provincial seclusion at Reading. Ernest Palmer had resigned the vice-chairmanship in 1906 on being appointed Deputy Chairman of the Great Western Railway, and he later became Vice-President of the Royal College of Music. He was thus constantly meeting people of many kinds, and was able to see the company's problems in a fresh light. He had been the one who had told the Board it should have a Chairman, and in 1913, when rival biscuit manufacturers seemed much more able to get new varieties on to the market, he proposed setting up a committee to overcome the 'lack of an effective connecting link between the commercial side of the business and those actually concerned in the production of novelties'.

Charles Palmer for his part had inherited his father's skill in purchasing ingredients at a time when many large firms, notably J. Lyons, the caterers and food manufacturers, were competing in the market for high-quality ingredients at keen prices. Like his father he was a juror at several international food exhibitions. In 1906 he was awarded the Greek Order of the Redeemer for his services to trade with Greece: his bulk purchases of that country's currant and fruit crops represented a valuable support to its weak economy. Among the suggestions he made to the Board was for the establishment of a workers' canteen (see Chapter 15) and of a Reserve Fund, as mentioned earlier. These were both turned down: perhaps because he felt himself so isolated, in 1912 he resigned from the deputy chairmanship and was succeeded by Eustace Palmer.

The changes in organisation which followed Howard Palmer's election to the chairmanship took place at the outset of the difficult economic conditions of the later Edwardian era. Huntley and Palmers Ltd. had been launched in a trade boom, which had turned out to be short-lived, so that the years up to 1902 were remembered as a peak which was followed by a protracted decline.[2]

Between 1903 and 1905 trade throughout Britain was said to be more depressed than for at least a generation—according to some authorities, since the Crimean War, when poor harvests and high commodity prices, combined with heavy taxation, had provoked a sharp consumer recession. The Co-operative Wholesale Society at Manchester stated that purchasing power generally had so diminished as to affect even the demand for sugar. Now regarded as a necessity, sugar was being consumed at twice the rate per head of fifty years ago, at over $1\frac{1}{2}$ lb. a week; yet in 1905 consumption fell by more than 10 per cent compared with

1904. Sales of luxuries such as biscuits were therefore even more likely to suffer, and when this happened, biscuit manufacturers' reactions were not unexpected: to demand protection from foreign competition, and industry-wide collaboration as an alternative to a damaging commercial war.

As to protection, Britain was still a free-trade country, importing goods without restriction from abroad, although having to pay tariffs on her exported manufactures in most overseas countries. George William Palmer, although a life-long Liberal free-trader, was so determined to support home industries that he insisted on all possible equipment, down to the office furniture, vehicles and even fire-fighting apparatus, being made within the factory.[3]

The issue of protection for home industry came to a head in Reading at the parliamentary by-election of 1904 for George William Palmer's successor. The Conservative candidate, C. E. Keyser, declared that Britain's export trade in biscuits, especially with American and Continental countries, was being gradually strangled by those countries' high tariffs. Worse still, he continued, biscuit sales at home, where Huntley and Palmers had had—with some platform licence—'a monopoly', was being undermined by the French manufacturers' practice of dumping biscuits, notably sugar wafers. Guillout, the Parisian manufacturers, were said to be offering for sale in Reading itself sugar wafers at a price nearly a penny a pound cheaper than those made on the spot. Other Continental firms were also making inroads into the British market, including the French quality firm Lefèvre-Utile.[4]

However, although over 1500 of Huntley and Palmers' employees were estimated to have the vote, Mr. Keyser's arguments left them unmoved, and instead they elected the Liberal candidate Rufus Isaacs—the celebrated advocate who later became Marquess of Reading. Guillout's attempt about this time to manufacture in England, too, proved a failure after a few years. Indeed, Huntley and Palmers' Board, although Conservatives except for George William Palmer, opposed protection as calculated on balance to harm the company's trade: the higher cost of ingredients would more than outweigh the relief from foreign dumping. The supporters of Joseph Chamberlain's Tariff Reform proposals about this time set up a Tariff Commission. This commission called for evidence from biscuit manufacturers, among other business men, but received no encouragement from Reading. The company had earlier protested when in 1901 Lord Salisbury's Government levied a duty of $\frac{1}{2}$d. a pound on sugar, although it was entitled to drawback (or a refund of the tariff) on its substantial volume of exports. The nominal duty on imported wheat and flour, introduced in the following year, made less impact on Huntley and Palmers, most of whose wheat came from home sources: nevertheless, it was very relieved when that duty was repealed a year later.

The second reaction of biscuit manufacturers to the economic depression was a movement towards co-operation by setting up a trade association. At first sight, biscuit-making did not appear to be a promising area for cartels, or collective agreements by manufacturers to control markets, output and prices, for as Alfred Marshall pointed out in his *Industry and Trade* (discovering a hitherto unnoticed resemblance between biscuits and ladies' hats) there 'versatility is demanded as well as high quality'.[5] Nevertheless, informal consultation between individual firms on such topics as prices and discounts was not much younger than wholesale biscuit-making itself.

Chapter 6 showed how even in the 1840s firms were regularly swapping information about their own and competitors' prices and were complaining bitterly to one another when third parties indulged in such practices as 'cutting up the trade'. Huntley and Palmers, whose irreproachable business conduct earned the respect, if not always the emulation, of its rivals, was often appealed to in this way, but invariably told the complainants that they should speak to the offender direct. Thus there had never been true 'perfect competition' (so beloved of economic theorists) in the biscuit trade, which despite its 'versatility' resembled other nineteenth-century industries by indulging in what Sir John Clapham has called 'a good deal of quiet price-fixing without formal association'.[6]

Biscuit firms had taken joint action to meet specific challenges from outside, such as the 1877 joint delegation to the Home Secretary about the Factories Bill mentioned in Chapter 10. Twenty years later they were becoming restive at the increasing power of the Federation of Grocers' Associations, which was exerting pressure on them over such matters as discounts and charges for returned tins. Things came to a head in the early years of the century, when the extra capacity created in England by the Scottish firms, combined with the gathering recession, began to pose grave problems of over-production relative to demand. 'Association is almost always a sign of tribulation', the historian of Unilever has written of a similar reaction by the soap manufacturers.[7] The current and prospective trials of the biscuit industry were plain enough when the Association of Biscuit Manufacturers was set up in 1903.

The Association's three objects were to promote the interests of the trade through common policies and combined action; to keep an eye on legislation affecting the trade; and to create a central organisation through which grievances could be ventilated and cleared up. Its thirty-five original members reveal the structure of the biscuit industry at that time. In geographical terms sixteen were in Scotland, six in Ireland and nine in the North of England. Only four had head offices in southern England, and none of these was in the 'quality' range: the National Bakery Co. Ltd. in London, Palmer Bros. of Bristol, Serpell's of Reading and the Cornubia Biscuit Ltd. (Messrs. Hosken, Trevethick and Polkinthorn) of Hayle, near Penzance, in Cornwall.

In size, only Jacob's of Dublin (with over 2000 employees), McVitie & Price, Macfarlane Lang and Carr's of Carlisle (with about 1500 employees each) and William Crawford's were medium-sized firms; the remainder were small, with localised markets and often precarious prospects. Two went bankrupt in 1905, and in the following year Middlemass's profits amounted only to £78 and those of Mackenzie & Mackenzie to £41. The former remained in business until it closed down in the depression of the 1930s, but the latter went into liquidation in 1911 and was bought up by William Crawford's. Again, in 1909 Cornubia's profits were scarcely adequate to cover its preference dividend.

What of the two large-scale firms in the industry? Peek Frean (with 3000 employees) declined to join the Association since its own system of discounts did not fit into the general pattern; however, it very cordially received delegates from the Association and assured them of every co-operation. Huntley and Palmers (with 6000 employees), on the other hand, despite a personal approach from H. O. Serpell of the Reading firm, remained aloof and flatly declined even to meet a deputation.

The company's refusal to co-operate was perhaps understandable in the circumstances. Its highly centralised system of decision-making made the working directors quite unwilling to share with outside firms decisions on such matters as prices and discounts. Huntley and Palmers was still the acknowledged price leader among the quality firms, and by adhering consistently to a policy of stable prices (stable, that is, in relation to demand), had probably saved the industry from a disastrous cycle of price wars, bankruptcies and forced amalgamations. However, the rigid price structure that tended to alter only with changes in raw material prices and other costs, had forced firms to compete by other means, chiefly through offering higher discounts to distributors.

The retailer's basic margin between the manufacturer's bulk price and the retail price to the public amounted only to 15 per cent. Most biscuit firms granted handsome additional discounts. Huntley and Palmers offered none at all to nearly half its 3600 retail accounts in London and as much as 5 per cent only to one-sixth of these. Only in 1902 did it consent to offer even an additional $1\frac{1}{4}$ per cent discount for settlement in cash within a month; not until 1908 did it raise this 1¼ per cent to 2½ per cent and lower the minimum volume of trade at which it was willing to grant a 2½ per cent quantity discount. In the poor state of business prevailing in 1907–9 it ought not to have been surprised that nearly a quarter of all its accounts remained unpaid over one month.

Now that the company was having to rely more and more on wholesalers, the discount it offered them—5 per cent plus 1¼ per cent for cash—scarcely covered their working expenses, notably the expenses of operating many small accounts. Moreover, it was derisory compared with the 15 per cent granted by Carr's and William Crawford's and the 12½ per cent of Peek Frean, Jacob's and Macfarlane Lang. Thus Huntley and Palmers was placing a great strain on the loyalty of its distributors.

As the price leader, the company was increasingly irritated by the current activities of Peek Frean. As early as 1902 the Carr family was extending its aggressive policy into the area of prices and discounts, which for so many years the two companies had 'harmonised'. That year Huntley and Palmers happened to learn from certain customers that Peek Frean was offering a 7½ per cent discount for monthly settlement, and straightway wrote with some asperity to ask if this was true. Peek Frean retorted that while the trade generally would benefit from some uniformity in prices, each individual company should be free to make its own terms over discounts. When the Palmer directors requested a personal meeting to thrash out the whole matter, they found themselves in the novel and disagreeable situation of being rebuffed.

The subsequent coolness between the two companies did not preclude them from agreeing on a price reduction for certain lines in 1904; yet each took pains to inform Association members that its hand had been forced by the other. The next round in the contest occurred three years later, when Huntley and Palmers curtly refused Peek Frean's request for a general price increase to take account of the continued high cost of ingredients. The company claimed that Peek Frean and other manufacturers had in the meantime increased their discounts so greatly that net prices to traders could not longer be compared as in the past. This refusal struck Peek Frean where it hurt most, in its profits, which in 1908 were little more than enough to pay the preference dividend, and therefore put the firm in the same category as the insignificant Cornubia.

In the distinctly chilly exchange of letters which followed, each party stubbornly failed to grasp the other's point of view. When, therefore, at the beginning of 1909 the Association thought of asking Huntley and Palmers to agree to an industry-wide increase, Peek Frean on being consulted had to admit that it was not on the same friendly footing with the company as previously. Although Association members recalled earlier snubs from Reading, they did steel themselves to send a deputation to Huntley and Palmers; this time the company did not decline to receive them.

There had been nothing Machiavellian in the company's lack of cordiality towards the Association, yet Howard Palmer could not have sought a more opportune moment to press home his views. The deputation arrived in Reading to discuss biscuit prices, for the cost of flour was at its highest since 1891, but they found themselves talking about discounts instead. He brushed aside the contention that the present high discounts arose from past refusals to adjust prices often enough, and asserted that his firm and Peek Frean were 'in honour bound to consult together before altering discounts'. However, he was willing to propose a *quid pro quo*. He would agree to confer in future over prices and other matters of common interest, on condition that Association members fixed their maximum discounts at $12\frac{1}{2}$ per cent, which would have to include the $1\frac{1}{4}$ per cent for cash.

By then some Scottish firms were offering over 20 per cent and even up to 25 per cent to van agents in Glasgow, while $17\frac{1}{2}$ per cent was not uncommon in England. This, then, was a bold proposal. Yet he meant exactly what he said: as he commented privately afterwards, 'I suppose that no such conferences have ever taken place in the biscuit trade before, and I hope there may be no necessity of their being frequently repeated.' His hopes were not to be fulfilled, for in the years to come he found himself increasingly conferring with, and giving a lead to, the rest of the industry.

The agreed advance in prices duly took place a few months later, but on the question of a maximum discount the Association was split right down the centre. Nine member firms—broadly speaking, those of medium size making quality biscuits—unconditionally accepted Huntley and Palmers' terms, no doubt with some relief at a truce in the discount war. These firms (later reduced to seven by Mackenzie & Mackenzie's going into liquidation and Middlemass's resignation) became the Executive Committee of the Association, while the smaller firms at the cheaper end of the scale which refused to accept the new discounts broke away to form the so-called London Branch. This agreed to fix maximum discounts at 15 per cent, plus $7\frac{1}{2}$ per cent to any van agents.

It may have been a coincidence that about the same time a firm of London brokers, Mitchell Hain & Co., put forward to the various biscuit concerns a proposal for amalgamating them all into a public company. The brokers employed the time-honoured technique of pretending that all concerns would welcome 'with something like enthusiasm' a nation-wide combine under Huntley and Palmers' leadership, similar to the Imperial Tobacco Company under W. D. & H. O. Wills: an enthusiasm which (they claimed) each on its own dared not express to the others. Mitchell Hain also played on the quality biscuit manufacturers' fears about the rapid growth of the 'cheap' trade, which would require concerted action for the sake of self-preservation, and about the possibility of the Government's introducing protection, which they could resist more effectively as a combine rather than as individual firms.

Howard Palmer felt that his company 'had better remain outside any combine for the time being', and the scheme therefore collapsed, but mutual lack of trust throughout the industry was also partly to blame. Such mistrust was still widespread two years later when Arthur Carr, who had succeeded his father John Carr as Chairman of Peek Frean, approached the five leading firms, namely Crawford's, Huntley and Palmers, Jacob's, Macfarlane Lang, and McVitie & Price. Although still unwilling to join the Association, he believed that sooner or later they should all merge; once again, the Imperial Tobacco Company was quoted as a model.

Arthur Carr's three objectives were respectively financial, social and managerial: to maintain profits—no doubt as Imperial Tobacco had done, by 'regulating the market'—to improve the conditions of all workers in the biscuit trade, and to safeguard the future management of the business, since the various generations of directors in the firms concerned were roughly of similar age. George William and Eustace Palmer had an exploratory meeting with him on the whole proposal and reported back to their Board. The Board was unenthusiastic and in November Howard Palmer wrote to say that they could not go further than 'friendly co-operation on the lines followed at present'. Some of the other firms did allow Sir William Plender, senior partner of the top-ranking accountants Deloitte Plender and Griffiths, to report to one another their aggregate turnover, profits and fixed asset figures, but one by one they had second thoughts, so that no more was heard of the proposals.

Thus the economic recession led to biscuit firms paying much heed to the question of protection and of working much more closely together. It also provoked labour troubles in the industry, of which Reading had its share. The decline in Huntley and Palmers' physical output was particularly steep after 1909; it was able to maintain the value of turnover fairly well only because it made periodical increases in retail prices as commodity prices continued to drift upwards. But little of the extra revenue had gone to the workpeople.

Between 1898 and 1911 the price of food on average increased (according to the official indices of retail prices) by almost exactly 10 per cent, that of clothing by nearly 16 per cent and that of coal by 18 per cent. These indices are very rough since they apply only to the London area. Two Board of Trade surveys of working-class living costs in Reading, for 1905 and 1912 respectively, show that the relation with London prices remained fairly constant. The actual increase in rents and retail prices in the town between those years was 7 per cent, but the earnings of Huntley and Palmers' workpeople did not follow suit.[8]

In September 1900 the lower-paid workers had been granted wage increases, notably those under twenty-one and unskilled adults earning less than 21s. (£1·05) a week. The directors felt the more highly paid hands, such as machine men and bakers, to be adequately remunerated. No increases in the basic rates were made in the next eleven years. Employees had relied also on overtime payments, normally a regular occurrence in the busy weeks leading up to Christmas. However, the depression in trade since 1903 had severely curtailed the amount of overtime done. Then in 1909 and 1910 there was much short time, and 400 men and boys had to be laid off just after Christmas 1910.

This combination of low basic wages, short time and heavy redundancies created an explosive situation, just at a time when similar conditions in many other industries had set in motion 'the gravest strike movement that till then the country had known'.[9] The summer of 1911, the hottest for nearly half a century, was in any case likely to foment disgruntlement in all the overcrowded back-to-back working-class housing districts throughout the country; the normally tranquil Reading proved to be no exception. Even Peek Frean, although its wages were relatively high for London and it had a good welfare record, was forced to close its factory for several days in August.

During that autumn the National Union of Gas Workers and General Labourers organised a mass meeting of townspeople to prepare for opening a branch in Reading. The union had four years previously achieved a noteworthy success at Carr's factory in Carlisle. There its agitation had been effective enough for the Board of Trade to appoint an arbitrator, who had awarded a general wage increase. It now vigorously campaigned to recruit Huntley and Palmers' employees, with the aim of raising wages and improving conditions within the factory.[10]

The agitation came to a head when 200 temporary hands, both men and women, were discharged in December at the end of the busy season. The company rather ill-advisedly took the opportunity to get rid of a number of other workers, apparently with between ten and forty years' service, whose work or conduct was considered to be in one way or another unsatisfactory. The union's district secretary immediately charged the company with victimising these long-service employees because they were trade unionists, and listed other grievances, such as putting girls into men's jobs, overworking them, and instituting spy systems throughout the factory. Certainly the proportion of women and girls employed in the factory had nearly quadrupled, from 8 to 23 per cent of the total, between 1898 and 1911.

The workers' cause was vociferously taken up by a bewildering variety of outside sponsors. These ranged from the redoubtable socialist Countess of Warwick to the editor of the *Berkshire Chronicle*, who week by week reported the dispute in great detail and never tired of pointing out how Reading's low wages were prolonging the trade depression from which the town had been suffering for so many years. When prominent outsiders, such as the Archdeacon of Oxford, wrote to the company on these matters, it retorted that the *Chronicle*'s partisanship sprang from the editor's pose as a Tory Democrat, since he was a disappointed Conservative parliamentary candidate for the Borough.

The very violence of the agitation soon provoked counter-demonstrations. Immediately after Christmas over 1200 employees met to protest indignantly against the 'shameless and lying statements' being circulated about conditions of work in the factory. Some of these employees, including one or two girls, wrote letters to the local press strongly refuting specific allegations. These reactions must have been wholly spontaneous and unaided by the directors, who did virtually nothing to prevent an admittedly unprecedented situation from getting out of hand and chose to let public opinion decide the issues. Thus two sets of people, apparently without any conscious distortion of the truth, were asserting entirely conflicting views.

Were wage rates in the factory on the whole too low? The Board of Trade report on working-class living costs merely commented that since many of the occupations were unskilled or semi-skilled in Reading, rates of wages were not high, although family incomes were often supplemented by women's and girls' wages. Far more specific evidence comes from a survey carried out in Reading by the distinguished statistician A. L. Bowley, then a lecturer at the University College.[11] The survey was taken in the autumn of 1912, or nearly a year after the events just related. He drew a sample of 840 houses in the borough, or just under one in twenty; of these about 600 working-class homes were actually visited. Taking a definition of overcrowding as more than one person on average per room (children under eighteen being counted as a fraction), Reading was found to be among the best of the County Boroughs, as less than one in seven houses could be considered overcrowded. Rents were correspondingly high, representing nearly 25 per cent of the earnings of the 20s. to 30s. (£1·00 to £1·50) a week category. However, the town came off much more badly when incomes were considered.

During the disturbances Huntley and Palmers had revealed that the average earnings of men, including overtime and lost time, in the previous twelve months had been 24s. 2d. (£1·21) a week. Since the company employed directly between a quarter and a fifth of the town's working-class population, and since (as non-statisticians were startled to discover) up to 50 per cent were earning less than the average, Reading had an unusually high proportion of unskilled workers on low wages. Hence more than one person in every four of the working classes and nearly one in five of all families in Reading were living in primary poverty; that is to say, below the minimum level of income considered necessary—by the undemanding standards of the day—to maintain physical health. This group comprised nearly half the schoolchildren and 45 per cent of children under school age. Since the main incidence of want therefore fell on families with large numbers of young children, the proportion of children who at some stage in their lives had experienced poverty must have been very much higher.

Dr. Bowley further showed that a half of these households were living in poverty because the breadwinner's wages were so low that he was unable to support a family of three children or more. Such poverty was therefore 'not intermittent but permanent, not accidental or due to exceptional misfortune, but a regular feature of the industries of the towns concerned'. He rightly condemned these results for Reading, and for certain other towns where similar circumstances applied, as 'shocking' and declared that 'to raise the wages of the worst-paid workers is the most pressing social task with which the country is confronted today'.[12] Thus the workpeople who were asserting that wages were sufficient probably belonged to thrifty households where the children—or most of them—no longer constituted a financial burden, whereas the opposing group were pointing to the poverty suffered by those with a large number of dependants. It is significant that the Board of Trade report noted how Reading's birth-rate was markedly lower than that for the seventy-six large towns it covered.

Throughout the troubles of 1911–12 George William Palmer had been on an extended trip abroad. Although local people had hoped that his return would bring about a rapid settlement of the dispute, in fact he did not become involved in it. He was giving most of his attention now to his estates and supporting handsomely any organisation which upheld country life, from the Royal Counties Agricultural Society (of which he was president in 1909) to the humblest flower show. Detesting the motor car, he was regularly to be seen driving his carriage and pair from Marlston to Newbury station, where he caught the train to Reading or London.

The story of how in those years he and Alfred Palmer jointly contributed well over £200,000, in addition to property and land, to endow Reading University College has been told elsewhere. Then he suffered without warning a severe attack of cerebral haemorrhage and died in October 1913; he was only sixty-two. The college's principal, William Childs, wrote in *The Times* of his 'straightforward simplicity of character' and 'singular modesty', unusual in a man of such shrewd and thorough mind, great wealth and influence. 'Here, indeed, was one who had the largeness of view and the largeness of heart of an ancient founder.'[13]

The company did raise wages, for the first time since 1900, from October 1912, at the time of the normal bi-annual revision of wages. These averaged about 12 per cent for lower-paid workers, so that the adult wage (at twenty-one in manufacturing and twenty-two in packing) was now 21s. (£1·05) for men and 11s. (55p.) for girls. The skilled men did no better than about 5 per cent. Thus the question of wage rates could not remain dormant for long. A further rise in living costs by mid-1914 led to requests from several departments for wage increases, but the directors refused to take any notice of them. Memories of the earlier agitations were still raw enough for the Chairman to be convinced that the union was 'conducting an active propaganda amongst our workpeople and endeavouring to excite discontent amongst them as to their conditions of labour'. However, the company had little to fear from that direction as long as the number of union members in the factory was relatively small. A more real threat was of Government attention being drawn towards the industry's wage rates.

In 1909 Winston Churchill, as Home Secretary, had piloted into law the Trade Boards Act, which had the object to abolishing 'sweated' trades where wages were abnormally low. Huntley Boorne and Stevens now anticipated that the provisions of the Act would be applied shortly to the tin-box-making industry, so as to secure a minimum rate of 6d. (2½p.) an hour for adult male labour. That firm therefore decided to

Pre-War 1906–14

anticipate any official action by introducing a 50-hour week without loss of pay.

At a special meeting on 28th July 1914 Huntley and Palmers' Board authorised Howard Palmer, at some opportune moment, to adopt a 48-hour week for adult males, with a standard weekly wage of 24s. (£1·20). Female labour was already working 48 hours, and young women at eighteen were now given a standard rate of 12s. (60p.) a week. It also authorised the Chairman to seek agreement with Peek Frean and the Association members over hours, and over increases in the price list to meet the consequent extra cost. Yet as a result of events that few at that moment could have foreseen, more than four years were to pass before the 48-hour week was finally introduced, in December 1918.

14
The Great War and its Aftermath: Business Mainly as Usual 1914–16

On Monday, 22nd June 1914 there was a general exodus of Huntley and Palmers' employees from Reading on the annual factory excursion. At a time when more than 5000 hands—including 3350 men over eighteen—were employed in the factory itself, the outing was important enough to close all the local primary schools for the day, so that children could accompany their parents.

From 3.30 to 6 that morning people were arriving at Reading station, to be greeted by the strains of the Temperance Band. Ten special trains were standing by, five destined for Margate and Ramsgate, with nearly 4000 passengers, and another five for Portsmouth, with just over 3000 passengers.[1] Some 500 had travelled on the previous Saturday for the weekend, but many families chose not to go at all: the ones who could not afford the expense, who were themselves too old or had very young children, or who felt that a long and arduous day was no pleasure, with work due to be resumed at 6.30 a.m. on the Tuesday.

Those bound for the Kent coast encountered continuous rain and thunderstorms from 10 a.m. onwards, whereas at Portsmouth the weather was ideal; yet all of them had been cheered by the recent improvement in biscuit sales. Although the cost of living remained high, grocers were prepared—according to the Manager of the Country Trade—to 'give our goods a better chance'. This had secured the company a welcome increase in home sales, from £773,000 in 1912–13 to £829,000 in 1913–14, and thus higher employment in the factory.

Unfortunately, the increase had been more than matched by rival firms. Peek Frean's home sales exceeded £900,000 in 1913. Jacob's, after some months' complete shut-down in Dublin caused by strikes and civil troubles there, was now building a branch factory at Aintree, near Liverpool. McVitie & Price, too, were planning a third factory, this time near Manchester, to supplement their plants in Edinburgh and London. Thus the pressure of competition was likely to be intensified, especially as the new factories were to be fitted with the most up-to-date—and therefore economical—types of machinery which Huntley and Palmers had hitherto declined to introduce.

For the Reading factory the improvement in business had only bred serious problems. The packing department, already strained to near the limit by the growing demand for packets, assortments and 'fancy varieties', was now often in arrears. As the invoice clerks could not complete their work each day until packing was over, the *average* time of their departure was about twenty-five minutes later than in the previous year, or 7.20 p.m. and 2 p.m. on Saturdays. The manufacturing department found that the already marked shortage of female labour was getting worse, so that men were having to be employed on women's jobs. Profits on turnover had therefore declined from 12·7 to 12·5 per cent as a result of the additional expenditure involved.

Moreover, an excessive regard for economy had allowed stocks of biscuits to fall too low in the summer of 1913. When trade therefore began to revive seasonally that autumn and remained at a higher level than in recent years, demand could be met only with an inordinate amount of overtime. The Board did respond to the rising demand for chocolate biscuits by doubling the number of chocolate coating machines, and by planning a new four-storeyed chocolate factory. The valuers, in a report only just received, had pressed strongly for all new buildings to be on one floor, to provide better lighting and ventilation and to minimise handling, and electrically driven machines to be installed, so as to economise in power lost when driving heavy and lengthy lines of shafting. The new chocolate factory, which followed neither of these recommendations, was started in June 1914; only the foundations had been completed when work was halted that same August.

There was one major reform, however: a strengthening of top management through an unexpected happening. One of the junior directors had, without consulting his colleagues, become joint master of the South Berks Hunt; this office would make considerable claims on his time and therefore contravene the provision in the Articles of the Association which required junior directors to work full-time in the business. It provoked the most serious row that ever erupted in the Board room, a row that was smoothed over with great diplomatic skill by the Company's 'elder statesman' since his brother's death, Alfred Palmer, who calmed tempers by blandly agreeing with all parties in turn.

As the director concerned was in charge of manufacturing, packing, stores and the laboratory, the Board now gave his Assistant Directors full responsibility for their respective departments: F. B. East in manufacturing, C. F. Newman in packing and E. A. Wrottesley in the stores. These three would all report directly to a committee of the top management, who were to be formally known as the Executive: the Chairman, Deputy Chairman and the General Manager. No one could have foreseen how soon this new managerial organisation was to be put to the severest imaginable test and prove highly workable.

Six days after the factory excursion, on 28th June, the Archduke Franz Ferdinand of Austria was assassinated in Sarajevo. In an era when foreign affairs were largely ignored by the British public outside Westminster and Whitehall, this incident and the gradual drift towards war passed virtually unnoticed in Reading itself. As late as 28th July, when a special Board Meeting debated the proposed introduction of the 48-hour week, the possibility of a general European conflict was not even mentioned, or at least not minuted. To Huntley and Palmers, then, the declaration of war on 4th August appears to have come out of an almost unclouded sky.

The South African War, although it had lasted nearly three years, and required a total of 450,000 British troops to be mobilised, had passed over the factory with scarcely a tremor: less so, indeed, than the Crimean War, which had damaged sales because of a recession at home and problems over shipping and had affected supplies through shortages of certain ingredients. In 1899-1900 the company had fulfilled several government contracts for army biscuits, but these had taken less than two weeks in all to complete. Out of the gross profit of 18·4 per cent on these contracts it had donated to the Berkshire Regiment a thousand tins of fancy biscuits and subscribed to a number of war charities. The Board had forbidden any employees to enlist for service overseas with the Yeomanry and allowed only part-time service with the Volunteers. Thus the company's labour force had not been disrupted at all.

A general war in Europe, on the other hand, was an alarming prospect; above all, just as during the Crimean War, there was the problem of safeguarding ingredient supplies. To economise on costs the firm had been steadily reducing stocks of ingredients ever since 1899; these were now at a dangerously low level, varying from six weeks' supplies in the case of butter and sugar to three weeks for flour and a mere ten days for eggs and syrup. Within a week sugar and egg prices more than doubled and flour was costing half as much again. The Association of Biscuit Manufacturers had already granted full powers to its president, James Macfarlane—Chairman of Macfarlane Lang—to agree price increases with Huntley and Palmers. On 4th August—the same day that war was declared—Howard Palmer met him but would not allow cheaper varieties, costing 6d. (2½p.) a pound or less, to be raised by more than 10 per cent, since higher prices would be 'very serious for the poorer classes'. However, he agreed to raise the more expensive kinds, and also cakes, by the 15 per cent which the Association had sought for the whole range of biscuits.

Meanwhile orders were 'pouring in from all over the kingdom' for an aggregate of two or three times what the Reading factory could possibly produce. The company tried to spread the orders over the longest possible period by despatching in instalments all orders that appeared to be inflated. Orders from overseas, on the other hand, had been falling off heavily ever since the onset of the crisis, and were abruptly halted on 6th August by a Government ban on exports of all foodstuffs. Although this ban was lifted a fortnight later, the company's overseas trade began a steady decline from which it never recovered. The average tonnage of its exports in the five war years 1914-15 to 1918-19 was a third less than in 1913-14, and at the end of 1916, during the worst months of the submarine menace, came almost to a standstill when exports of biscuits in quantities larger than 7 lb. were prohibited except under special licence.

Since the company was unable to divert export orders immediately, in August 1914 it had to put some factory operatives on to short time. Certain packing girls did not have enough work to occupy them even for half the day; the wives of the three Executive members therefore opened a workshop on the packing floor of H factory, to make clothes for employees who had gone to the war and for their dependants who had been left in distress. This charitable work soon came to an end as all factories gradually returned to full time.

On 12th August the War Office gave the company substantial orders to manufacture army biscuits, which involved working continuously day and night for several weeks. In all over £84,000 worth of such orders were fulfilled to the end of March 1915 and £653,000 worth by November 1918, nearly 6½ per cent of total turnover. At the same time it was asked specially to pack 250,000 tons of basic rations, consisting of tea, granulated sugar and Oxo cubes. The rations were provided by the Government, and the labour and packing materials by the company on a cost-plus basis; the tins came from Huntley Boorne and Stevens.

The company was soon experiencing a drain on its labour force. By September 1914 no less than 184 reservists and territorials had joined the colours, while it provided the local military depot with 150 labourers, checkers and clerks as other ranks in the Army Service Corps. In addition to promising these men their jobs back after the war, the company undertook to supplement official dependants' allowances to at least 13s. 6d. (67p.) a week for wives without children and at least 20s. (£1·00) for those with children. In that month total employment in the factory had risen to over 5100 for the first time since 1909—and incidentally for the last time in the company's history; the fall in the number of men had been very largely offset by an increase in women employed, and to a lesser extent by boys and girls under eighteen. By December 1914 no less than 515 men, one in seven of the male employees, were in the forces. The proportion from the building department was as high as one in five; the General Manager reminded the directors that these were 'not very easily replaced'.

Despite these unprecedentedly large dislocations in supplies of ingredients and labour and in overseas sales, the company rapidly adjusted itself to its new routine. To ease demand in the still overheated home market, it severely curtailed the number of Christmas tins, offering fewer than 340,000 for sale, compared with nearly 580,000 in 1913. The number for Christmas 1915 was as low as 220,000: a serious loss of profit for a firm which relied so much on its Christmas trade. Overseas business in general had by the second quarter of 1915 settled at the diminished level which was broadly to be maintained throughout the war. As in the very earliest days of exporting, many of these fancy biscuits were being consigned to military rather than to civilian destinations abroad.

Shortly before the war Howard Palmer had called for two reports on overseas trade, and in accordance with their recommendations he now offered more attractive discounts to exporters by raising it from 9 to 11 per cent for shippers who paid cash. This step was also intended to reduce the company's dependence on C. & E. Morton and Crosse & Blackwell, who between them accounted for nearly a third of the trade outside Europe. As to the management of exports, the London office was to be supervised by Cecil Palmer, Ernest Palmer's elder son, who after an apprenticeship in the factory had trained as a chartered accountant before becoming a director in 1911. However, Emsley Lea and the export manager, C. B. Hebb, were considered to possess enough of an 'intelligent grasp' of affairs in the office to undertake its day-to-day running.

At Reading top management was now effectively concentrated in the hands of the Executive: Howard Palmer as Chairman, Eustace Palmer as Deputy Chairman, and Herbert Pretty as General Manager. The other directors seem to have played only a minor part in everyday affairs for the remainder of the war. W. Bullivant Williams was now approaching eighty and died two years later in March 1917. Three of the other directors, Albert Palmer and Eric and Geoffrey Palmer were away at the war. Cecil Palmer was heavily committed with his work at the London office and also with Huntley Boorne and Stevens at a time when the company's nominee as director there, Clement Williams (son of Bullivant Williams), was also absent on active service. The Chairman had his small, harmonious and capable team which was apparently equal to every emergency as it arose. Yet the strain was such that it was the oldest and least burdened of the three, Herbert Pretty, who outlived his two younger colleagues.

The 'London contingent', Ernest and Charles Palmer, now had no executive duties in the company. From time to time they dropped hints that perhaps the company was not making the fullest use of some directors 'who are in a position to render real assistance', and that the organisation of the business needed examination, presumably because it was too centralised. To such points the Chairman's invariable reply was that they most certainly merited very careful consideration—*after* the war.

Alfred Palmer, still in charge of the engineering department, naturally enough knew what the Executive was doing, but while loyally supporting all its decisions, never sought to interfere in any way. For six months he acted as Deputy Chairman during a long illness of his son, but he gave up the office more readily than he had accepted it. The sensitive character sketch which William Childs, Principal of the University College, wrote of this 'big leisurely man', illustrates perfectly the part he played in the factory at this time. 'His style, through and through, was home-spun and uncoloured; expression, except through kindly blue eyes, never came easily to him; and it was not his way to intrude, or to overrule, either his opinions or himself. His rooted habit of doing things well, and as they should be done, had nothing in it of display . . . He had an eye for beauty and seemliness, depth and glow of feeling, and that kind of imagination which can see the finished thing before it has begun.'[2]

This imagination and sense of fitness found its outlet during the war. His department, employing in 1914 close on a thousand men, had to be on call to maintain and repair plant that was being used to the limit, or beyond, and to manufacture any minor piece of machinery that might be required. Over and above this responsibility, in September 1915, following the 'shell scandal' and the appointment of the dynamic Lloyd George as Minister of Munitions, he agreed to make shell cases as sub-contractors of the Pulsometer Co. in Reading. He also arranged for the company's railway system to be used as a marshalling yard for munitions made in the town, to provide easy despatch to the Ordnance Depot at Bristol.

The general shortage of men forced him to transfer some girls from the Packing to the Engineering department and to train them on the spot: an unheard of step for a firm which had always segregated male operatives from female ones. Beginning with a modest output of fifty shells a week, eventually he was turning out no less than 900 a week. The company rightly took pride because of the 60,000 shells in total that were delivered, the ministry rejected less than a hundred as substandard. One tester was so impressed by their quality that he reported: 'Every Huntley and Palmers' shell is like a piece of jewellery.'[3] He could not more aptly have summed up the company's strength and weakness. Only the best would do, even in a world which seemed to go for the good (or less than good) in preference to the best, mainly because it was cheaper. The engineering department also machined parts for aircraft engines and apparatus for gun rifling. Fortunately Alfred Palmer felt none of the scruples which beset the aged Samuel Beavan Stevens at Huntley Boorne and Stevens. Since his Quaker conscience forbade him to make weapons, after some hesitation Stevens consented to make cases for smoke bombs, which did not themselves take life; during 1915 his firm also made some of the first steel helmets issued to British troops at the front.

The period until the end of 1916, when Lloyd George became Prime Minister, has been described by Sir William Beveridge, in his classic account of *British Food Control* in the First World War, as one of 'business mainly as usual'.[4] The country then had no general food shortage and no overall Government control as such.

The company did everything it could to co-operate with the authorities: the value of army biscuits it produced rose from £10,000 a month in 1914–15 to £12,000 a month in 1915–16. Its No. 4 standard biscuit, measuring roughly four inches square and half an inch thick made out of whole-wheat flour, was often issued as an emergency ration. The ex-serviceman who said that his least happy memories of the Great War were the trenches, the mud and Huntley and Palmers' No. 4 biscuit was not being entirely fair to the last named; if it was excessively hard, it was also highly nutritious, and when soaked in water or stronger liquids made a sustaining meal, or could be made into a pudding. It was undoubtedly better than many army biscuits made by rival firms, which (the Association learnt in November 1916) were so unpalatable, because they did not contain enough fat, that they were only worth using as firelighters at the front.

Of the company's fancy-biscuit output, a high proportion was despatched to canteens of the British Expeditionary Force, the Young Men's Christian Association and similar organisations or to military hospitals, or else were sent privately to members of the forces in small tins. Regimental canteens submitted very heavy orders for small packets; the number of 2 oz. packets, for instance, soared from 300,000 to nearly 875,000 in the first year of war. In addition, all the biscuits sent from Britain by the Central Prisoners of War Committee were manufactured in Reading.

All these commitments, on top of a heavy civilian demand at home and abroad, strained to the limit the company's none too flexible or up-to-date productive capacity. In 1915–16 the output of biscuits and cakes, at 25,650 tons, was only a little short of the record outputs in the boom years 1899–1903 and in 1908; it was not to be exceeded again until 1954, in the quite different conditions of automatic production. The numbers of factory employees had fallen by September 1916 from 5100 shortly after the beginning of the war, to under 4800, and male employees from nearly 3800 to 2765: the number of women was now double that in 1913. Thus the company had to work much overtime to reach these output levels: in the three principal factories of the manufacturing department during 1915–16, no less than 115 nights were worked until 11 p.m., and in the packing department 91 nights to 9.30 p.m.

Rather short-sightedly, the Government was intensifying the company's difficulties by stepping up recruitment to the armed forces and neglecting the equally vital task of safeguarding essential services at home; these could fairly be held to include at least part of the biscuit industry. Such pressures for recruitment increased as the casualty lists mounted: not unexpectedly, many outsiders—chiefly those above military age and without sons—were soon complaining that Reading had fallen behind towns of comparable size.

As a London paper put it in September 1915, 'one sees many young fellows about the streets [of Reading] who would look much better in khaki than slouching along in soft felt hats, turned up trousers, and highly coloured socks';[5] yet it is improbable that many of these so-called slouchers were Huntley and Palmers' employees. Of the 3003 men employed at that time, 1000 had in fact more than thirty years' service with the firm and were therefore beyond military age. Of the younger ones, a considerable number had offered themselves and had been rejected. Baking for long stretches of time in very high temperatures was not conducive to building up a martial physique. Moreover —and this was often overlooked despite the disquieting facts that various official enquiries during and after the Boer War had revealed about working-class physical standards—perhaps half of those in Reading had lived in poverty, especially during the formative years of childhood.

The Chairman, in his report for 1915–16, noted that he had held prolonged negotiations with the authorities to let the company keep essential employees, with some success. However, the Home Office kept up pressure on Huntley and Palmers and its competitors to release more men from their factories by replacing them by female labour. For the first time the company allowed women to be employed on manufacturing, as well as engineering. The authorities willingly relaxed the stringent regulations on overtime worked by women, as set out in the Factory Act of 1901. Yet despite these relaxations, by the beginning of 1916 the company was faced with a distinct labour shortage of males and females alike.

One of the early wartime casualties was Ronald Poulton Palmer, George William's nephew and adopted son. He had entered the business as an apprentice in 1912 and after training in a Manchester engineering firm, Mather & Platt, was due to join the engineering department in the autumn of 1914. Here was an entirely new type to become a potential director, one who had been brought up in an academic household in Oxford and educated at Rugby and Balliol, where he obtained an honours degree in engineering. He was already a celebrity in his own right: the outstanding Rugby international of his generation, who captained the English side to victory in four classic games during 1914. To the company he gave promise of offering two major contributions. The first was the capacity, and will, to translate into practice the conviction of his father, (Sir) Edward Poulton, a distinguished Professor of Zoology, that British industry had not 'appealed to' pure scientists to help in technological matters.[6]

The company had, it is true, its own scientists, for biscuit-making, like food manufacture in general, requires among other things regular chemical analysis of ingredients and also attention to problems connected with keeping qualities. Sir Walter Palmer had been an able analyst and inventor, but he had died in 1910, and the laboratory had been under the direction of Dr. E. F. Armstrong until 1914, when he joined what later became Imperial Chemical Industries Ltd., ending up as a Managing Director. Armstrong was succeeded by Dr. R. T. Colgate, who remained with Huntley and Palmers until his retirement in 1957. Yet, as we have seen, it was on the mechanical side above all that the company required modernisation. With increasing experience and as Alfred Palmer's successor in the engineering department Ronald Poulton could have made it more receptive to technology and science generally.

His other potential contribution sprang from an abiding interest in social work: he is said to have established the first boys' club in Reading.

He was the only member of the family who would have ploughed through Alfred Marshall's lengthy treatise, the *Principles of Economics*, during his apprenticeship, in order to qualify him to discuss social and economic questions with an old man working next to him in the factory. Nor would any of the others have ventured to express openly, as he did, the view that 'men who had worked long and faithfully at their job were not receiving, and were not likely to receive, adequate payment', and that the company's practice of offering 'general comforts' rather than good wages was degrading. He was therefore tolerantly regarded in the family as a 'bit of a socialist', although he came to recognise that it was not so much the system that was at fault as ignorance and lack of mutual understanding between employer and employee.[7]

Eustace Palmer already knew him well, and looked forward to working with him after the war, as did many other people inside and outside the factory. It is a commonplace to enlarge on the irreparable losses which the nation incurred from the sacrifice of so many talented young men in the First World War; yet here was a unique combination of talents which could have served the company well.

15
The Great War and its Aftermath: Food Control 1916–19

During the 'Business Mainly as Usual' period from the outbreak of war to December 1916 the Government exercised no direct control over materials or labour, which were becoming increasingly scarce, or prices which continued to rise. Manufacturing firms therefore grew ever more anxious on these counts as the war dragged on. At Huntley and Palmers the greatest worry was over sugar. Although before the war two-thirds of Britain's supply had come from Germany and Austria-Hungary—now the two principal enemy powers—a Sugar Commission set up by the Government was able to purchase enough in other markets to hold off any real shortage until well into 1916. This was at the cost of steep increases in sugar prices, which reached 86 per cent above the pre-war average in March 1916; nevertheless, civilian consumption remained virtually unchecked. Thus when in that month U-boat sinkings reduced stocks of sugar to unprecedentedly low levels, the Sugar Commission was forced to restrict industrial users to 75 per cent of their 1915 consumption.[1]

Peek Frean immediately proposed to Huntley and Palmers that they should jointly discontinue production of all their most expensive biscuits. Huntley and Palmers, which had scarcely reduced the number of its varieties at all, refused to accept such a drastic measure. Instead, to save 250 tons of sugar, it decided to strike off most of its iced products, namely ninety kinds of biscuit and forty-four of cake.

In fact, the company had just begun a drive to meet the exceptionally large volume of orders from overseas markets, notably the more distant ones in the Far East. Its competitors were taking great advantage of its difficulties in fulfilling export orders, and it could not afford to neglect the problem any longer. As the Chairman said in his report for 1916–17, 'after the war, all our energy and intelligence will be required to ensure a continuance of our dominating position in export markets'. It therefore obtained the permission of the War Office to cut down its output of army biscuits, the value of which fell from an average of £125,000 in the previous two years, to £44,000 in 1916–17.

Army biscuits presented few ingredients problems because they required no sugar, whereas the export effort, on top of an almost unparalleled level of orders at home, caused the company's sugar stocks to fall alarmingly after the 25 per cent cut in March 1916. Four months later these stocks were down to the equivalent of four weeks' consumption; worse still, for a while it could buy only half the weekly allocation. To add to these difficulties, more and more men were with the colours—nearly 1000 in March 1916 and over 1500 a year later—thus intensifying in particular the problem of key workers. At the Annual Meeting in June 1916, Alfred Palmer declared that the past twelve months' work had been more consistently strenuous than any he could remember in well over forty years' service with the firm. Then in March 1917 food exports were prohibited to non-official destinations except under licence, which would be very sparingly granted.

A worry of a different nature altogether was over finance. The company was having to make such heavy outlays for supplies as to deplete its liquid funds; in 1915–16 the value of biscuit and materials stocks rose by nearly £54,500. Indeed, only by offering a higher cash discount to customers and thereby getting in remittances more quickly, was it able to avoid having to raise new capital. Presumably that would have involved becoming a public company, since as a private company it could not offer its shares for sale in the open market. It was prudently beginning to build up a general reserve, which reached £34,000 at March 1916, in addition to a £26,000 reserve against prewar Continental debts in enemy hands and funds in allied countries, notably France, which could not be repatriated owing to the depreciation of their currencies.

Amidst all these preoccupations came an outbreak of labour unrest. In March 1915 the company had conceded a war bonus, of 4s. (20p.) to men and 2s. (10p.) to women on short time, and half these rates—or roughly 8 per cent—to those on full time. Even though food prices generally had by then risen by a quarter since July 1914, both Ernest and Charles Palmer grumbled in the Board at these additions to the firm's standing charges: it may have been purely a coincidence that Board meetings thereafter were held only once a month instead of every fortnight.

Three months later, the company rejected a request from a deputation of workpeople for a further wage increase and ignored letters from union representatives who sought an interview. In November, when increases in food prices had crept up to over 40 per cent, Howard Palmer did meet the union representatives, but only to tell them that his was a private company, and that as every employee had the right of access to the directors, he and his colleagues knew all that was necessary about labour conditions within the factory. Earnings, he stated, were quite adequate: the heavy overtime being worked, often at time-and-a-half rates, in conjunction with the regular half-yearly rises in wages went far towards meeting the continual advance in the cost of living.

So matters rested until July 1916, when the cost of food was on average over 60 per cent higher than two years before. Labour relations suddenly reached breaking point.[2] A girl in H factory left work early without permission, and the forewoman had her sacked: fifteen other girls who protested at her dismissal were also discharged. All her fellow workers then came out on strike, and paraded in front of the factory, indulging in what a local newspaper called 'some boisterous but good-humoured merriment'. The next day they called off their strike after the forewoman had been moved and the sixteen reinstated.

The Reading branch of the union seized the opportunity to open a recruiting campaign, and had soon enrolled three hundred extra employees. A few days later, on the Sunday, the largest demonstration of workers ever held in Reading ended in passing resolutions for higher pay and better working conditions. It seemed as if the 1911-12 troubles were about to recur. Yet Howard Palmer, who now had a free hand in these matters, handled the crisis with a sureness of touch that had been wanting in the earlier incident.

He categorically refused to discuss a wage increase with union officials. Instead, he called together representatives from each department in the factory, in order to propose the setting up of a Factory Committee. This committee was to confer at regular intervals with the Executive about all matters that could not be settled in the ordinary way by foremen or managers.

The principle was not entirely new in the company. A consultative committee, of eight members, had been in existence since 1911, to advise the management on welfare questions after the passing of the National Insurance Act, with its provisions for sickness benefit, had brought to an end the Sick Fund after more than sixty years; it was thus a successor to the old Sick Fund Committee. Then in 1915 a General Committee of fifty-two members, one from each department, had been formed to consider the best means of getting operatives to take up the Government's National War Loan. The company had agreed to contribute £1 extra for every £4 subscribed, and allowed 5 per cent interest instead of the $4\frac{1}{2}$ per cent coupon value. Despite fears that the bonds were likely to have little appeal because they could not easily be turned into cash, the committee did succeed in selling nearly £6000 worth to 750 employees. The unprecedented feature of the new factory committee was its power to discuss freely wide areas of the company's business.

Howard Palmer's initiative took the union aback at a time when it appeared to hold the tactical advantage. At a meeting on 4th July, after his offer of raising the bonus to 4s. and 2s. (20p. and 10p.) respectively had been turned down, he offered a straight 5s. (25p.) increase for men and 3s. (15p.) for women, with the abolition of the war bonus. The union representatives demanded this increase on top of the existing bonus, and called out all the company's employees on strike from mid-day on Friday, 7th July.

The directors once again refused to treat with outside representatives of the union, and therefore at 1 p.m. that day a deputation of workpeople went to see them. The deputation's spokesman was A. T. Knight, also chairman of the union's local branch as well as president of the Reading Trades and Labour Council: he must have wondered what kind of reception he would get from his employers. He and his delegation accepted the Chairman's wage offer; he then asked Howard Palmer whether he was to be regarded as a rebel. 'Banish the thought from your mind,' the Chairman replied; 'as one of my employees I respect you more than ever I did before.'[3]

In the meantime the strikers, in a 'solid phalanx' outside the factory entrance, were hustling any supervisory staff that happened to be recognised. Of the non-strikers who tried to enter the factory, the men had their hats knocked off and the women their faces slapped. The hatpin, that formidable little weapon which for centuries had been a girl's best friend, was also said to have been used to great effect. Then a party of men and girls broke through the cordon across the entrance. The Chief Engineer, Cyril Byham, had the fire hoses played on them as they advanced across the bridge, but the hoses were seized and turned on him instead. In the mêlée a group of invaders slipped past, to spoil some of the biscuit mixings and throw tins into the river before being finally ejected. Altogether they did about £140 worth of damage.

The company had already telephoned for the Reading Constabulary, but the size of the posse sent was quite inadequate to restore order. Once their representatives had announced the wage agreement the strikers went back to work; the company immediately served a bill for the amount of the damage on Reading Corporation because of its alleged negligence in not sending more police. The Corporation argued that the police were given no prior warning and declared that it would resist the claim. Huntley and Palmers, determined not to advertise discord at that critical stage of the war, agreed to forgo it.

The new Factory Committee, now named the Workers' Representation Committee, adopted its rules three months later, in October 1916. It met once a month on its own, and the women's section at first met separately from the men's, but after a while the two sections united for the regular quarterly meetings with the Executive. The rules specified that if any employee were summoned to the Board room in connection with any dispute, he should be accompanied by the Committee's chairman, A. T. Knight. Committee members could transmit any complaints to the General Manager, and failing a satisfactory settlement, the chairman of the Committee was to take the matter to the company's Chairman.

The wartime minutes of the Committee from 1916 to April 1918 have survived in a Minute Book, the later pages of which were hrovidently used for those of the Wembley Exhibition Committee of 1923-4. The book highlights factory conditions and issues of the day. The Committee was not very willing to act as creatures of the Executive, although in the initial stage the Executive's attitude was still strongly paternalistic. Howard Palmer was immediately urged to insist that all workpeople should be members of a trade union. He maintained that the directors' practice was 'never to exercise any pressure upon their workpeople in any matters of personal opinion and judgement', and stood ready to investigate all genuine complaints of an employee 'rendering himself or herself obnoxious to a fellow-worker by provocative language or molesting attitude with regard to the other's feelings or convictions'. However, he did allow union funds to be collected in the firm's time.

Among the topics discussed, the more trivial items are often the most revealing. The Executive had, for example, found it necessary to stamp out the 'pernicious habit' of employees giving presents to foremen. Again, when one representative asked for hot water to be laid on for afternoon tea, Howard Palmer (who doubtless never went without a cup of tea in his office) retorted that there was a war on, but he undertook to consider the request on its merits. The committee did not directly discuss the question of wages, but when in November a wage increase was requested, and partly conceded, Howard Palmer promised Mr. Knight that a committee would be set up to investigate the whole wage structure.

As to the women's side, some matters raised were almost as old as Eve: Mr. Knight had to impress on all girls and their representatives 'the necessity for suppressing little petty jealousies'. Other problems, however, were of more recent origin. By July 1917 only 700 of the 1900 women and girls had been with the company since before the war; among those taken on later, there was a great deal of bad time-keeping, 'deliberate idling' and failure to get through the work allotted. One woman, incredibly enough, had lost 503 hours in three months, an average of 42 hours out of each 54-hour basic working week. Yet all categories of workers were guilty of irregular time-keeping. Badgered by his older colleagues on the Board, Howard Palmer again and again drew the Committee's attention to this problem, and especially to the common practice of leaving work before the three-minute warning bell rang; he even took it up with the secretary of the union. Moreover, he constantly threatened that when the combatants returned from the war, the offenders would be the first to go.

Several Committee members, who had paid a visit to the Co-operative Wholesale Society's biscuit works at Crumpsall, near Manchester, pointed out how machines and ovens were attended by boys and girls, who apparently earned higher wages than at Reading for a 48-hour (as opposed to a 54-hour) week, while the few men employed there were all mechanics or those on heavy duty with the dough mixers and the brakes. Conditions of work and welfare facilities were undoubtedly better than at Reading; for instance, a proper dining hall and cheap dinners were provided. Howard Palmer was quick to point out that Crumpsall was a modern factory, where it was easy to create good conditions. On the welfare side he reminded them of Huntley and Palmers' own Great Social Scheme. The company had in March 1916 given much publicity to that scheme, for which it had set aside a reserve of £50,000.[4]

Undoubtedly one of the prime movers was Charles Palmer, who—as mentioned in Chapter 13—ever since his visit to the United States in 1908 had been pressing for a workers' canteen to be provided. For some years the company had been buying up property in Kings Road opposite the factory's main frontage, as well as land on the west side of Watlington Street towards the town centre. It object was partly to co-operate with Reading Council over widening the King's Road and Watlington Street bridges across the canal, and partly to build an E-shaped block of buildings, the three wings of which would point towards the factory. The central wing, with a main entrance on King's Road, was to contain a recreation hall, kitchens and administrative quarters, and the other two wings dining and rest rooms for the men and the women respectively. The connecting block would overlook a terrace which ran along the canal. On the other side of Watlington Street a Great Hall would seat 2500 people, nearly twice the accommodation of Reading's large Town Hall.

This was in some ways a corollary of the endowments which members of the family had given to the University College. Its proposed amenities were no more than adequate for the company's present size.

It had to cater not only for the employees who were coming from greater distances than before, but also for those—especially girls—with a better education and therefore higher recreational standards. The sports facilities at King's Meadow were regarded as excellent, but the existing breakfast room near the North Gate—outside which groups of wives and children could be seen, waiting to hand in and collect dishes and cans of victuals—was no longer a substitute for proper dining and changing rooms. That room was also too cramped and unsuitable for dances, lectures and concerts. Once a Great Hall was built, the company looked forward to musical activities comparable with—although on a somewhat different plane from—those provided by the Reading Temperance Band, sponsored as it was by the company.

In the end the Great Social Scheme came to nothing. The licensing authorities refused to transfer elsewhere in Reading the licences of two public houses on the site, and the company was forced to postpone taking possession of the area for five years. In fact the negotiations with both vendors and the Council were more long-drawn-out still. Not until 1938 did the company open a Social Centre on a far less ambitious scale, in an office building which became vacant when the new Office Block was erected. Only £30,000 of the original £50,000—or about a third in real terms—was ever spent. The site earmarked for the Great Hall was sold and converted to commercial uses.

Reading is not so well endowed with attractive public buildings that it could easily afford to be deprived of these. According to the drawings, they would have formed a harmonious and pleasing group, in a style familiar to townspeople, for they were designed by Charles Steward Smith, the local architect of most of the University College's buildings, including Wantage Hall and the Library which Alfred Palmer and his family were to erect after the war in memory of George William Palmer. Nevertheless, the garden represented a genuine, if under-utilised, amenity of the firm, and allowed a view from the canal of the well-proportioned office buildings through a row of very handsome trees.

According to Beveridge, the second phase of food control began in December 1916, when a Ministry of Food was set up to allay severe public discontent with ever-rising prices and the growing scarcity of food.[5] Beveridge has christened this phase 'The Expert in Charge', for a former business man, Lord Devonport, was appointed Food Controller as political head of the ministry. He had founded the multiple grocery firm Kearley and Tonge, which before the war had been Huntley and Palmers' second largest customer in the home market. He was immediately confronted with the problem of grain shortages, and had to take measures that were unprecedented in Britain, notably stockpiling wheat and taking over the flour mills for the remainder of the war. Moreover, he increased the extraction rate for wheat from 70 to 81 per cent in January 1917, thereby using more of the bran and making flour darker and coarser, although more nutritious.

Very soon after taking office, Lord Devonport personally met the leading biscuit manufacturers and persuaded them to carry out tests on making biscuits with the 81 per cent flour and to accept a reduction in the sugar ration from 75 to 50 per cent of their 1915 use. Howard Palmer readily agreed to these proposals. When the Association had earlier urged him to protest at the raising of the extraction rate, he had replied that manufacturers would be ill-advised to make themselves conspicuous at that juncture. Eventually the company succeeded in making with 81 per cent flour standard varieties of biscuit, namely Osborne, Petit Beurre and Marie, which passed the exacting scrutiny of the Board.

The Ministry now followed this up with a number of restrictive orders. The Cake and Pastry Order in January 1917 reduced the allowable sugar content of cakes and biscuits. More onerous was the Sugar Restriction Order, which a few months later cut the sugar allocation from 50 to 40 per cent. A depressing piece of arithmetic revealed what this cut would mean to Huntley and Palmers. In 1913–14 it had used on average 82 tons of sugar a week, and in 1915, 71 tons; its permitted weekly use until the end of the year would now be only 28 tons. Yet the orders placed by the Army Canteen Committee, the Y.M.C.A., the Church Army, the Prisoners of War Committee and the War Office would probably absorb half that quantity and leave no more than 14 tons for the civilian market at home and overseas instead of the pre-war 82 tons. The company therefore planned to manufacture sweet biscuits without sugar, for instance by reintroducing a form of honey biscuit which (in the more agreeable form of Honey Drops) had won it an award in the International Health Exhibition of 1884.

The consequent reduction of output, on top of rising prices for flour, timber and paper, added markedly to the cost of production per ton of biscuits. By March 1917, the Executive had closed the Cake Factory and had discontinued a total of 242 kinds of biscuit. At that moment, delegates from the employees and union representatives demanded a further increase in wages. Howard Palmer maintained that to meet the union would be tantamount to giving it recognition. The Board, for once consulted on a policy matter, decided that he should meet such a deputation, but that the union representatives must be members of the national executive and not local officials. J. R. Clynes, M.P., was therefore one of those who attended—curiously enough, he was in a few months' time to become closely involved in the industry's affairs as Parliamentary Secretary of the Ministry of Food and later on as Food Controller. In advance of this deputation, a mass meeting of workpeople passed resolutions calling for a minimum wage of 30s. (£1·50) a week for men over twenty-one and 16s. (80p.) for women and youths over eighteen, with a general rise of 3s. and 2s. (15p. and 10p.) respectively; all these to be restricted to union members. Howard Palmer conceded the bonuses but not the minimum wages, and insisted that they should apply to all employees. This increase raised wage rates to nearly 40 per cent above the pre-war level. Moreover, the lower paid office staff were granted a 30 per cent in place of a 20 per cent bonus, which was scaled down for those with higher salaries.

In June 1917 the very serious losses at sea forced the Ministry of Food to reduce yet again the sugar allocation for biscuit making, to 25 per cent of the 1915 level. The same month saw the departure of Lord Devonport, who had not proved much of a success as a minister, for he had relied on voluntary rationing schemes combined with undue interference in industrial matters. A colliery owner, Lord Rhondda, took his place, thus ushering in what Beveridge has named the 'Heroic Age of Food Control'.[6] He was soon busy imposing proper control and rationing schemes for many foodstuffs, although not biscuits.

Now that the flour mills were under Government control, he was able to subsidise flour and hence bread in order to keep down living costs. He intended the subsidy on flour to apply to biscuit manufacturers as well as bakers, but Howard Palmer together with a spokesman of the Association went to see him and pointed out that the burden of this subsidy would fall on the Exchequer. Of his own company's output, he said, at least two-thirds was for official uses, while the remainder destined for the civilian trade was inessential; even if retailers passed on to the public the reduction of $\frac{1}{2}$d. per lb. which the subsidy represented, it could only result in an increase in orders. The ministry therefore agreed to issue biscuit manufacturers with licences for flour at the cost of 18s. (90p.) a sack, the value of the subsidy.

The meeting which settled these matters was in fact epoch-making, since the Association's president, James Macfarlane, was unable to attend, but felt that the 'interests of the biscuit trade would be considered safe' in the hands of Howard Palmer and of Arthur Carr of Peek Frean, neither of whom were Association members at all. Indeed, every shift in the industry's fortunes arising out of Government measures or changes in the market seemed to establish more securely Howard Palmer's authority to speak for the biscuit industry as a whole.

In November 1917 he proposed to the Association price increases to offset substantial rises in wage rates and in the cost of fruit, eggs and milk. James Macfarlane said of this meeting: 'This was perhaps the most satisfactory I ever attended. The utmost frankness was shown on all sides to exchange confidence about costings, profits and general policy.'

It was just seven and a half years since Howard Palmer had hoped that meetings between firms would not have to be held very often, and the measure of his conversion was that he now suggested that the leading biscuit manufacturers ought to act together after the war either as members of a Trade or Industrial Board or in an employers' association to negotiate with trade union representatives. He unfolded his own detailed plans a month or so later, after the publication of the Whitley Report. That official report recommended that industrial councils of employers and employees should be formed, and he now called for the setting up of a body for the biscuit industry. On the employers' side, if the two halves of the Association—the seven quality firms and the London Branch of cheaper manufacturers—would reunite, Huntley and Palmers and Peek Frean would be willing to join.

As a result of his initiative, a new trade association, the National Association of Biscuit Manufacturers, was formally incorporated in July 1918, with forty-two members. He was unanimously elected its first president, and had the time-consuming duty of drawing up its constitution. He took up with the recently established Ministry of Labour the question of forming without delay an industrial council for the biscuit trade. The ministry replied that it had no powers to act, and in any case a council could be set up only when an employees' side had been organised. This posed difficult problems: the National Union of General Workers, for instance, did not claim to represent all employees, notably the craftsmen who had their own unions. At the end of 1920 the ministry, speaking through one of its senior officials, the poet Humbert Wolfe, was still insisting that in the absence of an employees' organisation, a Trades Board would be more practicable. Like many other matters, the industrial council went into limbo, to be resuscitated some decades later.

Meanwhile, in June 1918 Howard Palmer was asked to become a member of an advisory committee on fats at the ministry which—at this late stage in the war—was seeking to impose control over butter, lard and cocoa butter. These new duties were over and above his commitments at Reading. There he was involved with a Reconstruction Committee, set up in August 1917 to consider, among other topics, hours of work and wages after the war. The members were the Executive on the one side and the chairman, secretary and one elected member of the

Workers' Representation Committee on the other. In all it held about seventy meetings at weekly sessions spread over fifteen months. Apparently the two sides were often wide apart in their views, so that discussions had to be adjourned for further consideration; yet eventually unanimous agreement on all matters was reached.[7] These agreements were incorporated in a booklet, setting out conditions of work in the factory.

In preparation for introducing the 48-hour week after the war, employees who had served continuously since 1914 were allowed to vote on whether the dinner hour should be an hour or an hour and a quarter. In the end hours were to be from 8 to 12.30 and from 1.45 to 6, and on Saturdays from 8 to 12.15; the bad old days of a 6.30 a.m. start would be gone for ever. The office hours would be from 9 to 6 with 9 to 1 on Saturdays. All workers would receive a week's holiday on full wages; the old excursions were automatically abolished.

At the beginning of 1918 Huntley Boorne and Stevens finally passed into the company's ownership. Samuel Beavan Stevens had recently completed seventy years with his firm, and now that he was eighty-five, he told Huntley and Palmers that he would be willing to sell the business outright. Howard and Eustace Palmer, together with Cecil Palmer, held consultations with their solicitors and accountants, and within a few months agreed to buy the 10,000 shares. Eustace Palmer became the chairman and Cecil Palmer the deputy chairman; the vendor's son Ewart Stevens was the managing director. Its sales and net profits were both declining, for Huntley and Palmers' business accounted for 60 per cent of turnover, and the number of tin boxes sent out in 1917–18 was only 40,000, compared with 90,000 in the previous year. Its own war contracts were probably not much more than 10 per cent of its total work, and at this stage in the war there were few fresh Government contracts that could be gained by a firm of its kind.

Huntley and Palmers' lower output of 22,000 tons in 1916–17 had been due to the concentration on exports. Then it achieved one of the highest tonnages in its history to date during 1917–18; over 25,000 tons, while profit on turnover reached the highest percentage, namely 17·5 per cent, since the late 1840s, although Excess Profits Duty offset much of its benefit to the company. However, about three-quarters of this output was destined for Government or semi-official bodies, and nearly 12 per cent, or £239,000, comprised army biscuits. Yet after the war factory buildings and machinery would have to be overhauled, so as to provide increased and more economical production. These had stood up to the stringency of wartime conditions with great robustness. The valuers that year reported that, taking into account the depleted maintenance staff, plant was in remarkably good condition; 'the machinery is fortunately so substantial that the wear and tear is not so heavy as on [other firms'] lighter makes'. Now the company appointed an architect and an engineer to report on 'remodelling and improving the factory and plant'.

On the marketing side, too, when in October 1918 the end of the war was at last in sight, Sir Ernest Palmer (as he had now become) and Charles Palmer insisted that the company must take measures to rebuild its sadly neglected home trade. As the Board had just received two reports on the future of the home and the overseas trade respectively, it set up two small committees to make detailed recomendations, but the Armistice was declared on 11th November, before they had a chance to meet.

The company noted some of its achievements during the war in its booklet *Our Work in the War and Reconstruction*. Almost 40 per cent of all men employees, namely 1833, went away on active service; of these 145 were killed. On the production side, having started the war with a dangerously low level of stocks, it had succeeded in honouring its commitments to the Government and other public bodies, only halting its stream of army biscuits in 1916–17 in a rescue attempt on the declining export business. Moreover, it had never had to close down completely because vital ingredients had run out.

An even more impressive fact, not recorded in the booklet, was that the company had unwittingly come to dominate the industry, in a way that had never happened before and rarely since. This domination was due partly to its towering size and reputation, which had made it the price leader. But also the personality of Howard Palmer had contributed. Events ever since the Association's establishment had helped to expand his outlook from provincial exclusiveness to active leadership of the whole industry, just as within the company he had developed from a rigid paternalism to belief in a form of joint consultation which anticipated the Whitley Report. It had not been a natural transition for a man who had entered middle life by the end of the Victorian age. No doubt much was also owed to the tact and forbearance of Association members and officials in their discussions with this prickly and stand-offish family.

Yet even at this pinnacle of its influence, the company was having to pay for the earlier neglect of its opportunities. It had chosen the 'easy' long-term decisions: to concentrate on the export market in preference to a sustained effort in the domestic market, to produce many varieties rather than limiting itself to a small number of fast sellers backed up by intensive advertising, to rely on trustworthy but uneconomical plant rather than introducing more up-to-date machines. It was thus standing still at a time when tastes, production and marketing methods, and distribution channels were altering rapidly. The dislocations and social changes caused by the war merely intensified the company's difficulties; they were not wholly responsible for them. However, it was encouraging that the top management now recognised the main problems that it would have to face. Indeed, in the next few years it showed signs of resilience and an acceptance of change that would have seemed unthinkable as recently as 1906 or even 1914.

16
The Associated Biscuit Manufacturers Ltd. 1919–29

Undoubtedly the most important change in Huntley and Palmers' organisation since 1914 had been the concentration of top policy-making in the hands of the Executive: namely, the Chairman, Deputy Chairman and General Manager. The Executive did not abdicate its functions when the three directors Albert, Eric and Geoffrey Palmer returned from the war and Howard Palmer's son Reginald was elected to the Board soon after being demobilised. For Alfred Palmer, now approaching seventy, retired from active work in the business he had served for fifty years, and Albert and Geoffrey Palmer were appointed Chairman and Deputy Chairman respectively of Huntley Boorne and Stevens. Thus only three younger directors were available for full-time service in the company, and they did not take part in the Executive's decisions. However, changes in its legal status were about to precipitate a major reform of the relations between the Executive and working directors.

In July 1919—the month in which the company paid all its work-people an extra week's wages to commemorate the signature of the peace treaty—Howard Palmer was actively discussing with his solicitors and accountants the possibility of conversion into a public company. As the number of family directors—and shareholders—seemed to be shrinking with each generation, they could well risk a possible loss of family control as long as the company remained a private one and hence legally debarred from offering the company's shares publicly for sale. Now that estate duty had risen to 20 per cent on estates worth £1 million and above, a series of premature deaths—like that of George William Palmer in 1913, aged sixty-two, only three years after Sir Walter Palmer's, aged fifty-two—might necessitate the sale of shares to meet taxation. A potential buyer of shares would therefore expect to have a say in policy-making.

A further problem was that raw material prices were continuing to rise and more and more of the company's liquid funds were being swallowed up in stocks. The company could achieve complete financial security only by amalgamating with sister firms, preferably under a holding company. Howard Palmer therefore asked Arthur Carr, Chairman of Peek Frean, if he wanted to revive his scheme for merging all the leading biscuit manufacturers, which Huntley and Palmers had turned down so unceremoniously in 1912.

Arthur Carr responded with alacrity. Years of collaboration within and outside the Association encouraged him to consult immediately with James Macfarlane, who proceeded to see in succession the Chairmen of Carr's, Crawford's, Jacob's and McVitie & Price. The last-named, Alexander Grant, proved the least forthcoming of them all. A crusty individualist, he staunchly resisted any idea of having to accept the control of a central Board: he himself 'must always be supreme—the first and the last word in McVitie & Price'. In any case, he added cannily, his business was not yet ripe for selling. His intransigence, coupled with Crawford's hesitation, undoubtedly deterred the others from coming in.

Howard Palmer meanwhile was preparing his co-directors at a private meeting. Their main worries were about safeguarding their shares, and for the younger ones about the possibility of being downgraded from full-time managers to merely part-time company directors. Being reassured on these points, they did not challenge the motives for amalgamation. They unanimously rejected a third alternative, of selling out to an American syndicate which had asked the accountants Price Waterhouse to approach likely firms. However, when the failure of Arthur Carr's approaches became apparent, they resolved to go ahead with converting Huntley and Palmers into a public company on its own.

The junior directors—the five who belonged to the third generation—now unexpectedly seized the initiative. Before the public company was set up, they declared, the company's administration must be reorganised. They therefore induced the Board to set up two committees. The first, a Finance Committee under the chairmanship of Cecil Palmer, himself a chartered accountant, was to determine the company's exact financial circumstances and prospects, which even the directors did not know precisely, as events in the next year or two were to reveal.

The second was a Committee of Management, to take over permanently the Executive's function. It was to comprise not only the Executive—including Herbert Pretty, who had very deservedly been promoted to the Board as Managing Director—but also the junior directors themselves and seven of the senior managers. The seven were a Chief Works Manager, the Manager of the 'Outside' departments, the Stores Buyer, the Home and Overseas Trade Managers, the Chief Engineer, and a representative of Huntley Boorne and Stevens. The sponsors were above all anxious to develop a greater sense of responsibility among these managers, each of whom would take entire charge of his function, while the directors should merely stand 'ready to give guidance and advice'.

The post of Chief Works Manager was a new one, to control manufacturing, packing and stores; the individual managers had before 1914 reported straight to the director responsible, who had taken all the main decisions. The geographical division between various factories, particularly those north and those south of the river, had for years been made the pretext for not centralising production. This reform therefore required the right man, who was prepared to match his opportunities. The first holder of the post, Richard Le Mare, was not. Brought in from outside, he served a year of apprenticeship under Frank East, who had been in charge of manufacturing since 1914, and was about to retire. He then took over in mid-1921. However, having come straight from the army and finding that the highly idiosyncratic organisation did not respond at all well to being run on military lines, he resigned eighteen months later, confessing that the 'ramifications of the business were too extensive'.

E. A. Wrottesley, who had served in the company since 1898 and who had taken over as ingredients buyer from Charles Palmer, was appointed in his place. An energetic man of forty-three, he demanded exceptionally high standards from everyone, including himself. He induced his managers to report to him direct rather than to the Board members concerned—Eric and Reginald Palmer—by always being on hand to deal with any labour troubles, a task which the managers tended to shirk. He proved so effective that even when he was appointed a director in 1931 he continued to exercise the same functions.

The senior directors did not resist this virtual take-over of the business by the younger generation, for they had enjoyed little real influence over policy ever since the Executive had been set up. Their average age was now sixty, whereas that of the next generation was thirty-five, of whom the Deputy Chairman, Eustace Palmer, was the eldest at forty-three. The only working directors of riper years were therefore Howard Palmer, aged fifty-six, and Herbert Pretty, aged sixty-seven. Speaking through Sir Ernest Palmer, the elder directors delegated full responsibility for setting up the public company to Howard and Cecil Palmer, with power to co-opt; not surprisingly, they co-opted *en bloc* the remaining members of the Executive and junior directors.

Howard Palmer was meanwhile keeping open negotiations with Peek Frean, and at a special Board meeting at the end of November 1920 he obtained his colleagues' unanimous agreement to starting formal talks with the object of a merger. Arthur Carr once again warmly welcomed his approach, and soon the whole scheme was moving forward under its own momentum: the former idea of becoming an independent public company faded away. The two sets of directors held a series of meetings from December onwards at the Great Western Hotel, Paddington. By April they were able to instruct their respective accountants (Sir William Plender, of Deloitte Plender & Griffiths, and Sir Albert Wyon, of Price Waterhouse) to calculate each party's relative interests in the new holding company, on the basis of the past eleven years' balance sheets and profit figures. Since both companies already had preference shares, and Peek Frean had debentures as well, the holding company would merely control each company's ordinary shares.

The two units (as the subsidiary companies came to be known) exchanged their ordinary shares for those of the holding company, on the basis recommended by the accountants: namely $52\frac{1}{2}$ per cent to Huntley and Palmers and the remaining $47\frac{1}{2}$ per cent to Peek Frean. Of the authorised capital of £2,500,000, £1,050,000 was issued to Huntley and Palmers' ordinary shareholders and £950,000 to those of Peek Frean. The remaining £500,000 was subscribed in cash and met the expenses of formation.

Directors were busy trying to decide on a name for the holding company. On Huntley and Palmers' side Howard Palmer suggested the British (or possibly United) Biscuit Co., as did Herbert Pretty. His colleagues favoured alternative designations, which ranged from Amalgamated, British Empire and Imperial to National. However, Alfred and Eustace Palmer pressed for Associated Biscuit Companies Ltd. In the circumstances this most nearly reflected the new company's form, and the Associated Biscuit Manufacturers Ltd. was incorporated on 1st December 1921.[1] Everyone concerned took great pains to deny that Peek Frean had been in any way taken over by Huntley and Palmers. Thus while Howard Palmer was elected the first Chairman, Arthur Carr became the Vice-Chairman, and Herbert Pretty and C. V. Jones (Managing Director of Peek Frean), became joint Managing Directors.

The Group Board similarly contained equal representation from each unit. Those from Reading comprised all the directors who were on the Committee of Management. Huntley and Palmers' solicitors required that this committee should become its Executive Committee and be delegated all the powers of Huntley and Palmers' Board. That Board, which included the older generation of the Palmer family met only once a quarter, chiefly to conduct formal business such as accepting the Chairman's Report and the accounts or appointing new directors.

Disappointed as they were that other firms had not come in, Howard Palmer and Arthur Carr—who were constantly rubbing shoulders with their fellow chairmen at meetings of the trade association—kept open the doors of communication with them. In particular, the firm of Jacob's had split into two legally distinct companies after the Irish Free State had been set up, with separate but interlocking boards of directors. In June 1924 Arthur Carr felt that the time was ripe to propose amalgamation to the Chairman of Jacob's, George Jacob, who took up the proposal with his respective boards. Dublin would consider a merger only on condition that each unit was given virtually complete autonomy. This would involve maintaining the existing arrangement whereby the Dublin company was allocated enough of the total orders to permit continuous operation, while the Liverpool company looked to the British market for its orders.

Howard Palmer's solicitors concluded from the ensuing correspondence that 'Jacobs are evidently at this moment very nervous and suspicious. . . . You have got to make it quite clear to them that they cannot expect you to buy their business and yet not get control of it.' In an official letter to be forwarded to Jacob's, the solicitor explained that if a holding company acquired all Jacobs' ordinary shares, it would obtain 'no more and no less right to interfere' in a subsidiary's management than the existing ordinary shareholders of Jacob's enjoyed.

Arthur Carr tried to calm George Jacob's apprehensions by pointing out how Huntley and Palmers and Peek Frean had had to make up their minds 'on what was a momentous step, and a step, I may add, almost into the unknown. . . . The real point is the spirit which animates the people who come to an agreement.' Despite this reassurance that a leap in the dark could land safely on *terra firma*, George Jacob was not convinced that he could win over the more intransigent members of his Dublin and Liverpool boards, and early in 1925 Arthur Carr, while accepting that this was the end of the round, declared that he intended to keep negotiations going. Just a third of a century later, under Arthur Carr's grandson and Howard Palmer's son, negotiations sprang into life again and were successfully concluded.

Although undertaken primarily for financial reasons, the general advantages of the amalgamation gradually became apparent to Huntley and Palmers as economic difficulties began to mount. While money incomes remained high immediately after the war, there was a buoyant demand for goods such as biscuits that had been scarce for so long; this demand was often hard to meet because of supply difficulties. The poor quality of butter and other fats prevented the company from reopening the cake factory until October 1920, and although the extraction rate for flour had been rapidly restored to very near its pre-war level, the surcharge on flour was not abolished until a month later, shortly before the dissolution of the Ministry of Food. In 1918–19 the company's output, at 24,400 tons, was only slightly below the record level of 1917–18, despite the termination of War Office contracts after the Armistice and the depressed state of Continental trade because exchange rates had moved against sterling and thus made British goods much dearer on the Continent. Indeed, fears of further depreciation and the company's financial stringency forced it to repatriate, at a loss of £66,000, the considerable export proceeds locked up in France and Belgium since 1914.

By mid-1920 the post-war boom was over. Yet the cost inflation persisted to the end of the year, during the whole of which distributors were feverishly stocking up with biscuits in advance of further price rises. Even so, in 1920–21 the company's tonnage was only half the 1917–18 level, namely 12,773 tons, including 165 tons of cake from the newly opened cake factory. Then prices tumbled. Between December 1920 and June 1922 the trade association approved one general and four partial reductions in biscuit prices: grocers began to buy from hand to mouth in anticipation of further reductions. Thus whereas the *volume* of orders remained buoyant, the average *value* of each was low, which kept the company's distribution and office costs high. Abroad, merchants who had overbought at peak prices were unable to liquidate their stocks, to allow them to order more. Although the number of factory employees fell from a post-war peak of 5000 in September 1919 to 3500 two years later, from August 1920 onwards the company had to reduce hours of work to two-thirds, or 31 hours a week, with a complete shut-down on Saturdays and Mondays.

Since the company appeared to be under greater difficulties from the recession than its quality competitors, the directors were inevitably worried about whether its costs were too high. A costings committee, headed by Howard Palmer himself, carefully investigated the costings of a number of biscuits and the rate of profit on each, to see what price reductions might be possible. Then at the end of 1920 the Board asked whether the factory machinery was up-to-date and economical. The very muted response was an order for two automatic machines for making ice cones, to be staffed entirely by female labour. The full enquiry, by an architect and engineer, started in 1918 to explore the possibility of remodelling the factory and plant achieved little, apart from rearranging work so as to allow biscuit cutting machines to be started immediately at the beginning of each shift.

The company's accounting methods appeared to be in no better shape than its production methods. At the end of the financial year 1920–21, in common with many firms, it had to write down stocks so drastically that it incurred a loss: the only one in the whole of its history. Directors seem not to have suspected this loss until the accounts were actually drawn up. They were largely to blame for not giving more powers to William Lea, the company secretary ever since 1898. With his domed head and highly polished boots, he appeared the epitome of a family firm's confidential clerk, but such a key position now required a more expert and less deferential figure. That figure was soon forthcoming.

In 1921 Bennet Palmer, a practising chartered accountant who was quite unrelated to the family, was appointed secretary of Huntley Boorne and Stevens, with the task of introducing a costing system there. Under the long Stevens regime, no proper check had been kept on costs and prices, and Bennet Palmer's first step was to cost precisely each order or job that went through the factory. He could then have the original estimates for these orders checked against actual costs, which made sure that estimates were realistic and that costs did not get out of hand.[2] Since accurate costing and estimation are the lifeblood of any company, what was good for a tin works was good for a biscuit factory, even though the latter made for stock while the former made to order. At the end of 1921 he therefore became joint secretary of Huntley and Palmers, and sole secretary when William Lea died in harness the following March. He soon introduced a system of monthly profit estimates, which were to be of considerable value during the next difficult decade.

From all the data now available, the company concluded that about the only practicable method of reducing costs was to economise in labour, for instance by putting women on to men's work. This would pose two problems. The first was that, except during the war period, women had not come forward in large enough numbers. Second, and more important, as the town's main industrial employer the company would be creating large-scale redundancies, since the men in their fifties and sixties who could most profitably be dispensed with were precisely those for whom no alternative work now existed; they would merely swell the growing ranks of the unemployed. As older factory hands became redundant, therefore, they were 'sent down the yard'; that is, attached to a pool of labourers in the building and engineering departments, where they did little productive work. Alternatively, they were kept on in the factories although managers knew they were dispensable. As late as 1931 an informed observer estimated that 120 men, or over 6 per cent of male employees, fell into one or other of these categories.

A further economy would be to reduce wages. In March 1921, the management therefore discussed the matter with the Workers' Representation Committee and the union, and obtained agreement for bringing down basic wages from 60s. to 57s. (£3·00 to £2·85). This was still well above the 48s. (£2·40) fixed at the end of the war. They agreed a further reduction of 2s. (10p.) in June after the official cost of living index had fallen by 26 points in the six months from October 1920. Managers and the office staffs similarly had their salaries cut. The Board also made a number of trifling economies: for instance, it disbanded the Cadet Corps, but it did not touch the Boys' Club, to which Eric Palmer had donated premises in 1918 as a memorial to Ronald Poulton.

The Recreation Club had quickly revived after the war. Since it was an important means of promoting good understanding between employers and employees, Howard Palmer was anxious to extend its scope, and therefore had a salaried official appointed as secretary; owing to the need for economies, the official now had to be replaced by an honorary secretary. More important, the King's Meadow grounds had frequently been unusable owing to flooding, but in 1919 the former Berkshire Cricket Club ground in Kensington Road, Reading, had come into the market and was in danger of being converted into housing sites. However, Howard Palmer acquired it and in 1920 agreed to make it over to the company on long lease. Its good amenities were therefore assured to the Recreation Club for at least a century to come.

Thus the top management found that economies and higher efficiency were not easy to come by. It was worried that in 1923, for instance, 3750 factory employees on average were needed to produce just under 12,000 tons, while in 1913–14 less than 5000 had been needed for almost exactly double that output: a fall in labour productivity of a third, from 4·8 tons a year to 3·2 tons. The company therefore needed to be able to compare more accurately the extent of the company's 'inefficiency', and of the 'economies' that should be made. Peek Frean now provided a standard of comparison, as the two units came to share figures of their relative performances. A report by J. R. Gales drew some telling comparisons in September 1922, a year or so after he succeeded H. J. Morton as Manager of the Home Trade. A young man of thirty, he had all the drive and singlemindedness that his post required, and was never afraid to speak his mind, least of all to the Board. He was not put off even when, in the late 1930s, the Board curtly instructed him to confine his reports in future to statistical matter.

In his report he pointed out that whereas in 1901–2 Peek Frean's gross home tonnage had been less than one-third of Huntley and Palmers', from 1919–20 onwards they were approximately equal. Moreover, both McVitie & Price and Macfarlane Lang, formerly much smaller firms, now probably had a home turnover comparable with that of the company. Rivals had eroded the company's trade not only by granting higher discounts but also by giving the public what it wanted: namely, shorter and slightly sweeter varieties. Huntley and Palmers' were felt to be too 'dry and plain', and he himself believed that they tended to be overbaked. This was particularly resented in the North of England, where customers disliked anything that could be labelled as 'burnt'.

Unlike Peek Frean, the company still seemed incapable of producing any really successful novelties. Looking at the company's four largest sellers in the sweet range—Ginger Nut, Marie, Milk and Petit Beurre—no less than thirteen rival firms were making ones with identical names. The numbers were similar with other popular varieties such as Osborne and Thin Arrowroot.

The company's present reliance on wholesalers was, in Gales's view, shortsighted, for any medium- or small-sized retailer asking for a direct account was referred to a wholesaler. This policy meant that the company was seriously under-represented in many areas of the country. It did over £350 worth of trade per thousand inhabitants in Exeter, £170 in Oxford and £145 in Bath, but only £19 in Liverpoool, £10 in Glasgow and £6 in Bolton. Glasgow had over 2000 grocers, yet the company had fewer than 125 direct and indirect accounts there. Even in the Baedeker-type cities where the bulk of provincial business was done, the family grocers who still survived were finding that it paid better to stock competitors' goods. Gales cited a letter from Grimbly Hughes, the Oxford grocer whose predecessor in the Cornmarket had been selling Huntley's 'read-ing' biscuits in the 1830s, which pleaded for higher discounts. By contrast, Selfridges in London—the typical department store of the inter-war period—refused to stock the company's biscuits any longer in its Bargain Basement, as it could devote space far more profitably to biscuits on which better terms were offered.

Gales believed that the company could easily increase the numbers of direct accounts. Peek Frean had 40,000 distributors, whereas Huntley and Palmers had less than 25,000 of which 16,000 were direct accounts. Numbers of travellers had been increased the previous year from thirteen to fifteen in London and from thirty-four to thirty-eight in the country, yet they were still below those of Peek Frean, and even so they were often deployed inefficiently. Again, Peek Frean had twenty-three depots in the country whereas Huntley and Palmers had none; rivals had introduced motor deliveries well before the war, but the company refused to follow suit until the 1920s, despite the maxim that 'the motor always follows the traveller'. The company's advertising, too, was so ineffective that many North Country people did not even know what Huntley and Palmers manufactured.

The directors did pay some attention to Gales's report. They accepted the need to go to retailers direct and to canvass them more intensively since in the main wholesalers were not 'actively and efficiently' bringing in business to the company. As to discounts, they agreed to increase those of the company and to press competitors, through the Association, to reduce theirs. They also authorised a further increase in the number of representatives and to retire some of the more elderly ones, as well as to employ more motor vans. Advertising expenditure was also increased by £40,000, and Mather & Crowther were called on to organise a special campaign. As a result, Ginger Nuts were advertised intensively in the North of England; by 1925 their total tonnage sold was over a fifth higher than before the war. In his report for 1923 the Managing Director was able to mention the 'aggressive policy' which the company was now pursuing. For the time being, the decline in home tonnage was reversed, rising above the 1920–1 level once again in 1925.

On the financial side the company and Peek Frean were sharing information to some effect. In December 1923 the two Costs Managers produced a thorough report, and concluded that the costing system at Reading was still very primitive: there was, for instance, no proper dissection of wages in each department. Sometimes one unit had to pay more for the different ingredients and supplies and sometimes the other; yet on balance Reading was spending £25,000 a year more for them. On wages, Huntley and Palmers' ability to hire labour at the lower provincial rates was offset by the fact that men were employed on jobs that could just as well be done by women and boys: the under-employment of boys in manufacture, for instance, was costing the company about £15,000 a year. Thus Huntley and Palmers' products had in the aggregate a lower profit-earning capacity than those of Peek Frean, namely 11·8 per cent compared with 18 per cent.

Such comparisons as these helped to restore to the company the sense of direction it seemed recently to have lost. Yet Howard Palmer did not live to guide it on its new course. He had been incapacitated since shortly after the merger had taken place, and he died in March 1923, aged only fifty-seven.[3] His achievements can best be gauged by contrasting the company's essentially nineteenth-century aspect when he took over from George William Palmer in 1906 with the will for modernisation that now existed. Even if the machinery was much the same, management was acquiring a new spirit. Undoubtedly he regarded as his greatest service to the company the establishment of the Workers'

Representation Committee some years before Whitley Councils were officially proposed, and he did not at all mind keeping his own managers waiting while he talked things over with members of the committee.

Eustace Palmer, who had been a director for twenty years and Deputy Chairman for ten years, was elected Chairman. Two joint Deputy Chairmen were appointed: Eric Palmer in charge of the factory and Cecil Palmer in charge of trade and finance. The new Chairman is remembered as a genial and tactful man of gentle but far from passive disposition, very much in the mould of his father, Alfred Palmer. Yet he was not a robust man: he had been seriously ill for six months in 1917 and he now suffered from pernicious anaemia. Nevertheless, he pressed on resolutely with the task of collaborating more closely with Peek Frean. In particular, he had the potentialities of joint production and joint delivery thoroughly investigated. Only in marketing did the two companies insist on maintaining their old rivalry.

They finally decided that it would not be feasible at that time to integrate their production processes, although they sought advice from Imperial Tobacco, whose various productive units had been integrated to a considerable extent. They did agree to some slight rationalisation: for instance, Peek Frean agreed not to make Breakfast biscuits—still one of Huntley and Palmers' best sellers—for at least two years, while the latter's new policy of dealing directly with retailers was being put into effect. On the other hand, joint delivery offered much scope for economies, provided that it was not used as a stepping stone to joint marketing. The joint Stock Depot set up in Reading at the end of 1923, to cover a radius of twenty-five to thirty miles, was the first move towards a radical reshaping, and speeding up, of Huntley and Palmers' delivery services. By 1929 twenty-six such Stock Depots and twenty-one Transfer Sheds were in being.

Meanwhile, however, the company's profits were continuing to decline. In 1917–18 to 1919–20 they had averaged £425,000 a year, but by 1923 they were running at only half that figure, or just under 10 per cent of turnover as against an earlier 16 per cent. The costing enquiry showed that the Reading unit's most popular varieties frequently showed big losses or only small profits, and that there were the varieties that should be looked at first of all. The Group Finance Committee therefore set up a committee of Huntley and Palmers' Chairman, Managing Director and Chief Engineer (A. W. Blackmore), to see if production costs could be reduced by removing any existing buildings and erecting a brand-new factory. The committee recommended the closure of the South Factory, which was shut down in 1925—almost twenty years after the valuers had first made this suggestion. It also proposed that fifty-three men over or approaching seventy should be pensioned, and that girls should take over biscuit sorting from men; moreover, boys should be invariably discharged at the age of eighteen if they were unfit to be trained for skilled work. Almost at the same time, a Buildings Committee recommended that a four-storeyed Central Warehouse should be erected at a cost of £175,000, and that the obsolescent buildings for storing and washing returned tins should be replaced at a cost of £40,000. In addition, the factories should be electrified: that would involve the expenditure of a further £30,000.

In the short run, however, the brunt of any economies would continue to be borne by the workpeople. This was at a time when an inquiry, similar to A. L. Bowley's 1912 survey of Reading households, showed that unskilled wages had on average more than kept pace with living costs. In 1912 the usual wages between 20 and 23s. (£1·00–£1·15), had been enough to support only two or three children. By 1924 comparable wages, around 45s. (£2·25), would support three to four children. Since the average size of families had tended to diminish, only 8 per cent of working-class families were in poverty instead of 23 per cent in 1912. Of this 8 per cent, only a quarter (as against 69 per cent) owed their poverty to inadequate wages. On the other hand, a further 24 per cent were poor because of unemployment, compared with a mere 2 per cent in 1912.[4]

The implication of this survey was that a large-scale transfer of work from males to females, clearly the next stage in Huntley and Palmers' reforms, would cause the amount of poverty in the town to soar. The Workers' Representation Committee, fearful of large-scale redundancies, asked that its members should sit on the Committee of Management. The directors did not agree, but promised to confer with them when important matters such as substantial changes in output were to be discussed. The union seemed unable to take any effective action. Its already low membership in the factory had declined, and the company maintained its refusal to discriminate in any way against non-union employees. The Board would not even agree to meet the national leaders J. R. Clynes and Will Thorne when they asked for an interview.

Industrial relations under the new conditions came under the first test in August 1924 when some girls in the packing room, after their piece work rates had been cut, refused to work their new 'lots', while others refused to handle trolleys in place of some old men who had just been pensioned off. The same afternoon the union stationed pickets at the gates, in preparation for a complete stoppage. Eustace Palmer reacted decisively: he closed the factory at 6 p.m. and declared that it would not be reopened until new conditions of work had been agreed. '[Negotiating] machinery already in existence in the factory', he declared, 'was the best and proper means of settling the details of the matter in dispute.' A mass meeting of employees in the Town Hall thereupon gave an overwhelming vote of confidence, with only a few abstentions, to the Workers' Representation Committee: the fact that they had very little option does not make their action any less touching.

The management then agreed with the committee to confer with the managers of each department concerned about any part of the new scheme likely to cause hardship or undue loss of wages; meanwhile, the new 'lots' in the packing room must be given a fair trial. A further mass meeting of workers then approved this agreement. The Reading factory had no further large-scale labour dispute; when in May 1926 the union attempted to call out the workpeople during the general strike, after an appeal by the management they remained at their posts.

A commemorative history would make much of the surface events of these years. In 1924 the British Empire Exhibition was held at Wembley, and at the company's stand a Baker Perkins machine manufactured the Wembley and other biscuits. A model of the Duke and Duchess of York's wedding cake was also on view; all employees were given a Saturday off with full pay to permit a visit. This was the era when the Christmas tins were at their most fanciful: they included a garden roller, a penny-in-the-slot machine which released a biscuit for every penny inserted, a hand camera and a Huntley and Palmers' delivery van.

With the coming of the British Broadcasting Company, a Radio biscuit was issued, and a juvenile idol of the silent films, Jackie Coogan (star of such tear-jerkers as *The Kid* and *My Boy*) lent his name to a biscuit that was shaped like his head; in the showbusiness language of *The Cinema* magazine, 'each cranium is enclosed in a grease-proof little bag'.[5] This unusual shape was not repeated fifteen years later for the Shirley biscuit which commemorated another infant phenomenon, Shirley Temple: hers was a straightforward rectangular shortcake. Further ceremonial followed in 1926 when the company, under the mistaken impression that the Huntley shop had been established in 1826, celebrated its centenary. Each employee received an extra week's wage, a banquet was held, and the Prince of Wales visited the factory.[6]

Yet below the surface all was clearly not well with the company. Profits were still diminishing; between 1924 and 1926 they averaged only £191,000, or under 9 per cent of turnover. Then in June 1926 Eustace Palmer resigned as Chairman, because of deteriorating health. During his brief tenure of the chairmanship, he had taken some useful steps to modernise the company, the fruits of lengthy experience at the centre of affairs. For a few years he remained a member of the Executive Committee, but he died in July 1931.

Eric Palmer became Chairman at the age of forty-two. Cecil Palmer was appointed the sole Deputy Chairman, and Reginald Palmer took over control of the factory. Eric Palmer's long period of office continued until after the Second World War, and he correctly judged that a more informal approach was needed in relations both within and outside the factory. A professional in every aspect of his work, he never stood on his dignity as Chairman, and was not above some discreet clowning to break the ice in difficult negotiations.

Almost his first act was to set up an Economy Committee, headed by Cecil Palmer. The other members were Clement Williams, the Managing Director's Chief Assistant since his return from Huntley Boorne and Stevens in 1922 and now designated General Manager, and Bennet Palmer as secretary. This high-powered committee, which thus had two chartered accountants on it, was intended to be thorough rather than expeditious in its work. In all it produced eight detailed reports on suggested economies in the various parts of the business, and did not complete its deliberations until early in 1932.

While the long-term problems were being investigated, however, the outlook in the short run was far from encouraging. After a slight improvement in 1926, tonnage produced, absolute profits and profits as a percentage of turnover all fell year by year to 1929. The company had increased discounts (at the expense of profits) as part of its aggressive policy at home and overseas, and fuel prices were high owing to the coal strike which dragged on throughout the latter part of 1926. Cheap manufacturers were doing well; most of them had already left the Association and were therefore not bound by its rules, and between them they were exploiting the general public's steadily increasing demand for biscuits. Some of Huntley and Palmers' directors visited various parts of the country to see for themselves how greatly cheap biscuits were harming the company's sales and to suggest what could be done. The company finally obtained the Association's agreement to nine varieties being retailed at 1s. or 10d. (5p. or 4p.) a pound in the home trade.

However, the introduction of the Bedaux system achieved a considerable and relatively painless economy on the labour side in the late 1920s. Based on time and motion study, it was designed to increase output by eliminating unnecessary movements by each employee and lay down 'normal' amounts of work. It would thus help to economise in wages.[7] An experimental trial, lasting a month, was held in the Rusk Packing Room; as this proved a success, a member of the Bedaux firm explained the whole system to the Workers' Representation Committee. The committee accepted it in exchange for an assurance that if any hands thereby became redundant, they would not be dismissed. Over the next few years the system was gradually extended to the whole of the factory; in 1932 it was estimated that over the five years since its inception, it had achieved a cumulative net saving of £95,000 when the cost of the Bedaux engineers and staff was deducted. At a time when profits were averaging less than £130,000 a year, this annual sum of nearly £20,000 represented a major economy.

The decline in overseas trade during the 1920s, in both absolute and relative terms, has already been mentioned. Since the rearrangement of duties in 1920, the Overseas Manager had been P. A. Spaul and the director responsible had been Geoffrey Palmer. He was a specialist in this field; he had served in Joseph Leete's firm, making a number cf tours throughout Leete's Continental and Near Eastern territory, before he began his apprenticeship. Leete himself had died in 1913, aged eighty-two, but his firm continued to undertake Huntley and Palmers' Continental business. When this fell off drastically during the war, the company paid it a retaining fee of £3000. These subsidies continued at much higher rates, namely £9500 a year in 1923 and 1924 and £8000 in 1925, for the average gross tonnage sold to the Continent during 1923–5 was less than 800 tons compared with nearly 6000 tons a year in the three years before the war. Huntley and Palmers then resolved to place its Continental trade in other hands, and in 1927, J. Leete and Sons Ltd. was wound up. The company helped to find alternative jobs for the clerical staff, pensioned off the older men and compensated the directors. Instead of despatching travellers from Britain, it engaged local representatives, who received a commission of $7\frac{1}{2}$ per cent on net sales.

In the export markets outside Europe, too, the company sought to bring its arrangements up to date by breaking its long-standing agreements with C. & E. Morton and Crosse & Blackwell. However, as an interim measure the two firms undertook to offer more favourable discounts to certain dealers nominated by Huntley and Palmers, mainly those in Far Eastern countries. Then in 1929 they both accepted six months' notice to terminate their agreements, except for the trivial case of 'trade with small clubs, missionaries etc.'. All other business was to be handled by representatives on the spot.

A particularly taxing problem was the company's trade with France, where sales had declined from £268,000 in 1919 to under £14,500 in 1923. This decline was due partly to the continuing unfavourable exchange rates and partly to heavy tariffs on certain leading varieties such as Breakfast biscuits and sugar wafers. In 1923 a committee of the Group Board investigated all the possible solutions to this problem, such as withdrawing from the French market until such time as it improved, and manufacturing in France. Early in the following year the

Group decided to set up, not a British subsidiary, but entirely French company controlled by and bearing the name of Huntley and Palmers.

It then purchased a factory for the equivalent of £39,000, at La Courneuve, in the industrial belt of Paris near St. Denis. Huntley and Palmers (France) S.A. was formed, with a capital equivalent to £235,000 of which the company subscribed £135,000. With some old machinery shipped out from Reading, fifteen of the most important varieties were manufactured; the quantities represented about half the pre-war sales of these varieties to France. Huntley and Palmers would receive royalties of between $2\frac{1}{2}$ and 5 per cent on all biscuits produced; this provision was afterwards waived to help the new subsidiary accumulate cash reserves.

About a year later a prominent United States banker tried to interest the company in setting up a manufacturing plant in that country. These negotiations foundered partly because managers would have had to be sent from Reading, and this would have represented a serious 'drain on the home organisation'. The company considered various schemes over the next decades for manufacture in a wide selection of countries, but none on closer examination turned out to be practicable. Thus Huntley and Palmers has never manufactured, except under licence, in any overseas country apart from France.

17
Depression Years 1929–39

The year 1929—midway between the wars—is a convenient stage for taking stock of the biscuit-making industry generally at that time and of Huntley and Palmers in particular. Accurate figures of all biscuit firms' total tonnage do not become available until the late 1930s, but in 1921 Huntley and Palmers and Peek Frean together seem to have produced nearly one-eighth of the whole. The following table gives estimates of total consumers' expenditure on biscuits for certain inter-war years.

UNITED KINGDOM: CONSUMERS' EXPENDITURE ON BISCUITS 1920–38[1]

	Consumers' Expenditure (£m.)	Percentage of Total Expenditure on Food		Consumers' Expenditure (£m.)	Percentage of Total Expenditure on Food
1920	19·7	1·2	1931	22·1	1·8
1921	20·2	1·3	1934	23·5	2·0
1922	17·4	1·3	1935	26·4	2·2
1926	21·7	1·6	1937	29·8	2·3
1929	23·5	1·8	1938	27·6	2·1
1930	24·1	1·9			

Both absolutely and as a percentage of people's spending on food in general, expenditure on biscuits showed a fairly constant upward trend between 1920 and 1937. Broadly speaking, twice as much of the food budget was going on biscuits at the end of the period as at the beginning. Even though the structural decline of Britain's staple industries was creating very large pockets of high unemployment in the depressed areas, south-east England and the Midlands at least seemed to enjoy a fair amount of prosperity arising from a host of newer and mainly light industries. Thus there was on the whole much purchasing power available for this convenience food.

However, Huntley and Palmers was not receiving an adequate share of the increased trade, as the accompanying figures show.

BISCUITS: NET TONNAGE PRODUCED[1]

	HOME TRADE	OVERSEAS TRADE		
	Huntley and Palmers	Total U.K.	Huntley and Palmers	Huntley and Palmers as % of whole
1914	14,239	19,921	9300	46·6
1926	10,715	8473	3011	35·5
1929	10,469	10,087	2828	28·0

TURNOVER (£000s)

	HOME TRADE		OVERSEAS TRADE			% of whole		
	Huntley and Palmers	Peek Frean	Total U.K.	Huntley and Palmers	Peek Frean	Huntley and Palmers	Peek Frean	Others
1914	829[2]	916	1166	759	250	65·1	21·4	13·5
1926	1601	1923	1083	578	261	53·4	24·1	22·5
1929	1495	1769	1177	482	358	41·0	30·4	28·6

Notes
1. Total U.K. Overseas Trade from *Annual Abstract of Trade* (H.M.S.O.). All other figures from internal sources.
2. 1913–14.

In Britain, total expenditure on biscuits rose by 35 per cent from 1922 to 1929, but the value of the company's home sales by less than 10 per cent. The tonnage which it sold in the home trade fell by a quarter between 1914 and 1929, while its tonnage sold overseas was by 1929 only 30 per cent of the 1914 level. In money terms, Peek Frean's aggregate turnover had been only 10 per cent higher than Huntley and Palmers' in 1913–14 but was 20 per cent higher by 1926 and 1929.

The Home Trade Manager, J. R. Gales, was still battling to reverse this relative decline. His report for 1928—in his opinion 'one of the worst years for general trade' in biscuits since the war—detailed the reasons for the company's poor results. Some reasons were familiar enough: that quality competitors, notably the 'Scotch makers', were better suiting the public's tastes than Huntley and Palmers were, and that the cheaper manufacturers (principally Kemp's, the International Stores and the Co-operative Wholesale Society) were making headway at the lower end of the price scale.

He did mention, as an example of the continuing disappearance of the family grocer, that thirty-four such grocers had between them bought almost £9000 worth of the company's biscuits, and had the previous year been absorbed by various multiples; virtually the whole of their trade had consequently been lost to the company. A new development was the very large number of complaints received about the condition of the company's biscuits: an unwelcome falling off from the one-time insistence on the highest standards.

In the longer term, Gales believed that definite shifts in consumers' wants would adversely affect biscuit sales in general. He cited the growing habit of smoking, particularly among women, and the demand for fresh fruit, now that the fruit trade was exploiting the current slimming craze through an 'Eat More Fruit' campaign. His fears were not entirely justified, for another publicity campaign, to 'Drink More Milk', was shortly to bring about the establishment of milk bars throughout the country. Biscuits were so much in demand in these bars that the company appointed an extra representative to canvass them. The problem therefore remained of how much of the potential business Huntley and Palmers could hope to capture.

The Chairman's report for 1929 pointed out how since 1921, when the Group had been set up, the company had expended no less than £735,000 on capital items, such as rebuilding, electrification and new plant and machinery. The whole sum had been met out of income and reserves, without the necessity of asking the Group for more capital. Already these schemes—as well as the Bedaux system—had brought in substantial cost reductions. He therefore felt very optimistic about the future. However, in October 1929 the great economic depression was heralded by the Stock Market crash in the United States. The preceding fever of activity and speculation is illustrated by the fact that the company's exports there had doubled from 164 tons in 1922–3 to 312 tons in 1929. These exports then fell steadily to 132 tons in the worst year of 1933, and even by 1936 had not revived even to the level of 200 tons.

As the depression spread throughout the world, the prices of primary products (including tin and rubber) began to tumble, thus further weakening the capacity of producing countries to import luxuries such as biscuits. In 1930 both the value and the tonnage of the company's total exports therefore fell by a quarter, the decline being concentrated mainly in Far Eastern territories, notably India.

At home, however, the effects on the British economy were delayed.

In October 1929 the trade association had, after much discussion, sanctioned the introduction of four new varieties of biscuits at popular prices, as a counter-measure against the cheap manufacturers. Over and above its annual allocation of £45,000 for advertising at home and £23,000 overseas, Huntley and Palmers set aside £14,500 for an intensive national press campaign to promote these varieties, which Gales by some able planning put into the shops ahead of rival Association members. Initial sales were therefore gratifying, and did not appear to be at the expense of the dearer varieties. As a result, the company's home sales held up well during 1930, and its net profit on turnover went up slightly from 6·9 to 7·2 per cent.

In comparative terms, however, Huntley and Palmers remained a high-cost firm, at a time when Peek Frean was becoming the most technically advanced of all biscuit manufacturers. Peek Frean's Chief Engineer, Laurent Rondolin, was a Frenchman who had worked at Bermondsey since 1909 and was the most able technician that firm ever employed. His skill lay not merely in making old and tried machines work at unprecedented speeds, but also in inventing new machinery, including a patent long oven which later became standard equipment throughout the industry. Thus when in 1931 Arthur Carr's grandson Rupert, seconded from Peek Frean for a period as an apprentice, wrote a detailed report on Huntley and Palmers' organisation, he judged its production methods by very demanding standards.

These methods he found old-fashioned but of very great interest. Most of the machinery had been made in the factory, and its makers had displayed 'wonderful ingenuity'. However, having been installed piecemeal, it was completely inflexible and unco-ordinated. Since the company required uniform excellence of quality, each worker was an expert in his own line, thoroughly familiar with the idiosyncracies of his piece of machinery but never moved around to gain new experience. 'It seems almost as if each line has been studied separately and the process altered and altered until the exact result is obtained,' he commented.

One consequence was that there was too much plant altogether. As the ovens were only 40 to 50 feet long, the number of machines exceeded the available oven capacity; hence either one machine in two had to be kept out of use, or else all machines were set to operate at a very slow and uneconomic speed. Practically all these ovens were coal-fired and suitable only for certain kinds of biscuit—which led to even more inflexibility and needless cost. For instance, 'every oven that is likely to be used is kept fired'.

It was not only plant operatives who were strong individualists, for each factory and department tended to be segregated from all others. Members of one department were not allowed even to set foot in any other department. Whereas recent reforms had to some extent broken down this departmental isolation, in one or two parts of the business 'organisation has to yield to personalities'. In particular, the manager of the Chocolate Factory was typical of the old school, for he behaved as an autocrat until his death in 1933, after which the factory was completely reorganised and modernised.

Similarly, Rupert Carr felt that the areas of managerial responsibility were too ill-defined. The production and the sales sides remained unco-ordinated. In manufacturing, there was an excess of machinery and of male labour, while in packing, the popularity of assortments and the Christmas trade caused shortages of female labour and factory space.

Manufacturing tended to ask the Stock Office for work in order to keep output going; biscuits therefore often accumulated and lost their crispness before being packed. Since 1929, however, the Stock Office was issuing a work schedule to each section, thus helping to achieve balance between the two sides. However, no account was taken of the available labour supply, and hence whether overtime or transfers from other departments would be required. Since the Stock Office was not yet fully acquainted with each section's productive capacity, section managers often blithely disregarded the work schedules and used their own judgement when they felt too much or too little was being ordered.

Instead, Rupert Carr recommended, the Stock Office should itself oversee the flow of labour between departments as well and build up enough experience of trends to undertake some 'intelligent forecasting'. Thus a strong Stock Office could act as the nucleus of a Planning Office, which could adjust production levels more nearly to market conditions. However, changes of this magnitude were far in the future. In March E. A. Wrottesley did persuade the Board to improve the storage of unpacked biscuits by extending the cool storerooms.

On the question of labour relations, Rupert Carr noted that the Workers' Representation Committee, despite its steadily growing value as a system of communications, was in some ways unsatisfactory because its members tended to bypass the managers, who if consulted would have been able to prevent much time-wasting and many misunderstandings. There should therefore be a joint council of managers and committee members in equal numbers. In fact, a Joint Advisory Council was not set up until 1949, at the suggestion of the National Joint Wages Council which had by then become the industry-wide negotiating body.

Perhaps the company's most urgent problem at this time was its shortage of ready money, which had caused its overdraft to rise to £100,000 by mid-1930. It hoped to fund part of this debt by offering its own preference shares on the open market. However, this proved difficult because the Stock Exchange would only give permission to deal in them if the company were to disclose its balance sheet to intending purchasers. While the company itself had nothing to hide, it did have in train three 'weak sisters', namely Pulp Industries Ltd., the French subsidiary, and Huntley Boorne and Stevens, all of which were unduly dependent on the company.

Pulp Industries, a very small firm, made packages out of woodpulp for Peek Frean and for Huntley and Palmers, which had a few years before acquired about £3000 worth of its ordinary shares. Despite steady losses from the outset, it did eventually become more or less self-supporting from 1936 onwards. The two larger sisters were far more costly to maintain, and it is not scarcely surprising that Huntley and Palmers in those difficult times should have tried to shed the burden by seeking to marry them off.

The main problem with the French factory was that it produced a limited output with some obsolete machinery imported from Reading. Its machinery was therefore expensive in terms of labour, and even though it operated inside France's high tariff walls, had little prospect of becoming profitable. Huntley and Palmers took steps to strengthen the management in Paris and to impose tighter control from Reading, and then amalgamated the French company with a local subsidiary of McVitie & Price. The merger, as sensible as it was unexpected—for McVitie & Price, with a turnover now roughly equal to that of Huntley and Palmers, was one of the company's main 'outside' rivals at home—involved the formation of a new company, the Union des Biscuiteries, with an enlarged capital. Even so, the losses continued and during 1936–7 in particular, political and other difficulties in France multiplied, such as the devaluation of the franc, strikes and an imposition by Government decree of a 40-hour week and higher wage rates. Until the Second World War, therefore, no royalties were received from France and the deficit mounted year by year.

Huntley Boorne and Stevens' potential earnings, too, were severely restricted by the depressed condition of the tinplate industry. Like Huntley and Palmers, the firm was handicapped through possessing highly durable machinery which dated from the nineteenth century. Moreover, since Bryant & May had ceased to do business with it during the 1920s, its principal customer was Huntley and Palmers. Thus obsolescent machinery and relatively low output made it, too, a high-cost firm. A comparison with Peek Frean's manufacture of tins at the Bermondsey factory revealed the disagreeable fact that the company was having to pay out £20,000 a year more than it needed for the tins it bought from its subsidiary.

Depression Years 1929–39

Huntley and Palmers therefore approached Metal Box Ltd. to seek an offer for Huntley Boorne and Stevens. Subsequent negotiations were as protracted and as brim-full of misunderstandings as the matrimonial transactions in any French classical comedy. Yet the central point on which they foundered could not have been plainer. Metal Box wanted to buy the firm with Huntley and Palmers' trade included; the company, on the other hand, was willing to sever its century-old connection and make tins in its own factory.

This failure to pair off Huntley Boorne and Stevens, however much of a setback to the company's finances at the time, worked to the subsequent advantage of both Reading firms. Although Huntley and Palmers' requirements of tins were diminishing steadily as packets grew in popularity, the Government's defence programme from 1937 onwards and the consequent demand for metal products of many kinds revived Huntley Boorne and Stevens' turnover. During the Second World War, when the shortage of tinplate virtually halted production of biscuit tins, about 90 per cent of its output was for wartime purposes, and representatives of both the Admiralty and the War Office were permanently stationed in the factory. After the war, it was able to build up trade in many kinds of metal containers for outside firms, and also in new materials such as a laminated product known as Lamiplate.

In 1931 the company's Board was reinforced by the election of Clement Williams, the General Manager, and E. A. Wrottesley. The latter became works Director under the Production Director, Reginald Palmer: the two maintained a very harmonious relationship, for Wrottesley still acted as Chief Works Manager. One project on which they had been collaborating for some time came to fruition that year: a dramatic revival in cake output.

Cake-making had always been a very subordinate activity of the firm, and has therefore received little attention in this history so far. Thomas Huntley shortly before 1841 had been making three kinds of cake compared with nineteen kinds of biscuits; this excluded wedding cakes, then as now a highly regarded speciality of the firm. The first surviving breakdown of tonnage, for 1903–4, shows that cake output was only $3\frac{1}{2}$ per cent of the total, or 904 tons out of 25,000 tons. All cakes were made to order, so that each morning the manager would determine what was to be produced that day, depending on the type of orders received. Not unexpectedly, the cake factory was felt to lack initiative, but output scarcely improved at all when in the late 1900s a trained manager was recruited from outside, for the marketing problem remained. Macfarlane Lang, for one, was seriously undercutting sales.

Well-off consumers tended to buy their cakes at confectioners, or else had them baked at home; the less opulent made do with cheap grocers' cakes, which were said to be 'horrible'. Yet although cake sales were very unsatisfactory, the Board scarcely ever considered them before the 1920s.

Once cake manufacture was resumed in 1920—in the undoubtedly expensive price range of 2s. 7d. to 3s. 7d. (13p. to 18p.) a pound—output settled down at the even more depressing level of 167 tons on average. Reginald Palmer chaired various committees which hunted in vain for a 'cake of character'. People's tastes in cake, as in biscuits, had shifted; the company's cakes were felt to be not only too dear but also too dry and expensive. As Rupert Carr had pointed out in his report, this was largely because the cake factory was quite out of date. All its products were baked in obsolete hand ovens, on principles little different from those introduced in George Palmer's day.

The company achieved success when in July 1931 it put on the market a slab cake, happily named the New Era, and saw output rise immediately to nearly 1200 tons in 1932 and nearly 1900 tons in 1939. Its price, of 1s. (5p.) a pound, did not allow it to make a clear profit, but even the small part of the overheads which it carried was very welcome at that difficult time. From 1936 onwards the cake factory was partly reorganised, and by 1939 its cakes were being manufactured with some labour-saving machinery, and baked on draw-plate ovens. However, it was the mid-1950s before the first travelling oven for cakes was installed.

The British economy did not experience the full effects of the depression until 1931, and it was from then onwards that Huntley and Palmers' vulnerability as a high-cost firm became really clear. After the crisis of August 1931 the new National Government rather misguidedly cut official incomes and increased taxation sharply, so reducing purchasing power and further depressing the demand for biscuits at home. For the moment the company succeeded in maintaining its share of the home trade, although exports fell to less than half the 1929 level by 1932: a mere 15 per cent of that of 1914.

Yet what really mattered was the profit level, and this was still declining. As a percentage of turnover, profits had averaged 12·6 per cent between 1898–9 and 1913–14, but only 8·2 per cent on average between 1923 and 1930. In 1931 they fell to 6·1 per cent and in 1932 to 5·7 per cent: the worst result ever, apart from the loss in 1920–1. In October 1932 the Chairman had to tell a special Board meeting that the company's future depended on increasing its output or reducing its overheads drastically.

Depression Years 1929–39

The Board referred the problem to the Executive Committee which urgently studied every conceivable economy from transferring Peek Frean's manufacture bodily to Reading and closing down Huntley and Palmers' London office, to the joint buying of ingredients: the last step was felt to be no more opportune than the others. It did propose a joint Experimental Department, which the Group Board accepted, Dr. Colgate becoming consultant chemist to both units. Since sales of the company's 'popular' (and thus largely unprofitable) biscuits had been increasing by 11 per cent over the past year, at the expense of the more profit-making lines, it altered the recipes of some biscuits slightly to make them yield a profit, and took measures to reduce the abnormally high wastage from spoilt biscuits.

The Executive Committee also grappled with the perennial question of economising in labour. It rejected the proposal to introduce a 44-hour week, although much short time was then being worked; instead it pensioned off some of the older and less efficient men. The axe was not even spared at the top. Herbert Pretty, now almost eighty, handed over the managing directorship to Clement Williams; he died three years later, in 1935.

On the question of stimulating output, it did put in hand the John Ginger campaign, which proved to be very successful and helped to maintain Ginger Nuts as the company's top-selling variety, despite fierce competition from rivals. To help exports, it agreed to share representation with outside firms. The upshot was that tonnage sold scarcely fell at all in 1933 and started to revive slightly over the next few years. This was at a time when some old-established markets were being lost: the Home Trade Manager reported that Eton, Rugby and many other leading schools were now buying second-grade biscuits. It was almost a century since Thomas Worth had opened Huntley's first account in Eton, and other public schools had soon followed suit.

In mid-1933 the trade association agreed to a substantial reduction in prices, which helped the company to turn a decrease of 321 tons (compared with the previous year) in the first half of the year into an increase of 166 tons in the second half. Opposition to these reductions—presumably because they were not large enough—led Carr's of Carlisle to resign from the association; indeed, for some time it had found great difficulty in abiding by the Association's agreements. Since none of the cheaper manufacturers were now members, a succession of them acted in the 1930s as price leaders at the lower end of the scale. In 1933, for instance, the Betta Biscuit Co., specialising in biscuits at 6d. (2½p.) a pound, was soon forcing most of its immediate rivals to sell at 6d. also. J. R. Gales, looking back more in sorrow than in anger, declared that if the Board had paid heed to his warning in 1921 that Serpell's, Palmer

Bros. of Bristol, Lipton's, the International Stores, the Co-operative Societies and others were doing an 'enormous trade' in 1s. (5p.) biscuits, and had countered with some good varieties at that price, Betta Biscuits, Kemp's and other smaller makers would never have gained a foothold in the market. He also pointed to Jacobs' and Crawfords' success in converting a large proportion of the higher-class trade on to a shilling basis. The Board did consider the possibility of making 6d. biscuits, but not unexpectedly rejected it.

The price war reached a new phase in 1934, when W. Garfield Weston came to Britain from Toronto in Canada. He soon built up the industrial concern of Associated British Foods Ltd., which contained a number of plants for making very cheap biscuits. Four years later a financial paper drew a comparison between the thriving state of the four new biscuit factories which he had established or acquired in as many years, and the decline in The Associated Biscuit Manufacturers Ltd.'s earnings on capital from 12 to just over 3 per cent since 1931, and the parallel drop in its ordinary share values from 67s. 6d. (£3·37) in 1928 to 15s. 8d. (79p.)[2]. The article's allegedly misleading statements greatly irritated the Group Board, which resolved to make a pronouncement at some opportune moment; but the moment never arrived. Instead, the confident Garfield Weston leapt in with an offer to buy a controlling interest in the Associated Biscuit Manufacturers. This offer was not rebuffed—as it would have been in happier days—but it finally proved unacceptable and the price threat from this quarter persisted.

However, when biscuit prices fell as low as 5d. (2p.) a pound, a reaction set in among some better-class retailers. The largest grocery chain in London, W. H. Cullen, realised that the cheap trade was beginning to jeopardise its own turnover and profit margins in the longer run, and therefore began to push the more expensive varieties once again. J. Sainsbury, too, was now an important customer of the company, for of the limited selection of biscuits which its branches stocked, Huntley and Palmers provided the standard kinds. The company's trade with the leading London hotels, such as the Savoy, Ritz, Berkeley and Dorchester, also showed a revival. At the same time, the Home Trade Manager kept up his demand for novelties, which Peek Frean seemed so much more adept at producing, but the company's only response was to strengthen the experimental department at the end of 1935.

One of the major changes in people's diet between the wars was the widespread adoption of cereals, such as cornflakes, for breakfast. In 1934, therefore, the company introduced a breakfast food, Tribrek, with an advertising outlay of £20,000. Its initial success seems to have been almost wholly responsible for the improvement in home turnover during 1935, and the directors were encouraged to think about branching out into potato crisps, for they anticipated an extensive trade in licensed houses. They had earlier rejected a suggestion to buy crisps from an outside manufacturer and sell them under the company's name, so as to test out the market. Now a thorough investigation revealed that, however successful they might prove to be, crisps could only yield a slender margin of profit. J. R. Gales tried to resuscitate the proposal in 1938 with the plea that the company had everything, including the tins and the office and marketing staff, to make them apart from the potatoes and the handling plant. He also pressed for confectionery-type cakes, such as swiss rolls, gateaux and jam tarts, to be introduced. However, by then the company had other preoccupations besides diversification.

The company's total output gradually rose from its lowest post-depression level of 12,176 tons in 1933 to 14,322 tons in 1936. Exports did not contribute much to this improvement: a slight rise in primary product prices did, however, help to revive sales in some Asian countries. Trade with the United States fell because of a recession there in 1937, but improved early in 1939 after the duty on biscuits there had been reduced from 30 to 15 per cent.

At home, the coronation of George VI and the introduction of a special Coronation Assorted provided some stimulus to trade. Yet the year as a whole proved an unhappy one: in 1937 and again in 1938 tonnage remained below the 14,000 ton level. Like output, profits were disappointing. The average of 8·2 per cent, mentioned above, for the period from 1923 to 1930 had been succeeded by a 6·6 per cent average between 1931 and 1938. Indeed, in 1937 and 1938, when profits were 6·4 and 5·7 per cent respectively, the company made no profit at all, after charging preference dividends, until June and March respectively.

At a time when over half the population with radio sets listened regularly to the pirate stations Radio Luxemburg and Radio Normandie, Huntley and Palmers felt constrained to buy time on both channels. This included lunch-time and tea-time on Sundays, which commanded such high rates that the advertising grant had to be over-spent. Leslie Henson was the resident comedian, and in the correct tradition of marketing—which seeks to create in the public mind a problem which only the consumption of the advertised product can resolve—an ailment named Afternoon Fatigue was invented, to which the remedy was 'Have you had your Osbornes?' It is not known how far this expensive form of promotion helped sales.[3]

Yet towards the end of the decade action was taken to meet some of the company's most pressing problems. The directors had for many years been worried about the state of the offices. As long ago as 1929 they had considered a scheme to centralise all office work. They also knew that mechanisation was urgently needed; for instance, statistics ought to be produced by Hollerith machine instead of by hand. This was deferred because it would have meant discharging or pensioning off an unacceptably large number of clerks. Instead, they concentrated on some administrative improvements. In 1932 the Continental and Export Invoice offices were amalgamated, and a year later the Overseas Manager moved his headquarters to Reading in order to control all overseas trade from there. The Fenchurch Street premises then became the local office of the London District.

In July 1934 a committee of directors and managers was set up to recommend an improved layout for all the offices, so as to achieve more economical working. By November it reported that the existing buildings could not be adapted and ought to be replaced by something entirely new. However, the kind of building required really depended on the way in which the office administration was to be run. The company therefore called in the management consultants Urwick Orr & Partners.

Urwick Orr predictably pointed out that of the estimated net savings —about £8500 a year—the greater part would have to come from a reduction in clerical staff. It also proposed a single management structure for all the offices. The directors accepted both these recommendations and appointed G. W. Meatyard as Clerical Manager. The way was now clear for the new offices to be built. By the end of 1935 the Victorian office building on the Kings Road frontage had been vacated. Dingy and inconvenient as it had been inside, its exterior had for generations reflected a feeling of unpretentious prosperity that was out of tune with the present age.

Its successor, completed early in 1937 at a cost of £55,000, was a steel and reinforced concrete building of four stories, well lighted by large windows. The new Board room, directors' and managers' offices were on the first floor, and the invoice and ledger offices on the upper floors, while there was also room for the buying department and other clerical departments. This allowed the plans for the new Social Centre to be put into effect. The centre included not only a licensed bar, but also such amenities as a billiard room and a small theatre, where plays were regularly performed by the drama group 'The Bourbons'. In 1937, too, Kings Road was reconstructed and the long overdue road-widening schemes put into effect.[4]

Yet the key to Huntley and Palmers' future profitability still remained its machinery. L. Rondolin at Bermondsey was showing how new machines could bring about substantial cost savings, but no one at Reading possessed his kind of expertise and drive. Then in 1928, Neil Gardiner became an apprentice in the engineering department. He was the son of Alfred Palmer's daughter Phyllis and was the first of the fourth generation to enter the factory. Alfred Palmer himself was paralysed by a stroke in 1931 and died in 1936, aged eighty-four. Until his illness he had served as the first President of Reading University's Council, and William Childs, the first Vice-Chancellor, described him in his journal as 'the most generous, kind hearted, large-minded man I have ever known'.

Neil Gardiner, too, had a wide-ranging and inventive mind. While spending part of his training at Vicars, the suppliers of biscuit-making machinery, he became convinced that the kind of automatic plants which Vicars had developed would go far towards improving the company's poor profit record. When a few years later he recommended these plants to the Executive Committee, he was told in so many words: 'They will not make Huntley and Palmers' biscuits; only rubbish turned out by the cheap people.'

The reaction was understandable in so far as the 'cheap people' concentrated on standard varieties that needed only simple baking and packing and little quality control. Moreover, Huntley and Palmers had gone to the trouble as long ago as 1924 of acquiring a new type of machinery, the Fosse Plant, to produce four kinds of biscuit with special cutters made by Baker Perkins. Some new biscuit-handling plant was also bought and sited in H factory. This equipment had, however, proved quite unreliable and had had to be withdrawn four years later. Even though by the early 1930s Peek Frean had two automatic plants in working order at Bermondsey, Huntley and Palmers' directors showed no enthusiasm about following suit.

Then, in 1937 Reginald Palmer and Neil Gardiner at last persuaded the Executive Committee to approve an entirely new building on the South Factory site. This was to be equipped with two auto-band plants which involved continuous rolling and cutting, and travelling ovens 204 feet long, made by Vicars. Manufacturing costs would be only a quarter or a third of those from older machinery; thus the capital outlay of £33,000 was expected to be recouped within four to five years. The new machines were also more economical with sugar and dough, and produced a remarkably low percentage of spoilt goods.

These developments exacerbated, if anything, the perennial problem of female labour for packing, and in the late 1930s the company was having to import girls from the depressed areas. Most of them came from Wales, and the remainder were from north-east and north-west England, but their turnover was high. No doubt the solution, adopted twenty years later, of opening a factory in the north-west, to take advantage of adequate labour on the spot, would have seemed unthinkable at that time.

18
The Second World War 1939–45

Between the wars Huntley and Palmers had withstood a succession of difficulties, but by 1939 its long-term prospects seemed less than bright. Annual output was in physical terms only half what it had been in the best years—although not all years—between 1898 and 1914. To compare the second eight-year period of the Associated Biscuit Manufacturers Ltd. (from 1931 to 1938) with the first eight years (from 1923 to 1930), average annual production at Reading declined only from 13,388 to 13,178 tons; yet the drop in biscuit sales was as high as 10 per cent, even though largely offset by an improvement in the unremunerative cake sales.

Thus whereas total output held up fairly well in the 1930s, profits did not. The decline in average profits on turnover, from 8·2 per cent between 1923 and 1930 to 6·6 per cent between 1931 and 1938 has already been noted. They would probably have declined more steeply but for the substantial volume of investment in these years, paid for out of the reserves that had been prudently built up since 1918.

Yet most of this investment on such projects as the Central Warehouse and the offices, however important, left untouched the main problem, that Huntley and Palmers was technologically an out-of-date firm. Since cakes and many of the fastest-selling varieties of biscuits alike were making little direct contribution to profits, there was only one remedy: new machinery, such as auto plants, to provide massive cost savings on the production side. In fact, the first two plants came into operation in June and August 1939, a few weeks before the outbreak of the Second World War.

As background to the part which Huntley and Palmers played in that war, developments in the biscuit industry during 1939 must be noted.[1] It was divided into three main sections, each with its fairly well defined, although not entirely separate, market. At the summit were the national manufacturers of quality biscuits: the 'big six' (then the sole remaining members of the N.A.B.M.), whose standard price was 1s. 1d. (5½p.) a pound. The medium-priced manufacturers sold at 8d. ($3\frac{1}{2}$p.) and the cheap ones at 6d. ($2\frac{1}{2}$p.) a pound or less. Although the quality makers were able to maintain a more or less orderly market through the Association—by restricting themselves to non-price competition—price-cutting was very common at the lower end.

In an effort to halt this price-cutting, during the 1930s the non-quality manufacturers established the British Cake and Biscuit Association. That organisation was unrelated to the N.A.B.M., and maintained a fairly loose structure that resembled somewhat the pre-1918 London Committee of the old Association. Two unconnected events brought the whole industry together and re-established Huntley and Palmers' moral authority, of a kind it had lacked since 1919. The first was the Ministry of Labour's revival of the Trades Board notion; the second was the drift towards war.

The Ministry now proposed a Trades Board to include the baking industry as a whole. More specifically, it aimed to impose minimum wages in the many thousands of small bakeries where conditions of work, although far superior to those of a century before, still required improvement. There was to be no exemption for cake manufacture, which was partly in the hands of small establishments. In the biscuit industry the old era of unduly low wages was now past, and after meetings with the two associations the Ministry agreed to exempt biscuit manufacture from the Trades Board machinery, provided that the industry set up instead a Joint Industrial Council.

The British Cake and Biscuit Association readily agreed to the proposal, but the N.A.B.M. maintained that it would be unworkable, as the employees' side was still not properly organised. As a compromise, therefore, a voluntary Joint Wages Council was set up with the Ministry's agreement. This had an independent chairman, the Cambridge economist C. W. Guillebaud, with Reginald Palmer as leader of the employers' side.

Since methods of work and also grading in the biscuit industry had grown up over the years quite haphazardly, the Wages Council found that the composition of its labour force was very complex. The first need was therefore for members to agree on the titles and definitions of all relevant grades. Unfortunately, although the unions involved were anxious to play a full part in the Wages Council, none of their representatives had any technical knowledge of biscuit manufacture. All the employers' representatives, on the other hand, were men who had spent their lives in the industry.

Reginald Palmer therefore took the lead in educating the employees' side: not so very different from his father's role within Huntley and Palmers after the Workers' Representation Committee had been set up. The initial meeting of the Council was much delayed by all the members' heavy wartime commitments, in fact until July 1942, when it fixed minimum rates of pay: 70s. (£3·50) a week for men and 43s. (£2·15) for women, which included war bonuses of 10s. and 8s. (50p. and 40p.) respectively. By May 1943 he had obtained the agreement of both sides to a grading system for the industry, which remained intact for many years.

The other unifying factor for the industry was the prospect of war in Europe. Partly because another general war had long been anticipated, and partly because of its earlier experience, the Government's control of the industry was to be extremely thorough, and quite different from the improvised, inefficient and unjust system of the previous war. There were, for instance, fewer irksome regulations about the precise construction of biscuits, the amount of sugar (if any) that should be allowed on top or inside, or the occasions on which biscuits could lawfully be served in teashops. This time, although abrupt changes in controls were made from time to time, on grounds which in retrospect appear arbitrary or doctrinaire, the biscuit industry accepted them because it had a say into putting these controls into effect.

As the prospect of war grew clearer, so the Government began to shape its contingency plans. In 1936 a sub-department of the Board of Trade, the Food (Defence Plans) Department, was set up. It had no recorded dealings with the biscuit industry until the Munich crisis, provoked by Germany's threats against Czechoslovakia, erupted to the brink of war in September 1938.

J. R. Gales's initiative won for the company a £15,000 order for army biscuits. Civilian needs, however, had not been provided for in any way. The two associations managed to 'scrape together' from firms' stocks enough biscuits to supply a half-pound packet to just over a quarter of the mothers and children evacuated from London and the large cities.[2] Huntley and Palmers provided about a tenth of the 1000 tons thus collected, largely in the form of Fancy Lunch biscuits. After the Munich agreement had ended that particular crisis, the company agreed to take back any unissued biscuits without charging more than out-of-pocket expenses.

The secret inquest in Whitehall on the food aspects of the crisis led to Eric Palmer's involvement in official contingency plans. Within a month the Board of Trade formally asked him, as president of the N.A.B.M., to devise a scheme for controlling the biscuit trade in the event of war. Helped by the president of the British Cake and Biscuit Association, in January 1939 he set up an organisation to represent the whole industry. At first this new body was called, with more emphasis on accuracy than on euphony, the Cake and Biscuit Wholesale Manufacturers' Defence Committee.

The committee first of all had to make sure that fully adequate biscuit supplies would be available for all those to be evacuated on the outbreak of war. It then worked out plans for the fair distribution of edible oils and fats: a task which in the Great War had been neglected until 1918. This meant bringing on to the committee representatives of large-scale bakers who used more than 10 tons of these ingredients a month; all large manufacturers of biscuits, cakes and flour confectionery were asked to state—in complete secrecy—the amount of oils, fats and sugar which they used.

Other Government departments' plans were already touching the company as well as the industry. That same July the Ministry of Labour designated work in the Reading factory as a reserved occupation. The increasingly intensive recruiting campaign after 1914 had led to chaos throughout the industry, as elsewhere: now the company's employees were forbidden to volunteer for service, as their primary duty in the event of war was to remain at their work, at least until directed elsewhere.

In 1914–18 biscuit firms—with Huntley and Palmers as one of the main culprits—had been reluctant to reduce the number of their varieties so as to economise in ingredients. Now in April 1939 Eric Palmer's committee submitted to the Board of Trade a schedule of cakes and biscuits to be manufactured in wartime. The company went ahead with its own preparations, building air raid shelters and fitting dimmed lights in case of a black-out. Then after the Conscription Act had been passed in a month or two later, it reintroduced the principle of supplementing employees' pay while they were on full-time military or other national service.

Huntley and Palmers therefore moved into war fairly smoothly and with some sense of priority, which contrasted sharply with the improvisations and anxieties of twenty-five years earlier. Predictably, the initial result of the war was a sharp increase in orders for biscuits and cakes. Moreover, whereas last time people had tended to stay put at the outset, now everyone expected mass air bombing; the consequent shifts in population were bringing about many drastic changes in the pattern of biscuit distribution. In London, for instance, official evacuation schemes had helped to deplete the population of the East End and such neighbouring areas as Ilford, which was said to have lost 40,000 of its inhabitants.

More relevant to Huntley and Palmers' quality trade was the voluntary evacuation of more affluent districts. These included the West End and Jewish residential areas such as Golders Green and North Hampstead, which representatives estimated to have cost the company £4500 worth of business in the last quarter of 1939 alone:

say, 1 per cent of its total home sales for that period. Again, many London restaurants, hotels and theatres, as well as West End stores, were in difficulties since people were on the whole too preoccupied to go out much. Nevertheless, representatives felt that the company's sales were holding their own in the capital; instead it was Peek Frean which lost over £27,000 worth of its London turnover.

A Ministry of Food had come into being in September 1939 and prepared without delay to ration basic foodstuffs and to control ingredients and other essential materials. Ingredient supplies were bound to become scarce, as in 1914, but the Government had made considerable forward purchases and had begun to build up stocks. A chilling fact—mercifully known only to a few—was that food stocks actually in the country were at such a low level that an all-out German air or submarine attack in the winter of 1939 might have carried Britain to the brink of defeat.[3] Since rationing was not introduced at all until January 1940, stocks had diminished rapidly while unrestricted consumption was allowed.

Once again, it was sugar which caused the first worry, notwithstanding the Government's bulk purchase of the entire Commonwealth output. When sugar was rationed in January 1940, biscuit manufacturers were allocated only 60 per cent of their requirements. A deputation to the Minister of Food, W. S. Morrison, from the industries using sugar icing, failed to deflect him from this drastic cut; the biscuit representatives had probably never heard of Howard Palmer's advice to a similar kind of deputation in 1916 not to act as a pressure group. Huntley and Palmers as a result struck off its list all iced cakes, except birthday and wedding cakes; previously it had delayed introducing this measure until March 1916. It had now discontinued fifty types of biscuit in all. When butter rationing was simultaneously introduced for consumers, fats for the trade were both rationed and increased in price.

At this stage Government control sought primarily to minimise inflation, for during the First World War the relentless cycle of ingredient and food price rises had provoked almost as much irritation, notably among the less well-off, as physical shortages themselves. Not until March 1940 did the N.A.B.M. agree to any increases in biscuit prices, and member firms responded by promising restraint in advertising. These and subsequent price increases all helped to reduce the gap between cheap and quality biscuits. By 1941, when the first price 'standstill' Order was imposed in biscuits, some formerly sixpenny (2½p.) biscuits were costing 1s. (5p.) a pound, while at the other end of the scale, 2s. (10p.) varieties (such as Breakfast, Cocktail and various chocolate assortments) were normally no more than a penny or twopence (½p.–1p.) dearer. Not until May 1942 did the Ministry issue a specific Order to regulate the prices of biscuits as such.

Both Huntley and Palmers and McVitie & Price had an additional ground for worry when the German *blitzkrieg* in May 1940 swept across northern France and took the enemy to within range of Paris. Shortly before, when the Union des Biscuiteries was shown to have incurred yet another loss for 1939, Huntley and Palmers had reluctantly concluded that in its present form the French subsidiary was unlikely ever to become a profit-making concern, and might therefore have to be closed down. However, the evacuation from Dunkirk drove that particular problem into the background. The British managers in the subsidiary and their families numbered twenty-three, of whom nine were children; on the eve of the surrender of Paris they left the capital for unoccupied France. They were only just able to keep ahead of the advancing Germans, and having missed the last boat out of Bordeaux, travelled south to Bayonne, near the Pyrenees, where they succeeded in embarking for England.

On 21st May 1940, when Winston Churchill's new Government was already stiffening British resistance, the Ministry made a 10 per cent reduction in the sugar allocation, to 50 per cent. Simultaneously Huntley and Palmers accepted an urgent army contract, which involved the entire use of the auto plants twenty-four hours a day, seven days a week until it was completed. The rush also meant postponing all holidays for factory and office staffs alike.

With the fall of France and the consequent risk of a German invasion of Britain, the directors took measures to protect the factory. For the purpose, they recruited an armed posse of what later became the Home Guard. Meanwhile, the Mayor had defence works thrown round the borough; for the first time since the Civil War in the 1640s, Reading was directly in the front line. (The one or two zeppelins that had strayed over the town between 1914 and 1918 had been exciting rather than destructive.) One of the directors served on the Mayor's Defence Committee for Reading, and the company guaranteed part of the costs of the defence works, in advance of the promised refund by the Government.

Now that large-scale bombing and perhaps invasion were every day becoming more likely, the company had to make provision for unprecedented emergencies. Above all, it must safeguard its assets as far as possible. An irreplaceable asset was the well-being of the labour force which now numbered just over 3000; the bank was asked to keep a large enough reserve of cash for making up the week's wages at very short notice. Records of debtors were removed to safety, together with other essential documents. Intangible assets were not overlooked. The

Chairman had already asked the head of the experimental department, H. H. Cridge, to place in airtight tins samples of all the 400 varieties being made in 1939; whatever happened to the company in the meantime, therefore, when the war was over it would have precise examples of the correct weight and design of biscuits. These were in 1966 specially scheduled in the factory as reference material; an abundant harvest, perhaps, for researchers in the remote future.

By 1941 the Government was adopting a tougher policy towards the biscuit industry. Until then the emphasis had been on how to obtain the maximum possible economies *within* each firm: namely, saving ingredients and manpower by simplifying recipes and (in the words of the official historian) eliminating 'the more extravagant sorts'.[4] Despite the severe cuts in materials such as sugar and fats, therefore, industry-wide biscuit production mounted to just 20 per cent above the 1939 average.

However, experiments in co-operation *between* firms had so far been less successful. Ever since the outbreak of war, Huntley and Palmers had been urging all biscuit manufacturers to participate in its joint distribution system with Peek Frean, but had met with no response. Even when the Government tried to compel Association members to pool their transport, they still refused. However, Eric Palmer's committee eventually set up a Biscuit Delivery Pool; this took over all the leading manufacturers' transport manpower and premises and became responsible for distributing virtually all their biscuits. Reading's and Bermondsey's joint organisation formed the nucleus of the pool. A limited delivery system was then tried out in certain areas before the scheme was allowed to come into operation late in 1941. These events showed clearly how any inter-firm co-operation to achieve economies would have to be imposed firmly from above.

The Government had two principal aims in its general plans for the industry. The first involved concentrating production, so as to economise on manpower, and the second was to reduce biscuit consumption, in order to save materials, particularly imported ones that used up scarce shipping space.

The concentration plan had been in the air for some time, and arose from the Board of Trade's anxiety to minimise the consequences of any future cut in biscuit production. Such cuts would mean that labour and factory space would be under-utilised, unit costs for each plant would rise, and small firms whose output was forced below the economic level might perhaps go bankrupt. The Defence Committee, now the Cake and Biscuit Wholesale Manufacturers' Wartime Alliance and a powerful instrument of control, saw no objection in principle to this proposal. It was only after the Government published a White Paper on Concentration in March 1941 that the Alliance became alarmed at the need for some factories to be closed down completely and production transferred bodily to other units, although that was the whole object of the scheme.

The second official plan, for reducing biscuit consumption, necessarily involved rationing consumers. Strict controls over prices, in force since 1940, meant that excessive demand could no longer be choked off by price increases. Yet the problem at the moment was that while biscuits were far from plentiful—about the only biscuits openly available in the shops were certain varieties of less popular makers—any form of rationing at that time would have led to an embarrassing glut of biscuits at home. There was the further problem, which the Ministry had been discussing for some time with Eric Palmer and his committee, of trying to ration biscuits jointly with other less basic foodstuffs, from breakfast cereals to dried fruit and tinned foods.

When the Ministry first suggested zoning in July 1941, Huntley and Palmers showed the same opposition as it had to a similar proposal by Carr's of Carlisle in 1915. The company maintained strongly that all manufacturers should be allowed to deliver a certain proportion of their specialities outside their designated areas. It was not being entirely obstructive, for having learnt its lesson the hard way in the First World War, this time it was keeping its sales organisation in good shape to meet the very keen competition expected after the war.

After a direct hit on Peek Frean's Bermondsey factory in May 1941 had destroyed 40,000 feet of factory space and put a great deal of machinery out of action, Huntley and Palmers arranged to make four Peek Frean varieties with labour from Bermondsey, while packing was to be done by Huntley and Palmers' labour. Although this was specifically seen as an emergency measure and did not recur during the war, it showed conclusively that there was no great difficulty in producing another firm's biscuits.

By early 1942 the company was aiming to reduce the number of its main varieties to twenty. Such drastic pruning allowed output that year to reach almost 17,500 tons, only 900 tons less than in 1941. Similarly, the industry's total biscuit output was 358,000 tons compared with 361,000 tons in the previous year. The authorities now increased the rate of extraction for flour to 85 per cent. The company was most anxious to continue using white flour in Breakfast biscuits, and sought the help of the veteran Lord Horder, formerly the King's physician and now honorary adviser to the Ministry of Food, to extol their dietetic properties in official quarters. However, even Lord Horder's weighty recommendations failed to influence officialdom on this point, or to have Breakfast biscuits exempted from the zoning system.

Then the industry's and the Government's useful rather than thorough-going economy plans received a severe jolt from what the official historian has described as 'a rush of austerity to the head of higher authority'. The ultimate source of this rush to the head was in fact almost the loftiest quarter of all: the Lord President's Committee of the War Cabinet, in supreme control of Government economic policy. The Ministry of Food had hitherto not been over-zealous in enforcing further concentration, as it felt that the resulting dislocations would more than outweigh the few thousand employees saved. It had, however, selected five industries, including biscuit manufacture, for investigations into what could be done. Now that the war had entered a world-wide phase and German U-boat activity in the Atlantic was at its peak, shipping space had to be saved at any cost. The ministry therefore aimed to cut the allocation of fats and sugar by a further 40 per cent, and at the same time to reduce total biscuit output immediately to 200,000 tons, of which about 50,000 tons would be for the services. At a time when the aggregate annual output was running at about 350,000 tons, this would involve reducing civilian consumption by a half, or even more if service requirements needed to be increased.

In common with other firms, Huntley and Palmers was given an individual ceiling of production. People were quick to note that the biscuit industry was an easy prey for such stringent measures, being so highly organised through the Alliance and having such an influential and widely respected chairman as Eric Palmer.

The Ministry of Food, by now wholly dedicated to austerity, also planned to introduce within a month the rationing of biscuits according to a 'points' system. That meant putting into each ration book a quantity of points that could be used at choice on a variety of foodstuffs; overall demand could be balanced with supply by varying the value of points on each commodity. Biscuits were unusual among points-rationed goods in being both perishable and fragile. Since packs, cartons and small tins had been discontinued in order to save labour, the contents of large tins, bumped around under the rough conditions of war transport, sometimes arrived in poor condition. Nevertheless, few major problems arose when rationing actually began.

Huntley and Palmers was now startled to receive an official order to close down the factory under the concentration scheme. For the past two years four Government departments had occupied parts of the buildings as offices; the Ministry of Aircraft Production, for instance, had taken over the second floor of the new office block. They all clearly appreciated the factory's convenient situation and the comfort of the recently completed offices. Partly, too, the closure was intended to ease the pressure on labour in high-employment—or in official terms 'scarlet'—areas like Reading. Cadbury's factory at Bournville, in the Birmingham munitions area, was similarly threatened.

For one dreadful moment, therefore, it looked as if Reading after nearly a century and a quarter would temporarily cease to be the biscuit town which Huntley and Palmers had made it. However, the Mayor, the borough's Member of Parliament and the unions concerned all protested, and the decision was reversed. Yet it was not divine intervention, or even the pleas of such influential citizens, which brought about this change of heart. As Eric Palmer later made clear to Neil Gardiner, the two auto plants alone—now taking almost the whole burden of its wartime biscuit production—saved Huntley and Palmers from being shut down as inefficient.

In return for its reprieve, the company gladly agreed to reduce its labour force by a further 25 per cent. Even better than its word, it brought numbers in the factory down from 1733 in September 1942 to just over 1000 twelve months later. Managers with years of service behind them noted for the first time in their careers the absence of familiar faces among the operatives, since about the only labour left in the factory was unsuitable for more 'essential' work.

The Executive Committee therefore took further biscuits and a large number of cakes off the list in order to reach the twenty or so varieties that was the company's target, and by September had achieved a $12\frac{1}{2}$ per cent reduction in total output. It even debated whether to discontinue production of Ginger Nuts and substitute Petit Beurre, since a relatively greater output—and thus a higher profit—could be secured from the very restricted materials available. However, it felt that this would be a short-sighted measure, as Ginger Nuts (despite the competing brands produced by rivals) were too closely associated with the company's name to be discontinued as long as their output was at all practicable.

It seemed in keeping with the dreary aspect of that year that the Ministry of Food should allocate to the factory 550 tons of potatoes for use in cakes. The directors felt that nothing could be gained by refusing this allocation, and indeed, cake output rose steadily from 1558 tons in 1941 to 2252 tons in 1945. Nevertheless, it reflects the contrast with the First World War that the Executive Committee never considered discontinuing manufacture of cakes. Ingredients were normally bulk-purchased by official agencies, and were of far more uniform quality than in the past, while allocations were so tightly controlled that no competitor could make substantially better products.

Even at this sombre period the directors set up a Factory Reconstruction Committee in December 1942. The chairman was the Production Director, Reginald Palmer, who was virtually in charge of day-to-day affairs at Reading, since Eric Palmer was necessarily absent for much of the time on Alliance and other official business. The committee's principal task was to consider how the factory could reorganise production in peace-time at the lowest possible cost consistent with the company's traditional standards. As vital and far-reaching in its way as the Economy Committee from 1926 had been, the committee remained in existence even longer, in fact until 1963. However, whereas the Economy Committee had been charged with the negative task of reducing costs, the Reconstruction Committee was given a positive and forward-looking role.

Its first interim report, in September 1943, gave a very clear and full outline of the company's future strategy. Above all, to earn the kind of profit required, it would have to produce a far higher tonnage of biscuits and cakes: say, 17,000 to 18,000 tons, as compared with under 13,300 on average between 1923 and 1938. Biscuit and cake prices must therefore be kept to the minimum compatible with quality. It believed that a list of 110 to 130 varieties of biscuit and ten of cakes was the minimum that would 'satisfy the trade'. The dilemma here was the age-old one that since the company had in recent times maintained its reputation by the sheer variety of kinds that it offered, in addition to a good selection of Christmas goods, any proposal to pare down the list from 400 to nearly a quarter involved substantial risks.

Since very many of its inexpensive biscuits and cakes had lately been selling well but contributed little to profit, the committee declared that great efforts were needed to increase the high-class trade: namely goods which had been priced in 1939 at above 1s. 6d. ($7\frac{1}{2}$p.) a pound. While expensive varieties would be produced on existing machinery in the North Factory, most kinds could be made on the auto plants. Two further auto plants, which had been on order in September 1939, were partly made at Vicars, but could not be completed until after the end of the war, and the committee put forward plans for a third new autoplant as well as the centralised mixing of dough for all machines. It also considered cake manufacture. Since the company's goodwill in slab and small cake had so greatly increased during the war, it felt that these lines should be expanded rather than, for instance, trying to manufacture confectionery of the swiss-roll type, where such firms as J. Lyons were very well entrenched.

The Government's austerity drive—described by the official historian as a moral gesture that was 'the negation of planning'—predictably broke down. Its collapse was due not merely to the labour difficulties it caused, but also to soaring demands for service and welfare biscuits, notably those needed for relief as occupied countries were successively liberated from enemy occupation. Although the company's biscuit tonnage was therefore less than 11,200 tons in 1943, compared with the 16,000–18,000 tons in 1940–2, these demands averted a much more drastic fall in output. In the second half of 1943, too, the Ministry of Food increased the points allocation for biscuits, to give more variety to civilian diets at home.

In 1944 and 1945 output rose to an average of 12,660 tons a year, and the company's labour force rose slightly from 1015 to round about 1100. For the first time since 1917–18 the number of boys, women and girls combined almost equalled the number of men. Taking biscuits and cakes together, during the last two years of the war Huntley and Palmers was producing slightly more than the best tonnage between the wars—that of 1936—but with less than a third of the pre-war labour force. This was in common with the industry as a whole. While no one wished to maintain the limited and austere range of wartime biscuits once peace returned, the reduction in varieties and such concentration as did take place had yielded such vast economies that biscuit manufacturers could scarcely fail to profit by the lesson. As soon as post-war conditions allowed, therefore, the industry was likely to embark on rationalisation and mass-production.

19
Restriction 1945–52

When peace returned in 1945 Huntley and Palmers devoted no time, as it had done in 1919, to publicising its wartime achievements. Not only were there more urgent matters to deal with, but such publicity had small value for commemorating a war which had drawn no clear-cut distinction between combatant and non-combatant. Employees had served not only in the armed forces but also in a very diverse range of war work; a few ended up as temporary milk roundsmen. It is not even known how many of these became casualties, either as combatants or as civilians.

The younger directors maintained the fighting tradition of the previous war. Alan Palmer, Eric Palmer's son, a director since 1938, became a lieutenant-colonel and was awarded the D.S.O. for services as a liaison officer with the Albanian partisans. Neil Gardiner became a commander R.N.V.R. on the staff of the Commander-in-Chief, Portsmouth, in various technical capacities which made good use of his engineering expertise and unorthodox mind. Cecil Palmer's sons served as army officers, Raymond Palmer in the Grenadier Guards and Gordon Palmer in a number of senior General Staff posts, during which he was promoted lieutenant-colonel and awarded the M.B.E. On completing their apprenticeships both were elected directors, Raymond Palmer in 1945 and Gordon Palmer in 1948.

These new appointments to the Board helped to replenish the depleted numbers of family directors; those on the Executive Committee in 1940 numbered only six, compared with four from outside the family, including the recently appointed Bennet Palmer and J. R. Gales. Charles Palmer had died in 1938 and Albert Palmer two years later; their eldest brother, Lord Palmer, at nearly ninety was the sole remaining member of the Board who was not also on the Executive Committee. In June 1945 Clement Williams, now aged sixty-eight, handed over the managing directorship to J. R. Gales, and in 1948 was the first director in the company's history to retire from the Board. Thereafter, family and non-family directors alike retired at the close of their working lives.

All business men in 1918 had hoped to see 'normal conditions restored' as soon as possible, to use Howard Palmer's words to the Board just after Armistice Day. To them this had meant the unrestricted rule of the market: unrestricted, that is, by Government intervention. Official controls had been dismantled fairly rapidly after 1918, but the resulting shocks to a company in need of modernisation had made the succeeding inter-war period one of the roughest in Huntley and Palmers' entire history.

This time there was less desire for a dash to freedom, and little chance that those in authority would allow it. In 1944 the Ministry of Food submitted to the Alliance plans to 'unwind' controls gradually as supplies became easier. The Alliance's own ideas, expressed through Eric Palmer, were similar, but predictably stressed the need to release quickly all requisitioned factory space and to distribute fairly between firms the new machinery that they required. Capacity was released when the large Government contracts for army and welfare biscuits and for a kind of official-issue cake called Pacific cake came to an end with the conclusion of the war.

After its election in July 1945 the Labour Government's policy was to keep in existence the elaborate apparatus of wartime control for as long as it seemed necessary. In fact, plain biscuits remained on points rationing until March 1949 and sweet biscuits until May 1950; rationing thus continued for a total of nearly eight years. Official controls over the basic ingredients persisted for even longer: flour, sugar and fats were not freed from restriction until 1953–4.

In the period 1945 to 1950, therefore, Huntley and Palmers was grappling with successive restrictions, often severe and usually imposed at short notice. The most critical years were 1945–7. Now that the war was over, Britain's imports of basic foodstuffs were limited not only by the availability of shipping space, but also by the need to share food supplies with many recently liberated countries in Europe and elsewhere. In May 1945 the Combined Food Board met in Washington; its members included Lord Woolton's successor as Minister of Food, Colonel Llewellin, and a member of the War Cabinet and Minister of Production, Oliver Lyttelton. This meeting agreed broadly on the relative shares which countries should receive.[1] In consequence, the biscuit industry had its allocation of oils and fats reduced by $12\frac{1}{2}$ per cent.

Exactly a year later, in May 1946, when a world shortage of grain had emerged, the Ministry cut by $27\frac{1}{2}$ per cent the amount of flour for biscuits and cakes in civilian markets. It spared only supplies for the

N.A.A.F.I., ships' stores and exports. As the official account of this episode put it, 'Those in authority were never able to make up their minds whether biscuits, cakes and other pleasant semi-luxuries were an alternative form of nutriment or an incitement to frivolous eating'. Predictably, the authorities' views oscillated according to the stringency or otherwise of ingredient supplies. We have seen how, in the relatively easy conditions of 1944, they had been glad enough to augment the monotonous diet of British civilians by providing a slightly more plentiful biscuit ration.

Flour supplies were not fully restored until January 1948, and Huntley and Palmers' output declined gradually from 12,673 tons in 1945 to just over 12,000 tons in 1947. A further restriction was bread and cake rationing, imposed in July 1946 and maintained for exactly two years. Yet cake output actually improved, being 50 per cent higher in the first half of 1947 than in the first half of 1946. Nor did biscuit output at any time fall in proportion to the cuts. What saved the company from worse consequences?

One factor was that exports, which escaped the cuts, were rising; in general, however, there was much scope for reducing wastage—a fact recognised by an *ad hoc* Economy Committee set up to secure the most economical use of ingredients. That committee halted the reintroduction of certain varieties on the old and inefficient machines which had so intrigued but dismayed Rupert Carr. The operatives who had spent much of their lives on them had to go; in the laconic words of the Personnel Manager's diary: 'large number old employees retired owing to ovens knocked off'. In fact, a $12\frac{1}{2}$ per cent increase in the allocation of sugar allowed the company to produce more of the sweeter kinds on the auto plants.

Yet where the cuts did fall was on the company's profits. Higher unit costs followed because overheads had to be spread over a smaller volume of output. Output produced by each employee per month, for example, fell from $6\frac{1}{2}$ tons in April and May 1946 to $5\frac{1}{2}$ in July, and by December had crept back only to $6\frac{1}{4}$. This rise in costs was accentuated by higher delivery expenses now that zoning had been abandoned, and by another factor: a levy recently imposed on all sacks of flour used for biscuits.

In contrast with the 1917–18 period of food control, biscuit manufacturers had benefited from a subsidy on flour practically throughout the Second World War. The Ministry of Food would dearly have liked to limit this subsidy to bread on its own, but was in a dilemma. The thousands of bakers up and down the country for the most part kept entirely inadequate records; to rely on them for the necessary paperwork would have been an administrative nightmare. On the other hand, it seemed unfair to penalise biscuit manufacturers alone just because they happened to be very efficiently organised through the Alliance.

Not until October 1944 did the Ministry steel itself to be beastly to the biscuit industry by charging 20s. 3d. (£1·01) on every sack of flour it used, which just offset the subsidy. In May 1946 this levy was increased to 24s. (£1·20), at the time of the cuts in allocation; the following year it rose by stages to 45s. (£2·25).

The biscuit firms, through the Alliance, therefore asked the Ministry of Food to sanction price increases of 3d. (1p.) a pound. The Ministry demurred: in the words of the official historian, the biscuit industry during the war had proved 'exceptionally adroit' in extracting price increases as costs had risen. Indeed, this very adroitness had caused the Ministry's Costing Division to investigate the industry's costs in 1944, hence the imposition of the flour levy. Price increases were not approved until August 1946, and then only by 2d. (1p.) per pound. As a result, Huntley and Palmers' profits fell to 9·5 per cent of turnover for 1946, compared with an average of 13·7 per cent between 1939 and 1945, but 6·6 per cent in the depression years 1931 to 1938.

Almost as serious as the cost problem was the Ministry's repeated inability to provide the correct sort of flour to the industry. In 1946 Eric Palmer successfully protested after imported flour for the industry was suddenly cut off, while two years later trouble developed over the supply of British wheat. As will appear below, the extraction rate remained at the unacceptable level of 85 per cent for home use until August 1950.

A very serious, although fortunately brief, disruption of another kind occurred during the 'great freeze' in the winter of 1946. Like the equally hard winter of 1813, communications between Reading and the outside world were hampered for several months. When it looked as if the company's coal supplies would be so severely reduced as to close the factory for two days a week, the directors through the Alliance reminded the Ministry of Food that biscuits and cakes were essential; to no effect.

The fuel cut, when it came in February 1947, was combated in the factory by the ingenuity of Neil Gardiner, of a kind that would have won the approbation of his ancestors George Palmer and William Exall. He substituted for coal coke breeze sprayed with mineral oil: a device that over the next few years saved the company about £20,000 a year in fuel bills. In order to provide electricity he brought back into operation a generating engine of Alfred Palmer's, the one named Alice. Alice, an indestructible matron of sixty-five who was not finally put down until 1956, proved to be in excellent working order, although she had been out of service since the factory electrification of 1927. The moment when steam was raised for the first time by these experiments probably aroused greater personal anxiety among the directors—most of whom were standing on the firing platform of the boiler house—than any comparable one since Neil Gardiner's great-grandfather George Palmer had tried out his steam coil oven in the new factory just a century before. That oven had exploded in his face; Alice was made of sterner stuff, and soon the factory was up to 80 per cent of its former capacity. Later that year Neil Gardiner was invited to serve on the National Fuel and Power Committee, under the chairmanship of Lord Ridley.

After the thaw came floods, which in some parts of Reading reached a higher point than the previous record levels of 1894. Not only did they pollute the company's water supply, so that all water for manufacture and drinking purposes had to be boiled, but the Breakfast factory, nearest to the river on the north-east corner, was in imminent danger of closing down. One cheerful episode during this trying period was that the company gave another mayor to Reading. H. V. Kersley, manager of Huntley and Palmers' canteen and Chairman of the Workers' Representative Committee, had been a member of Reading Council since 1934 and served as mayor from 1947 to 1949.

In spite of—or perhaps because of—all these irksome restrictions, individual biscuit firms seemed extremely anxious to go their separate ways as rapidly as possible. The Biscuit Delivery Pool was wound up in April 1946. Its organisation—of operating as a limited company without share capital, receiving loans of cash, depots, vehicles and personnel from members, and sharing out operating costs on the basis of the number of tins delivered—had proved entirely workable: the pool was estimated to have saved not less than 30 million ton miles a year.

The other biscuit manufacturers, except Carr's of Carlisle, declined Huntley and Palmers' and Peek Frean's invitation to take part in a permanent joint delivery scheme. The wartime pool was therefore wound up, and firms were allowed an advance of four months' ingredients so as to allow stocks to be built up. Huntley and Palmers had already calculated that the likely savings of the pooling (or 'common user') scheme for tins, once tinplate was no longer scarce, did not justify its being continued any longer.

At the same time Sir Eric Palmer—whose knighthood was announced in the New Year's Honours of 1946 for his wartime services to the industry—was anxious, both as Chairman of the Alliance and as the original sponsor of his own Group's joint delivery scheme, to preserve what he could of the wartime pool. He therefore set up the Associated

Deliveries Ltd., in conjunction with Carr's of Carlisle and a number of confectionery and preserves manufacturers, such as J. Mackintosh & Sons Ltd., Chivers & Sons Ltd., and Joseph Terry & Sons Ltd. All these firms resembled Huntley and Palmers in having a very large number of customers who often submitted very small orders.

J. R. Gales, Chairman of the former pool, now became Chairman of the delivery company, which with its forty depots and 300 vans was soon enjoying economies comparable with those in wartime. The principal Scottish manufacturers were reported to be pooling their own deliveries as well as co-ordinating their marketing and distribution efforts in the North of England. It was not therefore entirely unexpected when two years later, in 1948, McVitie & Price and Macfarlane Lang merged under the control of a holding company named United Biscuits Ltd: one of the names rejected by Huntley and Palmers' directors in 1921.

Although ingredient supplies remained the most pressing of the company's troubles, the scarcity of labour was the main long-term problem. We have seen how conscription, planned reductions in the workforce, and the generally unsettled wartime conditions had caused an unprecedented turnover of labour since 1939. Several times during the final months of the war labour shortages had forced the company to make use of the Alliance's 'mutual aid' scheme, and to sub-contract with a rival firm the production of some army biscuits. Ironically enough, that firm happened to be Bilsland Bros. of Glasgow, then a subsidiary of the Home and Colonial Stores Ltd., and hence one which had benefited at Huntley and Palmers' expense from the family grocer's decline and the rise of the multiple retailer. The company also had to cut back on a civilian order from the India Office because it lacked certain skilled operatives, notably solderers. It unsuccessfully sent deputations to the Ministries of Food and Labour to ask for these operatives to be released from national service.

By September 1945, therefore, the company had the smallest number of factory employees—namely 1071—since 1867, apart from the sombre year 1943 when it had averted the official threat of closure by running down its workforce by 40 per cent. The gradual return of employees from the war eased the labour problem for a while. These were entertained, in parties of 120 at a time, to 'welcome home' dinners in 1946–7; however, many of those entitled to reinstatement did not return. Thus difficulties were likely to persist, and even to be intensified, once Vicars became free to deliver the half-completed third and fourth auto plants. The Board of Trade finally sanctioned their completion at the beginning of 1946, and the site to house them, in an extension to the South Factory, was cleared with the aid of German prisoner-of-war labour.

The plants came into operation before the end of the year. Significantly, it was Peek Frean which provided one of the ovens: a 165 feet poly-fuel type of original design. Like the first and second, they were soon working day and night, with only one hour off in the twenty-four for maintenance. Owing to the continuing scarcity of ingredients, they were responsible for virtually the whole of the company's biscuits, apart from one or two special kinds such as Breakfast biscuits, and were achieving substantial production economies. Men's and women's wages had both more than doubled, from 48s. (£2·40) to 108s. (£5·40) and from 32s. (£1·60) to 75s. (£3·75) respectively, while working hours had been reduced from 48 to 45 hours since 1946. Yet total wages per ton made, £24 7s. 11d. (£24·40) in 1938, had risen by less than a quarter, to £30 16s. 2d. (£30·81) by 1951, and for manufacturing only from £7 6s. 8d. (£7·33) to £8 13s. 4d. (£8·67).

Packing problems had had to be overcome during the war. In 1944 office staff and even boys from the Reading Blue Coat School, on their weekly half-holiday, helped out, and the same year the Production Director, Reginald Palmer, tried to arrange for an outside firm to pack some biscuits. By March 1946 matters had become critical, for 180 volunteers from the offices gave up two Saturdays and Sundays to packing, and a bus ran regularly to Bracknell and Wokingham in order to bring in girls from there.

The Executive Committee therefore approved the establishment of a hostel, so as to attract girls from South Wales and other areas of plentiful labour, as had been done before the war. This fell through, and the company had to set up packing stations in outlying areas, as far afield as Hartley Wintney, Bagshot, Theale and Iver. The extra costs were heavy; packing wages per ton went up by 46 per cent between 1938 and 1951, compared with only 18 per cent for manufacturing. Moreover, the biscuits themselves were less crisp than when packed in the factory itself. Putting biscuits into packets by hand was more expensive in terms of labour than packing loose biscuits in tins; the company therefore benefited from a dispute between the Alliance and the Ministry about selling prices which postponed the reintroduction of half-pound packets at home until 1949, and then allowed them only on a restricted basis.

Then a committee of directors investigated the company's labour prospects in some detail. Its findings were unequivocal. No amount of inducement would provide the number of women operatives required at Reading: therefore some at least of its production would have to be undertaken permanently outside the town.

Under the Distribution of Industry Act of 1945 the Board of Trade had been given powers to assist industry to operate in areas of high unemployment—the old Depressed Areas, now renamed Development Areas—by building factories and renting them out to firms at reasonable rents. In 1946, therefore, the committee began to prospect likely sites at Doncaster, in the Yorkshire development area. Two years later it shifted its attention to Middlesbrough; its conclusions at the beginning of 1949 revealed a fundamental difference of opinion among the directors as a whole. The majority felt that the labour shortage at Reading had eased appreciably, while ingredients were still as scarce as they had been in 1946. Moreover, a factory of the kind envisaged would not completely solve the labour difficulties at Reading, but would merely increase overheads generally. J. R. Gales, as Managing Director, disagreed strongly. As always he took the long view. The Reconstruction Committee had looked forward to substantial production increases, and these clearly could not be achieved at Reading. There was thus in his view a powerful case for opening a factory in a development area, provided that the Reading factory could be kept in full production. He did not win his case at that point. However, while the Board decided to drop the Middlesbrough negotiations, it kept in being the committee to investigate a subsidiary factory. Almost four years passed before the matter was reopened.

Cakes had by now been scrutinised by the Reconstruction Committee. Its objective was to produce a considerably increased tonnage of high-quality cakes at a competitive price. As a result, new machinery was purchased, including four more double-decker ovens of the drawplate kind, which raised the total to twelve. The last of the old stand-by peel ovens, which were obsolete as well as tending to dry out the cakes too much, were finally dismantled. The company also appointed a manager with sole responsibility for the marketing of cakes, although no representatives were specifically allocated to him. Some cake vans were also put on the road, in order to speed up delivery in certain areas, since railway transport was so unreliable. By 1951, output of cakes reached 3884 tons, over double the 1939 level of 1882 tons.

Official post-war control over exports was at first stringent. Huntley and Palmers' overseas trade had been purely nominal from 1942 onwards and totalled only £84,000—less than 5 per cent of turnover—in 1945. For several years thereafter virtually no biscuit exports were allowed, except to 'sponsored markets', arranged bilaterally between the governments concerned, and shared out among manufacturers in proportion to their pre-war export trade. The Government relaxed its ban on 'free' exports in January 1946, only to reimpose it a few months later when the crisis over flour erupted. Not until mid-1947 could they be resumed, even to hard-currency areas. The 'economic overlord', Sir Stafford Cripps, then set the Alliance an export target of 15,000 tons for biscuits, which was reached almost exactly, Huntley and Palmers providing over 23 per cent and Peek Frean a further 20 per cent.

In 1948 the company's exports soared to £840,000 worth, or nearly 30 per cent of turnover. Sadly much of this—a record for the company since 1914—comprised re-stocking by overseas customers after their wartime privations. Yet its exports remained above 20 per cent of turnover until 1952; in 1951 the proportion was as high as 25 per cent.

However, the early 1950s saw restrictions imposed by such former large importing countries as South Africa, India, Burma and Ceylon. India had remained the company's biggest overseas customer until it prohibited biscuit imports in 1949, after which Malaya took over top place. It was now restrictions, rather than a lack of consumer demand as such, that hampered the development of the company's export trade. Although the directors were complaining in 1950 that this trade was doing little more than cover its direct costs, their need to export had never been greater.

This need was as true of France as elsewhere. Immediately after the liberation of Paris in 1944 a party from Reading visited the factories there and found them to be in the main undamaged, while the French staff were safe and well. In 1940 it had been agreed to sell the Courbevoie factory, and the sale now went through, but Huntley and Palmers maintained the factory at La Courneuve for the time being, principally in order to fulfil a French army contract for *pain de guerre*. It held some negotiations with the French manufacturer Heudebert for a possible sale of the factory, but these failed to produce any result as long as France's political and economic outlook remained so uncertain.

By 1949 La Courneuve was again in trouble, as it had to write down excessive stocks and was in dispute with the French Government over a further official contract. Eventually the firm won its case, but doubts persisted at Reading about the size of the possible market in France, the price and quality of the biscuits being produced, and the ability of the management on the spot to overcome its problems. Nevertheless, while Huntley and Palmers sold off part of the factory, it modernised the remainder by sending over an auto plant for installation. Profitability did not improve, and at the end of 1951 Huntley and Palmers regretfully decided to close down the factory entirely. Adam Frères, the leading wafer manufacturers in France, bought its sugar-wafer machines and auto plants and arranged to take some of its varieties under licence.

This experiment of manufacturing abroad, spread over thirty years, had proved costly in funds and in the time of top management at Reading. Moreover, it had achieved a very meagre return on capital, in the form of profits and royalty payments remitted home, after double taxation had been taken into account. Yet it had kept the name of Huntley and Palmers before the French public during an exceptionally turbulent period, which included a disastrous depression (when total industrial production in France had fallen by a quarter), defeat, enemy occupation and the problems of rebuilding an economically and morally wrecked nation.

In September 1948 Sir Eric Palmer died. Early in the previous year he had made an extended sea voyage to Australia for health reasons. However, like Howard Palmer twenty-five years before, his constitution had been undermined by his untiring exertions throughout the war on behalf of the industry and the company alike.

In a tribute paid at a council meeting of the Alliance his successor, H. Oliver-King, who had worked very closely with him from the formation of the original Defence Committee in 1938 onwards, recalled the way he had grown in stature since then 'from company chairman to industrial statesman'. He also noted 'a very curious mixture of early Victorianism and shrewd business sense. When he was talking to people at Reading and the employees on his Estate, he always insisted, with a very fatherly touch, that they were all his people—and yet he was able to bring a very shrewd appreciation to bear on any business deal.'[2] Mr. Oliver-King saw only one side of Sir Eric Palmer's work, that with the Alliance; he did not appreciate that it was precisely this combination of bonhomie and paternal feelings towards his workpeople which evoked the loyalty that was still so noticeable in the factory, in spite of all the changes and disruptions of the war.

Next month Reginald Palmer was elected Chairman of Huntley and Palmers. He also became Chairman of the Biscuit Industry Council, a body set up by the two trade associations towards the end of the war as a bridge between the Alliance and a new association that was planned to represent the whole industry when the Alliance was eventually wound up. However, although the Biscuit Industry Council tried to deal with future policy, the Alliance—at that time concerned solely with the industry's day-to-day running—had proved too useful a mouthpiece to be disbanded. In 1949 it became a permanent organisation and dropped the word 'Wartime' from its name, while the Biscuit Industry Council quietly faded out in the early 1950s.

The change in Huntley and Palmers' chairmanship happened to coincide with the death of Lord Palmer, the last surviving member of the second generation, at the age of ninety. Reginald Palmer therefore dissolved the Executive Committee which had governed the company ever since the Group's formation in 1921. Once again the Board wholly determined the company's policy.

Lord Palmer's peerage descended to his son Cecil, who had been Deputy Chairman of Huntley and Palmers since 1926 and joint Vice-Chairman, with Reginald Palmer, of the Group. As a chartered accountant, he had played a key role in the financial affairs of the Company and Group alike; he was, for instance, chairman of the Group Accounts Committee. He also chaired two other bodies, the Alliance's biscuit and cake export committee, and an official body sponsored by the Board of Trade, the Cake and Biscuit Manufacturers' Export Group, which helped to promote biscuit exports of over 11,000 tons in 1950.

His maiden speech in the House of Lords was noteworthy: as the only biscuit peer, he supported a motion in April 1950 urging the Ministry of Food to lower the extraction rate of flour for use at home. Almost five years after VE Day the extraction rate was still at the wartime level of 85 per cent. He pointed out that this made for uneconomic production and imparted a musty flavour to biscuits.[3] That August the extraction rate was lowered to 81 per cent, the flour levy being raised to 53s. 4d. (£2·67) a sack, but the industry continued to press for a reduction to the pre-war level of 72 per cent. By then Lord Palmer had died, aged sixty-eight. He was succeeded in the peerage by his elder son Raymond, while Geoffrey Palmer became Deputy Chairman. About this time Reginald Palmer's two sons were elected directors, William Palmer in 1949 and Richard Palmer in 1951, while E. A. Wrottesley retired at the age of seventy-one; he died in 1957.

By the early 1950s rationing had been abolished, prices de-controlled and a revised scheme for allocating ingredients drawn up, on a basis that would encourage, and not stifle, competition. Yet the industry was anxious to throw off all remaining restrictions. Fortunately, the Korean materials and economic crisis of 1950–1 caused nothing worse than a temporary shortage of tinplate and a 10 per cent cut in sugar allocation. Then in 1953 flour was at last freed from control and the subsidy withdrawn.

The price of cake flour rose by 23s. 4d. (£1·17) a sack, but as biscuit flour had not been entitled to the subsidy since 1944, its price increase was small. The de-control of sugar and fats followed during the next twelve months, accompanied by slight reductions in their costs. As the company had raised its own prices in 1952, when price control had been removed, it was able to announce reductions in certain standard biscuits, such as Ginger Nuts. The industry now had 'normal conditions' once again, and it was for the company to make certain that it could surmount the period of fierce competition that was bound to follow.

20
Reappraisal 1953–60

In the early 1950s Huntley and Palmers' prospects seemed more assured than for several decades. Between 1950 and 1954 its biscuit output increased by almost half, from under 16,000 tons to 23,800 tons: it had not enjoyed a growth rate of this magnitude in any five-year period since the early 1870s. Then, the newly equipped factories on the north side of the river had come into operation, to satisfy the demand for biscuits created by changes in public tastes. Now again, a combination of new technology and public demand—at last free from all restrictions—brought about this dramatic improvement.

These changes in tastes were affecting all sections of the community, and not just the narrow category of the well-to-do. People were eating less food in general, partly because they were busier and partly because an improved knowledge of nutrition demonstrated the benefits of a lighter and more balanced diet. The growth of the slimming cult between the wars has been mentioned, and also the changes in breakfasting habits once packaged cereals became popular. Huntley and Palmers' cereal Tribrek sold just under 300 tons in 1939; say, a million and a half packets a year. However, the company discontinued its manufacture in 1943 when materials became very scarce, and did not resume it after the war.

Less sustaining meals meant snacks in between. Teashops, milk bars and snack bars catered for the myriads of office and other workers without canteen facilities. Girl typists in particular, having often dispensed with breakfast, fortified themselves with a mid-morning snack; the good old English word 'elevens'—the glass of ale enjoyed by the rural labourer at that hour—became corrupted into the inelegant but convenient 'elevenses'.

Biscuits were not only an agreeable and increasingly popular form of snack, but also part of the new type of meal. Yet until the war many people could hardly afford them. A sample survey carried out in 1936–7 by Sir William Crawford, of the celebrated London advertising agency, showed that of those in Social Class AA (the well-off with incomes exceeding £1000 a year), 13 per cent took biscuits or cakes with their midday meal, the same proportion at tea-time, and 26 per cent with their evening meals. For Class D people—those earning less than £125 a year—comparable percentages were, however, 1½ per cent, 1 per cent and 9½ per cent respectively.[1]

The cheap manufacturers had made great efforts to stimulate demand for biscuits among the lower-income groups. Their success was such that in 1939 the six quality firms, which thirty years before had been responsible for most of the worth-while trade, produced only just over 30 per cent of national biscuit output. Wartime controls held them back, while new entrants into the industry were permitted an allocation from the common pool of materials, and could also buy unrationed ingredients, which were sometimes inferior ones which the quality firms refused to purchase. The number of separate biscuit firms therefore rose from 71 in 1935 to 92 in 1951, and the proportion of net output contributed by the three largest firms declined by about a sixth.[2]

Wartime and post-war experience had shown the powerful underlying demand for biscuits. Almost consistently throughout the rationing period biscuits remained the most preferred good on points, despite being given increasingly unfavourable points values by the Ministry of Food. The Alliance kept this preference alive by spending a total of £250,000 on public-relations advertising during the war. In 1946 it allocated £50,000 to publicising the slogan 'Biscuits keep you going': one of the most popular cartoonists, David Langdon, depicted the value of biscuits to the shop assistant, window cleaner, shorthand typist, bus conductor and other harassed workpeople in the hectic post-war world. The Alliance planned to follow this up with an ambitious programme of 'combined operations' in the field of publicity, to cost £250,000 over the next three years to 1949.[3] However, member companies, anticipating the end of rationing, preferred to concentrate on their own brand promotion. Huntley and Palmers, for instance, felt that its potential share of £6000 a year would make too great inroads into its home advertising allocation of £50,000.

Now quality biscuits were at last coming into their own. The points scheme had encouraged shoppers to secure 'value for points' by buying quality biscuits whenever they could, although zoning and irregular deliveries often forced them to accept second best. People's real incomes were higher than before the war, and would remain so because of the Government's pledge to maintain full employment. Moreover, by the time that biscuits came off points, the price gap between quality and cheap manufacture was fairly narrow, as the introduction of automatic machinery, with consequent savings in costs, went far towards offsetting the cost advantages of using cheap ingredients.

Reappraisal 1953-60

Although as late as 1949 Huntley and Palmers' Board was still anxious about the activities of cheap manufacturers, its main rivals were now the quality firms. McVitie & Price, for instance, even before the abolition of controls had staked the whole of its ingredients ration on two varieties that were recognised as among the leaders of their kind: Digestive and Rich Tea. This gamble must have paid off, for twenty years later these two were claimed to be in the six top varieties.

Huntley and Palmers would have been unable to adopt such a strategy, even had it wished to do so, since its general appeal still rested on the large number of standard varieties it produced. Thus the technical staff at Reading, like the top management, recognised the need to remain in the forefront of technology. One such effort followed a decision by Neil Gardiner and Dr. Colgate (as Chief Technical Manager) to conduct some research into convected and radiated heat in ovens. They therefore arranged for one of the gas undertakings to measure the two types of heat, both in a brick and in a gas oven. The results of these experiments persuaded Neil Gardiner to try out a Spooner oven for the baking of biscuits. This oven had started life as a wool dryer made by the Spooner Dryer and Engineering Co. Ltd., but the principle of subjecting biscuits to blasts of hot air while moving along the band proved highly efficient. Indeed, it reduced baking time eventually by 35 per cent, equivalent to increasing output by a half. All Huntley and Palmers' existing ovens were in time replaced by Spooner ones.

Yet the company's greatest potential money-spinners were the specialities which, as we have seen, were currently being made on ancient machines with a loving care and disregard of cost which was no longer tolerable in the post-war competitive era. These included the Breakfast biscuit, Milk and Honey, Iced Gem and Sponge Finger. The Breakfast, after its earlier triumphs, was no longer realising the sales it deserved; worse still, it was losing 6d. (2½p.) on every pound produced. Because fermentation had to take place, the process was difficult to adapt to automatic working.

Neil Gardiner therefore paid a visit to Holland, to see if the plants there to make Dutch Rusks could suggest any solutions; this proved unproductive, but he eventually found that by carrying the pans on an endless chain through the height of a four-storey building the fermentation process could be completed satisfactorily. At the same time, a Vicars five-tier oven, with a total length of 300 feet, could take care of the baking.

For the first six months after its installation in 1952 the new Breakfast plant produced 40 per cent spoilt biscuits, but even so was beginning to break even. Some improvements by Dr. R. Falconer, who succeeded Dr. Colgate in 1957, reduced the proportion of spoilt to 5 per cent, which yielded an acceptable profit. Two additional Breakfast plants were installed in 1958 and 1960.

The dramatic increases in output, now being realised, only exacerbated the chronic labour shortage. Since 1949, when negotiations for the Yorkshire factory were abandoned, the company had to adopt a series of expedients for providing the necessary labour. An advertising campaign for workers was followed by unsuccessful approaches for temporary help to rival manufacturers in various parts of the country. At the beginning of 1953, when the abolition of controls became imminent, the Board was compelled to seek a permanent solution. The two likeliest choices were first, a subsidiary factory, for both manufacturing and packing, in the North of England, and second, an outpacking station, also in the north, with manufacture being carried out exclusively in Reading. The second had the grave disadvantage that packing costs would be even greater than with the existing scattered and uneconomic packing stations. The Board therefore preferred the alternative of a manufacturing subsidiary, and while making searches, ordered two new auto plants—the seventh and eighth—and left open the question of where they should eventually be sited.

The search was soon narrowed down to a development area on Merseyside, where the Board of Trade agreed to build and rent a factory. One Sunday in February 1953, therefore, J. R. Gales and William Palmer visited the locality in order to inspect three alternative sites. The one finally chosen was at Huyton, due east of Liverpool, in a pleasant, countrified area, free from the smoke and grime usually associated with the industrial north. Huyton contained a number of large housing estates, an overspill from Liverpool; these were likely to provide all the labour needed, especially that for packing. In the long term as many biscuits would be produced there as in the main factory, but none of the work was to be at the expense of running down Reading's output.[4]

The construction firm for the factory was Sir R. Costain & Sons, the same firm which had built the front office block at Reading in 1937. It was begun in November 1953. The Chief Engineer at Reading, R. G. Davis, supervised the installation of the plant, and by April 1955 the new factory was ready for the first trials of biscuits—Shortcake, Nice and Reading Shortbread—on the seventh and eighth plants; two more auto plants were added not long afterwards. At the end of the year, the factory was ceremonially opened by Lord Derby, on part of whose former estates it stood. During the building operations from 1953 onwards, the company had to make use of outside production, for its own sales were at that time increasing by between a fifth and a sixth per annum. Three plants, fairly near to Reading, were able to help out temporarily; the most important was that of the International Stores at Southall in Middlesex.

A completely new factory on a green field site might have been expected to present an opportunity for experimenting with further technological improvements. In fact, this did not happen. The whole of the initial plant at Huyton therefore showed little improvement over what was already at Reading. The completely automatic weighing and mixing process was a technique still at an experimental stage, and could not therefore be included in a new factory with all the inevitable difficulties of starting up.

Much of the packing at Huyton was of assortments, especially for the Christmas trade, which was now on such a scale that between August and December 1955 over 772,000 Christmas tins, plus 110,000 half-square specially decorated tins of Family Assorted, were packed. Most of the remaining output went into half-pound packets, and was then loaded into tins for despatch. There being no railway sidings at Huyton, the tins had to be put into containers, and then consigned to all forty of the Associated Deliveries Ltd. depots throughout the country.

William Palmer was the director in charge of the factory and G. W. Meatyard, formerly Office Manager at Reading, was the Production Manager. Meatyard became a director of the company in 1959, and when William Palmer returned to Reading in 1963 as Production Director responsible for both factories, took over the Huyton factory, until his death only a few months later.

One Reading tradition maintained at Huyton was to encourage members of the same family to work in the firm. Of the 450 Huyton employees in September 1955, there were thirty-seven families with two or more of their numbers serving together. At Reading, the fifth generation was already entering the factory. Neil Gardiner's son David began his apprenticeship in 1955 and was appointed a local director at Huyton in 1961. Like Ronald Poulton, David Gardiner had taken an honours degree in engineering, in his case at London University.

In 1955 Geoffrey Palmer retired and Alan Palmer succeeded him as Deputy Chairman. As Alan Palmer had been Works Director since 1945, a good deal of his time had been given up to re-equipping the Reading factory with new plant as rapidly as possible. Much still remained to be done. Now that the auto plants in both factories were operating on such a scale, it was increasingly difficult for the respective packing departments to keep up. It was in fact a friendly visit by Reginald Palmer and Neil Gardiner to one of their rivals in the N.A.B.M. which brought home to them Huntley and Palmers' relative disadvantage in this area, for the rival firm had S.I.G. automatic packing machines at the end of almost every one of its automatic plants.

Reginald Palmer lost no time: within a week he had ordered two S.I.G. machines from the Swiss manufacturers. Although problems arose in trying to mechanise the link between the company's Spooner ovens and the wrapping machines, these were eventually overcome. This mechanisation, combined with some method study by the Works Manager, allowed the number of girls in H Factory's packing room to be reduced from 350 to 50.

With Huyton in full operation, the directors were able to think about long-term plans for improving production facilities at Reading. The North Factory was the oldest manufacturing unit on the site since the rebuilding of the South Factory, having been erected in the early 1870s, and arrangements were made to demolish it. More important, now that manufacturing and packing had been mechanised, it was possible to carry the process back to the mixing stage.

The automatic mixing and bulk handling scheme, which eventually came into operation in 1960, was well in advance of anything of its kind in the world. A new Central Mixing Room, situated between the South and H factories, housed the new mixers and the electric weighing apparatus. The main ingredients no longer had to be brought in by hand: flour and sugar were delivered by tanker lorry and blown into silos, while liquid ingredients, such as condensed milk, syrup, glucose and fats, were pumped into storage tanks. Depending on the recipe being used, the Control Panel drew off the correct quantities of each ingredient; these were now blended into dough in the Baker Perkins mixing drums, one for each auto plant. The dough was carried in trolleys by a tilt-head fork-lift truck and tipped into a hopper which fed the rolling and cutting machines; these trucks made the whole operation completely flexible, since they enabled each mixer to serve any of the auto plants.

Thus fifty-five years later, the valuers' hope (quoted in Chapter 12) of seeing operations in the factory made completely automatic 'from the flour mixing, through cutting, baking and delivery into the packing room, ready for packing', became a reality. Yet the valuers could not have begun to comprehend the difficulties of devising such automatic production. During most of the 1950s for example, a team of four or five technical staff, under Neil Gardiner's direction, were constantly at work on the problems involved. But with the completion of the Central Mixing Room, every piece of the plant at Reading had been replaced since 1939.

All these developments were very expensive for the company: its capital costs between 1951 and 1959 averaged over £300,000 a year.

The highest annual figure was £600,000 in 1955, mainly for the plants and fittings at Huyton. Peek Frean, too, was investing heavily in new machinery and buildings. In the early post-war years both firms had been able to use the cushion of Government securities they had bought during the war with surplus funds; for the rest, they hoped to rely on retained profits.

Events overtook them. Huntley and Palmers' total output was still growing, and in 1956 for the first time topped the 30,000-ton level. Profits, too, at first improved, rising from £244,000 in 1950 to £590,000 in 1954, and averaged 8 per cent on turnover in the ten years from 1946 onwards. Although roughly the same as for 1923–30, this profit rate was inadequate to cover the company's massive capital requirements. In 1951 the Group therefore borrowed £1,500,000 on short term from the preference and ordinary shareholders. Of this sum £450,000 was earmarked for Huntley and Palmers' investment, and the remainder for building up both units' working capital, which had been strained by the recent increases in turnover.

Continuing financial stringency forced the company and Peek Frean to increase their bank borrowings, but these soon approached the overall limit of £3,500,000 imposed when the recent loan was made, so as to safeguard the lenders' interests. Then the 1957 economic crisis brought a 7 per cent Bank Rate and a severe credit squeeze, and the Group had to ask both units to run down their stocks of materials in order to economise on finance: Huntley and Palmers' target was a 20 per cent reduction in money terms. The units were also requested to look again at their future investment plans. Even so, a few months later they estimated that they would jointly need £3,500,000 over the coming five years.

The Group Board therefore sought the advice of a leading merchant bank on ways of raising the sums that would be required. That bank straightway pointed out that in order to improve its borrowing powers, the Group's financial structure would have to be changed. To raise funds by issuing ordinary shares would weaken the essential family control; yet other means were unduly hampered because the units still held their preference capital outside the Group's control. The technical point here was that, since the holding company relied for its income on the dividends paid over by both units, all the Group shares ranked lower than each unit's preference shares, dividends on which had to be found before any ordinary dividends were transferred to the Group. In April 1958, therefore, the Group took over both units' preference shares and amalgamated them with its own. More than thirty-six years after the original merger, Huntley and Palmers and Peek Frean at last became wholly owned subsidiaries of the Group.

The way was now clear for creating some debenture stock, which not only allowed the maturing debt of £1,500,000 to be paid off, but made available £2,000,000 of fresh funds. None too willingly—for the same individuals sat on both Group and unit Boards—the Group was being forced to exercise effective supervision over the units' capital expenditure. When a year later Huntley and Palmers' capital commitments turned out to be £330,000 greater than its retained earnings for 1958, the Group instructed the company to postpone any further investment until its earnings covered the excess commitments. The subsequent rules introduced—that projects must save at least $33\frac{1}{3}$ per cent of their cost each year—represented another step forward towards proper Group control.

Apart from finance, however, the units continued to function as separate entities: only in their delivery arrangements did they co-operate fully through the Associated Deliveries Ltd. In 1947 J. R. Gales persuaded Huntley and Palmers' Board to discuss with Peek Frean the possibility of a joint marketing organisation; but the Board turned it down on the grounds of the initial costs and the existing benefits of inter-unit competition in keeping both managements on their toes. Nine years later, the two companies had reached the point of agreeing to avoid duplicating each other's varieties or development work on new products.

For Huntley and Palmers, the second half of the decade ought to have brought constantly rising profits. In fact, it did not repeat the record level of £590,000 achieved in 1954. Despite all the technical improvements, one organisational defect was harming it: imperfect co-ordination between production and sales. In April 1956, for instance, some biscuits and cakes were reported to be going stale, because the actual volume of home sales had fallen short of the forecasts; by implication, output was not flexible enough to be changed at short notice. In June Gordon Palmer, who had specialised on the marketing side of the business, was designated Planning Director. His specific task was to bring the combined demands of the home and the overseas trades into line with Reading's and Huyton's productive capacities. This involved creating a degree of liaison between sales and manufacture which had been completely lacking then.

Within two months Gordon Palmer had organised the production plan for that year's Christmas trade, and arranged for it to be varied week by week according to the current sales and stocks. By November he was planning ahead for the 1957 Christmas programme, and making it clear to the Board that the company was missing trade because it could not supply the quantities demanded. In particular, he demonstrated that more auto plants were required at Huyton; as a result, the Board authorised the fifth and sixth auto plants there, which came into operation in 1957 and 1960 respectively.

The crisis year of 1957 soon put Gordon Palmer's planning to the test. That March a decline in sales caused biscuit stocks to rise sharply, so that output had to be run down. The Board agreed to share the reduction equitably between Reading and Huyton, and to cut night work before introducing any short time. Despite the credit squeeze later on that year, nation-wide biscuit production in 1957 did not fall compared with 1956, but the company's tonnage fell—for the first time in ten years—by nearly $7\frac{1}{2}$ per cent. At a time when the Board estimated the annual expense of carrying stocks to have risen to 12 per cent of their value (made up of bank interest at 7 per cent plus 5 per cent for depreciation, handling and cost of storage) high stock levels were exceptionally costly, while lower output meant shorter production runs and less economical buying of ingredients.

Huntley and Palmers' way out of this dilemma was to appoint in November 1957 industrial consultants, the Wallace Attwood Co. of London, to advise on how to improve sales generally. They carried out a preliminary investigation, which recommended that there should be greater co-ordination of marketing efforts and more market research. They were then instructed to go ahead with a full-scale enquiry. In the meantime, the Board sought to reduce overheads, by making each director responsible for tracking down and enforcing economies in his own department. In April 1958 the consultants submitted their full report.

They stated that the company's sales organisation had failed to keep pace with the recent radical changes on the production side. This was partly because J. R. Gales had had to combine the function of Sales Director with the onerous post of Managing Director. The Home Trade Manager likewise had too wide a field of responsibility: with seven senior executives directly responsible to him, he was burdened with administration at the expense of policy. His deputy, the Home Sales Manager, likewise had to look after eleven District Sales Managers as well as other headquarters staff.

In the field, sales districts varied considerably in size, and were not planned so as to make the most effective use of representatives. Nor did the company have uniform selling methods, adequate sales training or properly co-ordinated local sales promotions. Hence sales penetration—the extent to which the company's products actually penetrated into any given area—was particularly uneven; as in the past, the North of England was very sparsely covered. Nor did the company keep any central record of the potential sales outlets, or see that each was systematically canvassed and offered a full range of the company's products.

On the marketing side, the company was carrying out no effective market research and therefore had little systematic idea of what the consumer really wanted. Although an Advertising Committee had recently been set up to oversee advertising and selling activities generally, these had not expanded in step with the recent increase in trade. Wallace Attwood now urged the setting up of a Marketing Department, to be responsible for publicity, the packaging and presentation of goods, and market research.

In effect, the consultants were saying that they had examined the company's sales organisation and had found practically none. The Board therefore lost no time in putting their recommendations into effect. Gordon Palmer was appointed Sales Director. The post of Home Trade Manager was abolished, and the Home Sales Manager and a new Marketing Manager were both made directly responsible to the Sales Director. J. R. Gales retired as Managing Director at the end of 1958 (he died ten years later) and was succeeded by Gordon Palmer: the first time a member of the family had held the managing directorship. Some of Gordon Palmer's duties were reallocated so that he could continue to exercise the co-ordinating functions he had acquired since 1956: notably that of matching production with sales.

In the following year Wallace Attwood, which had been retained in order to put the new sales organisation into effect, was asked to carry out a similar inquiry into the whole field of production. The object was not only to co-ordinate sales and production more systematically than in the past, but also to make sure that the company's traditional standards of quality control were maintained under the new materials handling system. In accordance with the consultants' report, Richard Palmer became Production Director and was given a new managerial structure, so as to speed up decision-making. In addition, just as the Marketing Department had been established as a 'staff' function parallel to the Home Sales Department's 'line' function, so a Production Control Department was to specify to the Production and Packing Departments exactly what was to be produced, and when.

It worked to a Master Plan, produced three or four times a year by the Planning Manager—who reported straight to the Managing Director—and built up from previous sales experience, plus the Sales Department's forecast for the twelve or so major kinds. The Production Controller then broke down the overall plan into a series of programmes, one for each monthly period; ultimately a Daily Production Order was produced, together with a Daily Ingredients Order.

This system provided a detailed yet flexible plan. It also ensured that any discrepancies between the department's orders and actual production should be immediately investigated, since the orders were returned to Production Control with the actual figures filled in. The penalties for the company of any forecasting errors were considerable, now that the auto plants turned out Osborne biscuits, for instance, at the rate of 125,000 an hour.

Such changes took place at a time when competition from the quality firms had never been more intense. Price competition revived when in 1956 the Restrictive Trade Practices Act outlawed collective agreements over prices, so that the National Association of Biscuit Manufacturers became merely a consultative body, at least to do with the home trade. Nevertheless, the industry as a whole felt advertising and sales promotion to be far more important weapons than price cuts, and here the company was at a relative disadvantage. Its own advertising appropriation in 1951, £70,000, was in real terms below the £25,000 of 1910–11, and increased only to £170,000 in 1960. Yet in 1951 the national advertising outlay on biscuits and crispbreads had been estimated at less than £350,000, wholly in the press, but by 1960 was almost £2,000,000: over £1,100,000 on television and £875,000 in the press. Admittedly a non-specialist firm, Cadbury's, was the heaviest advertiser, in order to promote its chocolate biscuits and 'snacks'.

As had happened before, well-planned advertising campaigns proved very rewarding for the company. In 1959 it launched what it described as its first real sales promotion: this extolled the non-fattening properties of the Breakfast biscuit and encouraged slimmers to eat seven a day. The whole campaign consumed a third of the total home advertising budget: sales of the Breakfast biscuit shot ahead so fast as to overtake production, and it had to be rationed to suppliers for the last eight months of the year. A similar campaign with the Cornish Wafer in the following year established that biscuit as the company's best seller.

The pattern of Huntley and Palmers' sales was being gradually altered by the growth of self-service supermarkets. A Nielsen market survey showed in 1959 that, in common with the other quality firms, the company had maintained its hold on independent retailers, but was far less strong in multiple stores. As supermarkets began to spring up in the 1950s, it had some initial difficulty in getting its goods on to their shelves, many of which were already stocked with 'own brands' made specially for the chains.

A minor setback occurred in 1957, when the supermarkets controlled by Weston's were instructed to sell only Weston's biscuits. However, once it had accepted the often punishing discounts which supermarkets were able to exact, and their tendency to take 'the cream of the list'—say, the first five, instead of up to fifteen kinds—then the company soon came to terms with them. The development of the new voluntary groups of independent grocers, too, meant losing some direct trade with retailers, but in the long run did not harm the company's sales too seriously.

To complete their investigations into sales and production generally, Wallace Attwood about this time looked also at exports. They concluded that the Managing Director, although ultimately responsible in this field, had little time for overseas travel. He was therefore unable to formulate realistic policies and see that they were carried out. Moreover, there were only two representatives for the whole world based in Reading; both were in their sixties and needed to be replaced with younger and more vigorous men. To be sure, their efforts were gravely hampered by import prohibitions or very high tariffs in many foreign countries, but even in relatively 'open' ones the company was doing too little serious market research into local conditions and needs, nor did it carry out any public relations activities overseas. Its total advertising allocation for exports was no more than £35,000. The Board duly reorganised overseas sales, although it did not accept the consultants' recommendation for the appointment of a full-time Export Director. Instead, at the end of 1962, when the duties of top management were rearranged, the Overseas Sales Manager and his department came under the Marketing Director.

In 1958 the company was given the opportunity to acquire control of a world-famous potato-crisp firm. The time had now passed when it would have been happy to diversify production in this way, for it now had to concentrate on making the most of its existing assets. Quite by chance, the Group happened to be in touch with another quality biscuit maker: W. & R. Jacob & Co. (Liverpool) Ltd. It will be remembered that Jacob's of Dublin had opened their Aintree factory in 1914. When the Irish Free State became independent in 1922, Jacob's split into two separate companies, although they maintained contact through some directors serving on both boards. The Liverpool firm became a public company six years later.

Ever since the Association in 1909 had polarised into quality and cheap firms, Jacob's and Carr's of Carlisle had been the only two non-Scottish firms on the quality side: Huntley and Palmers and Peek Frean were not members until 1918. Carr's had been in and out of the Association several times; having been readmitted in 1953, it resigned again in 1960, a few years before it lost family control and became a subsidiary of Cavenham Foods Ltd. The value of sales in the 1950s had scarcely risen at all, whereas Jacobs' had more than doubled.

Jacob's, still a family firm, had never resumed the talks it had held with the Group in the 1920s about a possible merger; however, when a would-be overseas buyer appeared to be in the offing, it was glad to make highly secret approaches to the Group. Negotiations went so satisfactorily that by the beginning of 1960 Price Waterhouse and Jacobs' accountants, Harmood Banner Lewis and Mounsey, drew up a joint memorandum outlining the basis for a possible exchange of shares. For security reasons, the memorandum nowhere specified the exact nature of the two firms' business. It referred to the Group as PW and Jacob's as HB, after their respective accountants' names; someone then softened these rather forbidding initials into the more poetic Periwinkle and Hambone. In almost every respect Hambone fitted in well with Periwinkle's main activities. Appropriately enough, at the end of this decade of reappraisal, three highly esteemed family firms were combining in order to meet the no less arduous conditions expected in the 1960s.

21

Reconstruction: (i) A Programme of Change 1960–5

In 1960 W. & R. Jacob & Co. (Liverpool) Ltd. became a wholly-owned subsidiary of the Associated Biscuit Manufacturers Ltd. Since this was a genuine amalgamation of interests and Jacob's remained a family firm like the other units, it received no cash but simply exchanged its own shares for Group ones. The Group thereby increased its issued share capital by just under £1,500,000 to £7,200,000. Three of Jacobs' directors joined the Group Board; the Managing Director, Roderic O'Conor—a grandson of one of his firm's original partners—became a joint managing director together with Gordon Palmer and Rupert Carr.

The Group was thus fortified by the accession of a quality firm having a nation-wide market and concentrating mainly on biscuits. In addition, the range of top-selling lines was broadened. While Huntley and Palmers' and Peek Frean's most well-known specialities were savoury, semi-sweet, cream and assorted biscuits, those of Jacob's were the plain —notably Cream Crackers—and chocolate varieties.[1] Financially, the Group had become stronger because the value of its net operating assets had increased from less than £17 millions to just under £21 millions. Turnover, too, rose from £24,200,000 in 1959 to £31,600,000 for 1960. In terms of physical output, the enlarged Group now contributed 19 per cent of aggregate tonnage, compared with United Biscuits' 16 per cent.

Yet these additions to capacity were merely the prelude to a period of radical change. Business mergers are often compared to human marriages, and financial journalists had for some time noted that the marriage between Huntley and Palmers and Peek Frean had never been consummated.[2] Unusually for amalgamated companies of national repute, the units had kept their distance from each other, not in the sense of being aloof, but rather of refusing to trespass on the other's privacy. In consequence, there was little incentive to develop common interests and approaches. Their resolve to remain as outright competitors in virtually every aspect of the business, as much as their failure to persuade other firms to join, had dissipated the widespread fears of the 1920s that the Group would become a 'biscuit monopoly'.

After Jacobs' entry, however, things were changed for good. In the words of a non-family director who remembered clearly the time when Huntley and Palmers itself consisted of a series of watertight compartments, Jacob's acted as a 'catalyst'. Inter-unit communications, previously requiring no more than a telephone call between Reading and Bermondsey, became far more involved overnight. Even so, the will towards complete and thoroughly planned integration—instead of a lengthy and piecemeal approach—was born of one man's initiative.

That man was Rupert Carr. His perceptive comments on Huntley and Palmers in 1930 were mentioned in Chapter 17. Since then he had exercised his large vision not only at Bermondsey but also further afield. Having helped to administer the zoning of biscuits during the war, he had become so 'exasperated' with post-war controls that he went out to Canada in order to set up a factory at Toronto which became Peek Frean (Canada) Ltd. After his return, in 1957 he became Vice-Chairman of the Group in addition to his post as Managing Director of Peek Frean, so that he had an inside knowledge of the Group organisation. Wishing to learn more about how large enterprises work, four years later he enrolled for the three-month Advanced Management Program at the Harvard Business School, which trains senior executives in mid-career.

Those who have attended this course at Harvard, or more recently the six-week version held in Britain each summer since 1964, know the attention paid to 'corporate strategy': clearly defining policy within the framework of the firm's general objectives. The case study method is used—taking real (or life-like) situations in firms for thorough discussion. As important as the classwork itself is the opportunity to make contact with fellow-participants in the small syndicate groups and also outside working hours. As one of the more elderly members—he was then over fifty—Rupert Carr found himself in the same group as several top executives in very large corporations; he later admitted that 'a lot of their thinking rubbed off on me'.

On returning to Britain, he found that Peek Frean was running into 'troubled waters'. This gave him an opportunity to reshape the firm along Harvard lines, employing Urwick Orr as consultants. As at Huntley and Palmers, Peek Frean's profit margins had not really kept pace with the greatly increased scale of output, and he now proposed to introduce the kind of forward planning and financial control in force at Reading.

Huntley and Palmers had recently called in Urwick Orr again, this time to study the engineering department. The powerful traditions in that department have already been stressed: a succession of able Chief

Engineers, from W. Ruddock in 1846 to R. G. Davis who resigned in 1964, had worked with some no less able and inventive directors, including Alfred Palmer and later on his grandson Neil Gardiner. The company had made heavy professional demands on the department, perhaps more so recently when automatic machinery had to be installed and kept in repair, than in the old days of individual machines made in the factory for specific varieties. Yet the department's technical efficiency was not matched by an economic efficiency: until lately the costs of maintenance—which were far higher now than in the past—had not been separated from those of installation.

As a result of Urwick Orr's recommendations a Technical Development Division was set up, to be headed by Neil Gardiner. Under him came the Chief Engineer, and his team of designers, together with the Chief Chemist and the vital laboratory facilities. Although the engineers and chemists had always worked very closely together, this was the first time that they had come under the same organisation. The Production Manager was made responsible for maintenance, exercised by a Works Engineer, who supervised quality control.

At the same time, the consultants forced the company's top management to practise a kind of self-consciousness that did not come naturally. Apart from wartime service, all the directors had spent their working lives with the company, in full-time charge of some aspect or other of its work. Years of experience had taught them to recognise instinctively what needed to be done. Now the consultants were telling them: 'We cannot over-stress the danger of bringing a new function into existence without clearly defining what it is supposed to do and what effect it will have on other departments in the company.'

Huntley and Palmers also took action over its disappointing results. Although in the past three years annual biscuit tonnage produced in Britain had increased from 514,000 to 544,000 tons, the company's share of this had diminished from 5·8 to 5·4 per cent. Late in 1961, therefore, a small committee, consisting of Alan Palmer (the Deputy Chairman), Gordon Palmer (the Managing Director) and Hector Hanford (the Company Secretary, who had been appointed a director in 1960) set down the aims and policies to be pursued.

By May 1962 they had produced a Trade and Development Policy for the company, to cover the years 1962-4. In addition to setting a target of return on capital employed, to be achieved by 1964, they also sketched out a new top management structure that would be required to achieve it. A month later Urwick Orr, which the committee had already drawn into its discussions, were asked to submit detailed proposals.

These followed closely the ones which Urwick Orr had recently put forward for Peek Frean. There a managerial organisation had been created to allow Rupert Carr as Managing Director to stand back from day-to-day operations and act as 'prime mover or stimulator rather than in an operational or administrative role'. The Chairman of Peek Frean was Rupert Carr's father Philip Carr, now almost eighty and in a part-time role, whereas Reginald Palmer was very much a full-time Chairman at Reading. Urwick Orr therefore proposed that Huntley and Palmers' Chairman should be concerned mainly with forecasting and long-term planning, and therefore free from detailed executive control of the company's operating divisions; that function was now delegated to the Managing Director. We have seen how the chairmanship had passed through many phases, but in 1962 for the first time he had to confine himself to the long view. In his turn the Managing Director delegated to his managers much detailed work to do with marketing and production planning, so as to concentrate on broader supervision.

Below them, the company was organised into four clearly defined divisions. William Palmer was appointed Production Director and Richard Palmer Marketing Director; their two 'operational', or line divisions now came under the Managing Director. The two 'planning', or staff, divisions—Finance, and Technical Development—were placed directly under the Chairman. Lord Palmer, who had succeeded Geoffrey Palmer as Chairman of Huntley Boorne and Stevens, also reported directly to the Chairman. Hector Hanford, the Secretary, was responsible for finance, as he had been ever since Bennet Palmer retired as Financial Director in mid-1962, while Neil Gardiner remained in charge of Technical Development. For the first time, as had been recommended during the sales reorganisation, a Marketing Research Manager was appointed.

These four divisions did not re-establish any of the old watertight compartments within the company, for the directors stressed that managers at all levels must have free access to and complete liaison with their opposite numbers in other departments. Early in 1963 the *Company Organisation Manual*, drawn up by Urwick Orr, set out precisely the responsibilities and 'matched authorities' of directors and senior managers, as well as the procedures, management techniques and annual planning programmes that had to be followed. As a beginning, the company laid down an intermediate profit target for 1963; this was translated into a series of budgets, which were passed on to the directors and senior managers of each department concerned.

The concentration of the Reading factory into a more compact and profitable entity went ahead smoothly, and the last of the North Factory buildings were demolished. It was now the turn of chocolate and cream-filled biscuits to be given improved manufacturing methods; three large enrobeurs were installed, for coating the biscuits with chocolate, together with a creaming machine and a number of high-speed packing machines which wrapped the 'count lines' (sold individually instead of by weight) with foil at the speed of a hundred a minute. In 1966 the whole of chocolate manufacture was transferred to Huyton, which left Reading as a very highly automated factory for the more standard types of biscuit.

By the early 1960s all the Recreation Club's sports facilities at Reading, apart from some football pitches, were concentrated in the Kensington Road ground. There the directors contributed half the expense of constructing a new pavilion and bowling green. The popularity of different activities was changing over the years; the Choral Society, for instance, was disbanded—mainly because there were other very active choirs in the town. Yet although members' wives and children over school age had been given associate membership, the solitary sport of angling remained the favourite pastime of the largest group of members. A similar club, with a Recreation Centre provided by the company, had been established at Huyton in 1956.

That membership remained over the 200 mark, in spite of the fall in total numbers of employees, was partly due to the successful method of administering the club; this differed from that found in most other clubs of its type. The company was the landlord of all club premises, including the sports grounds, but charged no rent for them. It paid the salaries of all the staff and made an annual grant which helped to meet running expenses not covered by subscriptions. This allowed the club and the sections responsible for the various activities to be organised without interference by the company.

Meanwhile, Rupert Carr's thoughts were running ahead to reorganising the Group structure, in order to complement what was taking place in Huntley and Palmers and Peek Frean. In June 1962 he circulated a memorandum, entitled 'A Programme of Change'. A brief document—no more than 3000 words long—it outlined some possible ways of integrating the various units' operations.

His declared objective was to create a 'climate' of ideas. This climate must be fostered by the Board, since ' "what goes on at the apex" is vital', and operating managements would then receive favourably and consider with due care schemes for reducing costs through integration, and eventually put them into effect 'with whole-hearted enthusiasm and drive'. He then succinctly reviewed the Group's history, to highlight what needed to be done. With beautiful precision, born of decades of experience, he dissected the attitudes and practices of the past generation.

Reconstruction: (i) A Programme of Change 1960–5

After their amalgamation in 1921, he said, the two businesses deliberately promoted paternalism and company loyalties by encouraging rivalry instead of collaboration between units. Both companies were therefore regarded as 'citadels in which these qualities'—of paternalism and pride in one's unit—'were enshrined' instead of as 'tools, or fixed capital investments which were required to produce so much profit for shareholders'. Moreover, 'the National Association of Biscuit Manufacturers determined the basic commercial policy for the units and their immediate competitors, and the influence of its rules and regulations was reflected downwards through the respective managements as laws by which the business game should be played. Life was strenuous but not particularly uncomfortable for management.'

As a result (he continued) the Board of the Group, composed as it was of family directors from each unit, concerned itself principally with formal business, such as monthly financial statements and overall sales policy vis-à-vis the trade association. Only when major items of capital expenditure were being considered did the Group exercise any effective supervision, and then only by asking each unit for capital budgets, so as to keep some control over the re-investment of funds as these became available. The Group did not lay down any target return on re-investment.

On the other hand, where genuine Group integration had occurred, specifically Group loyalties had begun to spring up. The most noteworthy example was the joint delivery system. To some extent the Co-ordinating Committee, of the units' managing directors, had developed into 'a top-level communication system', supervising all other systems of inter-unit communication and reviewing all current operating problems. Although lacking specific authority and directives, the committee had over the years achieved 'a certain degree of integration of effort and a reduction of senseless inter-unit competition'. (It is fair to add that other, equally well informed, observers felt that successive managing directors—including Rupert Carr himself since 1940—had not taken full advantage of their opportunities until 1958, when he and Gordon Palmer were in harness together.)

The units' attitudes had been transformed by Jacobs' entry into the Group, and Rupert Carr now specified the Group Board's primary task as one of laying down clearly its objectives and providing the framework of an organisation by which these could be achieved. The objectives were maximum profits and in the longer term, maintaining the Group 'in a dynamic condition leading to further growth'. In this way it could make the most effective use of its very considerable material resources, as well as the immaterial ones like customer goodwill—among retailers and final consumers—the loyalty of employees, and technical expertise.

As to organisation, since the present was a time of 'terrific change', Group directors must fully understand what was happening and have the will to change. Only through them could the unit executives be made to shift their loyalties from the unit towards the Group.

On the matter of timing, he believed that his Programme of Change should be carried out in two stages. Stage I was essentially a preparatory one, and involved creating certain key Group committees. The managing directors' Co-ordinating Committee should be enlarged and be re-named the Executive Committee. A new Forward Planning Committee should comprise three unit representatives and a Financial Controller who would supervise the financial aspects of all developments. In Stage II the Group would take further action in the light of experience.

Rupert Carr's task as a pace-setter was eased by the sense of urgency which his Group colleagues shared with him. The two Huntley and Palmers directors were Alan Palmer and Gordon Palmer, both of whom —in their forties—strongly supported this kind of change. The latter, as a managing director, became a member of the Executive Committee, and both were appointed to the Group Forward Planning Committee: Christopher Barber, one of the three Jacob's directors appointed to the main Board in 1960, became Group Financial Director. The two committees were chaired by Reginald Palmer. As Group Chairman he was in many ways re-enacting the role played by his father Howard Palmer, the initial chairman of the Group from 1921 to 1923: of harnessing the drive of a younger generation to his own ample experience.

It will be remembered that Reginald Palmer had specialised on the production side; he had been behind Huntley and Palmers' various economy drives between the wars and had also helped Neil Gardiner to win their colleagues' agreement to the first auto plants in the factory. He was as outward-looking as any of his predecessors: in addition to his Group chairmanship, he was President of the National Association of Biscuit Manufacturers and since the 1940s had been chairman of the National Joint Wages Council of the Biscuit Industry.

However, just as Howard Palmer had been incapacitated shortly after the Group was formed, so Reginald Palmer had to undergo a serious operation in 1962, and retired through ill-health in mid-1963, at the age of sixty-five. He died in 1970. Alan Palmer succeeded him as Chairman of Huntley and Palmers, and also became Vice-Chairman of the Group when Rupert Carr was elected Group Chairman.

While these long-term plans were coming into effect, short-term problems still persisted. The Group's profits for 1964 fell by a third, to 3·5 per cent of turnover compared with an average of 5·6 per cent in the previous three years. The principal reason was a sharp rise in the cost of ingredients during the year, and prices could not be raised until the beginning of 1965 owing to official price controls. Indeed, these increases were the first of any consequence for ten years in the industry, which had thus enjoyed a period of extraordinary price stability thanks to its vast mechanisation programme.

At the same time, the limits of savings from mechanisation were now in sight, and the very intense product competition was forcing up selling costs. The 1960 figure of total biscuit advertising, namely £2 millions, was estimated to have risen by 50 per cent to over £3 millions by 1964; the Group's contribution to the 1964 figure was £370,000, or about $12\frac{1}{2}$ per cent. Apart from advertising, sales promotions aimed at the consumer—such as competitions—were still rare, except for chocolate biscuits. On the other hand, there were many inducements to distributors, such as cash bonuses, selling contests with large prizes, and special displays in shops. All these had to be paid for out of firms' earnings.

As a preparation for Stage II, early in 1965 the Group called in consultants, P.A. Management Consultants Ltd., to advise on long-term plans for achieving economies within the Group in production and marketing. They were also to look at the best way of strengthening the whole Group management structure through its reorganisation.

The consultants' report warned against the dangers of trying to preserve traditional attitudes now that competition was so severe. 'If the Associated Biscuit Manufacturers Ltd. were to set up today to make maximum long-term profit', they asked, 'would it consciously create its present structure and organisation?' Clearly not, since it was made up of three separate companies with their own marketing and selling agencies and three other 'autonomous functions', including Huntley Boorne and Stevens and Peek Frean's subsidiary Meltis Ltd. Moreover, there was no Group executive authority as such, so that no one was really responsible for seeing that policy decisions made in the Group Board or its committees were actually carried out. The full advantages of Group operations had therefore not been gained.

Two steps therefore should be taken urgently: the first was a feasibility study of each factory, and the second was the establishment of a Group 'executive arm', which should be kept small, and grow organically out of the existing structure. In addition, marketing and sales managers in the three factories had little idea of which lines made the highest contribution to earnings per production hour, and therefore could not plan their sales efforts so as to maximise profits.

The number of varieties therefore needed to be reduced, not indiscriminately but by cutting out the loss-makers and promoting more effectively the leading varieties known to earn high profits. Representatives, too, would have to be retrained to sell this diminished range of products, and eventually to travel for the Group as a whole. The low-selling lines which contributed little to profit should have their price increased: that would either reduce their sales to a point where they could be cut out, or alternatively make them profitable enough to be kept in production.

Huntley and Palmers (it may be added) had not yet fully come to terms with this problem. It believed that its main goodwill with the public sprang from the large choice it offered, particularly in assortments, so that even in 1965 it was still producing eighty-five different kinds of biscuit and twenty-one of cake. At the same time it had begun to build up a healthy trade with the supermarkets and voluntary chains of independent grocers. These were the distributors who wanted to take a limited number—say five, or 'the cream of the list' as it was expressed above—rather than stock the ample choice commonly found in older-established shops. A greatly reduced range would also allow the representative to make the most effective use of the very small amount of time that each retailer could now spare for him. Even now, the large retailing concerns were beginning to insist on doing business with one salesman for the whole Group.

The consultants' recommendations were broadly accepted, and in September 1965 the Group made the first moves towards creating the structure required. The Group Executive Committee absorbed the Forward Planning Committee and was enlarged to include not only three unit directors—who remained answerable to their units—but also three whole-time Group executives in charge of finance, production and marketing respectively. Christopher Barber, already Group Financial Director and chairman of the Group's Finance Committee, now assumed his duties full-time at Reading, as did Gordon Medd, also a director of Jacob's, who was appointed Group Production Controller. Gordon Palmer became Group Marketing Director; Alan Palmer took over the managing directorship of Huntley and Palmers in addition to remaining its Chairman.

The Group headquarters were moved from Bermondsey, their location ever since 1921, to Reading. From early in 1966 the three full-time executives occupied part of Huntley and Palmers' first floor offices. Their immediate task was to study in detail the consultants' proposals and recommend programmes and priorities in their respective fields. These they would then co-ordinate into an integrated policy by means of discussions among themselves, and present their joint policy to the

Reconstruction: (i) A Programme of Change 1960-5

Group Executive Committee and where necessary to the whole Board.

In essentials, the developments to date correspond with Stage I of Rupert Carr's 'Programme of Change', while in the Stage II period, the definitive form of Group organisation would be introduced, to embrace all sides of its work. A Group standing executive body was now in being, which could speed up action, since until then any decisions had had to wait until the Group committee concerned had its next meeting. Moreover, as the consultants had suggested, the Group now had some 'teeth' because the full-time executives could now follow through decisions taken in their areas. Rupert Carr as Group Chairman acted as leader of this team, but until a full-time Group Managing Director was appointed in due course, the inner organisation that was badly required could not be fully effective.

22
Reconstruction: (ii) Stage Two and After 1965–72

Stage II of the move towards Group integration lasted from September 1965 until the end of 1968. It thus stretched from the date when the three full-time Group executives were appointed, until Huntley and Palmers ceased to exist in its old form and was wholly merged into a biscuit division of the Group. During that period the national output of biscuits hovered just below 600,000 tons a year: twice as high as in 1939 but not appreciably above the 528,000 tons of 1960.[1]

The level of 600,000 tons could be regarded as an equilibrium one, for with the rise in real incomes since 1939 demand was no longer being held down artificially by a lack of purchasing power. Most customers now had enough disposable income to buy biscuits if they chose to do so. They were also free to choose quality biscuits, which in real terms—allowing for changes in the value of money—were very much cheaper than before the war. In 1968 the general index of retail prices was three and three-quarter times that of 1938; yet Breakfast biscuits were only a little over 50 per cent dearer, and Ginger Nuts and Cornish Wafers just over twice as expensive. The economies secured by the new machinery were so considerable that although the costs of ingredients had continued to rise, these had been partly offset by an increase of $32\frac{1}{2}$ per cent between 1958 and 1968 in the tonnage produced per worker in the industry, whose numbers fell by 15 per cent in the period.[2]

Thus quality biscuits were now within the range of most family incomes and quality manufacturers—those currently members of the N.A.B.M.—had increased their share of output (in physical terms) from under 30 per cent in 1939 to nearly 46 per cent in 1965: say, from less than 100,000 tons to nearly 265,000 tons. The percentage would have been even greater but for the substantial amount of 'own brand' biscuits which the supermarkets were now selling. Since the quality manufacturers were competing for shares of a virtually static biscuit market, rivalry between them was bound to be intensified. The increases in advertising and sales promotion have already been mentioned, but there were also strong moves towards amalgamation.

The official Census of Production data show that the numbers of specialist firms with more than 25 employees shrank from 77 in 1954 to 60 in 1958 and to 38 in 1963.[3] A number of independent producers went out of business altogether. For Reading the most poignant example was Serpell's, which closed down in 1959, only eight years after celebrating its centenary. Relations between the two Reading firms had always been cordial, and Serpell's had undertaken a small amount of production for Huntley and Palmers while the Huyton factory was being built.

The company might have been expected to take over Serpell's when it closed; however, neither the factory buildings or machinery nor its market for biscuits would have fitted into Huntley and Palmers' or the Group's pattern. Serpells' trade name was therefore acquired by Kemp's, now a subsidiary of Wright's Biscuits Ltd. of South Shields in Durham, which had also absorbed Middlemass.

Other biscuit firms had joined larger groupings. Carr's of Carlisle (as we have seen) became a subsidiary of a non-specialist firm in the food business, and Frears—which at one time seemed to be interested in joining the Group—of the National Biscuit Co. of America. William Crawford's, Macdonald's and Meredith & Drew were all merged into United Biscuits between 1962 and 1967. The 'concentration ratios' in the Censuses of Production showed that whereas in 1958 the top five firms had contributed less than 48 per cent of the value of total biscuit sales, by 1963 their contribution had risen to $65\frac{1}{2}$ per cent.[4]

Over and above this merger activity, the largest firms sought to diversify their production. United Biscuits, for instance, branched out in a number of directions: into the restaurant business through another subsidiary, D. S. Crawford, potato crisps through Meredith & Drew and processed nuts through yet another subsidiary. From 1965 onwards it was making strenuous and costly efforts to build up sales through grocery outlets of cakes with a relatively short life, such as cream-filled sandwiches.

Associated Biscuits, on the other hand, saw itself as largely a homogeneous business, for its cakes, puddings, confectionery (through Meltis Ltd.) and tin boxes represented only a small percentage of total turnover. Its main expertise—including that of management—lay in biscuit production. Moreover, because all its home units used broadly similar manufacturing plant and ingredients, and marketed their goods to similar types of customer, the Group had ample scope for coordinating and rationalising activities such as ingredients purchasing, manufacture and marketing. Some form of diversification was highly necessary, both as a means of growth and as a hedge against risk, but the Group felt that this was well served by expanding its overseas activities, which are discussed below.[5]

The reorganisation of the Group at home had continued to preoccupy Rupert Carr, who in May 1963 wrote a supplementary report to his 'Programme of Change'. There he observed that so far, all those concerned had paid perhaps too much attention to 'what we are going to do' at the expense of 'how we are going to do it'. He therefore felt that it was time to move on to the question of means. Those primarily concerned with policy—namely, the Group's Executive Committee and Forward Planning Committee (as long as they remained separate bodies) —had already given much thought to the organisation of the Group into the most effective 'line' and 'staff' functions. Their main task now was to produce detailed proposals for this reorganisation, which they proceeded to do with great energy.

The consultants had recommended that feasibility studies should be carried out in each of the factories, to see what modernisation was required. Of Huntley and Palmers' two biscuit factories, the Huyton one was well organised, particularly for assortments—including the Christmas trade—which demanded a considerable amount of packing labour.

The Reading factory, too, seemed fairly efficiently laid out to deal with the more straightforward biscuit lines, but when in 1963 Urwick Orr surveyed the whole site, they found that it was too large for its actual needs, bearing in mind that only half the company's total output was produced there. However, while they rejected any plan to leave Reading altogether or even to move to another site in the town, they believed that the company could secure worth-while economies in production by demolishing the obsolescent buildings which were so costly to maintain, and improving the layout of operations in the more up-to-date parts. The front office block provided good office accommodation, and should therefore be used to the best effect.

In fact, the studies revealed that the factory in greatest need of modernisation was Peek Frean's. Not only was it cramped, since it covered only ten acres as against Huntley and Palmers' twenty-four acres at Reading, but some of its buildings dated back to 1872; by then all Huntley and Palmers' factory buildings of that vintage had disappeared. In 1966 the Group therefore decided to embark on a complete reorganisation of the Bermondsey site, at a cost of £3½ millions, in order to create what was to be the most modern biscuit factory in Europe. The old multi-story buildings would be replaced by a factory on one floor to house the main baking and packing equipment, consisting of eight auto plants and other integrated machinery for biscuits.

Bulk storage was to be installed, similar to but more up-to-date than that at Reading, and ingredients would be mixed and delivered to the plants by computer. It was only sixty years since, as the Peek Frean film shows, employees had scooped up great lumps of butter with their hands, banged them on the scales to make sure that they were not underweight, and flung them into the mixing drum. At the distribution end, after the biscuits had been mechanically packed and loaded on pallets, they would be stored in a warehouse fully equipped with pallet racking and operated with fork-lift trucks capable of lifting the pallets 26 feet high. In mid-1971 the first part of this modernisation scheme at Bermondsey was complete when four auto plants had been installed.

Another obsolescent multi-story factory on a congested site belonged to Huntley Boorne and Stevens. By the early 1960s the provision of biscuit tins for Huntley and Palmers made up less than a third of its total output, for at home practically no biscuits were now sold loose out of tins; wrapped packets usually travelled in cardboard boxes, known as 'outers'. Nevertheless, Huntley and Palmers still had its very important Christmas trade in decorated tins, no longer highly unconventional shapes, but of the half-square type. The Family Circle assortment, packed in the same kind of tin for sale throughout the year, was by 1968 the third most popular variety, after the Osborne and the Cornish Wafer.

Huntley Boorne and Stevens produced many other articles for outside customers. Tins were lithographed—like the biscuit tins—by means of very high speed two-colour printing machines, while the other light engineering products included brake fluid tanks for certain makes of car. However, the firm's Lamiplate, a material of laminated plastic and metal introduced in 1958, had become so much in demand—especially for outside parts of consumer durables—that in 1966 the firm made an agreement with one of the largest American producers of laminated products, Arvin Industries Inc. of Indiana, to share technical and marketing expertise.

The layout of the London Street factory was thoroughly overhauled in 1961, but there was no room for expansion on the site. Six years later much of the work on Christmas tins, mainly the ones packed at Huyton, was therefore transferred to Aintree. Plans were also worked out for moving the remainder of the factory from London Street to Woodley, near Reading. There, in single-storey premises, a new laminating plant was laid down; by 1971, as forecast, Lamiplate had become almost as important to the firm as tin boxes. Unfortunately, the costs of removal and reorganisation caused Huntley Boorne and Stevens to make a loss of £365,000 in 1969. This loss was reduced to £243,000 in 1970, partly by closing the Aintree branch factory, but for a few years longer, although now trading at a profit, it was likely to be by comparison a 'weak sister', as it had been in the 1930s.

Since other factories were more in need of major reorganisation, therefore, those of Huntley and Palmers could not expect to achieve any spectacular economies in the short term. However, the company did take one important step in 1966 to smooth out the rate of manufacturing at Huyton, and so minimise the need for undue overtime and fluctuations in labour, particularly before Christmas. This involved setting up storage units with low temperature and humidity.

At the same time, the company's marketing policy was capable of improvement. The Group Marketing Director, Gordon Palmer, had the specific task of integrating the sales efforts of all the units, but some years were likely to pass before this could be done. In fact, an integrated Group sales force for Scotland was in being by the autumn of 1969 and for the whole of Britain by the end of 1970: much sooner than forecast. Meanwhile, it was clear that Huntley and Palmers' sales reorganisation of 1958, intended to make the company orientated towards sales rather than production, had not completely achieved its object.

In particular, the new management structure since 1962—when the four divisions were set up—was not entirely effective for providing goods when and where they were demanded. The Master Plan suffered from the disadvantage that it was jointly drawn up by the Planning Manager, who belonged to the Production Division, and the Marketing Research Manager, who belonged to Marketing.

Despite the aspirations about free access and liaison, these two managers were subject to all the natural conflicts of interest between their respective divisions. Thus the company needed to establish close and regular links between divisions as well as improved sales forecasting and planning techniques. To this end C. D. van Namen, who had been Home Sales Manager since 1958, was made a director of the company while holding the same post. Also a Marketing Manager, whose post had not survived the 1962 reorganisation, was appointed to take charge of the company's overall marketing strategy. This included drawing up a profit and promotional plan for each of the top ten products.

As to planning, the company's Planning Manager was re-named Budget Controller and transferred from the Production to the Marketing Division. His principal function was to prepare and issue sales forecasts, both for the whole year and for each four-week period on which all the operational data, and especially cost accounting, were now drawn up. Moreover, he estimated and controlled finished stocks, both in the factory and in the depots.

In the Production Division, the Product Design and Quality Control Manager was designated Assistant to the Production Director. While retaining his earlier functions, he had to keep regularly in touch with the Home Sales Manager about any shortages and with the Budget

Controller when major fluctuations of demand took place. This closely knit team, with their interlocking functions, were therefore to be responsible for the whole of production planning on a co-ordinated basis, and to see that the plan as it unfolded kept broadly in step with sales trends.

At last, therefore, the company was beginning to integrate its marketing and production planning. In 1961 around half the home turnover, including cakes, was accounted for by twelve varieties of biscuit, but in 1968 by the top six varieties. This improvement had been helped by some successful sales promotions; one year of the Lemon Puff, so that it moved into the top six, and another year of the Osborne, which in 1962 had been given a shorter texture and renamed the Butter Osborne. With some good sales promotion the latter leapt into first place by 1967, narrowly outstripping the Cornish Wafer which had been in the lead since 1954.

Thus the company now had every inducement to curtail the number of varieties. By the end of 1968 it produced only two basic kinds of cake and less than forty different kinds of biscuit: twenty baked in ten ovens at Reading, compared with the 400 kinds in 150 ovens before the war. These changes reflected as well the fact that whereas in 1963 the six largest multiple retailers had accounted for $11\frac{1}{2}$ per cent of the company's home trade, in 1968 over 12 per cent was going to the largest four, of which J. Sainsbury was still comfortably in the lead.

The company had also reduced the number of delivery points—that is, individual customers—in a few years from more than 91,000 to 76,000. Yet some 34,000 of these bought less than £100 a year each, and therefore hardly recompensed the company for the costs of representatives' visits and deliveries. At the same time the proportion of trade done through wholesalers, which had fallen so dramatically from over 30 per cent in 1921 to 15 per cent as recently as 1964, had now recovered slightly to 19 per cent, owing to the growth of the voluntary chains. Predictably, the members of these chains tended to be the most enterprising independent retailers in their area.

Changes were taking place in the company's overseas trade, which in 1967 passed the £1 million mark, for the first time since the export bonanza of the early 1950s when biscuits once again became available without restriction. This represented $11\frac{1}{2}$ per cent of its total turnover, as against 4·8 per cent (in tonnage terms) for the biscuit industry as a whole, and more than 12 per cent of Britain's total exports of biscuits and cakes. Some of the company's most important traditional markets, such as India, Ceylon and Burma, had now vanished, mainly because of import prohibitions. Indeed, nearly a third of its exports now went to the United States. There its biscuits tended to have a wider sale than in the past, for the average household could buy them in the main supermarkets at prices which—despite the import duties—were not too uncompetitive with American-made ones. The value of sales thus more than doubled between 1963 and 1966, and helped to consolidate the Group's position as the largest exporters of British biscuits.

The succession of representatives sent out from England and later on the American agencies had never produced a really satisfactory volume of business and a New York sales office had taken their place. However, as part of the integration process for the Group, in 1967 the company joined with Peek Frean in establishing Huntley and Palmers (America) Ltd., which later became A.B. (America) Ltd. Its object was to market jointly the Group's products—including Peek Frean's biscuits produced in Canada—throughout the United States, by means of a large network of brokers and distributors.

In France and New Zealand the company had its biscuits manufactured under licence; of the other 140 or so countries throughout the world to which it despatched its exports, all but half a dozen maintained import duties. By the mid-1960s for the first time the British Government recognised exporting achievements as suitable grounds for honours. Over the years various directors of Huntley and Palmers had been honoured, but usually for some public service or other. Sir Eric Palmer's knighthood, for instance, had been granted for his wartime work with the industry as a whole through the Alliance, and his son Alan Palmer was awarded the C.B.E. in 1969 while Chairman of the Alliance for furthering exports and productivity in the industry. Lord Palmer, too, was awarded the O.B.E. in 1968 for his work in promoting National Savings. The first honour specifically relating to the company itself was the M.B.E. awarded in 1966 to Sidney Bartlett, Export Manager throughout the strenuous period from 1949 onwards.

The Group made a change on the distribution side in 1966, when it formed a new delivery company in conjunction with John Mackintosh & Sons Ltd. This was known as ABMAC Deliveries Ltd., and the Group's share was 70 per cent. Associated Deliveries Ltd. continued to function independently of the ABMAC firms, which still used its depots in a few areas. To ease the work of transition, Lord Palmer remained as Chairman of Associated Deliveries Ltd. until 1968. In 1966, too, David Gardiner returned from Huyton, where he had been a local director, to take charge of the Group's operational research. His initial task was to plan a new network of depots; these eventually numbered only seventeen instead of thirty-three. Just as Associated Deliveries had been the first—perhaps the only—really successful example of integration after the Group's establishment in 1921, so ABMAC led the way in the integration of the three units after 1960.

It made use of the latest materials handling techniques. For instance, cases of biscuits were loaded on to pallets so that they could be handled in the factories by fork-lift trucks as economically as possible. Maximum-capacity road vehicles undertook most of the 'trunking', or long-distance distribution to depots, where the bulk loads were broken down for local delivery. These arrangements showed substantially reduced costs compared with the rail distribution which—except at Huyton—Huntley and Palmers and Peek Frean had formerly used. When Mackintosh's amalgamated with Rowntree's in 1969 it withdrew from the delivery system which became solely a function of the Group.

Huntley and Palmers' reorganisation at this time was intended to complement that taking place within the Group, where by 1968 Stage II was being carried forward very rapidly. The structure which the Group created in that year has been described as 'very simple, but very clever', with its activities centred on three divisions; namely Biscuits, Overseas, and Tins and Light Engineering. The Biscuit Division took over the home and export sales of biscuits, cakes and puddings made in Britain, Overseas looked after the Australian, Canadian and Indian subsidiaries, and Tins and Light Engineering comprised Huntley Boorne and Stevens.

Roderic O'Conor, currently Chairman as well as Managing Director of Jacob's, was appointed as the Biscuit Division's first Managing Director. During the course of 1968 he moved from Aintree in order to join the three full-time executives in the Group offices at Reading. He formed the keystone of the Group structure, for while Rupert Carr and Alan Palmer as Chairman and Vice-Chairman respectively remained free of operational duties, he and his team took full control of day-to-day operations. Between them they completed their immediate work within the year. This included planning the detailed organisation required, and also choosing the people who were to fill the various Group posts.

The Managing Director was assisted by three main divisional committees, to deal with planning, operations, and product-marketing respectively. Planning took in all aspects of future activities from the development of new objectives to specific items such as budgeting and capital expenditure. Operations was shorter-term, in that it involved reviewing and analysing recent outcomes, and evolving a forecast for the immediate future. Product-marketing, as the name suggests, was concerned with product policy—for instance, changing the types of products and developing new ones—and with major changes in the organisation of sales representatives. Each director also held 'functional' meetings from time to time in order to deal with specific topics, such as productivity and cost control. The technical development meetings involved 'sharing ideas and "brain storming" '.

On 1st January 1969 the Biscuit Division, known as Associated Biscuits Ltd., formally came into existence. Simultaneously the three units disappeared as independent trading entities; however, since their brand names would continue to exist, they were re-established as agent companies for marketing the Group's products. Neil Gardiner and Hector Hanford retired, the former remaining as a consultant.

After the reorganisation, Huntley and Palmers' other directors all played their full part in the new structure. Alan Palmer and Gordon Palmer were still Vice-Chairman and Marketing Director respectively of the Group, while Lord Palmer, a member of the Group Board since 1966, became the Establishment Director for Reading and Huyton, being responsible for local matters within these factories; he was also a divisional head as chairman of Huntley Boorne and Stevens, as well as chairman of the new Huntley and Palmers. William Palmer was the Works Director for Reading, and Richard Palmer was the Export Sales Director, both of Associated Biscuits Ltd. David Gardiner remained as the Group's Operational Research Engineer, while C. D. van Namen was the Group Sales Executive for Southern England.

Not only did these directors have to be whole-time professional managers—in a way that their ancestors had not been—but their outside activities, which encroached on their leisure time, tended towards public duties and no longer included week-day sports such as regular hunting and cricket. These duties ranged from serving on the bench, the University Council or school governing bodies to membership of the Council of the Alliance or the Confederation of British Industries or several of their specialist committees, the Regional Council of National Savings, the Territorial Army, or the Duke of Edinburgh's Award Scheme.

Thus at the beginning of 1969 Reading became the 'biscuit town' in a new sense undreamt of by George Palmer, still less by Joseph Huntley senior in 1822: as the headquarters of a great enterprise which by the end of 1970 controlled net assets of £26 millions and had a turnover of £54 millions. It was fitting that the Group chairman at that point of time should have been Rupert Carr who, as a young apprentice from Peek Frean forty years before, had remarked on the great pride in biscuit-making and the 'wonderful loyalty' shown to the family by employees at Reading.

These employees, having seen almost as many changes in the 1960s as had occurred in the previous 140 years, were now being asked to transfer their pride and loyalty to the Group: an entity, moreover, that would not be static but was bound to evolve even further. As Roderic

O'Conor pointed out while explaining the new structure to managers, 'organisations, like living organisms, must adapt to change in their environment or perish. Rigidity is the attribute of a corpse.' As prime mover of all these changes, Rupert Carr had looked forward to directing the Group's further evolution well into the 1970s. However, in mid-1969 ill-health forced him to retire. Alan Palmer succeeded him as Group Chairman, charged with the onerous task of seeing through to completion these long-term corporate plans that he had helped to devise.

The whole reorganisation had now created a truly family firm: one in which the interests of the three controlling families had been evenly balanced. One of its main strengths, discussed above, was the loyalty and goodwill between employer and employee. Another was that very able members of the family would be attracted into the firm, through ties of heredity, even though they could have found more remunerative opportunities elsewhere. At the same time, they were now expected to be professionally trained or qualified in other ways; they did not have positions as of right merely through birth. Instead, they would be in competition for advancement with professional managers recruited from outside.

Managers, whether of the family or not, were now being brought forward and where necessary given additional training, so as to take full responsibility as soon as their aptitudes and experience allowed. So often in the past, elderly top management had failed to grasp opportunities as they arose and younger men had in consequence been frustrated because they could not be given their head during their most useful years. Such risks were now being minimised by more flexible retirement policies.

In this way the family firm was trying to combine the advantages of loyalty and continuity with the equal opportunities found in more heterogeneous types of firm. It was no longer, as Huntley and Palmers had been before until 1914, a bastion of private enterprise proof against almost any outside interference. Death duties and the obligations of trustees make any long-established concern liable to take-over attempts which, if successful, can uproot what has been built up over decades, in order to secure quick returns.

A family firm can, if it has clear objectives, often give a lead to the rest of the industry. In the field of technology, the various processes of biscuit manufacture in the mid-1960s did not differ basically from the ones which George Palmer had first devised in the 1840s. As his great-grandson Neil Gardiner reminded the technologists' conference of the

Alliance in 1965, machinery suppliers had of late worked closely with individual biscuit firms in order to introduce auto plants, wrapping machines and the automatic handling and mixing of ingredients. Even so, the whole process remained essentially mechanical rather than automated.

Now for the first time it was possible to visualise the central activities of a biscuit firm being entirely controlled by computers. The flow of orders, coming into the factory from representatives and other sources, would be scanned and fed into a computer, which would specify the precise requirements of materials on which the ingredients buyer would have to act, the most economic production programme, and the optimum stock levels and delivery schedules. A different computer, equipped with more sophisticated 'logical' parts than are required with data processing computers, would supervise a completely automated production plant. The process would need to be monitored while it was under way, in order to note how the most important variables that affected biscuit-making deviated from the standards laid down. Once the monitoring equipment had notified the computer of the deviations, it would calculate a new balance of the different variables and pass the necessary corrections to the remotely controlled points of adjustment. A substantial saving in labour costs and also a reduction in the number of defective biscuits and overweight packets would follow.

Arising out of Neil Gardiner's suggestions, in 1966 the industry began carrying out experiments, for instance to measure and correct the thickness of the dough sheet just before the biscuits were cut out, and to test the quality of biscuits after baking by mechanically extracting a certain number every minute. Where experiments needed to take place under working conditions (rather than, say, in the laboratory of a research unit) these were largely carried out at Huntley and Palmers' factory in Reading.[6]

Within a few years of its 150th anniversary, therefore, two major themes in Huntley and Palmers' history could be clearly seen. One theme was the very gradual maturing of its links with Peek Frean; exchanging information about prices from the 1870s onwards; their strange inert relationship as units within the Group between 1921 and 1960; and finally, after Jacobs' entry into the Group, a thorough-going integration of the three firms in every aspect.

The other theme related to Huntley and Palmers' dealings with the industry as a whole. Well into the twentieth century it had refused all contacts, except with one or two individual firms. Since 1918, however, the Palmers had a distinguished record as industrial administrators; Howard Palmer's pioneering work with the National Association of Biscuit Manufacturers was paralleled by Eric Palmer's creation of the

Cake and Biscuit Alliance to speak for the industry as a whole. Practically all the senior directors since then had contributed their expertise to one or other body. Now the company's initiatives—within the framework of the Group—were fostering this collaboration of the whole industry in technical innovations as far-reaching as any it had ever seen. It was appropriate that some of the key experiments for these innovations should have been carried out on the very site where George Palmer had started the biscuit industry as we know it today.

Notes to Chapters

INTRODUCTION

1. The general background to this Introduction is based largely on Arthur Raistrick's *Quakers in Science and Industry, Being An Account of the Quaker Contributions to Science and Industry during the 17th and 18th Centuries* (1950; new edition 1968). Although Quaker enterprise was necessarily more diffused after 1800, the later phases of the Industrial Revolution will not be fully understood until the Quaker part in it has been systematically explored.
2. *Rules of Discipline of the Religious Society of Friends, with Advices* (3rd ed. 1834) pp. 206–13, 252–3, 268–79. Cf. Raistrick, op. cit., pp. 46–8.
3. *Rules of Discipline*, pp. 2, 216–21.
4. Raistrick, op. cit., pp. 338–9.
5. C. & J. Clark Ltd. *Clarks of Street 1825–1950* (1950), p. 7.
6. The Bristol and Somerset Books of Sufferings are in Somerset Record Office, Taunton (Ref. BB/SFR) and the Berkshire and Oxfordshire Books of Sufferings in BRO (Berkshire Record Office), Reading (Ref. D/F2A/3/5, and for Reading D/F2B/3/22).
7. Paul H. Emden, *Quakers in Commerce, A Record of Business Achievement* (1939) p. 231.
8. Isabel Grubb, *Quakerism and Industry before 1800* (1930) pp. 167–8; *Rules of Discipline*, pp. 214–15.
9. *Rules of Discipline*, p. 47.
10. Adam Smith, *The Wealth of Nations*, Book I, Chap. X, Part II.
11. *Rules of Discipline*, p. 221; Raistrick, op. cit., pp. 27, 45.
12. *Morning Star*, 26 Sept. 1860.

CHAPTER I

1. *Reading Observer*, 7 Nov. 1891.
2. P. L. Payne, 'The Emergence of the Large-Scale Company in Great Britain, 1870–1914', *Economic History Review*, XX (New Series), 1967, Table I, pp. 539–40. The figures, which actually refer to 1905, show Huntley and Palmers as 38th in order of capital size of British manufacturing companies.
3. Will of John Huntley, proved 1638, in Gloucester City Libraries. John Huntley, labourer of Oddington, is mentioned in John Smith (compiler), *The Names and Surnames of All the Able and Sufficient Men in Body Fit for His Majesty's Service in the Wars, within the County of Gloucester* (1902).
4. Gloucester City Libraries, Gloucester Diocesan Records 243, p. 319.

The Huntleys' genealogy comes from FHL (=Friends' House Library) Port. C/120, James Boorne to J. J. Green, 21 Mar. 1897.

5. *Articles of Enquiry Addressed to the Clergy of the Diocese of Oxford and the Primary Visitation of Dr. Thomas Secker, 1738* (Oxfordshire Record Society, 1957), pp. 112–13.

6. *The Great End and Design of the True Gospel Ministry Demonstrated, from the Testimony of Holy Scripture, the Practice of the Primitive Church and the Nature of Christianity* (1741), in FHL. The quotation and further particulars are in FHL *Testimonies Concerning Ministers,* Vol. I.

7. The other school was that of Jonah, and later his son Thomas, Thompson of Compton, near Sherborne, Dorset. See J. Smith, *A Descriptive Catalogue of Friends' Books* (1867), II, p. 736.

8. The Stuffed Owl quality of his English verses can be seen from the one composed while meditating in the garden where his schoolroom once stood, which began:

> This spot, where Science long had rear'd her head,
> Is now with Flora's blooming gifts o'erspread.

(FHL J. T. 272). As to Latin verses, the preface to his Latin Grammar (also in FHL) contains fifty-seven elegiac couplets in dedication to his book, together with six pages of Ciceronian prose.

9. *Dictionary of National Biography,* XXVIII, p. 51, s.v. Luke Howard.

10. FHL *Testimonies Concerning Ministers,* Vol. V, p. 18.

11. For Hannah Huntley see ibid., Vol. VI, p. 68. The advertisement for the school and the school bill (for Jonah Thompson junior) are in FHL Vol. N, 173a, and particulars about clothes in J.T. 295, Thomas Huntley to Thomas Thompson, 9 Aug. 1798.

12. Joseph Huntley's story has had to be pieced together from many sources, e.g. Reading St. Giles Rate Books in BRO D/P 96/11, the wills of Binfield Willis senior (d. 1786) and Elizabeth Speakham (d. 1815) in PRO (The Public Record Office, London), and the Quaker records in BRO. The two sides of the *fracas* are in Reading MM 1810–17 (BRO D/F 2B 3/9) and Banbury MM 1804–23 (Oxford Record Office BMM 1/4). The Quaker school at Sibford Ferris is mentioned in MS Oxf. Dioc. Papers d. 707 fo. 174 and Joseph Huntley's overseer's accounts (Apr.–Oct. 1801) in MS DD Par. Sibford Gower b. 1, both in the Bodleian Library, Oxford.

13. M. R. Mitford, *Belford Regis, or Sketches of a Country Town* (1835) I, pp. 294–5.

14. (W. Turner), *Reading Seventy Years Ago: A Record of Events from 1813 to 1819* (1887), pp. 15, 30, 32.

15. T. Strutt, *Peregrinations of a Kiddy* (c. 1900, MS in Uxbridge Museum), p. 31–2. It is not true that both Thomas Huntley and Thomas Perry were apprenticed to F. Lemann of London, as asserted in FHL B. 25, W. White (of White & Pike, Birmingham) to J. J. Green, 25 Feb. 1895.

16. Elihu Burritt, *A Walk from London to Land's End and Back, with Notes by the Way* (2nd ed. 1868), pp. 68–9.

7. Goldwin Smith, *Reminiscences* (1911), pp. 2–3.

18. Mrs. Gaskell, *Cranford* (The World's Classics ed. 1916), pp. 4, 10, 31, 80, 166.
19. M. R. Mitford, op. cit., I, p. 181, cf. II, pp. 201–2.
20. J. Burnett, *Plenty and Want, A Social History of Diet in England from 1815 to the Present Day* (Pelican Books 1968), p. 96.
21. *The Star*, 26 Sept. 1812, and *Morning Chronicle*, 2 July 1819. James Cocks's will (proved 1827) is in PRO.
22. FHL *Testimonies Concerning Ministers*, Vol. VI, p. 404.
23. A. Beesley, *History of Banbury* (1841), p. 568.

CHAPTER 2

1. Survey of Long Sutton Manor, in Somerset Record Office DD/X/BB.
2. William Palmer II's will (proved 1816) is in Somerset Record Office, which also has an Inclosure Map of the parish for 1814 and a Tithe Map for 1842.
3. *Reading Observer*, 7 Nov. 1891. The Grant of Administration for William Isaac's goods (affirmed 1815) is in Dorset County Record Office.
4. C & J. Clark Ltd., *Clarks Comments*, No. 58, Nov. 1961, and No. 60, Feb. 1963 respectively. For loans to C. & J. Clark see *Clarks of Street 1825–1950*, p. 166.
5. The Tithe Map for 1840 for Elberton is in Bristol Archives Office, the Council House, Bristol, as is William Palmer III's will (proved 1826).
6. Francis A. Knight, *A History of Sidcot School: A Hundred Years of West Country Quaker Education 1808–1908* (1908), pp. 61, 80–1.
7. Ibid., pp. 93–4.
8. *Taunton Courier*, 4 July 1838. Particulars of George Palmer's early life were given in *Reading Observer*, 7 Nov. 1891, partly from his own reminiscences.
9. Knight, *Sidcot School*, p. 92; *Reading Observer*, 5 Jan. 1893.
10. *Annual Monitor* (obituaries of members of the Society of Friends) 1845, pp. 85 ff.

CHAPTER 3

1. Joseph Leete, *The History of Huntley and Palmers' Trade upon the Continent of Europe etc. 1865–1911* (1911, typescript), I, pp. 26, 89–90.
2. Ibid., p. 26.
3. *Minutes of Proceedings of the Institution of Civil Engineers*, LXVII, Session 1881–2, Part I.
4. John Snare (compiler), *The Post-Office Reading Directory* (1842) *Advertiser* (at back of directory, p. 16); *The Times*, 10 Feb. 1844. For 'superior' see George Eliot, *Middlemarch* (Everyman's ed. 1930), I, p. 85.
5. For John Fry Wilkey see *Annual Monitor*, 1886, pp. 147 ff.
6. The Rev. A. G. L'Estrange, *Life and Letters of M. R. Mitford* (1870), III, p. 221.
7. *Annual Monitor*, 1845, pp. 85 ff.

8. W. M. Childs, *The Town of Reading during the Early Part of the Nineteenth Century* (1910), p. 42.
9. Ibid., p. 23.

CHAPTER 4

1. Jacob Schmookler, *Invention and Economic Growth* (1966), p. 197.
2. C. Lloyd (Ed.), *The Health of Seamen*: Navy Records Society, CVII (1965), pp. 2, 4, 15.
3. *As You Like It,* Act II, Scene vii.
4. J. L. Lowes, *The Road to Xanadu* (1927), pp. 137–8, 454. M. Lewis, *The Navy in Transition 1814–64, A Social History* (1965), p. 265.
5. A. F. Fremantle, *Trafalgar* (1933), pp. 49–50.
6. Lloyd, *Health of Seamen*, p. 160.
7. *London Gazette,* Nos. 1606, 7–11 Apr. 1681, and 4332, 8 May 1707, cf. *Oxford English Dictionary*, I, p. 877, s.v. biscake and biscuit.
8. The Rev. T. H. Croker, T. Williams and S. Clark (Ed.) *Complete Dictionary of Arts and Sciences* (1769), s.v. biscuit.
9. D. A. Baugh, *British Naval Administration in the Age of Walpole* (Princeton, U.S.A., 1965), pp. 411 ff.
10. The accounts of the process at Deptford in Peter Barlow, *Encyclopaedia of Manufactures* (1836), pp. 801 ff., and of that at Portsmouth (*Transactions of the Society of Arts*, XL, 1833–35, pp. 97 ff., agree with one another, but S. Giedion, *Mechanisation Takes Command* (New York 1948), pp. 87 ff., quoting from *The Book of Trades, or Library of the Useful Arts* (1804), uses different terminology: the 'chucker' and the 'depositor' are the names of the pitcher and furner respectively.
11. H. G. Harris and S. P. Borella, *All About Biscuits* (c. 1910), p. 166. They describe this particular method as 'awful', but say that it was then common in some small coastal towns.
12. Croker, Williams and Clark, *Complete Dictionary of Arts and Sciences,* s.v. biscuit.
13. cf. refs. in *O.E.D.* I, p. 877, s.v. biscuit: 4. biscuit bread.
14. *Morning Star,* 26 Sept. 1860.
15. J. Burnett, 'The Baking Industry in the Nineteenth Century', *Business History*, V, 1962–4, pp. 98–108.
16. *Report on the Grievances of the Journeymen Bakers,* H.C. 3027 (H.M.S.O. 1862), pp. 160, 170, 173, 176, 198.
17. Burnett, *Business History*, V, p. 102.
18. *Reading Observer,* 21 Aug. 1897. For legislation see Burnett, *Business History*, V, pp. 106 ff.
19. e.g. *Reading Mercury,* 10 Oct. 1814, 8 Apr. 1816, 20 July 1816.
20. N. Penney, *Pen Pictures of London Yearly Meeting 1789–1833* (1930), pp. 2, 8.
21. *Report on the Grievances* . . . (1862), p. 176.
22. Jane Austen, *Mansfield Park* (ed. R. W. Chapman, 1923), p. 413.
23. See refs. to Peter Barlow and *Transactions of Society of Arts* in fn. 10 above.

24. e.g. *Irish Grocery World*, 2 Mar. 1912.
25. *Christian Messenger*, 1865, pp. 163–4.
26. Schmookler, *Invention and Economic Growth*, pp. 10 ff.

CHAPTER 5

1. *Reading Examiner*, 25 May 1872.
2. *Victoria County History: Stafford*, VIII, p. 304; *Berkshire Chronicle*, 14 Mar. 1857.
3. *Daily Mail*, 20 Aug. 1897; *Christian World*, 26 Aug. 1897.
4. Giedion, *Mechanisation Takes Command*, pp. 176–7, 190–1.
5. *Royal Album of Arts and Industries of Great Britain* (1887), p. 102; Augustus Muir, *The History of Baker Perkins* (1968), pp. 10 ff.
6. *The Grocer*, 15 Apr. 1905.
7. *British Workman* No. 459, Mar. 1893.
8. *Annual Monitor*, 1886, pp. 147 ff.; H. Holme, *Henry Lea of Reading, A Sketch of His Life* (1890), esp. p. 17.
9. *Hants and Berks Gazette*, 21 Oct. 1882.
10. *Christian World*, 26 Aug. 1897.
11. *Reading Mercury*, 9 Feb. 1850.
12. *Annual Monitor*, 1858, pp. 127 ff.
13. *Reading Mercury*, 14 Mar. 1857.
14. *Reading Standard*, 8 Mar. 1913.

CHAPTER 6

1. *Christian Messenger*, 1865, p. 165.
2. *Grocers Review*, 13 Feb. 1940.
3. *Clarks of Street, 1825–1950*, pp. 162–3, 166, 176–7.
4. The Hon. Arnold Palmer (son of the first Lord Palmer), *Movable Feasts* (1952), pp. 70 ff. See also Jane Austen, *Emma* (ed. R. W. Chapman 1923), Appendix: 'The Manners of the Age', p. 499, and G. M. Young (Ed.) *Early Victorian England 1830–1865* (1934), I, pp. 77 ff.
5. Board of Trade, *British and Foreign Trade and Industrial Conditions* (H.M.S.O. Cd. 2337, 1904), pp. 21, 25.
6. Earl Stanhope, *Notes of Conversations with the Duke of Wellington 1831–51* (1888), p. 204.
7. *The Grocer*, 20 Oct. 1883; E. F. Benson, *As We Were* (Penguin ed., 1938), p. 66.
8. *Royal Album of Arts and Industries of Great Britain*, p. 102.
9. *London Gazette*, 27 Jan. 1885, p. 361.
10. *Morning Star*, 26 Sept. 1860.
11. Ford Madox Hueffer (later F. M. Ford), *Ancient Lights and Certain New Reflections* (1911), p. 274.
12. A. Trollope, *The Eustace Diamonds* (World Classics ed. 1930), p. 572.
13. *Daily Mail*, 20 Aug. 1897.
14. *The Hour*, 17 Nov. 1873; *Reading Mercury*, 22 Nov. 1873.

CHAPTER 7

1. Beesley, *History of Banbury*, p. 568.
2. *The Times*, 10 Feb. 1844; cf. advertisements for J. Purssell and James Turner in *Ainsworth's Magazine* (advertisement pages), May and Aug. 1842.
3. *Great Exhibition of the Works of Industry of All Nations 1851, Official Descriptive and Illustrative Catalogue* (1851), II, p. 796 (Class 29, item No. 107).
4. Leete, *History of Huntley and Palmers' Trade*, I, p. 29. Leete's subsequent exploits on the Continent are fully described in the two volumes of this work.
5. *Daily Telegraph*, 28 Oct. 1878 (re 1878 Exhibition). For the Exhibition of 1867 see *Daily News*, 3 May 1867, and *Morning Post*, 12 June 1867.
6. *Illustrated London News*, 12 July 1873; *Morning Post*, 30 Aug. 1873.
7. *The Globe*, 6 July, and *The Grocer*, 27 July 1878.
8. *European Mail*, 2 Aug. 1878.
9. *The Grocer*, 26 May 1900 (Supplement).
10. Leete's book gives monthly statistics of the Continental trade from 1864 onwards, but there are no comparable figures for those of the Export department. Figures of total overseas trade have been computed from the end-of-year balances for the two departments combined, given in the firm's ledgers. Data of balances and of actual trade are available from 1896–7 to 1914–15 (19 observations) and simple regression analysis yields the equation

$$Y = \frac{X - 8313 \cdot 4}{\cdot 1098}$$

where Y = trade and X = balances. R^2 = 0·872 (0·560 with first differences).
11. *Commerce*, 31 Jan. 1900, pp. 245–71.
12. R. L. Nelson, *Merger Movements in American Industry 1895–1956* (Princeton U.P. 1959), p. 161.
13. Report of U.S. Consular Agent at Caracas, Venezuela, in *American Exporter* (New York), May 1885.
14. *The Graphic*, 27 Dec. 1879; illustration, p. 628.
15. Elihu Burritt, *A Walk from London . . .*, pp. 71–2.
16. *Cunard Steam Ship Album and Guide* (1875), p. 160.
17. *Reading Examiner*, 25 May 1872.
18. *Reading Mercury*, 30 Nov. 1872.
19. *The Times*, 31 Oct. 1898.
20. *Morning Post*, 12 June 1867.
21. Leete, *History of Huntley and Palmers' Trade*, I, p. 100; *The Standard*, 8 Feb. 1878.
22. Peter Fleming, *Bayonets to Lhasa* (1961), pp. 233, 267.
23. *Reading Standard*, 12 Nov. 1937.
24. Lord Redesdale, *Memories* (1915), pp. 740–1.
25. Oscar Browning, 'An Alpine Parliament', *Pall Mall Gazette*, 16 Sept. 1886; cf. L. Bromfield, *The Rains Came* (1938), p. 427. For Prince Henry of Battenberg see D. Duff, *The Shy Princess* (1958), p. 173.
26. *Pall Mall Gazette*, Aug. 1896.
27. E. W. Hornung, *Raffles* (1901), p. 158.

28. *The People*, 22 Sept. 1901; *Reading Standard*, 26 Feb. 1902.
29. *Hull News*, 15 June 1878.
30. MS. Journal of Chief Petty Officer A. F. Fanstone (*c.* 1900–10, copy in Reading University Library).

CHAPTER 8

1. C. H. Wilson, *History of Unilever*, I, p. xx.
2. E. J. Hobsbawm, *Industry and Empire* (1968), p. 66.
3. *The Reading Examiner*, 25 May 1872.
4. *Chambers's Edinburgh Journal*, 1846, p. 173.
5. For the hours of work at Carlisle see ibid. For those at Huntley and Palmers see *Reading Standard*, 8 Mar. 1913.
6. *Daily Mail*, 20 Aug. 1897.
7. The 1913 figure is deduced from a letter by H. Pretty in *Daily Mail*, 21 Feb. 1914.
8. *Reading Mercury*, 10 Oct. 1857.
9. *The Grocer*, II (1862), p. 211.
10. *Reading Mercury*, 2 July 1864.
11. *Knife and Fork*, 11 May 1872, p. 52.
12. *Reading Mercury*, 27 Mar. 1858.
13. Ibid., 21 July 1855.
14. Ibid., 19 July 1856, 8 Aug. 1857, 31 July 1858.
15. Ibid., 1 Aug. 1863.
16. *Hastings Mail & Times*, 25 June 1904.
17. *Reading Observer*, 5 Feb. 1881.
18. *Reading Mercury*, 21 July 1855.
19. *Victoria County History*: *Berkshire*, II, pp. 319, 322.
20. Iolo A. Williams, *The Firm of Cadbury 1831–1931* (1931), Chap. VII, esp. p. 187.
21. Hobsbawm, *Industry and Empire*, p. 69.
22. *The Age*, 25 Jan. 1885.
23. *Reading Standard*, 20 Dec. 1919; *First Name News* (Huntley and Palmers' house magazine), Vol. 3, No. 6 (Dec. 1959), pp. 20–1.
24. *Reading Standard*, 8 Mar. 1913.

CHAPTER 9

1. P. Gorb, Review of *Courtaulds*: *An Economic and Social History* (by D. C. Coleman), *Management Today*, Nov. 1969, p. 148.
2. Many details of George Palmer's career are given in *Reading Mercury* and *Reading Observer*, 7 Nov. 1891 and 21 Aug. 1897.
3. *Reading Mercury*, 18 Dec. 1847.
4. J. R. Vincent, Pollbooks: *How Victorians Voted* (1967), and review in *The Economist*, 6 May 1967, p. 575. The controversies are mentioned in *Reading Mercury* and *Berkshire Chronicle*, 4 Aug. 1849.
5. *Reading Mercury*, 19 Sept. 1846.

6. Reading Public Libraries, *Berkshire Local History Recording Scheme* R 1A—20.
7. W. S. Darter, *Reminiscences of an Octogenarian* (1888), p. 8.
8. *Return of Owners of Land 1873* (H.M.S.O. C.1097, 1875), I, p. 14, II, pp. 15, 29.
9. J. Travis Mills, *John Bright and the Quakers* (1935), II, pp. 34–5.
10. *Hansard's Parliamentary Debates*, Vol. 240, Col. 1826 (19 June 1878).
11. *Daily Mail*, 20 Aug. 1897.
12. *Reading Mercury*, June 1883.
13. *Reading Observer*, 4 Nov. 1879.
14. Ford Madox Hueffer (later Ford), *Ancient Lights and Certain New Reflections*, pp. 3–4, 17–18.
15. *Christian World*, 26 Aug. 1897.
16. *The Epicure*, Sept. 1897.
17. *Reading Examiner*, 25 May 1872.
18. Papers of 3rd Marquess of Salisbury, Christ Church, Oxford Y/1/P. esp. letters from W. Dorchester, 27 June 1885 and later, and Y/2/P ibid., 25 Nov. 1886 and later.
19. *Reading Mercury*, 1 Dec. 1887; *The Christian*, 19 Jan. 1893.
20. *Pall Mall Gazette*, 6 Jan. 1893; *Temperance Record*, 12 Jan. 1893.
21. *The Grocer*, 11 and 18 Apr. 1903.
22. Arnold Palmer, *Movable Feasts*, pp. 101–3.
23. V. Holland, *Son of Oscar Wilde* (1954), pp. 39–40.
24. Leete, *History of Huntley and Palmers' Trade*, II, pp. 13–130 *passim*.

CHAPTER 10

1. Value of total production figures are calculated from the 'Indices of Industrial Production' B. R. Mitchell and P. Deane, *Abstract of British Historical Statistics* (1962), pp. 271–2, fitted to the 1907 *Census of Production* data.
2. S. G. Checkland, *The Rise of Industrial Society in England 1815–1885* (1964), pp. 51–60.
3. Statistics of Bread and Biscuits exported from the U.K. are from the *Annual Statements of Trade* 1853 onwards. Huntley and Palmers' exports are estimated as described in Chap. 7, fn. 10. Other figures are from Mitchell and Deane, *Abstract of British Historical Statistics*.
4. In the calculations relating to Ginger Nuts and Osborne biscuits three-year averages have been used.
5. *Cunard S.S. Album and Guide*, p. 162.
6. *Reports of Reading School Board* and *Education Committee*, 1896–1904, in Reading Public Libraries.
7. e.g. remarks of Alfred Palmer in *Reading Observer*, 7 July 1877.
8. H. R. Edwards, *Competition and Monopoly in the British Soap Industry* (1962), p. 170. This is challenged by A. E. Musson, *Enterprise in Soap and Chemicals: Joseph Crosfield & Sons Ltd. 1815–1965* (1965), pp. 287–8.
9. Alfred Marshall, *Principles of Economics* (8th ed. 1920), pp. 299–300.

10. G. Bernard Shaw, *Major Barbara* (Penguin Books 1945), p. 122.
11. Kenn Rogers, *Managers—Personality and Performance* (1963), pp. 54, 152.
12. Marshall, *Principles of Economics*, pp. 210, 299 n.
13. *Biscuit Maker and Plant Baker*, Aug. 1967, pp. 574–8.
14. P. Redfern, *The New History of the CWS* (1938), p. 34; *Co-operative News*, 18 Mar. 1905.
15. P. Mathias, *Retailing Revolution* (1967), esp. p. 316.
16. *The Times*, 3 Oct. 1883; *Punch*, 13 Oct. 1883. 'Punch's Fancy Portraits—No. 157'.
17. Lady Charnwood, *Call Back Yesterday* (1937), pp. 286–7; M. Holroyd, *Lytton Strachey, A Critical Biography* (1968), II, p. 183.
18. E. Partridge, *Dictionary of Slang and Unconventional English* (1937), p. 416.

CHAPTER 11

1. A chart showing the long-term trends in the British price level between 1661 and 1959 can be seen in P. Deane and W. A. Cole, *British Economic Growth 1688–1959* (2nd ed. 1967) Fig. 7.
2. *First Name News*, Vol. 1, No. 8 (June 1956), pp. 2–3.
3. H. H. the Dayang Muda of Sarawak (née Gladys Palmer), *Relations and Complications* (1929), p. 24.
4. Leete, *History of Huntley and Palmers' Trade*, II, pp. 51 ff.
5. *Commerce*, 31 Jan. 1900, pp. 245 ff.
6. William Page, *Commerce and Industry*: Tables of Statistics for the British Economy from 1815 (1919), II, p. 232.
7. *Morning Leader*, 21 May 1896; *Daily Telegraph*, 29 Oct. 1896; *Liverpool Journal of Commerce*, 31 Oct. 1896.
8. *The Grocer*, 13 May 1893. For winding-up see ibid. 21 Aug. 1897 and subsequent issues.
9. *Berkshire Chronicle*, 13 Aug. 1892.
10. *Reading Mercury*, 2 Nov. 1889; *Reading Observer*, 7 Nov. 1891.
11. *Reading Observer*, 5 Apr. 1890.
12. *Berkshire Chronicle*, 27 June 1891.
13. Salisbury Papers, Christ Church Oxford, Class E, corr. with Sir Edward Bradford, 1897–8. For honours generally, see H. J. Hanham, 'The Sale of Honours in Late Victorian England', *Victorian Studies*, III, 1959–60, pp. 677–89.
14. Dayang Muda of Sarawak, *Relations and Complications*, pp. 19, 30–33.
15. L. Stevenson, *The Ordeal of George Meredith* (New York 1953), pp. 303, 327; C. L. Cline (Ed.), *The Letters of George Meredith* (1970), pp. 1728–9.
16. Louise Jopling, *Twenty Years of My Life*, (1925), p. 80.
17. Elihu Burritt, *A Walk from London . . .*, p. 66.
18. H. Montgomery Hyde, *Oscar Wilde: The Aftermath* (1963), esp. p. 107.
19. G. M. Young (Ed.), *Early Victorian England*, II, p. 414.

CHAPTER 12

1. Edwards, *Competition and Monopoly in the British Soap Industry*, pp. 144, 154; see also Chapter 1, fn. 2.
2. *Report of the Company Law Amendment Committee* (H.M.S.O. Cd. 3052, 1906), §§ 45, 51.
3. H. Ausubel, *In Hard Times, Reformers among the Late Victorians* (Columbia Univ. Press 1960), p. 32.
4. *Daily Mail*, 27 May 1904 and 25 Nov. 1905.
5. Lorna Houseman, *The House That Thomas Built, The History of De La Rue* (1968), pp. 95 ff.
6. Clapham, *An Economic History of Modern Britain*, III, p. 301; A. L. Levine, *Industrial Retardation in Britain 1880–1914* (1967), pp. 145 ff.

CHAPTER 13

1. *Berkshire Chronicle*, 11 Oct. 1913.
2. Clapham, *An Economic History of Modern Britain*, III, pp. 41–2.
3. *Reading Standard*, 7 Mar. 1908.
4. *Daily Mail*, 5 Aug. 1904 and 18 Sept. 1906.
5. Alfred Marshall, *Industry and Trade* (1919), p. 549.
6. Clapham, *An Economic History of Modern Britain*, III, p. 302.
7. C. Wilson, *A History of Unilever* (1954), I, pp. 59–71.
8. *Report of an Enquiry by the Board of Trade into Working Class Rents, Housing and Retail Prices* (H.M.S.O., Cd. 3864, 1908), pp. 386–91. For 1912 see H.M.S.O., Cd. 6955, 1913, pp. 226–7.
9. R. C. K. Ensor, *England 1870–1914* (Oxford History of England, XIV, 1936), p. 437.
10. The whole dispute can be followed in the Reading newspapers from Dec. 1911 to Jan. 1912, and in certain pamphlets (e.g. The Reading Trades and Labour Council, *The Victimisation at Huntley and Palmers,* and three counterblasts) in Reading Public Libraries. For the trouble at Carr's see *Carlisle Journal*, 11 Oct. 1907.
11. A. L. Bowley and A. R. Burnett-Hurst, *Livelihood and Poverty* (1915), p. 42.
12. Ibid., p. 16. Reading's low birth-rate is mentioned in H.M.S.O., Cd. 3864, pp. 388–9.
13. *Reading Standard*, 15 Oct. 1913, W. M. Childs, *Making a University* (1933). Some fragments of Childs's unpublished journal are quoted in T. A. B. Corley, 'The Palmer Family and the University of Reading', *Staff Journal* (University of Reading), No. 6, Nov. 1968, pp. 6–12. Childs's (anonymous) tribute to G. W. Palmer is in *The Times*, 10 Oct. 1913.

CHAPTER 14

1. *Daily Chronicle*, 23 June 1914.
2. Childs, *Making a University*, pp. 271–2.

3. Huntley and Palmers Ltd., *Our Work—The War and Reconstruction* (1919), p. 14 (reproduced in *Reading Standard*, 7 June 1919).
4. Sir W. Beveridge, *British Food Control* (Economic and Social History of the World War, 1928), p. 5.
5. *The Standard* (London), 20 Sept. 1915.
6. Levine, *Industrial Retardation in Britain 1880–1914*, p. 71.
7. *The Life of Ronald Poulton* (1919), a pre-Freudian biography written by his father (Sir) Edward Poulton.

CHAPTER 15

1. Beveridge, *British Food Control*, pp. 120 ff.
2. *Reading Standard*, 22 June 1916.
3. Ibid., 7 July 1916.
4. Ibid., 18 Mar. 1916. See also J. Oster, 'The History of the Recreation Club', *First Name News*, Vol. 4, No. 3 (Mar. 1961), pp. 21–5.
5. Beveridge, *British Food Control*, pp. 2, 32 ff.
6. Ibid., pp. 51 ff.
7. Huntley and Palmers, *Our Work—The War and Reconstruction*, p. 16.

CHAPTER 16

1. *The Grocer*, 3 Dec. 1921. For fears of a 'biscuit combine' see letter in *Daily Express*, 8 Dec. 1921.
2. Bennet Palmer, 'Costing System for a Tin Works', *Accountants' Journal*, XXXIX, Jan. 1922, pp. 537–60.
3. *The Times*, 19 Mar. 1923; *The Grocer*, 24 Mar. 1923, and *Reading Standard*, 24 Mar. 1923.
4. A. L. Bowley and M. H. Hogg, *Has Poverty Diminished?* (1925), pp. 109–32.
5. *The Cinema*, 13 July 1922.
6. *Reading Mercury*, 26 June 1926.
7. C. A. Oakley, *Men at Work* (1945), p. 175.

CHAPTER 17

1. Richard Stone, *The Measurement of Consumers' Expenditure and Behaviour in the U.K. 1920–39* (1954), p. 27.
2. *Financial Times*, 18 Feb. 1938. The rise of Weston's is discussed in R. Evely and I. M. D. Little, *Concentration in British Industry* (1960), pp. 274 ff.
3. *Radio Pictorial*, 18 Mar. 1938.
4. *Reading Standard*, 2 Apr. 1937.

CHAPTER 18

1. The Cake and Biscuit Manufacturers' War Time Alliance Ltd., *Reports* for years ending 30 June 1942 to 30 June 1945.

2. R. J. Hammond, *Food* (History of the Second World War, U.K. Civil Series), I, *The Growth of Policy* (1951), p. 42.
3. Ibid., I, p. 77.
4. Ibid., III, *Studies in Administration and Control* (1962), Chap. XXXVIII, 'The Control of Biscuits'.

CHAPTER 19

1. Hammond, *Food*, I, p. 251, III, Chap. XXXVIII.
2. Cake and Biscuit Manufacturers' Wartime Alliance Ltd., 'Tributes Paid to the Memory of Sir C. Eric Palmer, D.L., J.P., at the Council Meeting Held on 24th Sept. 1948', p. 3.
3. *The Parliamentary Debates*, 5th Series, Vol. 166, Cols. 1083-5, 1092 (20 Apr. 1950).

CHAPTER 20

1. Burnett, *Plenty and Want*, pp. 342-3.
2. Evely and Little, *Concentration in British Industry*, pp. 273 ff.
3. The Cake and Biscuit Manufacturers' Wartime Alliance Ltd., *Combined Operations by the Biscuit Industry* (1946).
4. *First Name News*, Vol. I, No. I (Sept. 1954), p. 11 and later issues for developments both at Reading and at Huyton.

CHAPTER 21

1. *Financial Times*, 11 May 1960.
2. 'Rupert Carr—Getting the Right Biscuit Mix', *The Director*, Apr. 1967.

CHAPTER 22

1. Cake and Biscuit Alliance Ltd., *Annual Reports* for years ending 30 June 1965 onwards; *H. & P. Herald*, No. 1 (Apr. 1965) to No. 23 (Feb. 1968) when it ceased publication.
2. These crude productivity figures have been calculated from data of production and employment in the Cake and Biscuit Alliance's *Annual Reports*.
3. Board of Trade, *Report on the Census of Production for 1958*, part 9, 'Biscuits' (1960). Similar data for 1963 is in part 9 (also 'Biscuits') of the *Report on the Census of Production for 1963* (1968).
4. Ibid., part 131 (1969), p. 98.
5. *Management Today*, Sept. 1969, p. 20.
6. *Biscuit Maker and Plant Baker*, Mar. 1966 and Mar. 1967; *Food Trade Review*, Mar.–May 1968.

Appendix I
Wage Rates in Huntley and Palmers' Factory 1844–1914

Some of the difficulties involved in trying to calculate wage rates in the factory have been mentioned in Chapters 8 and 10. Until the early 1870s, for instance, these were decided by the partners for each individual employee, according to their assessment of his worth. Only after that period did the partners introduce standard wages, according to age or to type of job. Some specialised employees, too, were paid piece rates or had variable wages according to systems of bonuses and penalties. Nevertheless, a summary of wage rates for selected years may be of interest.

The primary source of this summary is the wages books for the mid-1840s or from 1857 to the early 1870s. These give individual names and basic wages, together with dates of any changes. The exact numbers can be checked from independent sources, e.g. the number of employees stated by George Palmer in the 1851 and 1861 Censuses and in the hand-outs for various Exhibitions, as quoted in Joseph Leete's volumes.

A comparison of weekly wages with Carr's of Carlisle in the 1840s is as follows:

	Carr's[1] 1846	Huntley and Palmer 1844	1847
Foremen	23s.–25s.	40s.	40s.
Engineers	—	—	32s.
Journeymen	18s.–20s.	20s.–23s.	20s.–27s.
Men	up to 17s.	10s.–17s.	10s.–19s.[2]
Boys	3s.–5s.	2s. 8d.–9s. 6d.	2s. 6d.–9s.

The following tables show the numbers of employees and average wages, first for the factory as a whole, and then for individual departments.

	NOS. OF EMPLOYEES				AVERAGE WAGES (s. per week)			
	Men	Boys	Women and Girls	Total	Men	Boys	Women and Girls	Total
1844	9	8	—	17	17s. 5d.[3]	4s. 3d.	—	11s. 3d.
1847	21	20	—	41	18s. 2d.[4]	4s. 9d.	—	11s. 7d.
1857	163	143	6	312	17s. 6d.	6s. 2d.	8s. 8d.	12s. 1d.
1861	308	217	10	535	16s. 9d.	5s. 11d.	8s. 8d.	12s. 3d.

303

	Men	Boys	Women and Girls	Total	Men	Boys	Women and Girls	Total
1867	610	300	10	920	18s. 7d.	5s. 6d.	11s. 11d.	14s. 3d.
1873	2430		70	2500 nearly	n.a.	n.a.	n.a.	n.a.
1878	(2900)		(75–100)	3000	n.a.	n.a.	n.a.	n.a.
1889	3855		198	4053	n.a.	n.a.	n.a.	n.a.
1893–94	3379	542	186	4107	20s. 1d.[5]		9s. 3d.[9]	19s. 7d.
1899–1900	4123	722	564	5409	[6]		[10]	18s. 8d.
1909–10	3617	253	987	4857	(24s. 2d.)[7]	n.a.	n.a.	19s. 7d.
1913–14	3406	361	1199	4966	[8]		[11]	22s. 0d.

NOS. OF EMPLOYEES　　　　　AVERAGE WAGES (s. per week)

	Men	Boys	Women and Girls	Total	Men	Boys	Women and Girls
1857							
Manufacturing	88	90	—	178	17s. 1d.	6s. 7d.	—
Packing	39	51	6	96	14s. 2d.	5s. 5d.	8s. 8d.
Other	36	2	—	38	22s. 1d.	3s. 9d.	—
1861							
Manufacturing	168	144	—	312	16s. 9d.	6s. 0d.	—
Packing	88	70	10	168	14s. 1d.	5s. 10d.	8s. 8d.
Other	52	3	—	55	21s. 9d.	5s. 0d.	—
1867							
Manufacturing	264	181	—	445	18s. 7d.	5s. 4d.	—
Packing	230	112	10	352	16s. 7d.	5s. 8d.	11s. 11d.
Other	116	7	—	123	22s. 1d.	6s. 7d.	—
1894							
Manufacturing	1808	272	33	2113	20s. 6d.		9s. 8d.
Packing	1109	263	153	1525	17s. 8d.		7s. 7d.
Other	462	7	—	469	25s. 6d.		—

Notes

1. *Chambers's Edinburgh Journal* 1846, p. 174.
2. One man at Reading, George P. Rickman (1784–1875), one of the handful of Quakers to be employed, earned as little as 8s.–9s. In his sixties, he clearly had a light job, and between times carried out the temperance work which was his lifetime's interest.
3. 15s. 10d. excluding wage of Richard Brown, the foreman.
4. 17s. 2d. excluding Richard Brown's wage.
5. 5s. at age 13 to 19s. at 21.
6. 5s. 6d. at 13 to 19s. at 21.
7. Men's earnings in 1911–12.
8. 6s. 6d. at 13 to 21s. at 21.
9. 4s. at 14 to 10s. at 20.
10. 4s. 6d. at 14 to 10s. at 20.
11. 5s. at 14 to 11s. at 20.

Appendix II
Employees' Counties of Birth 1851 and 1861

	Huntley and Palmers		Reading Iron Works
	1851	1861	1861
Reading	46	51	28
Berkshire	19	17	24
Hampshire	6	4	7
Oxfordshire	5	6	4
Adjacent counties	76	78	63
Buckinghamshire	4	—	4
Cornwall	—	1	1
Devonshire	1	2	3
Dorset	—	1	2
Durham	—	—	1
Essex	1	1	—
Gloucestershire	4	1	5
Hertfordshire	—	—	1
Kent	2	1	—
Lancashire	1	—	1
Lincolnshire	—	—	1
London (and Middlesex)	2	4	3
Norfolk	—	1	—
Nottinghamshire	1	1	—
Somerset	1	1	2
Surrey	1	1	2
Wiltshire	6	2	5
Worcestershire	—	1	1
Yorkshire	—	1	1
Wales	—	1	1
Ireland	—	1	1
Australia	—	1	—
France	—	—	1
Germany	—	—	1
	100	100	100
Numbers in sample	99	177	158
Total employees	143	535	c. 350

(SOURCE: Public Record Office—Censuses of 1851 and 1861)

Appendix III
Huntley and Palmers Turnover and Profits (£000s)

YEAR	TURNOVER	NET PROFIT	PROFIT AS % OF TURNOVER
1841–42[1]	2·7	—	—
1842–43	3·4	0·2	6·4
1843–44	4·6	0·3	6·9
1844–45	5·7	1·0	17·0
1845–46	6·9	1·0	15·0
1846–47	8·3	1·1	13·8
1847–48	12·7	1·5	12·2
1848–49	17·9	3·4	18·8
1849–50	34·4	7·5	21·9
1850–51	41·1	7·5	18·2
1851–52	48·5	7·4	15·3
1852–53	66·1 (of which overseas = 6)	7·4	11·3
1853–54	82·1	9·4	11·5
1854–55	92·3	11·7	12·7
1855–56	105·2	12·1	11·5
1856–57[2]	93·1	15·1	13·1
1857–58[3]	131·0	18·0	13·8
1858–59	143·3 (of which overseas = 20)	24·4	17·0
1859–60	163·7	24·2	14·8
1860–61	184·0	22·1	12·0
1861–62	194·8	32·5	16·7
1862–63	207·8	30·0	14·5
1863–64	220·3	34·2	15·5
1864–65	238·1	24·4	10·3
1865–66	292·6	30·3	10·4
1866–67	358·5	41·7	11·6
1867–68	401·2–417·7	47·2	11·3–11·8
1868–69	439·4 (of which overseas = 72)	41·9	9·5
1869–70	514·8	53·3	10·3
1870–71	539·6	63·6	11·8
1871–72	642·5	75·4	11·7
1872–73	743·0	67·7	9·1
1873–74	841·8	84·3	10·0
1874–75	919·1 (of which overseas = 230)	119·3	13·0
1875–76	965·7	134·4	13·9
1876–77	997·3	124·9	12·5
1877–78	1074·4	146·2	13·6
1878–79	1042·6 (of which overseas = 302)	130·0	12·5
1879–80	1085·7	142·2	13·1

Appendix III

YEAR	TURNOVER				NET PROFIT	PROFIT AS % OF TURNOVER
1880–81	1100·3				91·2	8·2
1881–82	1150·5				139·6	12·1
1882–83	1206·5				159·5	13·2
1883–84	1196·9				172·5	14·4
1884–85	1188·8				197·2	16·6
1885–86	1106·3				185·8	16·8
1886–87	1132·7				175·5	15·5
1887–88	1167·4				163·0	14·0
1888–89	1177·9 (of which overseas = 381)				171·8	14·6
1889–90	1218·3				189·3	15·5
1890–91	1304·1				204·3	15·7
1891–92	1269·7				179·1	14·1
1892–93	1228·3				162·8	13·3
1893–94	1173·3				173·9	14·8
1894–95	1121·1				186·0	16·6
	Home	Overseas	Total			
1895–96	812·1	340·6	1152·7		179·9	15·6
1896–97	826·1	329·3	1155·4		138·2	12·0
1897–98	913·1	362·7	1275·8		163·5	12·8
1898–99	938·5	372·3	1310·8		205·1	15·6
1899–1900	942·8	413·0	1355·8		230·0	17·0
1900–01	952·8	423·8	1376·6		158·5	11·5
1901–02	990·5	473·6	1464·1		232·4	15·9
1902–03	994·0	474·1	1468·1		200·2	13·6
1903–04	935·8	464·2	1400·0		154·6	11·0
1904–05	887·1	475·5	1362·6		149·2	11·0
1905–06	864·4	527·1	1391·5		114·0	8·2
1906–07	869·7	569·0	1438·7		155·9	10·8
1907–08	857·5	596·8	1454·3		131·1	9·0
1908–09	855·0	592·4	1447·4		118·3	8·2
1909–10	824·2	623·4	1447·6		195·9	13·5
1910–11	804·2	682·6	1486·8		242·1	16·3
1911–12	798·2	675·5	1473·7		212·1	14·4
1912–13	773·3	741·7	1515·0		192·7	12·7
1913–14	829·1	771·1	1600·2		199·3	12·5
	Home	Army				
1914–15	812·9	84·1	544·3	1441·3	147·2	10·2
1915–16	925·4	106·4	703·0	1734·8	155·7	9·0
1916–17	1075·2	25·5	891·6	1992·3	249·9	12·5
1917–18	1289·3	239·0	855·9	2384·2	417·5	17·5
1918–19	1454·4	197·5	888·0	2539·9	423·6	16·7
1919–20	1751·4		1372·8	3124·2	433·1	13·9
1920–21	1710·3		833·4	2543·7 (loss 10·8)		—
1921–22	1610·2		428·9	2038·1	259·9	12·8
1922–23	1461·3		435·2	1896·5	261·4	13·8
1923[4]	1200·1		365·1	1565·2	155·5	9·9
1924[5]	1575·9		519·0	2094·9	193·4	9·2
1925	1626·6		560·1	2186·7	183·0	8·4
1926	1600·5		600·9	2201·4	197·1	9·0
1927	1565·3		631·1	2196·4	187·8	8·5
1928	1551·6		589·6	2141·2	167·3	7·8
1929	1495·4		571·4	2066·8	142·2	6·9
1930	1492·3		429·1	1921·4	138·3	7·2
1931	1408·1		317·9	1726·0	105·2	6·1
1932	1385·7		271·8	1657·5	93·9	5·7

| YEAR | TURNOVER | | | NET | PROFIT AS % |
	HOME	OVERSEAS	TOTAL	PROFIT	OF TURNOVER
1933	1319·3	247·4	1566·7	106·3	6·8
1934	1348·1	253·7	1601·8	122·4	7·6
1935	1372·9	267.8	1640·7	133·0	8·1
1936	1471·0	283·1	1754·1	114·3	6·5
1937	1534·6	282·4	1817.0	116·0	6·4
1938	1457·1	262·8	1719·9	98·0	5·7
	Home	Army			
1939	1590·2	86·8	273·1	1950·1	159·8	8·2
1940	1920·9	135·9	228·8	2285·6	235·5	10·3
1941	1836·8	132·2	150·3	2119·3	201·7	9·5
1942	1602·1	160·0	33·0	1795·1	264·2	14·7
1943	965·4	317·9	16·9	1300·2	196·6	15·1
1944	1217·5	343·5	35·5	1596·5	333·3	20·9
1945	1400·2	224·2	84·1	1708·5	277·2	16·2
1946	1537·7	2·1	188·8	1728·6	164·3	9·5
1947	1797·2	21·6	455·7	2274·5	250·3	11·0
1948	2024·2		839·0	2863·2	227·3	7·9
1949	2391·7		625·2	3016·9	234·7	7·8
1950	2802·0		707·9	3509·9	244·5	7·0
1951	3237·4		1165·8	4403·2	321·2	7·3
1952	3725·5		1020·7	4746·2	334·4	7·0
1953	4180·8		1027·4	5208·2	412·3	7·9
1954	4786·2		956·3	5742·5	589·9	10·3
1955	5313·5		910·3	6223·8	288·3	4·6
1956	6002·5		973·2	6975·7	437·4	6·3
1957[6]	6138·2		885·5	7023·7	408·3	5·8

Notes

1. Year ended June (19th 1846; 24th 1842–5, 1848; 25th 1847; 29th 1850; and 30th 1849, 1851–6).
2. June–31st Mar.
3. 1st Apr.–31st Mar.
4. 1st Apr.–31st Dec.
5. Calendar year.
6. (In 1958, Huntley and Palmers Ltd. became a fully-owned subsidiary of The Associated Biscuit Manufacturers Ltd.).

SOURCES *Turnover* 1841-42–1867-68 Work and Wages Books, Pass Books, etc.
　　　　　　1867-68–1893-94 Estimates drawn up in offices by W. Bullivant Williams (overlapping figures are given for 1867-68).
　　　　　　1893-94–1957 Partnership and Company Accounts.
　　　　　　N.B. Turnover is net of value of boxes and tins sent out.
　　Profits Partnership and Company Accounts.

Appendix IV
Huntley and Palmers: Net Output (in tons)

Year	Biscuits (Cakes not given)	Year	Biscuits	Cakes	Total
1859[1]	2831	1900–01	24,108		
1860	3210	1901–02	24,012		
1861	3308				
1862	3553		Biscuits	Cakes	Total
1863	4040	1902–03	24,059	1021	25,080
1864	4683	1903–04	23,954	904	24,858
1865	5561	1904–05	23,701	915	24,616
1866	6407	1905–06	23,843	893	24,736
1867	6580	1906–07	24,650	864	25,514
1868	7036	1907–08	24,717	948	25,665
1869	8881	1908–09	24,657	902	25,559
1870	9103	1909–10	22,575	828	23,403
1871	10,328	1910–11	22,461	747	23,208
1872	11,518	1911–12	21,845	716	22,561
1873	12,180	1912–13	22,768	770	23,538
1874	13,790	1913–14	23,848	817	24,665
1875	14,605	1914–15	23,437	661	24,098
1876	14,991	1915–16	24,914	733	25,647
1877	15,313	1916–17	21,689	512	22,201
1878	15,351	1917–18	25,432	—	25,432
1879	16,485	1918–19	24,364	2	24,366
1880	16,562	1919–20	19,874	37	19,911
1881	17,316	1920–21	12,608	165	12,773
1882	18,303	1921–22	10,749	164	10,913
1883	18,381	1922–23	11,089	165	11,254
1884	19,129	1923	11,991	178	12,169
1885	18,004	1924	12,677	173	12,850
1886	19,189	1925	13,922	87	14,009
1887	19,566	1926	13,726	96	13,822
1888	19,483	1927	13,424	218	13,642
1889	19,776	1928	13,244	231	13,475
1890	20,967	1929	13,297	185	13,482
1891	20,670	1930	13,480	176	13,656
1892	19,759	1931	12,165	495	12,660
1893	19,212	1932	11,435	1184	12,619
1894	19,125	1933	11,068	1108	12,176
1895	19,368	1934	11,514	1179	12,603
1896	20,465	1935	11,859	1229	13,088
1896–97[2]	21,809	1936	12,657	1665	14,322
1897–98	22,933	1937	12,042	1826	13,868
1898–99	22,963	1938	12,108	1870	13,978
1899–1900	24,268	1939	15,732	1882	17,614

Year	Biscuits	Cakes	Total	Year	Biscuits	Cakes	Total
1940	18,422	1960	20,382	1955	26,797	3036	29,833
1941	17,490	1558	19,048	1956	29,136	3033	32,439
1942	16,186	1783	17,969	1957	27,000	3094	30,094
1943	11,198	1853	13,051	1958	29,482	2981	32,463
1944	12,654	1979	14,633	1959	30,415	2957	33,372
1945	12,673	2252	14,925	1960	29,911	2992	32,903
1946	12,451	1730	14,181	1961	29,289	2788	32,077
1947	12,092	2567	14,659	1962	34,267	2226	36,492
1948	12,821	3478	16,299	1963	32,967	2126	35,093
1949	13,403	3623	17,026	1964	34,086	2039	36,125
1950	15,860	3301	19,101	1965	35,601	1709	37,310
1951	17,370	3884	21,254	1966	33,181	1902	35,083
1952	17,393	3548	20,941	1967	29,654	2825	32,479
1953	20,472	3087	23,559	1968	34,772	2675	37,447
1954	23,802	2516	26,318				

Notes
APPENDIX IV
1. Calendar year.
2. April–March, to 1922–23.

Index

Compiled by the author

This index is in three sections, namely (1) Huntley & Palmers and associated companies, including Peek Frean, Jacob's and Huntley Boorne & Stevens, (2) Fancy biscuit industry generally, and (3) General.

Abbreviations used: A.B.M.=Associated Biscuit Manufacturers Ltd.; H.B. & S.= Huntley Boorne & Stevens; H. & P.=Huntley & Palmers; N.A.B.M.=National Association of Biscuit Manufacturers (the trade association).

1. HUNTLEY & PALMERS AND ASSOCIATED COMPANIES

ABMAC Deliveries Ltd., 284–5
Advertising (see Marketing: advertising)
Alice, Phyllis and Betty, generating engines, 141, 247–8
Armstrong, Dr. E. F., head of laboratory, 188
Associated Biscuit Manufacturers Ltd., 'The Group', 7, 78, 228
  accession of Jacob's, 268
  finances, 212, 261–2
  formation 1921, 206
  relations with units, 212–13, 262, 268–9, 272–4
  reorganisation 1960s, 272–89,
Associated Biscuits Ltd., biscuit division of A.B.M., 286
Associated Deliveries Ltd., 248–9, 259, 282

Barber, Christopher, financial director A.B.M., 274, 276
Bartlett, Sidney, export manager, 284
Bath buns, 21
Bedaux system, 216–17, 221
Biscuits, main types
  Abernethy, 48, 74–5
  Bath Oliver, 21, 48
  Breakfast, 141, 159, 162, 213, 236, 239, 250, 257–8, 265, 278
  Captain, 41, 48, 56, 74
  Chocolate, 160, 181, 223, 271–2
  Cornish Wafer, 265, 278, 281, 283
  Cracknel, 20, 48, 54, 56
  Cream Cracker, 134, 268
  Garibaldi, 135
  Ginger nut, 53–4, 61, 74, 127, 150, 162, 211, 227, 241, 254, 278

Iced Gem, 257
Lemon Puff, 283
Marie, 135, 162, 197, 211
Osborne (Butter Osborne), 53, 74–5, 127, 162, 197, 211, 265, 281, 283
Petit Beurre, 162, 197, 211, 241
Pic-Nic, 53, 61, 74, 99
Biscuits, number of varieties, 20, 78, 132, 134, 159, 235, 239, 241–2, 276, 283
Bitmead, William, workman, 36
Blackmore, A. W., chief engineer, 213
Boorne, James (see also Huntley Boorne & Stevens), 42
Bread: fancy rolls, 20, 40; patent unfermented bread, 40–1, 78
British institution, H. & P. becomes in 1880s, 137–9
Brown, Charles, factory manager, 73, 100
Brown, Richard, foreman, 17–18, 36, 64–6, 72–3, 97–8, 100–1, 108, 304
Byham, Cyril, chief engineer, 158, 193

Cakes, 20, 128, 225, 241, 251, 254, 276; cake factory, 96, 197, 207
Carr, Arthur, chairman of P.F., 161, 174, 198, 204–7
Carr, Ellis, director of P.F., 161
Carr, John, chairman of P.F., 78, 161, 174
Carr, Philip, chairman of P.F., 271
Carr, Rupert, chairman of A.B.M., 222–3, 246, 268–9, 271–4, 277, 280, 285–7
Colgate, Dr. R. T., head of laboratory, 188, 227, 257
Committees, economy, 216, 242; reconstruction 1917, 199; 1942, 241, 251

311

Conditions of work, etc.
  factory accidents, 109
  factory rules, 101–2
  holidays, 99, 200
  hours, working, 98–9, 179, 181, 187, 200, 227
  machinery, adverse effects of, 97, 110
  offices, staff in, 109–10, 133–4
  paternalism, 109
  wages, 100–1, 127–9, 175, 178–9, 191–3, 197–8, 209–10, 234, 250, Appendix I; bonuses, 106, 152, 203, 215; piece rates, 128
Cridge, H. H., head of experimental department, 238

Davis, R. G., chief engineer, 258, 270
Day, John H., representative, 73
Discounts to retailers, etc., 61, 171–3, 265
Distribution (see also Associated Deliveries Ltd., Biscuit Delivery Pool), 20–1, 43–4, 63, 80; joint delivery, 213, 283

East, Frank B., head of manufacturing, 181, 205
Employees (see also Conditions of work, Industrial disputes, Welfare)
  ages of, 97
  length of service, 101, 107, 187
  numbers of, 36, 40, 80, 96, 100, 128–9, 133–4, 208, 249, Appendix I
  places of birth 1851–61, 97–8, Appendix II
  turnover, 101
  women, employment of, 96, 99, 103, 176, 181, 185–6, 188, 231
Establishment of shop 1822, 17; of partnership 1841, 35; of Huntley and Palmers 1857, 71; of limited company 1898, 152.
Exhibitions, international, 1851, 82–3; 1855, 83; 1862, 84; 1867, 85; 1869, 52–3, 59–60; 1873, 86–7, 129; 1878, 86–8, 132; 1884, 197; 1892, 88; 1900, 88–9, 132; 1924, 194, 215
Exports (see Trade, overseas)

Factory, Reading, general extensions, 56–7, 66–7, 79–81, 136–7; survey of, 280
  Cake factory (see Cakes)
  Chocolate factory (see Biscuits, chocolate)
  Engineering department, 97, 141, 159, 188, 269–70; makes shells 1915–18, 185–6
  H factory, 96, 163
  Mixing room, central, 260
  North factory, 80, 96, 242, 260, 271
  South factory, 79, 96, 158–9, 213, 260
  Warehouse, central, 214, 232
Falconer, Dr. R., chief technical manager, 257
Fame, world-wide of H. & P., 11, 93
Finance, 21, 39–40, 57, 142, 203–4, 208–9, 223–4, 260–2
  capital structure A.B.M., 206, 261–2
  capital structure H. &. P., 35, 70–2, 130, 156, 158–9
  reserve fund, 163–5, 168, 191, 221, 232
Frean, George H., co-founder of P.F., 78

Gales, J. R., managing director, 210, 220, 227–9, 234, 244, 249, 251, 258, 262–4
Gardiner, David, operational research engineer, A.B.M., 259, 284, 286
Gardiner, Neil, technical development director, 230–1, 241, 244, 247–8, 257, 259–60, 270–1, 274, 286–8
Group, the (see Associated Biscuit Manufacturers Ltd.)

Hanford, Hector, director, 270–1, 286
Hebb, C. B., export manager, 184
Home trade, 82, 137, 161, 180, 210–11, 219–20, 264, 278; in Ireland, 39, 73
Horsfall, John, office manager, 64
Huntley, Joseph, founder of shop 1822, 5, 7, 9, 11, 14–22, 24, 31, 38–9, 57, 132, 145, 286
Huntley, Joseph, founder of tin-box firm (see also Huntley Boorne & Stevens), 5, 9, 14, 19, 31, 35–7, 42, 46, 57, 62, 69, 112
Huntley, Thomas, chief cashier, 155
Huntley, Thomas, partner, 1841, 3, 5, 7, 11–14, 29–30, 35, 43, 56–70, 100, 104, 106, 112, 119–20, 152
Huntley Boorne & Stevens (since 1872; Huntley & Boorne 1846–72. See also Joseph Huntley, James Boorne, S. B. Stevens, Lamiplate, Tins), 42, 133, 164, 178–9, 183, 185–6, 200, 203–4, 209, 224–5, 275, 281

Index

Industrial disputes, 175–7, 191–3, 214–15
Ingredients, 9, 39, 42, 78–9, 122–3, 132, 207–8; shortages 1914–18, 190–9; 1939–45, 236–43; post-1945, 245ff.

Jacob, W. & R. & Co (Liverpool) Ltd. (see also Associated Biscuit Manufacturers Ltd.), 207, 266–9, 273–4, 276, 285, 288
Joint Advisory Council, 223
Jones, Sir C. V., managing director of P.F., 206

Kennedy, William, representative in U.S.A., 90–1
Kenway, Gawen B., representative, 38, 73
Kersley, H. V., chairman of Workers' Representation Committee and mayor of Reading, 248
Knight, A. T., chairman of Workers' Representation Committee, 193

Le Mare, Richard, chief works manager, 205
Lea, Emsley, London office manager, 184
Lea, Henry, chief representative, 61–3, 66, 70, 73, 83–4, 87–8, 101, 119, 155
Lea, William, company secretary, 155, 209
Leete, Joseph, Continental representative, 39, 73, 75, 84–9, 92, 124, 141, 160, 217
London office, St. Benet's Lane 1847, 62, 71; Philpot Lane 1861, 71; Rood Lane 1865, 71, 130; Fenchurch Street 1883, 130, 184–5, 227, 230.

Machinery, steam-powered, 36–7, 181
auto plants, 159, 231, 241–2, 249, 258, 263
dough mixer, 37, 53, 63
oven, travelling, 53, 59, 63
Management
committee of managers, 157; of assistant directors, 167; of management, 204, 214
Executive, set up, 181–2
Executive Committee, set up, 206; dissolved 253–4
problems, first-generation, 21–2, 70; second-generation, 129–32, 142

reforms 1906, 167; 1914, 181–2
wages and tonnages book, 134, 158
Marketing, 20, 37–8, 58, 60, 63, 211–12, 228–9, 263–4
advertising, 37–8, 161, 256; radio and television, 229, 265, 275
co-ordination with production (see Production)
supermarkets, 265
Meatyard, G. W., director, 230, 259
Medd, Gordon, director A.B.M., 276
Meltis Ltd. (now Chocolat Tobler Meltis Ltd.), 275, 279
Moore, John R., factory manager, 80, 107
Morton, H. J., home trade manager, 162, 210
Moulton, F. D., & Co., U.S. agents, 160

Newman, C. F., head of packing, 181

O'Conor, Roderic, managing director, A.B.M., 268, 285–7
Offices, reorganisation of, 229–30
Overseas manufacture, France, 217–18, 224–5, 237, 252–3; New Zealand, 284
trade, 66, 73, 82–4, 137, 160, 183, 191, 217, 251–2, 283–4; division into Continental (under Joseph Leete, q.v.) and export departments 84; Continental trade, 84–9, 92–3, 160, 217; export trade, 89–93, 160, 217; trade with U.S.A., 83, 89–92, 126, 160, 221, 283–4; India and Far East, 82–3, 92–3, 221, 252, 283

Packing, 35–6, 159, 181, 250, 259–60, 281
Palmer, Alan, 244, 259, 270, 276, 284–7; chairman of H. &. P., 274; of A.B.M., 287
Palmer, Albert, 107, 130, 142, 155, 167, 184, 203, 244
Palmer, Bennet, director of A.B.M., 209, 216, 244, 271
Palmer, Cecil, 2nd Lord Palmer, 184–5, 200, 204, 213, 216, 254
Palmer, Charles, 89, 130, 142, 155, 163, 167–8, 185, 191, 201, 244
Palmer, Sir Eric, 184, 203, 205, 210, 213, 234, 238–42, 247–8, 253, 284, 286; chairman 216
Palmer, Ernest, 1st Lord Palmer, 107, 124, 129, 142, 155, 157, 163, 167–8, 185, 191, 205, 244, 253;

Palmer, Ernest 1st Lord Palmer—*cont.*
 baronet, 149, 201; peer, 149
Palmer, Eustace, 167–8, 174, 184,
 189, 200, 205, 215; chairman, 213
Palmer, Geoffrey, 184, 203, 217, 254,
 259, 271
Palmer, George, 3, 247–8, 286–7;
 attitude to women's rights, 116–17;
 character: irascible, 65–6, 80, 83,
 119, 147; open-handed, 119–20;
 childhood and apprenticeship,
 25–31; education, interest in,
 112, 115; death, 152; M.P., 116–18;
 mechanical aptitude, 28–9, 45,
 52–5; partnership 1841–57, 11,
 35–68; senior partner, 69–152;
 Reading councillor and mayor,
 72, 112–14
Palmer, George William, 106, 116,
 131–2, 151–2, 203, 212; apprenticeship, 86; character, 166, 178;
 chairman, 157, 166–7; M.P.,
 145–6; partner, 81, 129; privy
 councillor, 149, 166; Reading
 councillor and mayor, 145–6
Palmer, Gordon, 244, 262–4, 268, 270,
 273–4, 282, 286
Palmer, Howard, cricketer, 107;
 chairman, 166, 173, 184, 191–5,
 198, 200–1, 203–6, 208; death,
 212–13; 245; 253, 274, 286;
 partner, 130, 132, 141–2, 155, 157
Palmer, Raymond, 3rd Lord Palmer,
 244, 254, 271, 276, 284, 286
Palmer, Reginald, 203, 205, 216,
 225–6, 231, 233, 241–2, 250,
 259–60, 271, 274; chairman, 253
Palmer, Richard, 254, 264, 271, 286
Palmer, Samuel, 11, 25–7, 140; at
 Bristol, 42, 62; character:
 countrified, 124; jaunty, 69, 111,
 122, 151–2; home life, 123–4;
 ingredients purchasing, 66, 79,
 122–3; London office (q.v.)
 overseas trade, 66, 75, 83–6, 93;
 partner, 65, 69–72; shareholdings,
 71–2, 130, 156
Palmer, Sir Walter, 123, 130, 132,
 141–2, 146, 149, 155, 167, 203;
 baronet, 149
Palmer, William, 254, 258–9, 271, 286
Palmer, William Isaac, 11, 25–7, 87,
 111, 136–7, 147, 152; at Liverpool,
 62; character: conciliatory, 80,
 120–1; open-handed, 120–2;
 death, 122, 140; factory manager,
 66, 69–72, 109, 149; mother,
 relations with, 66, 121; partner,
 70–2; schooldays and apprenticeship, 29–31; shareholdings, 71–2,
 130, 156; temperance worker,
 29–30, 118, 121
Peek, James, co-founder, of P.F., 78
Peek Frean & Co. Ltd., 7, 50, 84,
 90–1, 106, 143, 159; as unit of
 A.B.M., 210–13, 220, 222, 224,
 227–8, 231, 236, 239, 248, 250,
 261–2, 266, 268–71, 279–80,
 284–5, 288
 co-operation with H. & P., 88, 135,
 179–80
 merger talks with H. & P., 204–7
 origins, 78
 rivalry with H. & P., 135, 161, 172
Premises (see also Factory); London
 Street, 56, 96; King's Road,
 Reading, 43, 56ff., Huyton,
 258ff.
Prices, biscuit, 59, 127, 182, 208,
 232–3, 236–7, 247, 254, 275, 278
Production (see also Machinery,
 Appendix IV for net output)
 co-ordination with marketing 264–5

Recreation (see Welfare and recreation)
Representatives, 38–9, 62–3, 161, 211
Resale price maintenance, 61, 265
Rickman, George P., workman, 304
Rondolin, L., chief engineer of P.F.,
 222, 230
Ruddock, William, chief engineer, 100,
 108, 270

Spaul, P. A., overseas manager, 217
Stevens, Ewart, managing director of
 H.B. & S., 200
Stevens, Samuel Beavan, partner in
 and chairman of H.B. & S., 186,
 200
Stone, Thomas, partner in P.F., 161
Supermarkets (see Marketing)

Tins (see also Huntley Boorne &
 Stevens), 19, 55, 84, 93–5, 224–5,
 240, 259, 281
 decorated, 132–3, 159, 164, 184,
 215, 281
Trade, home (see Home trade)
 overseas (see Overseas trade)
Trade credit, to customers, 21, 39,
 61–2, 171–2
Trade mark (garter and buckle), 93,
 133, 143, 145
Tribrek, breakfast cereal, 228, 255

Index

Valpy, Edward, representative in U.S.A., 91, 160
Van Namen, C. D., director, 282, 286
Visitors, factory, 137-8

Welfare and recreation,
  canteen, 168, 195
  cricket club, 107
  donations to employees, 102, 108-9
  excursions, 102, 105-6, 180, 200
  factory suppers and celebrations, 64, 80-1, 102
  library, 67, 104
  mutual improvement society, 104
  penny bank, 103
  recreation club, 108, 196, 272
  sick fund, 67, 80, 102-4, 108-9, 192

social centre, 195-6, 230
Wholesalers, 163, 211, 283
Wilkey, John Fry, 38, 62, 73
Williams, Charles, chief representative, 63, 73, 98
Williams, Clement, director, 185, 216, 225, 227, 244
Williams, William Bullivant, director, 63, 73, 84, 98, 155, 158, 184
Women (see Employees; George Palmer, attitude to women's rights)
Workers' Representation Committee, 194-5, 199-200, 212-16, 223, 233
Worth, Thomas, representative, 19-20, 38, 145, 227
Wrottesley, E. A., director, 181-2, 205, 223, 225, 254

2. FANCY BISCUIT INDUSTRY GENERALLY

A.1 Biscuit Co., London, 134
Associated British Foods Ltd., London, 228, 265
Association of Biscuit Manufacturers (see also National Association of Biscuit Manufacturers), 134, 170-3, 182-3, 197-9, 266

Belcher, Charles S., U.S. biscuit manufacturer, 89
Betta Biscuit Co. Ltd., 227-8
Bilsland Bros., Glasgow, 136, 249
Biscuit Delivery Pool, 238, 248
Biscuit Industry Council, 253
British Cake and Biscuit Association, 233-4

Cake and Biscuit Alliance (Defence Committee, Wartime Alliance), 234-5, 238-9, 247, 250, 253-4, 256, 289
Cake and Biscuit Manufacturers' Export Group, 254
Carr, Jonathan Dodgson (see also Carr's of Carlisle Ltd.), 52, 55, 78
Carr's of Carlisle Ltd., 6, 52-3, 61, 77, 97, 99, 135, 143, 171-2, 175, 204, 227, 239, 248-9, 266, 279
Cheap manufacturers, 136-7, 221-2, 256-7
Co-operative Wholesale Society, Crumpsall, Manchester, 136, 168, 195, 221, 228
Cornubia Biscuit Ltd., Cornwall, 171-2

Crawford, William & Sons Ltd., Edinburgh, 171-2, 174, 204, 279

Frears Ltd. (Nabisco-Frears Ltd.), 279

Grant, (Sir) Alexander, chairman of McVitie & Price, 204
Gray Dunn & Co. Ltd., Glasgow, 135
Guillout's, France, 86, 169

Hill & Jones, London, 50, 77-8, 134, 143

Imperial London Biscuit Co. Ltd., 134

Jacob, George, chairman of Jacob's, 207
Jacob, W. & R. & Co. Ltd., Dublin, 7, 134-5, 143, 171, 174, 180, 204, 207, 266

Kemp's Biscuits Ltd., Grimsby, 221, 228, 279

Label printers (see Printers of Labels, etc.)
Lefèvre-Utile, Nantes, 89, 169
Legislation, factory, 99, 135-6, 188
Lemann, F., London, 50, 134

Macdonald, William & Sons Ltd., Glasgow, 279
Macfarlane, James, chairman of Macfarlane Lang, 182, 198-9, 204
Macfarlane Lang & Co. Ltd., 135, 143, 161, 171-2, 174, 182, 211, 225, 249

Machinery suppliers (see 3. Joseph Baker & Son, Baker Perkins Ltd., A. M. Perkins & Son, T. & T. Vicars Ltd.)
Mackenzie & Mackenzie Ltd., Edinburgh, 135, 143, 171, 173
McVitie & Price Ltd., Edinburgh, 135, 161, 163, 171, 174, 180, 204, 211, 224, 237, 249, 257
Meredith & Drew Ltd., London, 143, 279
Middlemass, R. & Son, Edinburgh, 135, 143, 171, 173, 279

National Bakery Co. Ltd., London, 171
National Association of Biscuit Manufacturers (successor to Association of Biscuit Manufacturers, q.v.), 199, 201, 212, 216, 222, 227, 232, 234, 236, 259, 265, 273–4, 278, 288
National Biscuit Co., U.S.A., 91, 279
National Joint Wages Council of Biscuit Industry, 223, 274

Palmer Bros., Bristol, 171, 227–8
Perry, Thomas, biscuit baker of Reading, 18, 50
Printers of labels etc., (see 3. De La Rue Co. Ltd., White & Pike Ltd.)

Reading Biscuit Co. Ltd., 29, 143

Serpell, H. O. & Co. Ltd., Reading, 135, 171, 227, 279

Technological developments in, 45–55, 287–9
Trades board, threat of, 100, 178–9, 199, 233
Turner, James, biscuit baker of London, 52

United Biscuits (Holdings) Ltd., Edinburgh, 249, 279

Weston Biscuit Co. Ltd. (see Associated British Foods Ltd.)
Wright's Biscuits Ltd., South Shields, 279

3. GENERAL

Abernethy, Dr. John (see also 1. Biscuits: main types), 48
Ackworth School, Yorks, 13, 27
Addington, Henry, Viscount Sidmouth, 75
Anson, Hon. George, Prince Albert's private secretary, 75
Arvin Industries Inc., U.S.A., 281
Athlone, Earl of, 149
Austen, Jane, 51

Baker, Joseph & Son (see also Baker Perkins Ltd.,), 60, 159–60
Baker Perkins Ltd., biscuit machinery suppliers, 60, 215, 231, 260
Baking industry, 48–50
Banbury and Shipston Turnpike, 14
Banbury cakes, 21, 41
Barclay & Fry Ltd., London, 133
Barrett Exall & Andrewes (after 1864 The Reading Iron Works, q.v.), 37, 53, 57, 83
Batger & Co., London, 9
Baylis, Messrs.' silk factory, 43
Beesley, Samuel, Banbury, 21
Blandy, John Jackson, mayor of Reading, 80

Blandy, William Frank, of Reading, 80, 119
Boer War (see South African War)
Bowley, Sir Arthur L., statistician, 176–7, 214
Bright, John, 116
Brown, Rev. George, prison chaplain and go-between, 147
Bryant, Thomas, Quaker of Somerset, 4
Bryant & May Ltd., London, 133, 224
Burford, Oxon., 12–13, 27
Burritt, Elihu, American Quaker and traveller, 17, 150
Busvine, James, grocer of Bristol, 21, 29, 145

Cadbury Bros. Ltd., 6, 73, 108, 135, 160, 241, 265
Canals (see also Kennet and Avon canal), 20–1
Cannon brewery, Reading, 43, 67, 79
Chalmers, J. B., honours tout, 148–9
Childs, William M., Reading University (College), 146, 178, 185, 231
Chivers & Sons Ltd., Cambridgeshire, 249

Index

Claggett, Caleb, ship's biscuit maker, 47
Clark, C. & J. Ltd., shoe manufacturers of Street, Somerset, 6, 26, 72
Clark, Cyrus and James, co-founders of C. & J. Clark Ltd., 26
Clark, John, inventor, 26
Clynes, J. R., M.P. and food controller, 197, 214
Cocks, James, founder of Cocks & Co., 19, 145
Cocks & Co., Reading sauce makers, 19, 83, 133
Coffin, Sir Isaac, admiral and inventor, 59
Cook, Captain James, 46
Costain, Richard Ltd., 258
Cox, Edward William, lawyer, 28
Crawford, D. S. Ltd., caterers of Edinburgh, 279
Crawford, Sir William, advertising agent, 255-6
Crimean War, 67, 83, 168, 182
Crosse & Blackwell Ltd, food manufacturers and overseas agents of H. & P., 19, 60, 84, 86, 89, 156, 184, 217
Cullen, W. H., grocers, 228

De La Rue Co. Ltd., printers of labels, etc., 85, 133, 163
Deloitte Plender & Griffiths, accountants, 174, 206
Depression, great, 1874-95, 126, 140; 1929-35, 221
Derby, Earl of, 258
Devonport, Lord, food controller, 196-8
Dickens, Charles, 49-50, 112
Diet (see Tastes, changes in consumers')
Dimsdale Drewett Fowler & Barnard, bankers of London, 30
Dodson, Henry, baker of Southwark, 40
Dorchester, William, butcher of Reading, 120-1, 147
Doubleday, Benjamin, grocer of Epping, 16
Duncan, Isadora, dancer, 150

Edward VII, 93; as Prince of Wales, 129, 137
Edward VIII, as Prince of Wales, 215
Ellwood, Thomas, Quaker, 24
Eugénie, French empress, 93, 137

Exall, William, engineer (see also Barrett Exall & Andrewes), 37, 247

Fallières, Armand, French president, 93
Fardon, Edwin, ironmonger of Reading, 19
Farrar, Archdeacon, 118
Forbes-Robertson, Sir Johnston, actor, 150
Forster, W. E., and 1870 Education Act, 115
Fortnum & Mason, London, 60-1, 162
Fortt, William, Bath, 21
Fox, George, Quaker, 4
Foxwell, Herbert, professor, 161
Friends, Society of (see Quakers)
Fry, J. S., & Sons Ltd., Bristol, 6, 160

Gaskell, Mrs., author, 18, 51
George III, 18
Gillett, John and Martha, of Langport, Somerset, 25-7
Golder, James Ltd., booksellers, Reading, 104
Golding, William, ironfounder of Newbury, 39, 66
Goldney family, of Bristol, 26
Grant, Sir Thomas, inventor, 51, 55
Grant, Ulysses, president of U.S.A., 137
Great Western Railway (see Railways)
Greig, David Ltd., provision merchants, 136
Grocers Associations, Federation of, 136, 170
Guillebaud, C. W., economist, 233

Harcourt, Sir William, Chancellor of the Exchequer, 143
Harmood Banner Lewis & Mounsey, accountants, 267
Harrison, Thomas & Co., Liverpool, 59
Harrods Ltd., London, 145
Harvard Business School, attended by Rupert Carr, 269
Haslam, Dryland, estate agent of Reading, 147
Hawtrey, Mrs. Edward, of Eton, 75
Henry of Battenberg, Prince, 94
Hitchcock, Robert, confectioner of Taunton, 28
Home & Colonial Stores Ltd., 136, 163, 249
Horder, Lord, physician, 239

Howard, Luke, chemist, 12
Hudson Scott & Sons Ltd., printers of Carlisle, 52
Huntley, Augusta, née Ainsworth, 70
Huntley, Hannah, née Cowdry, 13, 25
Huntley, Hannah and Mary, 5
Huntley, Henry Evans, 7, 65–6, 70–1, 129, 152
Huntley, Jacob, 12
Huntley, Jane, née Evans, 8, 22, 29, 57, 152
Huntley, John, d. 1638, 4, 11
Huntley, John, fl. 1682, 11–12
Huntley, John, of Uxbridge, 17
Huntley, Joseph, d. 1756, 12
Huntley, Mary, née Lamb, 21
Huntley, Mary, née Willis, 14–16
Huntley, Sarah, fl. 1682, 12
Huntley, Thomas, d. 1813, 12–13, 27

Imperial Tobacco Co. Ltd., 174, 213
International Stores, 221, 228, 259
Irving, H. B., actor, 150
Isaac, William, tanner of Sturminster Newton, 25
Isaacs, Rufus, 1st Marquess of Reading, 169

Jee, Adam, merchant of Bombay, 92
Johnson, Dr. Samuel, 45–6, 48
Jones, Owen, industrial designer, 85–6

Kennet, river, 14, 37, 43, 79
Kennet and Avon canal, 20
Keyser, Sir C. E., M.P. for Reading, 169
Kubelik, Jan, violinist, 150

Lamb, Joseph, farmer of Sibford, 14
Lamiplate, made by H.B. & S., 225, 281
Lancaster, Joseph, Quaker educationalist, 112
Langdon, David, cartoonist, 256
Lear, Edward's nonsense-rhyme on H. & P., 138
Leopold II of the Belgians, 75, 85
Lever Bros. Ltd., 156
Lind, Dr. James, naval surgeon, 46
Lipton Ltd., provision merchants, 136, 163, 228
Long Sutton, Somerset, 24–5, 41
Lyons, J. & Co. Ltd., 168, 242

Macintosh, Charles, inventor, 26
Mackintosh, J. & Sons Ltd., 249, 284–5

Marsh Deane & Co., bankers of Reading, 16
Marshal, William, ship's biscuit maker, 47
Marshall, Alfred, economist, 130–1, 170, 189
Mary, Queen, d. 1953, 149
Mather & Crowther, advertising agents, 162, 212
Mather & Platt Ltd., engineers of Manchester, 188
Maypole Dairy Co. Ltd., 136
Meaby's, bakers of Reading (see also 2. Reading Biscuit Co. Ltd.), 49, 144
Mechanics Institution, Reading, 111; Taunton, 28
Meredith, George, author, 141, 150
Metal Box Ltd., 225
Milton, John, 24
Mitchell Hain & Co., brokers, 173
Mitford, Mary Russell, author, 15, 18, 40–1, 51
Morton, C. & E., overseas agents of H. & P., 89, 184, 217

Nall, J. G., commission agent, 90–2
Napoleon III, French emperor, 75, 83, 85, 88; gift to Madagascar, 93
National Union of Gas Workers and General Labourers (now National Union of General & Municipal Workers), 175, 178, 192, 197, 214
Nielsen, A. C. Co. Ltd., and market research, 265

Oddington, Glos., 11
Oliver, Dr. William, 48
Oliver-King, H., president of N.A.B.M., 253
Oxford, bishop of (J. F. Mackarness), 118–19, 138

P.A. Management Consultants Ltd., 275
Palmer, Alice, née Exall, 37, 141
Palmer, Betty, née Salter, 24, 70
Palmer, Elizabeth, nee Meteyard, 8, 64, 119, 151–2
Palmer, Jean, née Craig, 149–50
Palmer, Joseph, 26–7, 29
Palmer, Mary, née Isaac, 25–6, 29, 36, 39–40, 66, 111, 121, 151
Palmer, Mary Jane, née Marsh, 123
Palmer, Mary Ovens, 26–7, 29–30, 36, 41–2, 111, 120
Palmer, Richard, 24

Index

Palmer, Robert, 27
Palmer, William I, 24
Palmer, William II, 5, 25
Palmer, William III, 25-6
Patent Desiccating Co., engineers, London, 59
Pease, Joseph, Quaker M.P., 116
Perkins, A. M. & Son, London (see also Baker Perkins Ltd.), 60
Perry, Daniel, baker of Suffolk, 50
Pickfords Ltd., carriers, 63
Pius IX, Pope, gift to Madagascar, 93
Potin, F., emporium of Paris, 84
Price Waterhouse, accountants, 151, 204, 206, 267
Proust, Marcel, author, 150
Pulp Industries Ltd., 224
Pulsometer Pumps Ltd., Reading, 185
Punch cartoon, 138

Quakers, 3-10, 12-13
  characteristics in business, 10, 59, 65, 101, 109, 131
  cousinhood, 3
  rules of discipline, 3-4, 21, 118

Railways, 43, 63, 76-7, 142, 157
Reading, 14, 18, 29, 42-3
  development of, 113-14
  working-class conditions in, 174-7, 214
Reading Athletic Club, 107
  Blue Coat School, 250
  Dispensary, 57, 67
  Gas Co., 43, 57, 137
  Iron Works Ltd. (see also Barrett Exall & Andrewes), 150
  sauce (see Cocks & Co.)
  School, 115
  Temperance Band, 108, 180, 196
  University (College), Palmer benefactions to, 114, 178, 195-6
  Water Co., 113
  Working Men's Regatta, 108
Redesdale, Lord, 94
Rennie, Sir John, engineer, 51
Rosse, Earl of, astronomer, 75
Rowntree & Co. Ltd., York, 6, 90
Royal Berkshire Hospital, Reading, 67, 152
Royal Clarence Victualling Yard, Gosport, 47, 51-3

Sainsbury, J. Ltd., provision merchants, 136, 228, 283
Salisbury, 3rd Marquess of, 120, 147, 148, 169

Salter, James, of Podimore, Somerset, 24, 70
Schweppe, Jacob, founder of Schweppes Ltd., 19
Scott, William & Maxwell, engineers of Tranmere, 59
Selfridges Ltd., London, 211
Shakespeare, William, 46
Shaw, George Bernard, dramatist, 131
Ship's biscuits, 45-6
Sibford Ferris, Oxon., 14
Sidcot school, Somerset, 27-30
Simonds, George Blackall, sculptor and brewer, 146
Slocombe, William, solicitor of Reading, 70, 129
Smith, Adam, economist, 8
Smith, Goldwin, academic, 18
Smith, John, grocer of Reading, 9, 36, 42
South African War 1899-1902, 182
Speakman, Elizabeth, of Reading, 16
Spiers & Pond Ltd., London, 145
Spooner Dryer & Engineering Co. Ltd., Yorkshire, 257
Squire, George, baker to Queen Victoria, 49
Stanley, Henry, explorer, 87, 93
Stephens Blandy & Co., bankers of Reading, 39
Sturge, Joseph, Quaker philanthropist, 26
Sturminster Newton, Dorset, 25
Sutton, Martin Hope, seedsman, 115
Sutton & Sons Ltd., Reading, 115, 150
Swallowfield Mill, Berks., 39, 79

Talfourd, Sir Thomas, M.P. and judge, 112
Tastes, changes in consumers', 74-7, 160, 221, 255-6
Taunton, Somerset, 28-9
Teck, Duke and Duchess of, 149
Terry, Joseph & Sons Ltd., 249
Terry, Thomas, miller of Swallowfield, 39, 42, 58
Thorne, Will, trade unionist, 214
Times, The, 37-8, 138, 178
Trollope, Anthony, author, 76

United States (see also 1. Overseas trade; trade with U.S.A.), 204, 218
Urwick Orr & Partners Ltd., consultants, 230, 269-71, 280
Uxbridge, Middlesex, 17

Venua, Mr., musician of Reading, 118.
Vicars, T. & T. Ltd., biscuit machinery suppliers, 60, 78, 231, 249
Victoria, Queen, gift to Madagascar, 93; royal warrant to Carr's, 52; to H. & P., 75–6, 137; to other biscuit firms, 134

Wallace Attwood Co., consultants, 263–4, 266
Weedon, John, solicitor of Reading, 43, 58
Wellington, Arthur Duke of, 75
Wesley, John, 18
Wheatley Kirk Price & Co., valuers of London, 158
White & Pike Ltd., label printers of Birmingham, 9, 133, 163

Whiteley, William Ltd., London, 145
Whiting, John, physician, 40
Wilde, Oscar, author, 123, 149–50
Willis, Binfield, maltster of Reading, 14, 16
Willoughby de Eresby, Lord, 75
Wolfe, Humbert, civil servant and poet, 199
Wordsworth, Christopher, bishop of Lincoln, 75
World War, first, 180–202, 234, 245; army contracts, 183, 186, 190–1, 197, 200–1; H. & P. makes shells, 185–6
second, 234–44; army contracts, 234, 237, 245; factory concentration, 238–41; flour subsidy, 246–7; rationing, 239–40, 245; ends 254; zoning, 239

1 2 3 4 5 6 7
A B C D E F G H I J K

HUNTLEY AND PALMERS READING

HUNTLEY AND PALMERS READING ENGLAND

HUNTLEY AND PALMERS READING, ENGLAND.